P9-DFM-936

Myth and Measurement:
The New Economics of the Minimum Wage

Myth and Measurement

THE NEW ECONOMICS OF THE MINIMUM WAGE

David Card and Alan B. Krueger

PRINCETON UNIVERSITY PRESS

PRINCETON, NEW JERSEY

Copyright © 1995 by Princeton University Press
Published by Princeton University Press, 41 William Street,
Princeton, New Jersey 08540
In the United Kingdom: Princeton University Press, Chichester, West Sussex

All Rights Reserved

Grateful acknowledgment is made to the *American Economic Review* for their permission to reprint portions of the authors' previously published work.

Grateful acknowledgment is made to the *Industrial and Labor Relations Review* for their permission to reprint portions of the authors' work previously published in vol. 6, no. 1, pp. 6–21; vol. 46, no. 1, pp. 23–37 and 38–54; and vol. 47, no. 3, pp. 487–96.

Grateful acknowledgment is made to *Research in Labor Economics* for their permission to reprint portions of the authors' previously published work.

Library of Congress Cataloging-in-Publication Data

Card, David E. (David Edward).
    Myth and measurement : the new economics of the minimum wage /
David Card and Alan B. Krueger.
        p.   cm.
    Includes bibliographical references (p.) and index.
    ISBN 0-691-04390 (acid-free paper)
    1. Wages—Minimum wage.   2. Employment (Economic theory)
3. Wages—Minimum wage—United States.   4. Labor market—United
States.   I. Krueger, Alan B.   II. Title.
HD4917.C37   1995
331.2′3—dc20   94-40567
                                                                            CIP

This book has been composed in Palatino.

Princeton University Press books are printed on acid-free paper and meet the guidelines for permanence and durability of the Committee on Production Guidelines for Book Longevity of the Council on Library Resources

Printed in the United States of America

10 9 8 7 6 5 4 3 2 1

Dedicated to Richard Allen Lester—our colleague and friend

Contents

Preface

This book represents the culmination of more than five years of research on the subject of minimum wages. Our interest in the topic was sparked during the late 1980s, when a number of states responded to the decade-long freeze in the federal minimum wage by raising their own minimum wage rates. The next few years saw a spate of minimum-wage legislation, with more and more states raising their minimum wages and an eventual increase in the federal minimum rate. These historically unprecedented changes set the stage for a new kind of research on the minimum wage. Borrowing from the natural sciences, the idea of this new research is to compare the labor-market outcomes of the "treatment" and "control" groups that arise naturally when the minimum wage increases for one group of workers, but not for another. This analytical method recently has been applied very effectively to such issues as education, immigration, and unemployment. In fact, during the 1940s, Richard Lester and other economists used very similar research methods to study the effect of the newly imposed federal minimum wage. Since then, however, this very straightforward and telling methodology has been supplanted by alternative approaches that are more closely linked to econometric modeling.

What began as an attempt to bring a "new" methodology to an old question quickly turned into a puzzle. Our initial work on the 1988 increase in California's minimum wage, and on the 1990 and 1991 increases in the federal minimum wage, showed the anticipated positive effect of the minimum wage on the pay rates of teenagers and other low-wage workers. But in each case, the anticipated negative effect of a minimum-wage hike on employment failed to materialize. When New Jersey increased its minimum wage to more than $5.00 per hour in early 1992, we again set out to measure the effects of the minimum wage. Once again, we found that the increase in the minimum wage seemed to occur with no loss in employment—even among fast-food restaurants, which many observers view as the quintessential minimum-wage employers.

In the face of the mounting evidence, we began to question the applicability of the conventional models that are routinely taught in introductory economics textbooks. What does it mean if an increase in the minimum wage has *no* effect—or even a positive effect—on employment? This book synthesizes the studies on the minimum wage that we have published during the past five years and presents our own interpretations of the evidence on the effects of minimum-wage legislation. In writing the book, we have had the opportunity to revise and update our earlier research, and to expand the evidence on the effects of the minimum wage in many new directions. We also have broadened our lines of inquiry to include a reexamination of the previous literature on the minimum wage, an analysis of the distributional effects of the minimum wage, a study of the effects of minimum wages on shareholder wealth, and a discussion of the theoretical implications of our findings.

In conducting our research and writing the book, we have benefited from the assistance of many colleagues, friends, and students. Lawrence Katz coauthored two of the original articles that preceded this book and provided detailed comments on the manuscript. Orley Ashenfelter, Danny Blanchflower, Charles Brown, David Cutler, Ronald Ehrenberg, Henry Farber, Randy Filer, George Johnson, Mark Killingsworth, and Christina Paxson generously participated in a conference presentation of an early draft and gave us many suggestions that improved the content and exposition of the book. We are especially grateful to Orley Ashenfelter for arranging this forum. Anne Case, Daniel Hamermesh, Richard Lester, and Isaac Shapiro also commented in detail on various chapters. Earlier versions of many chapters were presented at workshops and conferences across the country, and we thank seminar participants at the National Bureau of Economic Research, Cornell University, and the Universities of Chicago, Michigan, and Pennsylvania for their comments and suggestions. During the past year, we received dedicated research assistance from Lisa Barrow, Gordon Dahl, Sam Liu, Jon Orszag, Norman Thurston, Tammy Vu, and Xu Zhang. We also gratefully acknowledge research support from the Industrial Relations Section of Princeton University, the Sloan Foundation, and the University of Wisconsin Institute for Research on Poverty.

Finally, we thank Lisa, Benjamin, and Sydney Krueger, and Cindy Gessele, for their patience and support.

CHAPTER 1

Introduction and Overview

> There are two excesses to avoid in regard to *hypotheses:* the one of valuing them too much, the other of forbidding them entirely.
> —The *Encyclopédie* of Diderot and D'Alembert

NEARLY 50 YEARS AGO, George Stigler implored economists to be "outspoken, and singularly agreed" that increases in the minimum wage reduce employment. The reasoning behind this prediction is simple and compelling. According to the model presented in nearly every introductory economics textbook, an increase in the minimum wage lowers the employment of minimum-wage workers. This logic has convinced most economists: polls show that more than 90 percent of professional economists agree with the prediction that a higher minimum wage reduces employment.[1] Such a high degree of consensus is remarkable in a profession renowned for its bitter disagreements. But there is one problem: *the evidence is not singularly agreed that increases in the minimum wage reduce employment.* This book presents a new body of evidence showing that recent minimum-wage increases have not had the negative employment effects predicted by the textbook model. Some of the new evidence points toward a *positive* effect of the minimum wage on employment; most shows no effect at all. Moreover, a reanalysis of previous minimum-wage studies finds little support for the prediction that minimum wages reduce employment. If accepted, our findings call into question the standard model of the labor market that has dominated economists' thinking for the past half century.

Our main empirical findings can be summarized as follows. First, a study of employment in the fast-food industry after the recent 1992 increase in the New Jersey minimum wage shows that employment was *not* affected adversely by the law. Our results are derived from a specially designed survey of more than 400 restaurants throughout New Jersey and eastern Pennsylvania, conducted before and after the increase in the New Jersey minimum wage. Relative to restaurants in Pennsylvania, where the minimum wage remained unchanged, we find that employment in New Jersey actually *expanded* with the increase in the minimum wage. Furthermore, when we examine restaurants within New Jersey, we find that employment growth was *higher* at restaurants that were forced to increase their wages to comply with the law than at those stores that already were paying more than the new minimum. We find similar results in studies of fast-food restaurants in Texas after the 1991 increase in the federal minimum wage, and of teenage workers after the 1988 increase in California's minimum wage.

Second, a cross-state analysis finds that the 1990 and 1991 increases in the federal minimum wage did not affect teenage employment adversely. The federal minimum increased from $3.35 per hour to $3.80 on April 1, 1990, and to $4.25 per hour on April 1, 1991. We categorized states into groups on the basis of the fraction of teenage workers who were earning between $3.35 and $3.80 per hour just before the first minimum-wage increase took effect. In high-wage states, such as California and Massachusetts, relatively few teenagers were in the range in which the minimum-wage increase would affect pay rates, whereas in low-wage states, such as Mississippi and Alabama, as many as 50 percent of teenagers were in the affected wage range. On the basis of the textbook model of the minimum wage, one would expect teenage employment to decrease in the low-wage states, where the federal minimum wage raised pay rates, relative to high-wage states, where the minimum had far less effect. Contrary to this expectation, our results show no meaningful difference in employment growth between high-wage and low-wage states. If anything, the states with the largest fraction of workers affected by the minimum wage had the largest gains in teenage employment. This conclusion continues to hold when we adjust for differences in regional economic growth that occurred during the early 1990s, and conduct the analysis with state-level data, rather than regional data. A similar analysis of employment trends for a broader sample of low-wage workers, and for employees in the retail trade and restaurant industries, likewise fails to uncover a negative employment effect of the federal minimum wage.

Third, we update and reevaluate the time-series analysis of teenage employment that is the most widely cited evidence for the prediction that a higher minimum wage reduces employment. When the same econometric specifications that were used during the 1970s are re-estimated with data from more recent years, the historical relationship between minimum wages and teenage employment is weaker and no longer statistically significant. We also discuss and reanalyze several previous minimum-wage studies that used cross-sectional or panel data. We find that the evidence showing the minimum wage has no effect or a positive effect on employment is at least as compelling as the evidence showing it has an adverse effect.

Fourth, we document a series of anomalies associated with the low-wage labor market and the minimum wage. An increase in the minimum wage leads to a situation in which workers who previously were paid different wages all receive the new minimum wage. This finding is difficult to reconcile with the view that each worker originally was paid exactly what he or she was worth. Increases in the minimum wage also generate a "ripple effect," leading to pay raises for workers who previously earned wages above the new minimum. More surprisingly, increases in the minimum wage do not appear to be offset by reductions in fringe benefits. Furthermore, employers have been reluctant to use the subminimum-wage provisions of recent legislation. Each of these findings casts further doubt on the validity of the textbook model of the minimum wage.

Fifth, we find that recent increases in the minimum wage have reduced wage dispersion, partially reversing the trend toward rising wage inequality that has dominated the labor market since the early 1980s. Contrary to popular stereotypes, minimum-wage increases accrue disproportionately to individuals in low-income families. Indeed, two-thirds of minimum-wage earners are adults, and the earnings of a typical minimum-wage worker account for about one-half of his or her family's total earnings. In states in which the recent increases in the federal minimum wage had the greatest impact on wages, we find that earnings increased for families at the bottom of the earnings distribution. The minimum wage is a blunt instrument for reducing overall poverty, however, because many minimum-wage earners are not in poverty, and because many of those in poverty are not connected to the labor market. We calculate that the 90-cent increase in the minimum wage between 1989 and 1991 transferred roughly $5.5 billion to low-wage workers (or 0.2 percent of economy-wide earnings)—an amount that is smaller than most other federal antipoverty programs, and that can have only limited effects on the overall income distribution.

Sixth, we examine the impact of news about minimum-wage legislation on the value of firms that employ minimum-wage workers. Stock market event studies suggest that most of the news about the impending minimum-wage increases during the late 1980s led to little or no change in the market value of low-wage employers, such as restaurants, hotels, and dry cleaners. In contrast, more recent news of possible increases in the minimum wage may have led to small declines in shareholder wealth—1 or 2 percent, at most.

If a single study found anomalous evidence on the employment effect of the minimum wage, it could be easily dismissed. But the broad array of evidence presented in this book is more difficult to dismiss. Taken as a whole, our findings pose a serious challenge to the simple textbook theory that economists have used to describe the effect of the minimum wage. They also provide an opportunity to develop and test alternative theories about the operation of the labor market. As a step in this direction, we present and evaluate several models that depart only slightly from the textbook model, and yet are capable of explaining a broader range of reactions to the minimum wage.

Why Study the Minimum Wage?

Economists in the United States have been fascinated with minimum wages at least since 1912, when Massachusetts passed the first state minimum-wage law. During the next decade, 16 states and the District of Columbia adopted legislation establishing minimum pay standards for women and minors in a variety of industries and occupations.[2] The constitutionality of minimum-wage legislation was challenged almost immediately, and in 1923, the U.S. Supreme Court declared the District of Columbia's minimum-wage law unconstitutional. The effects of this ruling were far-reaching and essentially struck down or curtailed most of the state laws (Davis [1936]). The Court reconsidered the issue several times before finally reversing itself in 1937, upholding a Washington state law and setting the stage for the national minimum-wage regulations that were enacted as part of the Fair Labor Standards Act of 1938. This law, as amended, forms the basis for federal minimum-wage legislation today.

At the heart of economists' interest in the minimum wage is the prediction that an increase in the minimum wage will destroy jobs. Indeed, this hypothesis is one of the clearest and most widely appreciated in the field of economics. Figure 1.1 illustrates the impact of the minimum wage on covered employment in a stylized market, using the conventional supply and demand apparatus. In the absence of a minimum wage, wages and employment are determined by the intersection of the supply and demand curves. Introducing a minimum wage forces employers to move up the demand curve, reducing employment and increasing unemployment. Note that this prediction holds *regardless* of the precise magnitude of the parameters that determine the shape of the supply and demand curves. If a minimum-wage increase does *not* reduce employment, the relevance

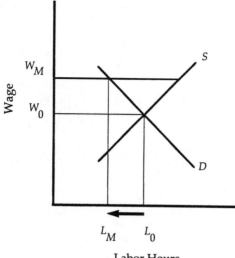

Figure 1.1 The impact of a binding minimum wage on employment in a market for homogeneous workers. The curve marked S is the supply curve, and the curve marked D is the demand curve. W_0 and L_0 represent the wage and amount of employment in the absence of a minimum, and W_M and L_M represent the minimum wage and amount of employment with a legal minimum.

of the textbook supply-and-demand apparatus seemingly is called into question.

The minimum wage is also of obvious importance to policy-makers. Countries around the world, including the United States and most other member nations of the Organization for Economic Cooperation and Development, maintain minimum-wage laws. Figure 1.2 shows the quarterly value of the U.S. minimum wage in constant 1993 dollars, from the the first quarter of 1950 to the last quarter of 1993. The minimum wage currently is at a relatively low level, and federal and state legislators recently have debated increases in the minimum. Each time an increase is discussed, there is renewed debate about whether minimum wages help or hurt the disadvantaged, and whether the labor market functions as smoothly as economics textbook writers assume.

Another reason for the prominence of the minimum wage in economics and policy discussions is the fact that, at some time during their lives, most individuals are paid the minimum wage. Indeed, we estimate that *more than 60 percent of all workers* have worked for the minimum wage at some time during their careers.[3] On any given

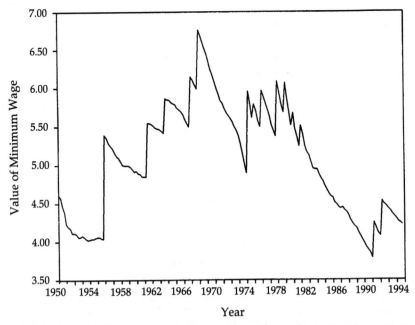

Figure 1.2 Quarterly value of the minimum wage from 1950 to 1993 in constant 1993 dollars, using the CPI as price deflator.

day, however, only about 5 percent of U.S. workers earn the minimum wage. Because those who earn the minimum wage tend to be disproportionately from low-income and minority families, the minimum wage has attracted the attention of social activists, as well.

What Does the Minimum Wage Do? Economists' Perspectives

If we imagine the total output of the economy as a pie, then the minimum wage can accomplish two things. First, it can alter the size of the overall pie. Second, it can change the size of the slice that different groups—low-wage workers, high-wage workers, and business owners—receive. Conservative economists generally argue that the minimum wage helps no one. They argue that it substantially shrinks the size of the overall pie *and* reduces the size of the slice that low-income people receive. For this reason, George Stigler called Michael Dukakis's support for a minimum-wage increase during the 1988 presidential campaign "despicable."[4] Finis Welch (1993) went even further, calling the minimum wage, "one of the cruelest constructs of an often cruel society."

Many liberal economists also find fault with the minimum wage.

They argue that, even though the minimum wage might give a slightly larger slice of the pie to some low-wage workers, other, equally deserving workers are shut out of the labor market by the minimum. In the 1979 edition of their introductory textbook, William Baumol and Alan Blinder explained, "The primary consequence of the minimum wage law is *not* an increase in the incomes of the least skilled workers but a restriction of their employment opportunities." Similarly, Robert Heilbroner and Lester Thurow (1987) wrote, "Minimum wages have two impacts. They raise earnings for those who are employed, but may cause other people to lose their jobs."

On the other side of the debate, social activists, policymakers, and other noneconomists often argue for an increase in the minimum wage. Advocates of the minimum wage have included Franklin D. Roosevelt, Martin Luther King, A. Philip Randolph, Walter Reuther, Edward Filene, and Beatrice and Sydney Webb. Within academia, social scientists from outside the field of economics often support minimum-wage legislation. Many noneconomists are skeptical of economic theory and downplay the predicted employment losses associated with a higher minimum wage, while emphasizing the potential pay increases for low-wage workers.

Most significantly, the general public does not widely share the negative opinion of the minimum wage that most economists hold. Surveys find that a majority of the public often supports increasing the minimum wage. A 1987 poll (Gallup [1987]), for example, found that three-fourths of the U.S. population favored an increase. Polls find even stronger support for the minimum wage among the low-income population, the group that many economists argue is hurt by the minimum. The general public is more evenly divided over the question of whether a minimum-wage increase reduces employment. A 1987 poll found that 24 percent of the public "agree a lot" with the statement that "raising the minimum wage might result in some job loss," whereas 22 percent "disagree a lot" with the statement.[5]

Where Do Economists' Views of the Minimum Wage Come From?

How can the general public, most governments, and many other social scientists disagree with the negative view of the minimum wage that is so widely held by economists? First, one should recognize that economists' views of the minimum wage are based largely on abstract theoretical reasoning, rather than on systematic empirical study. Indeed, introductory economics textbooks rarely cite any evidence for the hypothesized negative impact of the minimum wage. As we shall see throughout this book, close examination of the evidence reveals considerable uncertainty over the employment effect of the minimum wage.

Second, psychologists have found that people have a tendency to see patterns that support simple theories and preconceived notions, even where they do not exist. For example, the belief that basketball players shoot in streaks is widespread, even though empirical research has found no evidence of the so-called "hot hand" (Tversky and Gilovich, 1989). As another example, some investors continue to follow strategies that are based on recent trends in the stock market, even though economists have found that short-run stock market returns are essentially unpredictable. The weakness of this tendency is that researchers might discover patterns that support their theories, even if the theories are inaccurate. One way to overcome this shortcoming is to focus on empirical methods that all sides agree can provide a test of a particular theory *before* collecting and analyzing the data. In our view, this is an attractive aspect of the methodology used in our research, which relies on relatively simple comparisons among workers, firms, and states that were affected to varying degrees by a particular increase in the minimum wage.

Third, one should recognize that many models of the labor market have been developed, yet much of what occurs in that market remains a mystery to economists. Furthermore, many features of the labor market are at odds with the simple models that are presented in the introductory textbooks, and that most policymakers have in mind when considering a minimum-wage hike. The following passage, from the distinguished economist Paul A. Samuelson (1951, p. 312), suggests that the labor market has long posed a special challenge to economic theorizing:

> But I fear that when the economic theorist turns to the general problem of wage determination and labor economics, his voice becomes muted and his speech halting. If he is honest with himself, he must confess to a tremendous amount of uncertainty and self-doubt concerning even the most basic and elementary parts of the subject.

Social Economics Revisionists

The view that a higher minimum wage necessarily reduces employment was not always so strongly held by economists. Economists who led the field of labor economics during the middle half of the twentieth century—including Lloyd Reynolds, Clark Kerr, John Dunlop, and, especially, Richard A. Lester—believed that the minimum wage could increase employment in some instances, and reduce it in others. These so-called "social economics revisionists" believed that a number of noneconomic considerations, such as fairness and ability to pay, influence wage setting and employment.[6] These factors were believed to generate what Lester (1964) called "a range of indeterminacy," within which wages could vary with little effect on employment. Higher wages, for example, could reduce worker turnover and, therefore, improve productivity. Alternatively, increases in the minimum wage could "shock" some firms into adopting better management practices, leading to gains in output and employment.[7] According to the revisionist school, an increase in the minimum wage could cause some firms to increase employment, and others to reduce it. In general, however, the revisionists expected a modest increase in the minimum wage to have little effect on employment.

This view of the labor market and the minimum wage developed from empirical studies of individual firms and markets. Richard Lester, for example, analyzed the impact of the minimum wage on low-wage textile producers in the South, supplementing employment and wage data with survey information on firms' management practices. Judged against the empirical research on the minimum wage that was conducted during the 1970s and 1980s, the revisionists' style of research is surprisingly sophisticated, although their statistical methods are relatively simple. Nevertheless, the subsequent wave of neoclassical researchers has largely ignored the social economics revisionists' empirical research.[8]

The Neoclassical Model

As the influence of the revisionists waned during the 1960s, an alternative "neoclassical" view of the labor market rose to prominence. With this shift, the consensus view of the minimum wage changed radically. In contrast to the inductive reasoning of the institutionalist school, the neoclassical view of the labor market is based primarily on deductive reasoning. To understand the neoclassical view of the minimum wage, one must understand the theoretical logic that contemporary economists apply to the minimum wage. According to the standard model of the labor market, each employee is paid his or her "marginal product"—the contribution that he or she makes to the firm's revenue. If a worker is earning $3.50 per hour and contributing the same amount to the firm's revenue, and the government imposes a minimum wage of $4.25, then it is no longer profitable to employ that worker. In response to an increase in the minimum wage, employers attempt to adjust their operations so that workers are worth at least as much as the new minimum wage. They make this adjustment by cutting back on the employment of low-wage workers, and by substituting machinery and more highly skilled workers, whose wages are unaffected by the minimum wage.

The standard model makes a number of simplifying assumptions about the operation of the labor market that are important to this story. Firms have no discretion in choosing the wages that are paid to their workers. Workers are perfectly informed about wages at other firms and will readily move to a new job, if it pays more. In the standard model, workers are treated no differently than are other inputs that employers purchase, such as computers or electricity. The labor market is assumed to operate as smoothly and impersonally as the markets for these other inputs.

The assumptions of the standard neoclassical model lead to what is often called the "law of one price." It is easiest to understand this "law" in the context of a simple auction market, such as the commodities market or the stock exchange. In a frictionless auction market, each buyer pays the same price, and buyers can purchase all they want at the going price. When an investor goes to the stock market, she expects to be able to buy as many shares of AT&T as she wants at the "market price." If she isn't willing to pay the market price, she won't get any shares. And, she has no reason to pay more than the market price.

In the labor market, the law of one price translates into the assumption that employers can hire as many workers as they need at the market wage rate. Furthermore, workers of a given skill level receive the same wage rate at all firms. For example, janitors with the same training and skills earn the same pay at IBM as at McDonald's. The law of one price is in direct conflict with the revisionist economists' notion of a range of indeterminacy of wages. Indeed, the failure of the law of one price is what led many revisionists to abandon the simple neoclassical model, and to search for richer models, which could more readily explain the observed features of the labor market.

The standard model rules out a variety of other behaviors that might be important in understanding the workings of the labor market and the effect of the minimum wage. For example, the assumptions of the standard model imply that:

- Higher wages have no effect on worker productivity, or on the likelihood that employees shirk on the job
- Employees' productivity and turnover behavior are unaffected by inter-

personal wage comparisons. Employers need not worry about the perceived "fairness" of their wage structures.

- Employers always operate at peak efficiency and exploit every opportunity for profit. For example, they cannot negotiate lower prices from their suppliers if profits are squeezed by an increase in wages.
- Highly profitable firms do not share some of their profits with workers by offering higher wages or bonuses.

In the standard model, the role of a company's personnel department is exceedingly simple. A personnel manager need only observe the market wage and set pay rates accordingly. He or she need not worry about choosing wages to reduce turnover or motivate employees to work harder. Simply paying the going wage is the right strategy. This is clearly an abstraction of the personnel function. The key questions is: "Does this simplification matter?"

To be useful, a theoretical model can never capture all the nuances of the real world. Therefore, economic theory must abstract from many aspects of reality. A widely held view in economics is that theoretical models should be judged by the accuracy with which they can predict observed phenomena, and not necessarily by the realism of their underlying assumptions. Unfortunately, the standard model of the labor market does not always yield clear and unambiguous predictions, making it extremely difficult to test the model. The minimum wage is an exception, however, because the standard model makes strong and unambiguous predictions about the impact of a minimum wage on employment, wages, profit, and prices. Economists' fascination with the minimum wage arises in large part because it provides such a clear test of the standard neoclassical model.

What If Employers Set Their Own Wages?

The assumption that firms can hire all the workers they want at the going wage rate is widely adopted in modern discussions of the labor market. In fact, this assumption is the linchpin of the standard model of the labor market and underlies the reasoning that each worker is paid his or her "marginal product." Nevertheless, the standard model can be modified easily to include situations in which firms cannot recruit all the workers they desire at the wage they are paying their current work force. This modification allows firms some discretion in choosing the wages that they pay. A firm that wants to recruit more workers, or to recruit workers more quickly, will have to pay a higher wage.

This generalization of the standard model gives rise to what is known as a "monopsony" model. The term *monopsony*, which means a "sole buyer," was coined during the late 1920s by Joan Robinson, a British economist who first used the tools of neoclassical economic theory to analyze situations in which firms have some wage-setting power in the labor market.[9] Why might the buyers of labor, unlike the buyers of shares in large companies, have some monopsony power? In the simplest example of monopsony, there is only one employer in an area, and, in order to coax additional employees to work at the firm, the employer must offer a higher wage than he or she is currently paying. Some degree of monopsony power also arises in modern theories of the labor market that are based on "search theory"—formal models that take into account workers' and firms' lack of information about employment opportunities elsewhere in the market and the costs of moving between jobs and recruiting new workers.[10] As long as a higher wage helps firms to recruit workers, the firm has some monopsony power.

Monopsony power puts firms in an interesting position. On the one hand, if they offer a higher wage, they can recruit more workers, which, in turn, leads to higher output and profits. On the other hand, if they pay a higher wage to new recruits, then they must increase the wages of all their current employees.[11] A profit-maximizing firm will make a rational calculation and will raise wages to the point at which the wage paid to an additional worker is just equal to the worker's marginal product, *minus* the additional wages that must be given to all the current workers when this worker is added to the payroll. Each worker no longer is paid what he or she contributes to output, but something less.

In a monopsony situation, firms operate with ongoing vacancies. Although each employer would like to hire more workers at the current wage, it is not worthwhile to offer a higher wage, as the firm would have to pay the higher wage to all its current employees. Furthermore, different firms might choose to pay different wage rates, depending on the sensitivity of their recruiting efforts to the level of wages. Some firms might choose to offer a lower wage, and to operate with higher vacancies and higher turnover. Others might choose a higher wage, and to operate with lower vacancies and lower turnover. The result of these actions is a persistent range of indeterminacy for wages.

From our point of view, the most interesting aspect of the monopsony model is that it can *reverse* the predicted adverse employment effect of an increase in the minimum wage. In fact, in a monopsony situation, a small increase in the minimum wage will lead employers to increase their employment, because a higher minimum wage enables formerly low-wage firms to fill their vacancies quickly. The minimum wage forces these firms to behave more like the high-wage firms, which experienced lower vacancies and lower turnover rates. Of course, if the minimum wage is increased too much, firms will choose to cut employment, just as in the conventional model.

Economists typically take a dim view of the monopsony model. For example, Baumol and Blinder (1979) wrote, "Certainly the types of service establishments that tend to hire the lowest-paid workers . . . have no monopsony power whatever. While minimum wage laws can conceivably raise employment, few if any economists believe that they actually do have this pleasant effect." This view is based mainly on deductive reasoning. Most economists will ask the introspective question: How can a fast-food restaurant have any discretion in the wage that it pays for cashiers? In our view, the question is an empirical one. Do higher wages lead to more rapid recruiting rates and lower quit rates? Do different fast-food restaurants pay different wages? Does an increase in the minimum wage always lead to employment losses, as most economists believe, or can it lead to employment gains, as the monopsony model predicts?

PLAN OF THE BOOK

This book investigates the effect of the minimum wage on employment, prices, and the distribution of income. In chapters 2, 3, and 4, we summarize our research on the employment effects of recent increases in the U.S. minimum wage. This new research is based on comparisons across firms or across regions of the country that were affected by increases in the minimum wage to varying degrees. As noted, we believe that this research provides fairly compelling evidence that minimum-wage increases have no systematic effect on employment. Indeed, some of the research, based on employment changes at individual fast-food restaurants affected by an increase in the minimum wage, and on comparisons of employment trends in eating and drinking establishments across different states, suggests that a rise in the minimum wage may actually increase employment.

This is not to say that we believe that an increase in the minimum wage always leads to no change in employment at all firms. As our detailed microdata samples show, employment growth varies greatly across firms. In any given year, some firms grow, some shrink, some die, and some are born. A hike in the minimum wage could lead to an increase in employment at some firms, and to a decrease at others. As a result, it is always possible to find examples of employers who claim that they will go out of business if the minimum wage increases, or who state that they closed because of a minimum-wage increase. On average, however, our findings suggest that employment remains unchanged, or sometimes rises slightly, as a result of increases in the minimum wage. This conclusion poses a stark challenge to the standard textbook model of the minimum wage.

In chapter 5, we investigate other employment-related outcomes that are affected by the minimum wage. We find that the minimum wage has a "ripple effect" in many firms, leading to pay increases for workers who initially were earning slightly more than the new minimum wage. Although this effect is inconsistent with simple versions of the standard model, its existence is readily acknowledged by many low-wage employers. We also point out many other anomalies associated with the minimum wage. For example, we show that a large spike in the wage distribution occurs exactly at the minimum wage. The spike moves in response to minimum wage changes and becomes more prominent after a minimum-wage increase, as workers who formerly were paid less than the new minimum are "swept up" to the minimum wage. This pattern implies that workers who were paid different wages before the increase are paid the same wage afterward—seemingly at variance with the claim that all workers are paid in accordance with their true productivity. Even more puzzling, we cite research showing that firms that are exempt from the minimum wage often pay the minimum wage anyway. Finally, we find that minimum-wage employers are extremely reluctant to take advantage of subminimum-wage provisions. All these results complement our conclusion that recent increases in the minimum wage have not harmed employment. A variety of evidence suggests that the minimum wage does not have the effect on the labor market that would be predicted from the competitive neoclassical model.

What about the body of previous research that generally concluded that minimum-wage increases are associated with employment losses? For example, the 1981 Minimum Wage Study Commission concluded that a 10 percent increase in the minimum wage reduces teenage employment by 1 to 3 percent. Most of the research was based on aggregate time-series analyses of teenage employment. In this research, teenage employment rates in periods in which the minimum wage is relatively high are compared with rates in periods in which it is relatively low. In the past, this work generally found that the teenage employment-to-population rate was lower in periods of relatively high minimum wages. No systematic relationship was found for adults, perhaps because their wages were too high to be affected by the minimum.

In chapters 6 and 7, we reinvestigate previous empirical research on the minimum wage. We reach two surprising conclusions. First, the historical time-series relationship between minimum wages and teenage employment has become much weaker. If we use more recent data to estimate the same models that found negative effects of the minimum wage in the past, we no longer find statistically reliable evidence that the minimum wage reduces employment. To the extent that one found the past evidence convincing, the new evidence suggests a different conclusion. Second, some of the previous cross-sectional and panel-data studies rely on questionable assumptions and research methods. We have obtained and reanalyzed the data sets that were used in a number of these studies. Our reanalysis provides results that are generally consistent with the findings of our own studies.

One explanation for the small effect of the minimum wage in the U.S. labor market is that the minimum wage is set at a low level relative to average wages. Typically, only about 5 percent of workers are paid the minimum wage in the United States, compared with approximately 25 percent in Puerto Rico. In chapter 8, we investigate recent evidence of the impact of the minimum wage in other countries. We focus on Puerto Rico, which, because it is bound by U.S. minimum wage laws, has an extremely high minimum wage relative to average wages. We also review evidence with respect to the United Kingdom and Canada. The evidence for Canada is surprisingly similar to the aggregate time-series evidence for the United States: the same models that previously showed large negative effects of the minimum wage on teenage employment now show much smaller and statistically insignificant effects.

Of course, even if one believes that minimum-wage increases sometimes lead to employment increases, one need not support a minimum-wage increase. Likewise, some people may support a minimum-wage hike even if it is demonstrated to have a negative effect on employment. Given that our own and previous research find the magnitude of the employment effects of the minimum wage to be relatively small, opinions about the desirability of a minimum wage are based largely on distributional issues.

In chapter 9, we examine the effects of the minimum wage on the distributions of wages, earnings, and incomes. We use data from 1989–1992 to examine the family-income characteristics of minimum-wage earners and compare changes in the distributions of wages and earnings across different states after the 1990 and 1991 increases in the federal minimum wage. We also compare the family-income circumstances of workers whose wages were affected by the most recent increases in the minimum wage with those of workers who were affected by the 1974 increases. We find that, relative to the situation in 1974, workers affected by the recent minimum-wage increases are more highly concentrated in poorer families. We find strong evidence that an increase in the minimum wage raises pay rates for workers in the bottom 10 percent of the wage distribution. As a result, we conclude that recent increases in the minimum wage have contributed to a partial reversal of the rising wage inequality that emerged during the 1980s. The minimum wage has a similar effect on family earnings for families in the bottom 10 percent of the earnings distribution. Finally, we find some evidence that minimum wages reduce the poverty rates of families having at least one wage earner.

In chapter 10, we examine a different aspect of the distributional consequences of the minimum wage. We use a standard event-study methodology to evaluate the impact of news about minimum-wage legislation on the stock market values of a sample of firms in low-wage industries. We track news about the federal minimum wage, beginning in early 1987, when proposals to amend the Fair Labor Standards Act first appeared in Congress during the Reagan administration, and ending in 1993, with the most recent round of speculation about additional increases in the federal minimum. The standard model of the minimum wage predicts that the market values of firms employing low-wage workers should be very sensitive to changes in the relative likelihood of a minimum-wage change. On balance, we find only weak evidence of such an effect. One interpretation of our results is that the standard model overstates the profitability effects of a higher minimum wage. Another is that "news" about the minimum wage is released so slowly that it is difficult to capture discrete changes in investors' attitudes toward the probability of a change in the law.

In light of our new research, and our reanalysis of previous studies, we believe that the standard model of the labor market is incomplete. Chapter 11 presents a detailed discussion of alternative theoretical models of the labor market, and the implications of our empirical findings for the validity of these alternatives. We describe several versions of "the" standard model of the minimum wage, including a version that allows for covered and uncovered sectors of the labor market, and versions that explicitly take into account differences in skills across workers. We then present an alternative set of models, which share the common feature that employers have some discretion over the wages that they pay. We focus on a simple dynamic monopsony model, and on generalizations of this model that describe an equilibrium distribution of wages across firms. We highlight two important contrasts between the standard model and alternative models in which employers have some wage-setting power. First, all versions of the standard model lead to the prediction that an increase in the minimum wage will reduce employment of workers whose pay is increased by the minimum wage, whereas the alternative models suggest that employment can rise with modest increases in the minimum wage. Second, the alternative models provide a more natural interpretation of many other labor-market phenomena, including wage dispersion across seemingly identical workers, the existence of vacancies, and low-wage employers' use of a wide variety of recruiting tools. A rigorous evaluation of these alternative models will have to await subsequent research. Nevertheless, we hope that a careful consideration of the alternatives ultimately will lead to a better understanding of the labor market, and to better formulation of public policy.

In chapter 12, the concluding chapter, we summarize our research findings and consider the implications of our work for future policy discussions on the minimum wage. Finally, we evaluate the implications of our findings for the narrower debate within economics on the appropriate model of the labor market. We also outline some important areas for additional research on the effects of the minimum wage and the operation of the labor market.

CONCLUSION

Many of the findings in this book challenge the prevailing economic wisdom about the labor market and the effect of the minimum wage. Some of the research has provoked a great deal of critical comment and reaction. As a result, it is important to understand the strengths and weaknesses of the evidence on which we base our conclusions. For this reason, we describe our empirical findings in what many readers might consider excruciating detail. An important feature of the book is that our conclusions are based largely on the quantitative analysis of several data sources, in several settings. Our approach is to identify a series of "natural experiments" that would provide convincing evidence, even to a skeptic. We then analyze existing data sets and, in some cases, collect new data sets, in order to examine the impact of the minimum wage. The study of the impact of the New Jersey minimum wage is a good example of this approach. The fact that we designed the analysis in advance of collecting the data gives an added measure of credibility to the results, because the empirical findings could have supported one conclusion as easily as the other.

Judged against the standard of previous empirical research on the minimum wage, we believe that the new research that we present in this book is convincing. Nevertheless, all quantitative analyses have limitations. A major concern is that the minimum wage is never increased randomly for one group of employers. Consequently, we can analyze only "quasi-experiments," rather than classical randomized experiments, which routinely are used in the "hard" sciences. We try to probe the limitations of our analyses by using alternative "control groups" to compare the results. More importantly, we try to assemble a variety of evidence on different minimum-wage increases, which affect different groups of workers in different regions of the country at different times.

Some readers may be interested in exploring our analysis further, or in using our data sets for course work or problem sets. We will make the new data sets available via anonymous FTP until the end of the century. Specifically, the key data sets used in chapters 2, 4, and 6, are available in the MINIMUM directory of IRS.PRINCE-TON.EDU. The READ.ME file in that directory describes the data sets.

NOTES

1. See Kearl et al. (1979) and Colander and Klamer (1987).

2. Only the state of Wisconsin adopted a minimum wage covering adult male workers. For a detailed account of the state legislation, see U.S. Department of Labor, Women's Bureau (1928).

3. This estimate is based on data from the National Longitudinal Survey of Youth. Specifically, we tracked the 1964 birth cohort between 1979 and 1991 to estimate the percentage of workers who were ever paid within 5 cents of the minimum wage.

4. Transcript, "McNeil/Lehrer News Hour," September 28, 1988.

5. This poll was conducted for the Service Employees International Union in May 1987. See *Public Opinion Online*, accession number 0023319, question number 50.

6. The term *social economics revisionist* is used by Kerr (1994).

7. The "shock" theory of firm behavior recently has been endorsed by Alan Greenspan, chairman of the Federal Reserve Board. In describing the positive productivity effects of low inflation, Greenspan argued that low inflation causes businesses to become more efficient because they cannot raise their prices (see *New York Times*, June 9, 1994, p. D1).

8. The influential review article by Brown, Gilroy, and Kohen (1982), for example, does not mention Lester's work.

9. Robinson (1933, page 215, footnote 1) credits Mr. B. L. Hallward, of Cambridge, England, for the word.

10. One of the ironies of this line of research is that it was begun by George Stigler, who remained a staunch opponent of the minimum wage.

11. Of course, some employers actually try to pay higher wages for the new recruits than for their existing labor force. This practice often generates considerable turmoil in the work place, however.

CHAPTER 2

Employer Responses to the Minimum Wage: Evidence from the Fast-Food Industry

> The higher the minimum wage, the greater will be the number of covered workers who are discharged.
> —George J. Stigler

> Much of the experience under minimum wages fails to support Professor Stigler's conclusion.
> —Richard A. Lester

ECONOMISTS' thinking about the minimum wage is grounded in a simple theoretical model of employer behavior. According to this model, an increase in the minimum wage will lead to a decrease in employment at any firm that must raise pay rates to comply with the law. Although the tools of economic theory can be used to transform this microlevel prediction into a prediction about the labor market as a whole, the fundamental insight of the theory is at the level of the individual employer. In seeking to document the effects of the minimum wage, it is therefore most natural to begin at the firm level. This chapter presents two in-depth case studies of the effect of an increase in the minimum wage. Both studies use detailed data on individual fast-food restaurants that we collected to study the effects of the minimum wage. The choice of fast-food restaurants is deliberate: as suggested by the "McJobs" cliche, fast-food chains are the quintessential minimum-wage employers in today's labor market. Indeed, jobs in the fast-food industry account for a substantial fraction of all the minimum-wage jobs in the U.S. economy.

The first case study (based on Card and Krueger [1994]) focuses on the "natural experiment" generated by the April 1992 increase in the New Jersey minimum wage, from $4.25 to $5.05 per hour. Prior to the effective date of the new law, we surveyed 410 fast-food restaurants in New Jersey and eastern Pennsylvania. We resurveyed the restaurants roughly ten months later, to determine how employment had responded to the hike in the minimum wage. Comparisons between restaurants in New Jersey and those in Pennsylvania, where the minimum wage remained fixed at $4.25 per hour, provide direct estimates of the effect of the new minimum wage. A second set of comparisons, between restaurants in New Jersey that had been paying $5.00 or more per hour before the law took effect and lower-wage New Jersey restaurants, which had to increase their pay rates in order to comply with the law, provides a further contrast for studying the effect of the minimum. Remarkably, regardless of the comparison used, the estimated employment effects of the minimum wage are virtually identical. Contrary to the stark prediction of competitive-demand theory, we find that the rise in the New Jersey minimum wage seems to have *increased* employment at restaurants that were forced to raise pay to comply with the law.

The second case study uses the natural experiment generated by the April 1991 increase in the federal minimum wage, from $3.80 to $4.25 per hour. In collaboration with Lawrence Katz, one of us (Krueger) conducted a survey of fast-food restaurants in Texas, in December 1990 (see Katz and Krueger [1992]). We then conducted a second survey in July and August 1991, about four or five months after the increase in the federal minimum wage. More than 100 restaurants were interviewed in both surveys, permitting us to conduct a longitudinal analysis similar to the one conducted in the New Jersey–Pennsylvania study. Although the Texas analysis relies exclusively on the comparison between higher- and lower-wage restaurants within the same state to measure the effects of the minimum-wage hike, the results are similar to the results in the New Jersey–Pennsylvania study. Fast-food restaurants in Texas that were forced to increase pay to meet the new federal minimum-wage standard had *faster* employment growth than did those that already were paying $4.25 per hour or more, and that therefore were unaffected by the law. Again, the results seem to directly contradict the predictions of competitive-demand theory.

Testing Employment Demand Theory Using Natural Experiments

Before describing the two case studies in more detail, it is useful to outline the methodological basis of the natural-experiment approach that underlies the research in this chapter and later chapters of this book. The idea of using natural experiments is hardly new in economics. Indeed, the earliest research on the minimum wage, by Richard Lester (1946) and others, used that approach. Nevertheless, it is controversial—perhaps because studies based on the natural-experiment approach often seem to overturn the "conventional wisdom."[1] Readers who are mainly interested in the results of the studies, rather than in their methodology, can skip this section.

From an Ideal Experiment to a Natural Experiment

How can economists test the predictions of competitive-demand theory? Ideally, we would like to use the same experimental techniques that have revolutionized physics, medicine, and other "hard" sciences during the past century. In an experimental drug trial, for example, a sample of patients is randomly divided into two groups: (1) a treatment group, which receives the drug; and (2) a control group, which does not. The key feature of this classical experimental design is the random assignment of the original population into treatment and control groups. Because the two groups are randomly selected, there is no reason to believe that in the absence of the drug, the average behavior of the treatment group should differ from the average behavior of the control group. The experiences of the control group therefore provide a valid "counterfactual" for the outcomes of the treatment group if they had not received the drug.

In principle, a well-funded social scientist could design and implement a similar experiment to test the effect of the minimum wage.[2] A sample of low-wage employers could be randomly divided into a treatment group that is subject to a minimum wage, and a control group that is not. The effect of the minimum wage then could be deduced by comparing average employment levels in the two groups of firms. Budgetary and legal restrictions make it unlikely, however, that a "perfect" experimental evaluation of the minimum wage will ever be conducted. Furthermore, in contrast to a simple drug trial, one might expect the imposition of a minimum wage on employers in the treatment group to have some spillover effect on employers in the control group.[3] Control-group firms might gain a competitive advantage if firms in the treatment group are required to increase pay rates to meet the minimum wage. Thus, an idealized experiment would have to involve random assignment of entire (isolated) labor markets.

Nevertheless, the central feature of a classical randomized experiment—the existence of a control group to estimate what would have happened in the absence of the intervention—lies behind the idea of a natural experiment. In a natural-experiment evaluation, the analyst makes use of the differences in outcomes between a treatment group and a control group, just as in a classical experiment, but treatment status is determined by nature, politics, or other forces beyond the analyst's control. Examples of natural experiments in the labor market include the Vietnam-era draft lottery (Angrist [1991]), the 1980 boatlift of Cubans into Miami (Card [1990]), and compulsory-schooling laws (Angrist and Krueger [1991]).[4] In the case of the minimum wage, the simplest example of a natural experiment is the adoption of a minimum wage by a single state (for example, New Jersey, 1992). Low-wage employers in the state become the treatment group, and low-wage employers in a nearby state that does not raise its minimum wage provide an obvious control group. The effect of the minimum wage can be estimated by comparing employment outcomes in the two states after the imposition of the minimum. Another type of control group can be formed from similar firms in the "treatment-group" state that initially were paying more than the new minimum wage, e.g., because of their location in high-wage areas. The employment outcomes of these higher-wage firms provide a second, potentially useful counterfactual for the outcomes of affected firms in the state.

Assessing the Validity of a Natural Experiment

The critical question in any natural-experiment evaluation is the validity of the control group.[5] Treatment status in a natural experiment, unlike that in a classical experiment, typically is *not* determined by a randomizing procedure, but rather, through a political process or other mechanism. In the case of the minimum wage, for example, a state legislature might be more likely to vote for a minimum-wage hike if the state economy is expanding rapidly. Unless the economy in the "control-group" state is similarly robust, the comparison between employment levels in the treatment and control groups could be biased. Moreover, without random assignment, there is no guarantee that employers in the treatment group and those in the control group would be identical in the absence of the minimum wage. If employers in the two groups differ only with respect to their permanent characteristics (such as location), any differences between them can be eliminated by comparing *changes* in outcomes for the treatment group relative to the control group from a pre-intervention baseline to a postintervention period. The maintained assumption in this so-called "difference-in-differences" procedure is that growth rates in the two groups would have been the same in the absence of the intervention. More generally, one can assume that the treatment and control groups would behave the same way *conditional on a set of observed covariates*, including lagged outcomes.

The validity of a potential control group can be checked by determining the answers to several questions. First, are the pre-intervention characteristics of the treatment and control groups reasonably similar? Second, have the two groups tended to move together in the past? Third, was the intervention more or less "exogenous," or was it triggered by some phenomenon that differentially affects the treatment and control groups? Finally, is it possible to compare the control group against other plausible control groups? Although affirmative answers to these questions cannot guarantee the validity of the control group, careful consideration of the answers can lead to a more confident assessment of the credibility of a natural-experiment evaluation.[6]

Comparison with Other Approaches

In our opinion, the natural-experiment approach is an attractive one for studying the labor market in general, and for evaluating the effect of the minimum wage in particular. First, it is simple and clear-cut. Unlike the time-series approach that dominated the minimum-wage literature during the 1970s, a credible natural-experiment evaluation can be based on a comparison of means. A related advantage is that a natural-experiment evaluation is largely model free. The results can be construed as a test of a particular theoretical model, but their interpretation does not hinge on the maintained assumptions of a specific model. Another advantage is that the source of wage variation used to estimate the effect of the minimum wage is clearly spelled out.[7] As we explain in later chapters of this book, much of the literature on minimum wages can be criticized for failing to distinguish between wage differences caused by minimum-wage changes and wage differences caused by other, potentially endogenous labor-market forces. Finally, a natural-experiment approach focuses on a predetermined set of comparisons between the treatment group and the control group. In principle, the complete set of empirical specifications can be laid out in advance of the analysis. There is less need for specification searching, which can lead to biased statistical inferences if the same data set is used to derive an appropriate model *and* to perform hypothesis tests.[8]

Evaluations of natural experiments induced by government interventions possess an additional advantage that is particularly relevant for policy deliberations. Policy analysts are often asked to forecast the effects of a proposed intervention, such as an increase in the minimum wage. Most often, policy forecasts are constructed from a simple theoretical structure and a set of estimated behavioral parameters. The simulations rely on a series of assumptions and simplifications that can be difficult to evaluate. By its very nature, however, a natural-experiment evaluation provides reduced-form estimates of the effects of the underlying intervention on a wide variety of outcomes. These estimates can be used in subsequent deliberations to forecast the effects of a similar intervention without having to start from a particular theoretical framework.[9]

THE EMPLOYMENT EFFECTS OF THE NEW JERSEY MINIMUM WAGE

Legislative Background

After a decade of inaction on the issue of the minimum wage, the U.S. Congress and President Bush finally reached agreement in November 1989 on a bill that increased the federal minimum wage in two steps, from $3.35 to $3.80 per hour on April 1, 1990, and to $4.25 per hour on April 1, 1991.[10] Following a long-standing tradition, many states, including New Jersey, voted to raise their own, state-specific minimum-wage rates in lockstep with the federal law. The Democrat-controlled New Jersey legislature, buoyed by the strength of the state economy during the late 1980s, went one step further and voted an additional 80-cent increase, effective April 1, 1992. The scheduled $5.05 hourly minimum-wage rate gave New Jersey the highest state minimum in the country and was strongly opposed by its business leaders.

During the two years between the passage of the $5.05 minimum wage and its effective date, the New Jersey economy fell into recession. In addition, the Democratic majorities of both houses of the legislature were swept aside by a Republican landslide. Concerned about the possible impact of the scheduled minimum-wage hike, the lower house voted in March 1992 to split the increase over two years. The vote fell just short of the margin required to override a gubernatorial veto, and then-Governor Florio allowed the $5.05 rate to go into effect on April 1, before finally vetoing the two-step legislation. Faced with the prospect of having to roll back wages for minimum-wage workers, the legislature dropped the issue. Despite a strong, last-minute challenge, the $5.05 minimum rate took effect as originally planned.

We believe that this dramatic sequence of events underscores the value of a case study of the New Jersey minimum wage. In accordance with the simple hypothesis that legislators enact minimum wages when times are good, the $5.05 minimum was adopted when the state economy was relatively healthy. By the effective date of the actual increase, however, the U.S. economy was in recession, and New Jersey was mired in an even deeper regional slump. We suspect that, had it been voting in early 1992, the legislature would not have agreed to a $5.05 minimum. In our view, then, the April 1992 minimum-wage increase qualifies as a legitimate natural experiment.

It certainly seems unlikely that the effects of the higher minimum wage would be overshadowed by a rising tide of general economic conditions.

A Sample of Fast-Food Restaurants

Early in 1992—before we knew with certainty whether New Jersey's $5.05 minimum wage would be repealed—we decided to conduct a survey of fast-food restaurants in New Jersey and eastern Pennsylvania, to evaluate the effect of the new law. Our choice of the fast-food industry was driven by several factors. First, fast-food restaurants are a leading employer of low-wage workers: in 1989, they employed 20 percent of all workers in the restaurant (eating-and-drinking) industry, which, in turn, accounted for about one-third of all workers who earned at or near the minimum wage.[11] Second, most fast-food chains rigorously comply with minimum-wage regulations and would be expected to raise wages in response to an increase in the minimum wage. Third, the job requirements and product offerings of fast-food restaurants are relatively homogeneous, making it easier to obtain reliable measures of employment, wages, and product prices. The absence of tips greatly simplifies the measurement of wages in the industry. Fourth, it is relatively easy to construct a sample frame of franchised restaurants. Finally, experience with a survey in Texas (discussed later in this chapter) suggested that fast-food restaurants have high response rates to telephone surveys.

Although most Americans are familiar with fast-food restaurants, some of the characteristics of fast-food workers and their jobs may come as a surprise. The most thorough study of the fast-food industry was conducted by Charner and Fraser (1984). In 1982, Charner and Fraser conducted interviews with 4,660 fast-food employees at seven companies: Arby's, Del Taco, KFC, Krystal, McDonald's, Roy Rogers, and White Castle. Our survey of New Jersey and Pennsylvania fast-food restaurants (described in the next section) provides some additional information on workers in the industry.

Fast-food workers tend to be younger than workers in other industries, although a substantial fraction are adults. In the first wave of our survey of restaurants in New Jersey and eastern Pennsylvania, slightly more than one-half of nonsupervisory employees were age 20 or older.[12] Anecdotal evidence suggests that fast-food restaurants increasingly are hiring older workers in response to the decline in the relative size of the teenage population. With respect to other demographic characteristics, Charner and Fraser report that 66 percent of fast-food workers are female, 77 percent are white, and 65 percent are high school graduates.

Reliable information on job-turnover rates at fast-food restaurants is difficult to obtain, but by all accounts, turnover is extremely high. Charner and Fraser report that nearly one-half of surveyed fast-food workers were employed in their jobs for one year or less. They also find that 32 percent of fast-food workers employed at a given date separated from their jobs within approximately the next six months. (The turnover rate as traditionally measured will be higher than this figure because many of the employees who were hired to fill the vacancies created by the workers who separated also may have separated within the six-month period.) Charner and Fraser find that 90 percent of employee separations are reported by the workers as voluntary quits, and that 10 percent are reported as employer-initiated firings. These statistics suggest that recruitment and worker discipline are important issues in the industry. Evidently, many fast-food restaurants are involved in a continuous process of recruiting workers.

How do the restaurants find workers? Forty-one percent of the employees in Charner and Fraser's survey reported that they learned about their jobs from friends or siblings, 32 percent simply walked in and applied, 11 percent saw a sign in the restaurant, and 6 percent responded to a newspaper ad. The two most commonly cited reasons for quitting were to take another job (28 percent) and to return to school (21 percent).

Charner and Fraser (p. 22) observe that "most fast food employees perform multiple tasks within the store," such as sweeping and mopping (43 percent), cooking food (44 percent), cleaning equipment (55 percent), taking orders (65 percent), assembling orders (61 percent), and taking money (64 percent). The nature of the jobs requires that individuals work in teams, so morale and camaraderie are important work attributes. Although the typical fast-food job involves several different tasks, jobs do have primary lines of responsibility. About one-half of fast-food employees work in the front of the store, performing such tasks as taking orders and handling money. Workers with more seniority and females are more likely to be assigned to front-of-the-store tasks. Full-time workers are also more likely to be assigned to front-of-the-store tasks and administrative tasks than are part-time workers.

The fraction of part-time workers varies from restaurant to restaurant. About 30 percent of nonsupervisory employees work full time. Charner and Fraser find that fast-food workers' hourly wages typically are tied to seniority, rather than to job titles or responsibilities.

In addition, because the typical job tenure is short, a high fraction of workers are paid the entry-level or starting wage.

We constructed a sample frame of 473 fast-food restaurants in New Jersey and eastern Pennsylvania from the Burger King, KFC, Wendy's, and Roy Rogers chains.[13] The first wave of the survey was conducted by telephone during late February and early March 1992—slightly more than one month before the scheduled increase in New Jersey's minimum wage. The overall response rate to the survey was extraordinarily high (87 percent), resulting in a usable sample of 410 restaurants—331 in New Jersey, and 79 in Pennsylvania. Figure 2.1 is a map of the Middle Atlantic region showing the locations of the restaurants in our sample. There is a large concentration of sampled restaurants along the New Jersey–Pennsylvania border, and another in northeastern New Jersey. Additional details

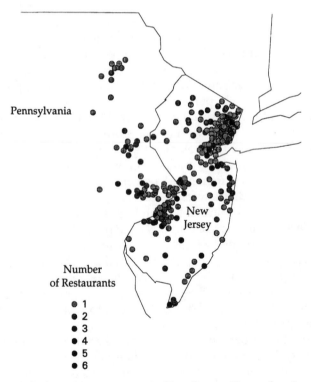

Figure 2.1   Location of restaurants in New Jersey–Pennsylvania survey.

of the survey, including information on response rates and the reliability of the answers to certain key questions, are reported in the Appendix to this chapter.

The second wave of the survey was conducted in November and December 1992, about eight months after the minimum-wage increase. Only the restaurants that responded to the first wave of the survey were contacted during the second round of interviews. We successfully interviewed 371 of these by telephone in November 1992. Our concern that nonresponding restaurants might have closed prompted us to hire an interviewer to drive to each of the 39 nonrespondents, determine whether the restaurant was still open, and conduct a personal interview, if possible. The interviewer discovered that 6 restaurants were permanently closed, 2 were temporarily closed (1 because of a fire, 1 because of road construction), and 2 were under renovation. All but 1 of the 29 stores open for business granted the request for a personal interview. Therefore, we have second-wave interview data for 99.8 percent of the restaurants that responded in the first wave of the survey, and information on closure status for 100 percent of the sample.

We stress the value of complete longitudinal data—including information on the closed stores—for a study of the effect of the minimum wage. George Stigler (1947) once remarked that studying the effect of an increase in the minimum wage on a sample of firms that remain open for business after the increase is like studying the effect of a war by analyzing the surviving veterans. By tracking *all* the restaurants in our initial sample, we are able to measure the overall effect of the minimum wage on average employment in the industry, rather than simply its effect on surviving establishments.

Table 2.1 presents the mean values of the key variables in our survey, taken over the subset of nonmissing responses for each variable. In these tabulations, we measure employment as full-time-equivalent (FTE) employment, counting each full-time worker (including managers and assistant managers) as 1, and each part-time worker as 0.5. We analyze the sensitivity of our findings to alternative measures of employment later in this section. Wave 2 employment is set equal to 0 for the permanently closed restaurants but is treated as missing for the temporarily closed ones. Means are presented for the full sample, and separately for restaurants in New Jersey and in eastern Pennsylvania. The fourth column of the table shows the *t*-statistics for the null hypothesis that the means of each variable are equal in the two states.

The first five rows of the table give the distribution of restaurants in the sample by chain and ownership status (company owned

TABLE 2.1
Means of Key Variables

	All (1)	New Jersey (2)	Pennsylvania (3)	t-test for NJ − PA[a] (4)
		Restaurants, by State		
1. Distribution of Restaurant Types (%)				
a. Burger King	41.7	41.1	44.3	−0.5
b. KFC	19.5	20.5	15.2	1.2
c. Roy Rogers	24.2	24.8	21.5	0.6
d. Wendy's	14.6	13.6	19.0	−1.1
e. Company Owned	34.4	34.1	35.4	−0.2
2. Means in Wave 1				
a. FTE Employment	21.0 (0.49)	20.4 (0.51)	23.3 (1.35)	−2.0
b. Percent Full-Time Employees	33.3 (1.2)	32.8 (1.3)	35.0 (2.7)	−0.7
c. Starting Wage ($/hr)	4.62 (0.02)	4.61 (0.02)	4.63 (0.04)	−0.4
d. Wage = $4.25 (%)	31.0 (2.3)	30.5 (2.5)	32.9 (5.3)	−0.4
e. Price of Full Meal ($)	3.29 (0.03)	3.35 (0.04)	3.04 (0.07)	4.0
f. Hours Open (weekday)	14.4 (0.1)	14.4 (0.2)	14.5 (0.3)	−0.3
g. Recruiting Bonus	24.6 (2.1)	23.6 (2.3)	29.1 (5.1)	−1.0

versus franchisee owned). The sample includes 171 restaurants from the Burger King chain, 80 from KFC, 99 from Roy Rogers, and 60 from Wendy's. Although not reported in the table, a detailed analysis reveals that restaurants in the Burger King, Roy Rogers, and Wendy's chains have very similar levels of employment, hours per worker, and meal prices, whereas the KFC restaurants are smaller, are open fewer hours, and charge more for their main course (chicken).

In the first wave of the survey, average employment was 23.3 FTE workers per restaurant in Pennsylvania, compared with an average of 20.4 in New Jersey. Starting wages were very similar among restaurants in the two states, although the average price of a "full meal" (a main course, a small order of french fries, and a medium-sized

TABLE 2.1
(continued)

| | All (1) | Restaurants, by State | | t-test for NJ − PA[a] (4) |
		New Jersey (2)	Pennsylvania (3)	
3. Means in Wave 2				
a. FTE Employment	21.1	21.0	21.2	−0.2
	(0.46)	(0.52)	(0.94)	
b. Percent Full-Time	34.8	35.9	30.4	1.8
Employees	(1.2)	(1.4)	(2.8)	
c. Starting Wage ($/hr)	5.00	5.08	4.62	10.8
	(0.01)	(0.01)	(0.04)	
d. Wage = $4.25 (%)	4.9	0.0	25.3	—
	(1.1)	—	(4.9)	
e. Wage = $5.05 (%)	69.0	85.2	1.3	36.1
	(2.3)	(2.0)	(1.3)	
f. Price of Full Meal	3.34	3.41	3.03	5.0
($)	(0.03)	(0.04)	(0.07)	
g. Hours Open	14.5	14.4	14.7	−0.8
(weekday)	(0.1)	(0.2)	(0.3)	
h. Recruiting Bonus	20.9	20.3	23.4	−0.6
(%)	(2.1)	(2.3)	(4.9)	

Note: Standard errors are shown in parentheses. See text for definitions.
[a]t-statistic for test of equality of means in New Jersey and Pennsylvania.

soda) was significantly higher in New Jersey. There were no significant differences between the states in the average number of hours of operation or the percentage of full-time employees. About one-fourth of the restaurants in both states reported that they offered their existing employees a cash bonus to help to recruit new workers.[14]

The average starting wage at fast-food restaurants in New Jersey increased by 10 percent after the rise in the minimum wage. This change is illustrated in Figure 2.2, in which we have plotted the overall distributions of starting wages in the two states from the two waves of the survey. In wave 1, the wage distributions in New Jersey and Pennsylvania were very similar. After the minimum-wage increase, virtually all the restaurants in New Jersey that had been paying less than $5.05 per hour reported a starting wage exactly equal to the new minimum, generating a sharp "spike" in the wave

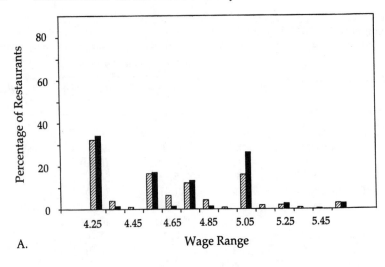

A.

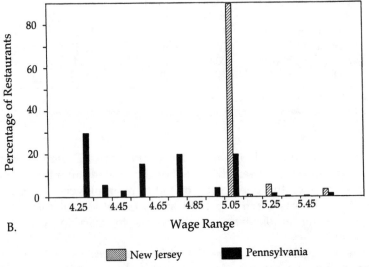

B.

New Jersey   Pennsylvania

Figure 2.2 Distribution of starting wage rates. A. February–March 1992. B. November–December 1992.

2 wage distribution for New Jersey. Interestingly, the minimum-wage increase had no apparent spillover effect on higher-wage restaurants in the state: the mean percentage wage change for restaurants that initially were paying more than $5.05 per hour was −3.1 percent.

Despite the increase in wages, FTE employment *increased* in New Jersey relative to Pennsylvania, as can be seen by comparing rows 2a and 3a of Table 2.1. Although restaurants in New Jersey initially were smaller, employment gains in New Jersey, coupled with losses in Pennsylvania, led to rough equality in wave 2. Only two other variables show a relative change between waves 1 and 2: (1) the fraction of full-time employees; and (2) the price of a meal. Both increased in New Jersey relative to Pennsylvania.

Difference-in-Differences Estimates

Table 2.2 presents a more detailed analysis of the levels and changes in average employment per restaurant in the two waves of our survey. Data are shown for the overall sample (column 1); by state (columns 2 and 3); and for restaurants in New Jersey, classified by whether the starting wage in wave 1 was exactly $4.25 per hour (column 5), between $4.26 and 4.99 per hour (column 6), or $5.00 or more per hour (column 7). We also show the differences in average employment between New Jersey and Pennsylvania restaurants (column 4), and between restaurants in the various wage ranges in New Jersey (columns 8 and 9).

Row 3 presents the estimated changes in average employment between waves 1 and 2. The entries are simply the differences between the averages for the two waves (i.e., row 2 minus row 1). An alternative estimate of average employment growth is presented in row 4. Here we have computed the change in employment over the subset of restaurants with nonmissing employment data for both waves, which we refer to as the *balanced subsample of stores*. Finally, in row 5, we present the average change in employment among restaurants with nonmissing data for both waves, setting wave 2 employment at the temporarily closed restaurants equal to zero, rather than treating it as missing.

As noted in the discussion of Table 2.1, New Jersey restaurants initially were smaller than their Pennsylvania counterparts but grew relative to Pennsylvania restaurants after the rise in the minimum wage. Average employment levels of the New Jersey and Pennsylvania restaurants before and after the minimum-wage increase are illustrated in the upper panel of Figure 2.3. The difference-in-differences of FTE employment between New Jersey and Pennsylvania restaurants, shown in the third row of Table 2.2, is 2.76 FTE employees (about 13 percent), with a t-statistic of 2.03. Inspection of the alternative calculations in rows 4 and 5 shows that the relative change between New Jersey and Pennsylvania restaurants is vir-

TABLE 2.2
Average Employment per Restaurant Before and After Increase in New Jersey Minimum Wage

| | All | Restaurants, by State | | Difference | Restaurants in New Jersey[a] | | | Differences Within New Jersey[b] | |
| | | PA | NJ | NJ − PA | Wage = $4.25 | Wage $4.26–4.99 | Wage ≥ $5.00 | Low − High | Midrange − High |
	(1)	(2)	(3)	(4)	(5)	(6)	(7)	(8)	(9)
1. FTE Employment Before, All Available Observations	21.00 (0.49)	23.33 (1.35)	20.44 (0.51)	−2.89 (1.44)	19.56 (0.77)	20.08 (0.84)	22.25 (1.14)	−2.69 (1.37)	−2.17 (1.41)
2. FTE Employment After, All Available Observations	21.05 (0.46)	21.17 (0.94)	21.03 (0.52)	−0.14 (1.07)	20.88 (1.01)	20.96 (0.76)	20.21 (1.03)	0.67 (1.44)	0.75 (1.27)
3. Change in Mean FTE Employment	0.05 (0.50)	−2.16 (1.25)	0.59 (0.54)	2.76 (1.36)	1.32 (0.95)	0.87 (0.84)	−2.04 (1.14)	3.36 (1.48)	2.91 (1.41)
4. Change in Mean FTE Employment, Balanced Sample of Restaurants[c]	−0.07 (0.46)	−2.28 (1.25)	0.47 (0.48)	2.75 (1.34)	1.21 (0.82)	0.71 (0.69)	−2.16 (1.01)	3.36 (1.30)	2.87 (1.22)
5. Change in Mean FTE Employment, Setting FTE at Temporarily Closed Restaurants to Zero[d]	−0.26 (0.47)	−2.28 (1.25)	0.23 (0.49)	2.51 (1.35)	0.90 (0.87)	0.49 (0.69)	−2.39 (1.02)	3.29 (1.34)	2.88 (1.23)

Note: Standard errors are shown in parentheses. The sample consists of all restaurants with nonmissing data on employment. FTE (full-time-equivalent employment) counts each part-time worker as 0.5 a full-time worker. Employment at six closed restaurants is set to zero. Employment at four temporarily closed restaurants is treated as missing.

[a] Restaurants in New Jersey classified by whether starting wage in wave 1 equals $4.25 per hour (N = 101), is between $4.26 and 4.99 per hour (N = 140), or is $5.00 per hour or higher (N = 73).

[b] Difference in employment between restaurants in low-wage ($4.25 per hour) and high-wage (≥$5.00 per hour) ranges; and difference in employment between restaurants in midrange ($4.26–4.99 per hour) and high-wage ranges.

[c] Subset of restaurants with nonmissing data on employment in wave 1 and wave 2.

[d] In this row only, wave 2 employment at four temporarily closed restaurants is set to zero. Employment changes are based on the subset of restaurants with nonmissing data on employment in wave 1 and wave 2.

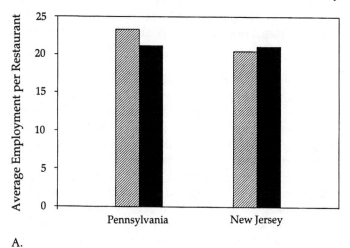

A.

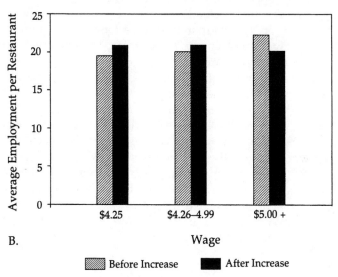

B.

Before Increase   After Increase

Figure 2.3 Average employment per restaurant, before and after increase in the minimum wage. A. Comparison of restaurants in New Jersey and Pennsylvania. B. Comparison of restaurants within New Jersey, by initial wage.

tually identical when the analysis is restricted to the balanced subsample of restaurants, and is only slightly smaller when wave 2 employment at the temporarily closed restaurants is set equal to zero.

From February to November 1992, employment increased at the low-wage restaurants in New Jersey (those paying $4.25 per hour in wave 1), was approximately constant at New Jersey restaurants in the middle of the wage distribution (those paying between $4.26 and 4.99 per hour in wave 1), and contracted at the high-wage restaurants in the state (those paying $5.00 or more per hour). Employment patterns at the three types are illustrated in the lower panel of Figure 2.2. The average change in employment among the high-wage restaurants (−2.16 FTE employees) is remarkably similar to the change among Pennsylvania restaurants (−2.28 FTE employees). Because high-wage restaurants in New Jersey were not affected directly by the new minimum-wage law, this comparison provides a potential specification test of the validity of the Pennsylvania control group. The test is clearly passed. Regardless of whether the affected restaurants are compared with restaurants in Pennsylvania or with high-wage restaurants in New Jersey, the estimated employment effect of the minimum wage is positive.

Our results suggest that fast-food restaurants that were *unaffected* by the rise in the New Jersey minimum wage—those in Pennsylvania and New Jersey restaurants that already were paying $5.00 per hour or more in wave 1—cut employment between February and November 1992. We believe that the source of this trend was the continued worsening of the economies of the Middle Atlantic states during 1992.[15] Unemployment rates in the three Middle Atlantic states rose between 1991 and 1993, with a larger increase in New Jersey than in Pennsylvania during 1992. Fast-food restaurant sales are highly procyclical.[16] Thus, in the absence of other factors, the rise in unemployment would be expected to reduce employment in these establishments.

Regression-Adjusted Models

The comparisons in Table 2.2 make no allowance for other sources of variation in employment growth, such as systematic differences across chains. These sources are incorporated in the estimates in Table 2.3. The entries in this table are regression coefficients from ordinary least squares (OLS) estimates of the following two equations:

$$\Delta Y = a + b\,X + c\,NJ + \epsilon \qquad (2.1a)$$

or

$$\Delta Y = a' + b' X + c' GAP + \epsilon', \qquad (2.1b)$$

where ΔY is the change in employment or the proportional change in employment or wages from wave 1 to wave 2 at a particular restaurant, X is a set of characteristics of the restaurant, and NJ is a dummy variable equal to 1 for restaurants in New Jersey. GAP is an alternative measure of the impact of the minimum wage at a given restaurant, based on the starting wage at that restaurant in the first wave of the survey (W_1):

$GAP = 0$ for restaurants in Pennsylvania

$\quad = 0$ for restaurants in New Jersey with $W_1 \geq$ \$5.05 per hour

$\quad = (5.05 - W_1)/W_1$ for other restaurants in New Jersey.

GAP measures the proportional increase in wages at restaurant i required to meet the new minimum rate. Differences in this variable across restaurants reflect both the New Jersey–Pennsylvania comparison and differences within New Jersey based on reported wages in wave 1.

The first 10 columns of Table 2.3 report models for the changes in employment at the fast-food restaurants in our sample, whereas the last two columns present models for the changes in starting wages. Beginning with the employment models, the estimated coefficient of the New Jersey dummy variable in column 1 of Table 2.3 is directly comparable to the simple difference-in-differences of employment changes in column 4, row 4, of Table 2.2. The minor discrepancy between the two estimates is due to the restricted sample in Table 2.3, which contains only restaurants that reported employment *and* wages in both waves of the survey. This restriction results in a slightly smaller estimate of the relative increase in employment in New Jersey.

The model in column 2 introduces a set of four control variables: indicators for three of the chains and another indicator for company-owned restaurants. As shown by the probability values in row 6, these control variables add little to the model and have no effect on the size of the estimated coefficient of the New Jersey dummy.

The specifications in columns 3–5 use the GAP variable to measure the effect of the minimum wage. This variable gives a slightly higher R-Squared coefficient than does the simple New Jersey dummy, although it implies a slightly smaller relative change in em-

TABLE 2.3
Estimated Reduced-Form Models for Changes in Employment and Starting Wages

	Dependent Variable: Change in Employment[a]					Dependent Variable: Proportional Change in Employment[b]					Dependent Variable: Proportional Change in Starting Wage[c]	
	(1)	(2)	(3)	(4)	(5)	(6)	(7)	(8)	(9)	(10)	(11)	(12)
1. New Jersey Dummy	2.33 (1.19)	2.30 (1.20)	—	—	—	0.05 (0.05)	0.05 (0.05)	—	—	—	0.11 (0.01)	—
2. Initial Wage Gap[d]	—	—	15.65 (6.08)	14.92 (6.21)	11.98 (7.42)	—	—	0.39 (0.26)	0.34 (0.26)	0.29 (0.31)	—	1.04 (0.03)
3. Controls for Chain and Ownership[e]	No	Yes	No	Yes	Yes	No	Yes	No	Yes	Yes	No	Yes
4. Controls for Region[f]	No	No	No	No	Yes	No	No	No	No	Yes	No	No
5. Standard Error of Regression	8.79	8.78	8.76	8.76	8.75	0.373	0.372	0.373	0.372	0.372	0.078	0.043
6. Probability Value for Controls[g]	—	0.34	—	0.44	0.40	—	0.14	—	0.17	0.27	—	—

Note: Standard errors are shown in parentheses. The sample consists of 357 restaurants with nonmissing data on employment and starting wages in waves 1 and 2. All models include an unrestricted constant (not reported).

[a] The dependent variable is the change in full-time-equivalent (FTE) employment. The mean and standard deviation of the dependent variable are −0.237 and 8.825, respectively.

[b] The dependent variable is the change in FTE employment, divided by average employment in wave 1 and wave 2. For closed restaurants, proportional change = −1.0. The mean and standard deviation of the dependent variable are −0.005 and 0.374, respectively.

[c] The dependent variable is the change in the starting wage, divided by the starting wage in wave 1. The mean and standard deviation of the dependent variable are 0.087 and 0.090, respectively.

[d] Proportional increase in starting wage necessary to increase starting wage to the new minimum rate. For restaurants in Pennsylvania, the wage gap is zero.

[e] Dummy variables for chain type (three) and whether the restaurant is company owned are included.

[f] Dummy variables for two regions of New Jersey and two regions of eastern Pennsylvania are included.

[g] Probability value of joint F-test for exclusion of all control variables.

ployment between restaurants in New Jersey and Pennsylvania. The mean value of GAP is 0.11 among restaurants in New Jersey, and 0 among those in Pennsylvania. Thus, the estimate in column 3 implies an average increase in FTE employment of 1.72 in New Jersey relative to Pennsylvania.

Because GAP varies within New Jersey, it is possible to add both the GAP variable and the New Jersey dummy to the employment model. The estimated coefficient of the New Jersey dummy then provides a specification test of the Pennsylvania control group. When we estimate these models, the coefficient of the New Jersey dummy is insignificant (with t-ratios of 0.3 to 0.7), implying that inferences about the employment effect of the minimum wage are similar whether the comparison is made either across states or within New Jersey between restaurants with higher and lower initial wages.

An even stronger test is provided by the model in column 5, which includes dummies representing two regions of New Jersey (central and south) and two regions of eastern Pennsylvania (Allentown–Easton and the northern suburbs of Philadelphia). These dummies control for any unobserved region-specific demand shocks and identify the effect of the minimum wage by comparing employment changes at restaurants in the same region of New Jersey with higher and lower starting wages in wave 1. The probability value in row 6 gives no evidence that the regional dummies are important predictors of employment growth. The addition of the region dummies leads to an attenuation of the estimated GAP coefficient and increases its standard error, however, so that it is no longer possible to reject the null hypothesis of a coefficient of zero. Nevertheless, measurement error in the starting wage normally would be expected to lead to some attenuation of the estimated GAP coefficient when region dummies are added to the model, because some of the true variation in GAP is explained by region. Indeed, calculations based on the estimated reliability of the GAP variable suggest that the decrease in the estimated coefficient of the GAP variable between column 4 and column 5 is just about equal to the expected change attributable to measurement error.[17]

The models in columns 6–10 repeat the previous analysis, using as a dependent variable the proportional change in employment at each restaurant.[18] The estimated coefficients of the New Jersey dummy and the GAP variable are uniformly positive in these models but are insignificantly different from zero at conventional levels. The implied employment effects of the minimum wage are also smaller when the dependent variable is the proportional change in employment. For example, the estimated coefficient of the New Jersey dummy in column 1 implies that the increase in minimum wages raised relative employment at New Jersey restaurants by 2.33 employees, or about 11 percent. The corresponding proportional model (column 6) implies only a 5 percent effect. As we show, the difference is attributable to heterogeneity in the effect of the minimum wage at larger and smaller restaurants. The proportional change in average total employment across all restaurants in New Jersey is approximately a weighted average of the proportional changes at individual restaurants, using as weights the initial employment shares of the restaurants. Weighted versions of the proportional-change models give rise to estimated employment effects that are very similar to the effects arising from the models in columns 1–5.

The models in columns 11 and 12 show the effect of the New Jersey dummy and the *GAP* variable on the proportional increase in starting wages between the first and second waves of our survey. In column 11, the estimated coefficient of the New Jersey dummy is 0.11, suggesting (as in Table 2.1) that the increase in the New Jersey minimum wage raised average wages in the state by 11 percent. The estimated coefficient on *GAP* in column 12 is 1.04. This estimate implies that wages were increased at restaurants in New Jersey by precisely the amount required to bring starting wages up to the level of the new minimum wage. Note that, because the mean of the *GAP* variable for restaurants in New Jersey is 0.11, the estimates in columns 11 and 12 have the same implications for the effect of the minimum wage on relative wages in New Jersey.

Specification Tests

The results in Tables 2.2 and 2.3 seem to directly contradict the prediction that an increase in the minimum wage will reduce employment. Table 2.4 presents a series of alternative specifications designed to probe the robustness of this conclusion. The first row of the table reproduces the "base specifications" from columns 2, 4, 7, and 9 of Table 2.3. These base specifications are models that include chain dummies and a dummy for company-owned restaurants. Row 2 presents alternative estimates when we set wave 2 employment at the four temporarily closed restaurants equal to zero (expanding our sample size by four). This addition has a small attenuating effect on the coefficient of the New Jersey dummy (because all four restaurants are in New Jersey), but less effect on the *GAP* coefficient (because the size of *GAP* is uncorrelated with the probability of a temporary closure in New Jersey).

TABLE 2.4
Specification Tests of Reduced-Form Employment Models

	Change in Employment		Proportional Change in Employment	
	NJ Dummy (1)	Wage Gap (2)	NJ Dummy (3)	Wage Gap (4)
1. Base Specification	2.30 (1.19)	14.92 (6.21)	0.05 (0.05)	0.34 (0.26)
2. Treat Four Temporarily Closed Restaurants as Permanently Closed[a]	2.20 (1.21)	14.42 (6.31)	0.04 (0.05)	0.34 (0.27)
3. Exclude Managers in Employment Count[b]	2.34 (1.17)	14.69 (6.05)	0.05 (0.07)	0.28 (0.34)
4. Weight Part-Timers as 0.4 × Full-Timers[c]	2.34 (1.20)	15.23 (6.23)	0.06 (0.06)	0.30 (0.33)
5. Weight Part-Timers as 0.6 × Full-Timers[d]	2.27 (1.21)	14.60 (6.26)	0.04 (0.06)	0.17 (0.29)
6. Exclude Restaurants in NJ Shore Area[e]	2.58 (1.19)	16.88 (6.36)	0.06 (0.05)	0.42 (0.27)
7. Add Controls for Wave 2 Interview Date[f]	2.27 (1.20)	15.79 (6.24)	0.05 (0.05)	0.40 (0.26)
8. Exclude Restaurants Called More than Twice in Wave 1[g]	2.41 (1.28)	14.08 (7.11)	0.05 (0.05)	0.31 (0.29)
9. Weight by Initial Employment[h]	—	—	0.13 (0.05)	0.81 (0.26)
10. Restaurants Around Newark Only[i]	—	33.75 (16.75)	—	0.90 (0.74)

TABLE 2.4
(continued)

| | Change in Employment | | Proportional Change in Employment | |
	NJ Dummy (1)	Wage Gap (2)	NJ Dummy (3)	Wage Gap (4)
11. Restaurants Around Camden Only[j]	—	10.91 (14.09)	—	0.21 (0.70)
12. Pennsylvania Restaurants Only[k]	—	−0.30 (22.00)	—	−0.33 (0.74)

Note: Standard errors are shown in parentheses. Entries represent the estimated coefficient of the New Jersey dummy (columns 1 and 3) or the initial wage gap (columns 2 and 4) in regression models for the change in employment or percentage change in employment. All models also include chain dummies and an indicator for company-owned restaurants.

[a] Wave 2 employment at four temporarily closed restaurants is set equal to zero (rather than missing).

[b] Full-time-equivalent (FTE) employment excludes managers and assistant managers.

[c] FTE employment equals the number of managers, assistant managers, and full-time nonmanagement workers, plus 0.4 times the number of part-time nonmanagement workers.

[d] FTE employment equals the number of managers, assistant managers, and full-time nonmanagement workers, plus 0.6 times the number of part-time nonmanagement workers.

[e] The sample excludes 35 restaurants located in towns along the New Jersey shore.

[f] Models include three dummy variables identifying the week of the wave 2 interview in November–December 1992.

[g] The sample excludes 70 restaurants (69 in New Jersey) that were contacted three or more times before obtaining a wave 1 interview.

[h] The regression model is estimated by weighted least squares, using employment in wave 1 as a weight.

[i] Sample of 51 restaurants in suburban Newark area only.

[j] Sample of 54 restaurants in suburban Camden area only.

[k] Sample of Pennsylvania restaurants only. *GAP* measure is the percentage increase in starting wage necessary to increase the starting wage to $5.05 per hour.

Rows 3–5 present estimation results using alternative measures of FTE employment. In row 3, employment is redefined to exclude managers. This change has no effect relative to the base specification. In rows 4 and 5, we include managers in FTE employment but reweight part-time workers as either 40 or 60 percent of full-time workers (rather than as 50 percent).[19] These changes have little effect on the models for the level of employment but yield slightly smaller point estimates in the proportional-change models.

Our sample design sometimes has been criticized because the second wave of interviews was conducted at a different time of year (just after Thanksgiving) than was the first wave (during late winter). Observe that this criticism is valid only if the pattern of seasonal employment is *different* among restaurants that were affected by the minimum wage and among those that were not. To probe the issue more fully, we performed a series of specification checks. Row 6 of Table 2.4 presents estimates obtained from a subsample that excludes 35 fast-food restaurants in towns along the New Jersey shore. The exclusion of these restaurants—which may have a different seasonal employment pattern than others in our sample—leads to slightly larger (i.e., more positive) minimum-wage effects. A similar finding emerges from the models in row 7, which include a set of dummy variables for the week of the wave 2 interview in November or December 1992. We also added dummies for the interview dates of the wave 1 survey, but these were insignificant and their addition did not change the estimated minimum-wage effects relative to the base specifications.

As we explain in the Appendix of this chapter, our interviewer made an extra effort to survey New Jersey restaurants in wave 1. In particular, a higher fraction of restaurants in New Jersey were telephoned three or more times in an attempt to obtain completed interviews.[20] To check the sensitivity of our results to this sampling feature, we reestimated the employment models, using the subset of restaurants in New Jersey and Pennsylvania that were called back twice, at most. The results, in row 8, are very similar to the base specifications.

Row 9 presents estimation results for the overall sample when the proportional employment changes are weighted by the initial level of employment in each restaurant. In principle, weighting of the proportional changes should give rise to coefficients that are similar to the implied proportional changes from the models estimated in levels. As expected, the weighted estimates from the proportional-change model are substantially larger than the unweighted estimates, and significantly different from zero at conventional levels.

The weighted estimate of the New Jersey dummy (0.13) implies a 13 percent relative increase in New Jersey employment—exactly the same effect as the simple difference-in-differences in Table 2.2.

One explanation for our finding that a rise in the minimum wage led to an apparent increase in employment is that unobserved demand shocks offset the disemployment effects of the minimum wage. Note that there is no evidence of these differential shocks at the regional level in New Jersey, as the specifications in Table 2.3 that include broad region dummies show positive employment effects. To further address the possibility that restaurants experienced unobserved demand shocks, however, rows 10 and 11 present estimation results for restaurants in two, narrowly defined subregions of New Jersey: towns around Newark (row 10), and towns around Camden (row 11). In each case, the sample area is identified by the first three digits of the store's ZIP code.[21] In both local areas, changes in employment are positively correlated with the increase in wages necessitated by the rise in the minimum wage, although in neither case is the effect statistically significant. To the extent that fast-food product-market conditions are similar within narrow geographic areas, these results suggest that our findings are not driven by unobserved demand shocks. Our analysis of price changes (reported later in this chapter) also supports this conclusion.

Another specification check is presented in row 12. In this row, we (incorrectly) define the GAP variable for Pennsylvania restaurants as the proportional increase in wages necessary to increase the wage to $5.05 per hour. We then fit the employment models to the subset of Pennsylvania restaurants. In principle, for restaurants in Pennsylvania, the size of the wage gap should have no relation to employment changes, and in practice, this is the case. We find no indication that our wage-gap variable is somehow spuriously related to employment growth.

We also investigated whether the first-differenced specification used in our employment models is appropriate. A first-differenced model implies that the level of employment in any period is related to the lagged level of employment with a coefficient of one. If employment fluctuations are smoothed, however, the true coefficient of lagged employment may be less than one. The imposition of the assumption of a unit coefficient could then lead to biases. To test the first-differenced specification, we reestimated models for the change in employment, including wave 1 employment as an additional explanatory variable. To overcome any mechanical correlation between base-period employment and the change in employment (attributable to measurement error), we instrumented wave 1 employment with the number of cash registers in the restaurant in wave 1 and the number of registers in the restaurant in operation at 11:00 AM in wave 1. In all the specifications, the coefficient of wave 1 employment is close to zero. For example, in a specification including the GAP variable and ownership and chain dummies, the coefficient of wave 1 employment is 0.04, with a standard error of 0.24. We conclude that the first-differenced specification is appropriate.

As a final check, we compared the fraction of restaurants in New Jersey and Pennsylvania in which employment declined, remained constant, or increased. By simply examining the fraction of restaurants with positive or negative employment growth, we greatly downgrade the influence of those that experienced exceptionally high or exceptionally low employment changes. These results are summarized in Table 2.5. During any time period, employment growth varies greatly, with some restaurants shrinking, and others growing.[22] Nevertheless, the results indicate that, relative to Pennsylvania restaurants, New Jersey restaurants were less likely to shrink between the time of the two waves of our survey, and were more likely to grow. Forty-one percent of Pennsylvania restaurants increased their employment during our sample period, compared with 52 percent of New Jersey restaurants. In addition, a higher fraction of Pennsylvania restaurants (53 percent) than of New Jersey restaurants (44 percent) contracted during this period. These results are consistent with our finding of a net increase in employment in New Jersey restaurants relative to Pennsylvania restaurants. Nevertheless, they indicate that many New Jersey restaurants did experience employment declines, even though the average employment level increased, both absolutely and relative to Pennsylvania restaurants.

To summarize, evidence from a variety of alternative specifications confirms the basic message of the simple differences-in-differences shown in Table 2.2. Regardless of whether low-wage restaurants in New Jersey are compared with those in Pennsylvania or with restaurants in New Jersey that already were paying as much as

TABLE 2.5
Pattern of Employment Growth in New Jersey
and Pennsylvania Restaurants

Percentage of Restaurants with	New Jersey	Pennsylvania
Decline in Employment	44.0	53.3
Constant Employment	4.5	5.3
Increase in Employment	51.5	41.3

the new minimum wage, we find that the rise in the minimum wage seems to have *increased* employment. In many of the specifications, including the basic difference-of-differences models, the estimated effect of the minimum wage is significantly different from zero, suggesting that our estimates are unlikely to have arisen by chance. In other specifications, however, the estimated effects are less precise. At a minimum, we believe that our estimates call into question the prediction that an increase in the minimum wage will lead to significant employment losses at affected firms. In particular, even our least precise estimates reject the hypothesis that the elasticity of demand for labor by fast-food employers is greater than 0.3 in absolute value.[23] To see this, note that the estimated *GAP* coefficients in our proportional-employment-change models can be interpreted as labor-demand elasticities, because the percentage increase in wages induced by the minimum wage is directly proportional to *GAP*. A two-standard error-range around the estimated *GAP* coefficients from column 8 or 9 of Table 2.3 is bounded below by -0.30.

OTHER EMPLOYMENT-RELATED EFFECTS OF THE NEW JERSEY MINIMUM WAGE

Full-Time and Part-Time Substitution

Our analysis so far has concentrated on FTE employment and has ignored possible changes in the distribution of full-time and part-time workers. An increase in the minimum wage could lead to an increase in full-time employment relative to part-time employment for at least two reasons. First, in a conventional employment-demand model, one would expect a minimum-wage increase to induce employers to substitute skilled workers and capital for minimum-wage workers. Full-time workers in fast-food restaurants typically are older and may possess higher skills than part-time workers. Thus, on the one hand, a conventional model predicts that restaurants may respond to an increase in the minimum wage by increasing the proportion of full-time workers. On the other hand, in the first wave of our survey, 81 percent of restaurants paid full-time and part-time workers the same starting wage.[24] This finding suggests either that full-time workers have the same skills as part-time workers, or that equity considerations lead restaurants to pay equal wages for unequally productive workers. If full-time workers are more productive but are paid the same as part-time workers, restaurants might substitute full-time workers for part-time workers for a second reason; namely, a minimum-wage increase enables the industry to attract more full-time workers, and restaurants naturally would want to hire a greater proportion of full-time workers, if they were available.[25]

Row 1 of Table 2.6 presents the mean changes in the proportion of full-time workers in New Jersey and Pennsylvania restaurants between waves 1 and 2 of our survey, and coefficient estimates from three, alternative regression models. The first model, reported in column 4, includes a New Jersey dummy, as well as chain dummies and a company-ownership dummy. The second model (in column 5) includes the GAP variable and the chain and ownership dummies. The third model (in column 6) includes the GAP variable, chain and ownership dummies, and four dummies representing different regions of New Jersey and eastern Pennsylvania. The results are ambiguous. As shown by the estimates in columns 3 and 4, the fraction of full-time workers increased in New Jersey restaurants relative to Pennsylvania restaurants by about 7.3 percent (t-ratio = 1.84). Regressions on GAP show only a weakly significant effect, however. Further investigation confirms that the average fraction of full-time workers increased at about the same rate among New Jersey restaurants with higher and lower initial wages.

Hours and Number of Cash Registers

Rows 2–4 of Table 2.6 present results for other outcomes that we expect to be related to the level of restaurant employment. In particular, we examine whether the increase in the minimum wage is associated with a change in the number of hours that restaurants are open during a weekday, with the number of cash registers in the restaurant, or with the number of cash registers in operation in the restaurant at 11:00 AM (a typical slack time, during which managers may have more discretion about staffing). Consistent with our employment results, none of these variables shows a statistically significant decline in New Jersey restaurants relative to Pennsylvania restaurants. Similarly, regressions including the GAP variable provide no evidence that the minimum-wage increase led to a systematic change in any of these variables. The results for the total number of cash registers in the restaurant and the number open at 11:00 AM actually differ in sign, although neither set of estimates is very precise.

Nonwage Offsets

A possible explanation for our finding that an increase in the minimum wage does not reduce employment is that restaurants can off-

TABLE 2.6
Effects of Minimum-Wage Increase on Other Outcomes

	Mean Change in Outcome			Regression of Change in Outcome Variable on		
Outcome Measure	NJ (1)	PA (2)	NJ − PA (3)	NJ Dummy (4)	Wage Gap[a] (5)	Wage Gap[b] (6)
Restaurant Characteristics						
1. Percentage of Full-Time Workers[c]	2.64 (1.71)	−4.65 (3.80)	7.29 (4.17)	7.30 (3.96)	33.64 (20.95)	20.28 (24.34)
2. Number of Hours Open per Weekday	0.00 (0.06)	0.11 (0.08)	−0.11 (0.10)	−0.11 (0.12)	−0.24 (0.65)	0.04 (0.76)
3. Number of Cash Registers	−0.04 (0.04)	0.13 (0.10)	−0.17 (0.11)	−0.18 (0.10)	−0.31 (0.53)	0.29 (0.62)
4. Number of Cash Registers Open at 11:00 AM	−0.03 (0.05)	−0.20 (0.08)	0.17 (0.10)	0.17 (0.12)	0.15 (0.62)	−0.47 (0.74)
Employee Meal Programs						
5. Reduced-Price Meal Program (%)	−4.67 (2.65)	−1.28 (3.86)	−3.39 (4.68)	−2.01 (5.63)	−30.31 (29.80)	−33.15 (35.04)
6. Free Meal Program (%)	8.41 (2.17)	6.41 (3.33)	2.00 (3.97)	0.49 (4.50)	29.90 (23.75)	36.91 (27.90)
7. Combination of Reduced-Price and Free Meals (%)	−4.04 (1.98)	−5.13 (3.11)	1.09 (3.69)	1.20 (4.32)	−11.87 (22.87)	−19.19 (26.81)

Wage Profile

8. Time to First Raise (weeks)	3.77	1.26	2.51	2.21	4.02	-5.10
	(0.89)	(1.97)	(2.16)	(2.03)	(10.81)	(12.74)
9. Usual Amount of First Raise (cents)	-0.01	-0.02	0.01	0.01	0.03	0.03
	(0.01)	(0.02)	(0.02)	(0.02)	(0.11)	(0.11)
10. Slope of Wage Profile (%/wk)	-0.10	-0.11	0.01	0.01	-0.09	-0.08
	(0.04)	(0.09)	(0.10)	(0.10)	(0.56)	(0.57)

Note: Standard errors are shown in parentheses. Entries in columns 1 and 2 represent mean changes in the outcome variable indicated by the row heading for restaurants with nonmissing data on the outcome in waves 1 and 2. Entries in columns 4 through 6 represent estimated regression coefficients of the indicated variable (New Jersey dummy or initial wage gap) in the model for the change in the outcome variable. Regression models include chain dummies and an indicator for company-owned restaurants.

[a]Wage Gap is the proportional increase in starting wage necessary to increase the starting wage to the new minimum rate. For restaurants in Pennsylvania, the wage gap is zero.

[b]Models in column 6 include dummies for two regions of New Jersey and two regions of eastern Pennsylvania.

[c]Fraction of part-time employees in total full-time-equivalent employment.

set the effect of the minimum wage by reducing nonwage compensation. For example, if workers value fringe benefits and wages equally, employers simply can reduce the level of fringe benefits by the amount of the minimum-wage increase, leaving employment costs unchanged. The main fringe benefits offered to fast-food workers are free and reduced-price meals. In the first wave of our survey, about 19 percent of fast-food restaurants offered their workers free meals, 72 percent offered reduced-price meals, and 9 percent offered a combination of free and reduced-price meals. Only 10 percent offered no meal program. Subsidized meals are an obvious fringe benefit that can be cut if the minimum-wage increase forces restaurants to pay higher wages.

Rows 5 and 6 of Table 2.6 present estimates of the effect of the minimum-wage increase on the incidence of free and reduced-price meal programs. Between March and November 1992, the proportion of restaurants offering reduced-price meals fell in both New Jersey (-4.7 percent) and Pennsylvania (-1.3 percent), with a somewhat greater decrease in New Jersey. Contrary to being an offsetting action, however, the relative reduction in reduced-price meal programs in New Jersey was accompanied by a relative *increase* in the fraction of restaurants offering free meals: up 8.4 percent in New Jersey, versus 6.4 percent in Pennsylvania. In both states, the fraction of restaurants offering a combination of reduced-price and free meals fell. On net, New Jersey employers actually shifted toward more generous fringes than did their Pennsylvania counterparts (i.e., toward free meals and combined programs and away from either no program or a reduced-price meal program only). None of the relative shifts is large or statistically significant.

We also find a statistically insignificant effect of the minimum-wage increase on the likelihood of receiving free or reduced-price meals in columns 5 and 6, where we report coefficient estimates of the *GAP* variable from regression models for the change in the incidence of the meal programs. The results provide no evidence that New Jersey employers offset the minimum-wage increase by offering fewer free or reduced-price meals.

The Wage Profile

Another possible employer response to a binding minimum wage is to reduce the amount of on-the-job training. A reduction in the amount of on-the-job training increases the net value of newly hired employees but ultimately lowers the value of more senior workers, leading to a flattening of the wage-tenure profile (see Leighton and Mincer [1981] and Hashimoto [1982]). To determine whether this flattening occurred, we analyzed restaurant managers' responses to survey questions on the amount of time before a normal wage increase was given, and on the usual amount of the increase.[26] In rows 8 and 9 of Table 2.6, we report the average changes between waves 1 and 2 for these two variables, as well as regression coefficients from models that include the GAP variable. Although the average time to the first pay increment increased by 2.5 weeks in New Jersey relative to Pennsylvania, the increase is not statistically significant. Furthermore, the difference in the relative change in the amount of the first pay increment between New Jersey and Pennsylvania restaurants is trivial.

We also examined a related variable—the "slope" of the wage profile, measured by the ratio of the typical first raise to the amount of time until the first raise is given. As shown in row 10, the slope of the wage profile flattened for both New Jersey restaurants and Pennsylvania restaurants, with no significant relative difference between the state groups. The change in the slope is also uncorrelated with the GAP variable. In summary, we find no strong evidence that New Jersey employers changed either their fringe benefits or wage profiles to offset the increase in the minimum wage. We return to the issue of the wage profile in our analysis of wage "spillovers" in chapter 5.

Price Effects of the New Jersey Minimum Wage

Although the implications of competitive-demand theory for the effect of a binding minimum wage are most directly tested by examining firm-level employment outcomes, the theory also makes a set of predictions for the effects of a minimum wage on prices. In an idealized competitive market, all firms in an industry receive the same price for their outputs. If all workers at all firms are affected equally by the minimum wage, then standard demand theory predicts that the industry price will rise by the percentage increase in wages, multiplied by labor's share of cost. If only a fraction of workers at each firm is affected by the increase in the minimum, then the share calculation must be modified to include only those workers affected by the minimum-wage hike. Before the increase in the minimum wage went into effect, a typical restaurant in New Jersey paid about half its workers less than $5.05 per hour. On average, to meet the new minimum wage, these workers' wages rose by 15 percent. Assuming that labor's share of total cost is 30 percent, we would expect fast-food prices in New Jersey restaurants to rise by no more than 2.2 percent ($= 0.15 \times 0.5 \times 0.3$) after the minimum-wage increase.[27]

The predictions of the theory are more subtle if different firms pay different wages and receive different prices for their outputs. To derive the implications of the theory, one must first develop a model of *why* wages and prices vary across firms. The simplest model of wage and price dispersion, and the one that most economists have "in the back of their heads," assumes that each firm is a perfect competitor in a local market characterized by homogeneous wages and prices, and that wages and prices vary across markets as a result of exogenous differences in the costs of living and doing business. If this model of wage and price dispersion is the correct one, then the previous calculation applies at each New Jersey restaurant in our sample, with a suitable modification for the fraction of workers whose wages rise with the minimum. Restaurants in low-wage markets that offered a starting wage rate of $4.25 per hour and that had a high fraction of affected workers are predicted to have a sizable price increase (as much as 5 percent). Those in high-wage markets that had starting wage rates of more than $5.00 per hour are predicted to have no change in prices.[28]

More complex models of industry equilibrium take into account endogenously determined differences in land rents paid by different restaurants (for example, higher-volume fast-food restaurants in large shopping malls versus lower-volume restaurants on nearby side streets). These models predict that an increase in the minimum wage will lower land rents for locations that are occupied by low-wage restaurants, and will raise land rents for locations that are occupied by high-wage restaurants. The rent changes in turn, will spread the cost of the minimum-wage increase across restaurants, leading to smaller price increases at the restaurants that were directly affected by the minimum wage, and to some increase in prices at high-wage restaurants that were not affected directly.

Price Data

During each wave of our survey, we asked managers about the prices of three standard items: a main course, a small order of french fries, and a medium-sized soft drink. The main course was a basic hamburger at Burger King, Roy Rogers, and Wendy's restaurants, and two pieces of chicken at KFC restaurants. We define the "full-meal" price as the after-tax price of a main course, a small order of french fries, and a medium-sized soft drink.

Table 2.7 presents average price data from the two waves of the survey for restaurants in New Jersey and Pennsylvania, and separately for New Jersey restaurants in three wage ranges. The format of the table is identical to that of Table 2.2. Relative to the Pennsyl-

TABLE 2.7
Price of Full Meal Before and After Increase in New Jersey Minimum Wage

| | All | Restaurant, by State | | Difference NJ − PA | Restaurants in New Jersey[a] | | | Differences Within New Jersey[b] | |
| | | PA | NJ | | Wage = $4.25 | Wage $4.26–4.99 | Wage ≥ $5.00 | Low − High | Midrange − High |
	(1)	(2)	(3)	(4)	(5)	(6)	(7)	(8)	(9)
1. Price of Meal Before, All Available Observations ($)	3.29	3.04	3.35	0.31	3.33	3.38	3.38	−0.05	0.00
	(0.03)	(0.07)	(0.04)	(0.08)	(0.07)	(0.06)	(0.07)	(0.10)	(0.09)
2. Price of Meal After, All Available Observations ($)	3.34	3.03	3.42	0.39	3.40	3.44	3.47	−0.08	−0.03
	(0.03)	(0.07)	(0.04)	(0.08)	(0.07)	(0.06)	(0.07)	(0.10)	(0.09)
3. Change in Price of Meal ($)	0.05	−0.01	0.06	0.08	0.06	0.06	0.09	−0.03	−0.03
	(0.02)	(0.05)	(0.03)	(0.06)	(0.05)	(0.05)	(0.06)	(0.08)	(0.07)
4. Change in Price of Meal, Balanced Sample of Restaurants ($)[c]	0.05	−0.03	0.07	0.10	0.06	0.06	0.08	−0.02	−0.02
	(0.02)	(0.04)	(0.02)	(0.04)	(0.03)	(0.04)	(0.06)	(0.06)	(0.07)
5. *Percentage* Change in Log Price of Meal, Balanced Sample of Restaurants	1.5	−0.9	2.0	2.9	1.9	1.9	2.5	−0.6	−0.5
	(0.5)	(1.1)	(0.6)	(1.3)	(0.7)	(1.0)	(1.6)	(1.7)	(1.9)

Note: Standard errors are shown in parentheses. The sample consists of all restaurants with nonmissing data on prices. A full meal includes a main course, a small order of french fries, and a medium-sized soda.

[a] Restaurants in New Jersey classified by whether starting wage in wave 1 equals $4.25 per hour, is between $4.26 and 4.99 per hour, or is $5.00 per hour or higher.

[b] Difference in prices between restaurants in low-wage ($4.25 per hour) and high-wage (≥$5.00 per hour) ranges; and difference in prices between restaurants in midrange ($4.26–4.99 per hour) and high-wage ranges.

[c] Subset of restaurants with nonmissing data on prices in both wave 1 and wave 2.

vania price, the price of a full meal in New Jersey increased by 8 to 10 cents, or about 3 percent. Because the sales-tax rate in New Jersey fell during 1992 by one percentage point, these data indicate that the pretax price increased by about 4 percent. The relative price increase is statistically significant if we use the balanced subsample of restaurants that reported price data in both waves of the survey.

Columns 5–7 present meal prices for restaurants in New Jersey. Comparisons of price data for restaurants in the three wage ranges indicate two interesting anomalies. First, average wave 1 prices between restaurants that were paying a starting wage of $4.25 per hour and those that were paying more than $5.00 per hour are insignificantly different. Second, after the increase in the minimum wage, prices increased at about the same rate at low-wage and high-wage restaurants. In fact, price increases at high-wage restaurants, which presumably were unaffected by the rise in the minimum wage, tended to be slightly larger than those at low-wage restaurants.

Table 2.8 presents reduced-form estimates of the effect of the minimum-wage increase on prices. The dependent variable in these models is the change in the logarithm of the price of a full meal at each restaurant. The key independent variable is either a dummy indicating whether the restaurant is located in New Jersey or the proportional wage increase required to meet the minimum wage (the GAP variable). The estimated New Jersey dummy in column 1 shows that, between February and November 1992, after-tax meal prices rose 3.3 percent faster in New Jersey than in Pennsylvania. The effect is slightly larger after controlling for chain and company ownership (in column 2). Like the simpler difference-in-differences estimates presented in Table 2.7, these estimates suggest that pretax prices rose 4 percent faster as a result of the minimum-wage increase in New Jersey—slightly more than the increase required to fully cover the cost increase caused by the minimum-wage hike.

Models that include the GAP variable implicitly assume that any price increase between February and March 1992 is proportional to the restaurant-specific increase in wages necessitated by the increase in the minimum wage. As we saw in Table 2.7, however, the pattern of price changes *within* New Jersey is less consistent with this "pass through" view of minimum-wage effects than is the pattern of price changes between New Jersey and Pennsylvania. As a result of this inconsistency, the estimated GAP coefficients in columns 3–5 of Table 2.8 are relatively small and insignificantly different from zero.

These results provide mixed evidence that higher minimum wages

TABLE 2.8
Estimated Reduced-Form Models for Change in the Price of Full Meal

	Dependent Variable: Change in Log Price of Full Meal				
	(1)	(2)	(3)	(4)	(5)
1. New Jersey Dummy	0.033 (0.014)	0.037 (0.014)	—	—	—
2. Initial Wage Gap[a]	—	—	0.077 (0.075)	0.146 (0.074)	0.063 (0.089)
3. Controls for Chain and Ownership[b]	No	Yes	No	Yes	Yes
4. Controls for Region[c]	No	No	No	No	Yes
5. Standard Error of Regression	0.101	0.097	0.102	0.098	0.097

Note: Standard errors are shown in parentheses. The sample contains 315 restaurants with valid data on prices, wages, and employment for waves 1 and 2. Entries are estimated regression coefficients for models fit to change in log price of a full meal (main course, small order of french fries, medium-sized soda). The mean and standard deviation of the dependent variable are 0.0173 and 0.1017, respectively.

[a]Proportional increase in starting wage necessary to increase wage to the new minimum rate. For restaurants in Pennsylvania, the wage gap is zero.

[b]Dummy variables for chain type (three) and whether the restaurant is company owned are included.

[c]Dummy variables for two regions of New Jersey and two regions of eastern Pennsylvania are included.

result in higher fast-food prices. The strongest evidence emerges from a comparison of New Jersey and Pennsylvania restaurants. On the one hand, the magnitude of the relative price increase is consistent with predictions from a conventional model of a competitive industry. Within New Jersey, however, we find no evidence that prices rose faster among New Jersey restaurants that were most affected by the increase in the minimum wage. One explanation for the latter finding is that restaurants in New Jersey compete in the same product market. As a result, restaurants that are most affected by the minimum wage are unable to increase their product prices faster than their competitors. In contrast, restaurants in New Jersey and those in Pennsylvania compete in separate product markets, enabling prices to rise in New Jersey relative to Pennsylvania when overall costs increase in New Jersey. Note that this explanation is consistent with the fact that average prices in New Jersey differ little between high-wage and low-wage restaurants. Importantly, however, the single-product-market explanation rules out the possibility that restaurant-specific demand shocks can account for the employment increases at New Jersey restaurants having initially lower wages.

Broader Evidence on Employment Changes in New Jersey

Our establishment-level analysis suggests that, if anything, the rise in the minimum wage in New Jersey increased employment in the fast-food industry. Is this finding simply an anomaly associated with our particular sample or a phenomenon unique to the fast-food industry? Data from the monthly Current Population Survey (CPS) allow us to compare statewide employment trends in New Jersey and surrounding states, providing a check on the interpretation of our findings. Using monthly CPS files for 1991 and 1992, we computed employment-to-population rates for teenagers and adults (aged 25 years or older) for New Jersey, Pennsylvania, New York, and the United States as a whole. Because the New Jersey minimum wage rose on April 1, 1992, we computed the employment rates for April–December of both 1991 and 1992. The relative changes in employment in New Jersey and surrounding states give an indication of the effect of the new law.

Teenage workers were much more likely than adult workers to earn a wage in the range that was affected by the increase in the state minimum. For example, during the three months before the increase, 37 percent of New Jersey workers aged 16 to 19 years earned between $4.25 and 5.05 per hour, compared with 5 percent of adult workers.[29] Thus, if the minimum wage affects employment, it should have a greater impact on the employment rate of teenagers than on that of adults.

Table 2.9 presents the estimated employment rates and their changes between 1991 and 1992. A comparison of the employment rates of adult workers shows that, during 1991–1992, the New Jersey labor market fared slightly worse than either the U.S. labor market as a whole or labor markets in Pennsylvania or New York. With respect to teenagers, however, the situation was reversed. In New Jersey, teenage employment rates fell slightly from 1991 to 1992. In New York, Pennsylvania, and the United States as a whole, teenage employment rates dropped more rapidly than in New Jersey. Relative to the rate in Pennsylvania, for example, the teenage employment rate in New Jersey rose by 2.0 percentage points, although the standard error is large (3.2 percent). Unfortunately, there is a fair

TABLE 2.9
Employment–Population Rates for Teenagers and Adults,
April–December 1991 and 1992

	Employment–Population Rate		
	1991 (1)	1992 (2)	Change 1992 − 1991 (3)
1. New Jersey			
a. Teenagers	37.7	37.0	−0.7
	(1.8)	(1.8)	(2.2)
b. Aged 25+	64.1	61.5	−2.6
	(0.5)	(0.5)	(0.6)
2. Pennsylvania			
a. Teenagers	48.0	45.3	−2.7
	(1.0)	(1.9)	(2.3)
b. Aged 25+	58.8	59.1	0.3
	(0.5)	(0.5)	(0.6)
3. New York			
a. Teenagers	31.4	28.6	−2.8
	(1.3)	(1.3)	(1.6)
b. Aged 25+	59.6	58.6	−1.0
	(0.4)	(0.4)	(0.5)
4. United States as a Whole			
a. Teenagers	43.5	42.4	−1.1
	(0.4)	(0.4)	(0.5)
b. Aged 25+	62.7	62.5	−0.2
	(0.1)	(0.1)	(0.1)

Source: Estimated from monthly Current Population Survey files for April–December 1991 and 1992.

Note: Standard errors are shown in parentheses.

amount of sampling variability in the state-level employment rates for teenagers, so it is difficult to draw a confident assessment from the CPS data. Nevertheless, consistent with our results for the fast-food industry, the relative employment of workers most heavily affected by the New Jersey minimum wage seems to have *risen*, rather than to have fallen.

The Effect of the Federal Minimum Wage on Employment in Fast-Food Restaurants: Evidence from Texas

The federal minimum-wage increases in 1990 and 1991 that preceded the 1992 increase in New Jersey provide a series of potential natural experiments for analyzing the effect of legal wage floors. In this section, we describe the results of one such experiment, based on the experiences of fast-food restaurants in Texas between December 1990 and early August 1991. In a study that preceded the New Jersey–Pennsylvania study, one of the authors (Krueger), and Lawrence Katz, of Harvard University, conducted a pair of surveys of fast-food restaurants in Texas. Like the increase in the New Jersey minimum wage, the increase in the federal minimum, on April 1, 1991, affected some fast-food restaurants, but not others. Restaurants that already were paying more than the new minimum rate therefore serve as a potential control group for measuring the effect of the minimum wage on lower-wage restaurants in the state. We have no out-of-state control group for stores in Texas, as we did in the New Jersey–Pennsylvania study. Indeed, the two-state design of our New Jersey–Pennsylvania study was motivated in part by a desire to improve on this aspect of the Texas study. Nevertheless, our finding in the New Jersey–Pennsylvania analysis—that a control group of high-wage restaurants in New Jersey led to the same conclusions as did a control group of restaurants from Pennsylvania, where the minimum wage was unchanged—gives us an added measure of confidence in the use of higher-wage restaurants as a control group in Texas.

The Texas Surveys

In selecting a state for a study of the 1990 and 1991 increases in the federal minimum wage, two features led to the choice of Texas. First, Texas is a large state, with many fast-food restaurants distributed across different cities. Second, it is a relatively low-wage state, with no state minimum wage. Thus, the federal minimum wage was likely to be a binding constraint on many fast-food restaurants in the state.

The first Texas survey was administered in December 1990, eight months after the 1990 increase in the federal minimum wage to $3.80 per hour, and four months before the scheduled April 1991 increase to $4.25 per hour. The sample frame for this survey included 294 restaurants in the Burger King, Wendy's and KFC chains, drawn from the metropolitan yellow pages telephone books for Texas. The response rate for the survey was 57 percent, yielding a usable sample of 167 stores.

The second survey was conducted eight months later, in July and early August 1991. Unlike the design of the New Jersey–Pennsylvania study, the second-round survey was not limited to restaurants that had responded during the first round. Rather, the sample frame for the second survey was *expanded* to include all 589 restaurants from the three chains that were listed in the 1990 Texas telephone books. The response rate for the second survey was 56 percent, yielding a usable sample of 330 restaurants. The response rate for firms that were included in the first-round survey was slightly higher (67 percent), leading to a subsample of 110 restaurants providing at least some information in both waves of the survey. No attempt was made to follow up respondents from the first wave who failed to respond in the second wave. This is an important limitation of the Texas sample relative to the New Jersey–Pennsylvania sample, although differential restaurant-closing rates were not an important source of bias in the latter study.

Employment Effects

We begin our analysis of the employment effects of the minimum wage with a set of difference-of-differences calculations. Table 2.10 presents data for the subset of 104 restaurants providing complete data on employment and wages in the two waves of the Texas survey, broken down by whether the starting wage in December 1990 was $3.80 per hour (the existing minimum wage), between $3.81 and 4.24 per hour, or $4.25 or more per hour. Over the entire sample of restaurants, average FTE employment increased slightly.[30] Among the highest-wage restaurants, however, average employment fell, whereas among the lowest-wage restaurants, it actually increased. The difference-in-differences of employment between the lowest-wage and highest-wage restaurants is 4.89 employees, or approximately 30 percent. As was the case in New Jersey, the increase in the minimum wage in Texas was associated with a relative expansion in employment at firms that were forced to raise pay in order to comply with the law.

Table 2.11 presents a series of regression models for the change in employment and wages between December 1990 and July–early August 1991 across the Texas restaurants. As in the New Jersey–Pennsylvania analysis, the key explanatory variable in the regression models is a measure of the proportional increase in starting wages necessary to meet the new minimum-wage rate:

TABLE 2.10
Average Employment per Texas Restaurant Before and After 1991 Increase
in Federal Minimum Wage

					Differences	
	All (1)	Wage = $3.80 (2)	Wage $3.81–4.24 (3)	Wage ≥$4.25 (4)	Low – High (5)	Mid – High (6)
1. FTE Employment Before	15.64 (0.65)	14.65 (1.03)	16.21 (0.88)	16.50 (2.34)	−1.85 (2.56)	−0.29 (2.50)
2. FTE Employment After	16.29 (0.63)	16.90 (0.97)	16.34 (0.88)	13.87 (2.09)	3.03 (2.30)	2.47 (2.27)
3. Change in Mean FTE Employment	0.65 (0.65)	2.25 (1.06)	0.14 (0.88)	−2.64 (2.07)	4.89 (2.33)	2.78 (2.25)

Note: Standard errors are shown in parentheses. FTE employment denotes full-time-equivalent employment and is equal to the number of full-time-workers plus 0.57 times the number of part-time workers. The sample size is 104 for column 1, 40 for column 2, 53 for column 3, and 11 for column 4.

$$GAP = (4.25 - W_1)/W_1 \text{ if } W_1 < 4.25$$

$$= 0 \qquad\qquad \text{if } W_1 \geq 4.25,$$

where W_1 is the reported starting wage in wave 1. Other explanatory variables in the models include dummies for the chain identity and ownership status of the store (franchisee owned versus company owned), and a measure of the population of the city in which the store is located. The two employment models presented in the table differ in the specification of the dependent variable. In column 1, the measure of employment is a simple "head count" of total employment. In column 2, the measure is FTE employment. The wage model in column 3 uses as a dependent variable the proportional change in the starting wage between waves of the survey.

As with the comparable specifications fit to the New Jersey–Pennsylvania data (e.g., columns 8 and 9 of Table 2.3), the estimated GAP coefficient in the employment models is positive. Moreover, in the model for FTE employment, the GAP coefficient is statistically different from zero at conventional significance levels.[31] The correlation between the GAP variable and store-level employment changes is illustrated in Figure 2.4. Each point in the figure represents 1 of the

TABLE 2.11
Estimated Reduced-Form Models for Change in Employment,
December 1990 to July–August 1991

	Dependent Variable		
	Proportional Change in Employment (1)	Proportional Change in FTE Employment (2)	Proportional Change in Starting Wage (3)
1. Initial Wage Gap[a]	0.44	2.48	1.07
	(0.22)	(0.96)	(0.07)
2. Company Owned	−0.02	−0.03	0.00
(1 = Yes)	(0.02)	(0.09)	(0.01)
3. Burger King	0.00	−0.07	−0.01
(1 = Yes)	(0.02)	(0.10)	(0.01)
4. KFC (1 = Yes)	0.02	0.02	0.02
	(0.03)	(0.11)	(0.01)
5. Log Population of	−0.04	0.01	0.05
City in 1986 (coefficient and standard error × 10)	(0.07)	(0.03)	(0.02)
6. Standard Error of Regression	0.087	0.376	0.027

Note: Standard errors are shown in parentheses. FTE employment denotes full-time-equivalent employment and is equal to the number of full-time workers plus 0.57 times the number of part-time workers. The sample size is 101.

[a]Proportional increase in starting wage necessary to increase starting wage to the new minimum rate.

101 stores in the longitudinal sample. For reference, we also show the estimated regression line from column 2 of Table 2.11. Although some outliers are apparent, the figure confirms the existence of a positive correlation between employment growth and the *GAP* variable. To check that the estimated regression line is not influenced unduly by one or two outlying data points, the models were reestimated by the least-absolute-deviations (LAD) method. The LAD estimates are smaller than the corresponding OLS estimates, but still positive. For example, the estimated *GAP* coefficient in an LAD version of the model in column 2 of Table 2.11 is 1.11, with a standard error of 0.69. This suggests that the positive employment effect is robust.

The estimated effect of the *GAP* variable on wage growth in Texas stores is comparable to the estimate in the New Jersey–Pennsylvania

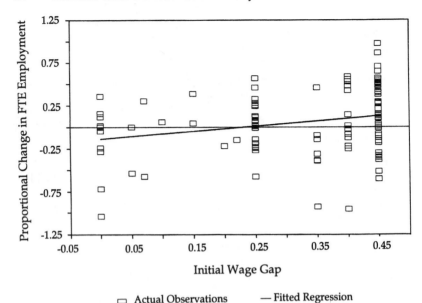

Figure 2.4   Employment changes in Texas restaurants, by initial wage gap.

study. The coefficient of 1.07 suggests that starting wages rose by as much as or just slightly more than enough to bring starting wages up to the level of the new minimum wage. The average value of the *GAP* variable across all Texas stores was 0.08. Thus, the increase in the federal minimum wage raised average starting wages in the state by about 8 percent.

Price Effects

A second issue that we use the Texas sample to examine is the effect of the minimum wage on fast-food prices. In the second wave of the survey, we asked about current prices for a main course (either a basic hamburger, at Burger King and Wendy's outlets, or six pieces of chicken, at KFC outlets), a medium-sized soft drink, and a small order of french fries. We also asked about prices as of January 1991, three months prior to the increase in the minimum wage. This retrospective design allows us to use responses for 266 restaurants that were interviewed in wave 2, at the cost of some potentially larger measurement error in the January price data.

Table 2.12 presents estimated regression models for the change in the logarithm of the price of a full meal (the sum of the prices for the three items in the survey), as well as for the changes in the prices of

TABLE 2.12
Estimated Reduced-Form Models for Changes in the Prices
of Standard Fast-Food Items

	Models for Change in Log Price of			
	Full Meal[a] (1)	Main Course (2)	French Fries (3)	Soda (4)
1. Initial Wage Gap[b]	−0.019 (0.028)	0.025 (0.042)	−0.077 (0.043)	−0.027 (0.047)
2. Company Owned (1 = Yes)	−0.014 (0.006)	−0.004 (0.009)	0.002 (0.009)	−0.033 (0.010)
3. Burger King (1 = Yes)	−0.001 (0.006)	0.020 (0.010)	0.006 (0.010)	−0.017 (0.011)
4. KFC (1 = Yes)	0.009 (0.007)	0.025 (0.010)	0.002 (0.010)	0.002 (0.011)
5. Log Population of City in 1986	−0.003 (0.002)	0.000 (0.003)	−0.007 (0.003)	−0.004 (0.003)
6. Standard Error of Regression	0.038	0.056	0.058	0.064

Note: Standard errors are shown in parentheses. All models include seven region dummies. The sample size is 266.
[a]A full meal consists of a main course (a basic hamburger at Burger King and Wendy's, or six pieces of chicken at KFC), a small order of french fries, and a medium-sized soda.
[b]Proportional increase in starting wage necessary to increase starting wage to the new minimum rate.

the individual items. As in the employment models presented in Table 2.11, the key explanatory variable is the *GAP* measure. The results are relatively imprecise but point toward the same conclusion as does our analysis of price changes in New Jersey. Contrary to a simple "pass through" model of price determination, average prices (for the full meal) seem to have risen more slowly at the stores that were most affected by the increase in the minimum wage. On the other hand, the estimated pattern of price adjustments is different for soft drinks and french fries than for the main course. Given this pattern, and the imprecision of the estimates, it is difficult to reach any firm conclusions about the effects of the minimum wage on pricing behavior in Texas fast-food restaurants.

EFFECTS OF THE MINIMUM WAGE ON RESTAURANT OPENINGS

An important potential effect of higher minimum wages is to discourage the opening of new businesses. Although the sample design of our New Jersey–Pennsylvania study allows us to estimate the effect of the minimum wage on *existing* restaurants in New Jersey, we cannot address the effect of the higher minimum wage on the rate of creation of new businesses in the fast-food industry.[32] To assess the likely size of such an effect, we used national restaurant directories for the McDonald's restaurant chain to compare the numbers of operating restaurants and the numbers of newly opened restaurants in different states during the 1986–1991 period. We chose this period because many states adopted state-specific minimum wages during the late 1980s. In addition, the federal minimum increased in this period. These policies create an opportunity to measure the impact of minimum-wage laws on restaurant-opening rates across states.

Each year, McDonald's Corporation publishes the *McDonald's Restaurant Guide*, listing the locations of existing restaurants and restaurants that are scheduled to open within the year. Using the 1986 and 1991 *Guides*, we calculated the number of new restaurants in each state (i.e., the number that were listed in the 1991 *Guide* but not in the 1986 *Guide*), the number of closed restaurants (i.e., the number that were listed in the 1986 *Guide* but not in the 1991 *Guide*), and the total number of outlets in each state in each year.

To test for the effect of the minimum wage on the growth rate of the number of outlets in a state, we developed two measures of the upward wage pressure exerted by minimum-wage changes during 1986–1991. The first measure is the fraction of workers in the state's retail trade industry in 1986 whose wages were in the range between the federal minimum wage in 1986 ($3.35 per hour) and the effective minimum wage in the state in April 1990 (the maximum of the federal minimum wage or the state minimum wage as of April 1990).[33] The second measure is the ratio of the state's effective minimum wage in 1990 to the average hourly wage of retail-trade workers in the state in 1986. In addition to these key explanatory variables, we included two other controls in our models: the rate of population growth in the state between 1986 and 1991, and the change in the state's unemployment rate during that period.

The results of our analysis are presented in Table 2.13. The first four columns present results using as a dependent variable the proportional change in the total number of restaurants in a state. Columns 5–8 present results using as a dependent variable the number of new openings divided by the number of outlets in the state in 1986. The results provide no evidence that higher minimum-wage rates exert a negative effect on either the net number of restaurants operating in a state or the rate of new openings. To the contrary, all

TABLE 2.13
Estimated Effect of Minimum Wage on the Number of McDonald's Restaurants, 1986–1991

	Dependent Variable: Proportional Increase in Number of Restaurants				Dependent Variable: Number Newly Opened Restaurants/Number in 1986			
	(1)	(2)	(3)	(4)	(5)	(6)	(7)	(8)
Minimum Wage Variable								
1. Fraction of Retail Workers in Affected Wage Range, 1986[a]	0.33 (0.20)	—	0.13 (0.19)	—	0.37 (0.22)	—	0.16 (0.21)	—
2. State Minimum Wage, 1991/Average Retail Wage, 1986[b]	—	0.38 (0.22)	—	0.47 (0.22)	—	0.47 (0.23)	—	0.56 (0.24)
Other Control Variables								
3. Proportional Growth in Population, 1986–1991	—	—	0.88 (0.23)	1.03 (0.23)	—	—	0.86 (0.25)	1.04 (0.25)
4. Change in Unemployment Rates, 1986–1991	—	—	−1.78 (0.62)	−1.40 (0.61)	—	—	−1.85 (0.68)	−1.40 (0.65)
5. Standard Error of Regression	0.083	0.083	0.071	0.068	0.088	0.088	0.077	0.073

Note: Standard errors are shown in parentheses. The sample contains 51 state-level observations (including Washington, DC) on the number of McDonald's restaurants open in 1986 and 1991. The dependent variable in columns 1–4 is the proportional increase in the number of restaurants open. The mean and standard deviation are 0.246 and 0.085, respectively. The dependent variable in columns 5–8 is the ratio of the number of new restaurants opened between 1986 and 1991 to the number open in 1986. The mean and standard deviation are 0.293 and 0.091, respectively. All regressions are weighted by state population in 1986.

[a] The fraction of all workers in retail trade in the state in 1986 earning an hourly wage between \$3.35 per hour and the "effective" state minimum wage in 1990 (i.e., the maximum of the federal minimum wage in 1990 [\$3.80 per hour] and the state minimum wage as of April 1, 1990).

[b] Maximum of state and federal minimum wage as of April 1, 1990, divided by average hourly wage of workers in retail trade in the state in 1986.

the estimates indicate *positive* effects of the minimum-wage measures on the number of operating or newly opened restaurants, although many of the point estimates are insignificantly different from zero. Although this evidence is based only on data from one chain, we believe that it is probably safe to conclude that new openings in the fast-food industry are not strongly affected by wage changes induced by modest changes in the minimum wage.

Summary, Criticisms, and Responses

This chapter presents the results of two, detailed case studies of the effect of an increase in the legal minimum wage. The first study uses firm-level data for fast-food restaurants in New Jersey and Pennsylvania, collected before and after the April 1992 increase in the New Jersey minimum wage to $5.05 per hour. The second study uses comparable data for fast-food restaurants in Texas, collected before and after the April 1991 increase in the federal minimum wage. Both studies focus on comparisons of the changes in employment at restaurants that were directly affected by the increase in the minimum wage with the corresponding changes at restaurants that were unaffected by the law. This simple "treatment and control group" methodology has many advantages for analyzing the effect of the minimum wage. Most importantly, the behavior of the unaffected firms (the control group) provides a counterfactual for what would have happened at affected firms (the treatment group) in the absence of an increase in the minimum wage. The existence of a credible control group is essential in any scientific study. Using a control group, for example, allows us to "difference out" any seasonal changes that might have affected employment levels in both groups of restaurants.

With respect to the critical question of whether an increase in the minimum wage causes a reduction in employment, the results of the two studies are remarkably similar. In the New Jersey–Pennsylvania evaluation, comparisons between restaurants in the two states show that employment actually expanded in New Jersey relative to Pennsylvania, where the minimum wage was constant. A comparison within New Jersey between high-wage restaurants that initially were paying more than $5.00 per hour and low-wage restaurants that had to raise their wages to comply with the new law yields the same conclusion. Relative to high-wage restaurants, employment increased at restaurants affected by the minimum wage. The same pattern emerges in the Texas study: relative to higher-wage restaurants that were unaffected by the law, restaurants that were forced to increase pay to meet the new federal minimum wage increased employment.

Despite the consistency of these findings, several criticisms—some valid and some not—have been raised about the studies and their underlying methodology. Here, we try to provide a summary of the criticisms and indicate which ones we think are most important. One criticism that is sometimes voiced is that the studies measured the impact of the minimum wage too soon after the new law took effect. In our opinion, this issue is minor, for three reasons. First, it is unlikely that employers would respond to a higher minimum wage by increasing employment in the short-run, if their long-run intentions were to cut employment. Second, fast-food restaurants can easily vary their staffing levels by cutting back on off-peak crews or store hours, and by allowing longer queues. We would expect these types of adjustments to be made within a few months of a higher wage. Moreover, high quit rates in the fast-food industry allow managers to trim employment without incurring large layoff costs (such as higher unemployment insurance premiums). All things considered, if the increase in the minimum wage has a negative effect on employment, we would expect to see some indication of the effect within four to eight months. Finally, the effect of an increase in the minimum wage will tend to fall over time, as inflation erodes the real value of the minimum. Thus, the impact of a modest minimum-wage hike may well be larger during the first few months after the increase than in subsequent years.

A related criticism is that the baseline surveys that we use to measure employment levels before the rise in the minimum wage were conducted too close to the date of the minimum-wage hike. Again, we think this point is minor. Because quit rates in the fast-food industry are so high, a manager who wants to reduce costs simply can refrain from hiring new employees for several weeks. There is no need to "pre-adjust" staffing levels far in advance of a minimum-wage increase. Furthermore, in the case of New Jersey, considerable uncertainty existed as to whether the minimum-wage hike would actually occur. This uncertainty was resolved only after we had conducted the first wave of our survey, so that our baseline employment estimates are unlikely to be fully adjusted to the impending rise in the minimum wage.

A more serious criticism is that an increase in the minimum wage might choke off new investment in the industry, even if it has little or no effect on existing restaurants. The design of our New Jersey–Pennsylvania study allows us to measure the total effect of the minimum wage on restaurants that were open for business prior to the increase in the minimum wage, including any effect on restaurant closings. However, it does not allow us to measure effects on new openings. Our analysis of teenage employment rates addresses this criticism indirectly, by testing whether overall teenage employment opportunities fell after the minimum-wage increase. Although the results are imprecise, they do not point to any relative reduction in employment opportunities for low-wage workers in New Jersey. We also address the issue of restaurant openings directly, by comparing interstate patterns of new openings for the McDonald's restaurant chain between 1986 and 1991 with state-level measures of the wage pressure exerted by minimum-wage changes during that period. The results show no indication that minimum-wage increases deter investment in the fast-food industry.

Another criticism of the results in this chapter is their narrow focus. Although we present some statewide data on teenage employment trends, our main estimates pertain only to franchised restaurants in the fast-food industry. As we noted in this chapter, fast-food restaurants are one of the largest employers of minimum-wage workers. Furthermore, because fast-food chains comply with minimum-wage laws and usually do not permit tipping, the minimum wage presumably has a stronger effect on fast-food outlets than on many other types of restaurants. Nevertheless, it is sometimes suggested that fast-food outlets may actually benefit from an increase in the minimum at the expense of other low-price restaurants. For example, the higher minimum might force some "mom and pop" restaurants to close, leading to an increase in business for the fast-food chains. If this is the case, however, we would expect to observe a relative increase in employment at the fast-food restaurants in New Jersey that already were paying more than the new minimum wage. In fact, higher-wage restaurants that were not affected directly by the minimum wage had the same employment growth as did restaurants in Pennsylvania. This comparison suggests that there was no relative demand shock that coincidentally increased the demand for fast-food employees in New Jersey—whether attributable to the minimum wage or to any other factor.

A final criticism is directed at the case-study methodology itself. The comparison of employment trends at affected and unaffected restaurants relies on the assumption that the control group and the treatment group would have exhibited the same trends in the absence of an increase in the minimum wage. There may be underlying differences between the two groups that periodically lead to shifts in employment in one group relative to the other. We can never rule out the possibility that unobserved shocks occurred during the course of our studies. Even if these shocks tended to average out between the affected and unaffected restaurants in our samples, the precision of our findings might be overstated, because we failed to take into account the potential sampling variability attributable to the unobserved shocks.

This criticism is potentially valid, although we believe that it is more likely to apply to the comparison between New Jersey and Pennsylvania restaurants than to the comparison of restaurants within New Jersey or to the similar comparison of restaurants within Texas. Our answer to this criticism is to obtain additional evidence by examining more case studies, and by using other types of data to study the effects of the minimum wage. In the next chapter, we present a third case study, based on the experiences in California after that state's adoption of a $4.25 minimum wage in July 1988. In chapter 4, we reexamine the 1990 and 1991 increases in the federal minimum wage—this time, combining data for all the states and correlating employment outcomes across different states with a measure of the impact of the minimum wage on low-wage workers in each state. Each of these studies has strengths and weaknesses that must be carefully considered in evaluating the weight of the evidence. To the extent that these disparate strands of evidence give similar answers about the effect of the minimum wage, however, the individual parts of the story are more compelling.

Appendix

This appendix describes in more detail the characteristics of the sample of fast-food restaurants used in our New Jersey–Pennsylvania study. We also present some data on the reliability of the responses to our survey questions and describe the differences in characteristics for various subsamples of restaurants in the data set.

Sample Frame and Response Rates

The sample was derived from telephone listings for New Jersey and eastern Pennsylvania as of February 1992. The frame included all Burger King, KFC, Wendy's, and Roy Rogers outlets listed in the white pages of the New Jersey telephone books, and outlets for the same chains in selected telephone books for eastern Pennsylvania. The original frame included 502 telephone numbers.

Table A.2.1 shows that 473 restaurants in the sample frame had working telephone numbers at the time that we tried to reach them for our first-wave interview, during February–March 1992. Because we were particularly interested in obtaining a large sample of restaurants in New Jersey, we instructed our interviewer to call back the

TABLE A.2.1
Sample Design and Response Rates

	All (1)	New Jersey (2)	Pennsylvania (3)
		Restaurants, by State	
Wave 1: February 15–March 4, 1992			
1. Number of Restaurants in Sample Frame[a]	473	364	109
2. Number of Refusals	63	33	30
3. Number Interviewed	410	331	79
4. Response Rate (%)	86.7	90.9	72.5
Wave 2: November 5–December 31, 1992			
5. Number of Restaurants in Sample Frame	410	331	79
6. Number Closed	6	5	1
7. Number Under Renovation	2	2	0
8. Number Temporarily Closed for Other Reasons[b]	2	2	0
9. Number of Refusals	1	1	0
10. Number Interviewed[c]	399	321	78

[a]Restaurants with valid telephone numbers only. Twenty-nine restaurants in the original sample frame had disconnected telephone numbers.

[b]Includes one restaurant that closed because of highway construction, and one that closed because of a fire.

[c]Includes 371 telephone interviews and 28 personal interviews with restaurant managers who refused an initial request for a telephone interview.

New Jersey restaurants "as often as necessary" to obtain an interview. We instructed the interviewer to call back those in Pennsylvania at least twice. The interviewer called back 70 restaurants three or more times before obtaining completed interviews—69 of the 70 were in New Jersey.

We obtained completed interviews (with some item nonresponse) from 410 of the restaurants, for an overall response rate of 86.7 percent. As expected, the response rate was higher in New Jersey (90.9 percent) than in Pennsylvania (72.5 percent), reflecting the more aggressive callback strategy used to contact New Jersey restaurants. Response rates per callback were almost identical in the two states. Among New Jersey restaurants, 44.5 percent responded to the first call, and 72.0 percent responded after two callbacks, at most. Among Pennsylvania restaurants, 42.2 percent responded to the first call, and 71.6 percent responded after two callbacks, at most.

The second wave of the survey was conducted during November and December 1992, about eight months after the minimum-wage increase. Only the 410 restaurants that provided data in the first wave were included in the second-wave survey. During November, we successfully interviewed 371 (90 percent) of these restaurants by telephone. We then hired an interviewer to drive to the 39 nonresponding restaurants in order to determine whether they were still in operation, and to conduct a personal interview, if possible. The interviewer discovered that six nonresponding restaurants (five in New Jersey and one in Pennsylvania) were closed permanently. She also discovered that four (all in New Jersey) were closed temporarily. Two were closed for renovations, a third was closed because of a mall fire, and the fourth because of nearby highway construction. By April 1993, the restaurant that had closed because of road construction and one of the restaurants that had closed for renovation had reopened.

RELIABILITY

We can assess the reliability of our survey questions by examining the responses of 11 restaurants that inadvertently were interviewed twice in the first wave of the survey. These outlets were interviewed twice because their telephone numbers appeared in more than one telephone book, and neither the interviewer nor the respondent noticed that a previous interview had been conducted. (We conjecture that the two interviews were granted by different managers or assistant managers at each restaurant). The first four columns of Table A.2.2 present the means and standard deviations of full-time-equivalent (FTE) employment, starting wages, and full-meal prices for our overall sample of 410 restaurants and for the subsample of 11 restaurants that were interviewed twice. The characteristics of the reinterview sample are remarkably similar to those of the overall sample.

The fifth column of the table presents the estimated "reliability ratios" for each of three key variables—FTE employment, starting wages, and prices. The reliability ratio represents the fraction of the cross-sectional variance in an observed variable that is attributable to true "signal," as opposed to measurement error. Assuming that the measurement errors in the two interviews are independent of each other and independent of the true value of the particular variable in question, the reliability ratio can be estimated by forming the simple correlation coefficient between the two measured values of the same variable in the two interviews. As shown in Table A.2.2, the estimated reliability ratios are fairly high—ranging from 0.70 for FTE employment to 0.98 for the price of a meal.

TABLE A.2.2
Estimated Reliability Ratios for FTE Employment, Wages, and Prices

	Overall Sample		Subsample of Double Interviews		
	Mean (1)	Standard Deviation (2)	Mean (3)	Standard Deviation (4)	Estimated Reliability[a] (5)
1. FTE Employment	21.0	9.7	21.1	9.4	0.70
2. Starting Wage ($/hr)	4.62	0.35	4.77	0.48	0.83
3. Price of Full Meal ($)	3.29	0.65	3.26	0.65	0.98

Note: Columns 1 and 2 are based on a sample of 410 restaurants. Columns 3 and 4 are based on first-interview results for the subsample of 11 restaurants that were interviewed twice.

[a] Estimated correlation between responses in first and second interviews.

Similar reliability ratios were obtained by Katz and Krueger (1992) in a more systematic reliability study of responses to their Texas questionnaire. Katz and Krueger randomly selected 30 respondents to the second wave of their Texas survey and readministered their survey questionnaire. The estimated reliability ratios in this analysis were as follows: for the log of FTE employment—0.76; for the starting wage rate—0.76; for the price of a medium-sized soda—0.72; and for the price of a small order of french fries—0.65.

CHARACTERISTICS OF SELECTED SUBSAMPLES

Table A.2.3 presents a variety of data for various subsamples of our overall sample, including the subsample with valid wage and employment data for both waves of the survey (column 2); the subsample with valid wage, employment, and price data for both waves of the survey (column 3); the subsample with valid employment data in wave 1 but missing employment data in wave 2 (column 4); the subsample with valid employment data in wave 2 but missing employment data in wave 1 (column 5); the subsample of six stores that permanently closed between waves 1 and 2 (column 6); and the subsample of four stores that were closed temporarily as of wave 2 (column 7). A comparison of columns 1–3 suggests that restaurants with valid employment, wage, and price data are similar in other respects to the overall sample of restaurants. Restaurants that reported employment in wave 1 but not in wave 2 were about average in size in wave 1, whereas those that reported employment in wave 2 but not in wave 1 were slightly larger than average in wave 2.

TABLE A.2.3
Means of Employment, Wages, and Prices for Various Subsamples

	Overall Sample (1)	Samples with Valid				Closed, Wave 2 (6)	Temporarily Closed, Wave 2 (7)
		Employment, Wages (2)	Employment, Wages, Prices (3)	Missing Wave 2 Employment (4)	Missing Wave 1 Employment (5)		
1. Mean FTE Employment, Wave 1	21.00 (0.49)	21.10 (0.53)	20.72 (0.52)	20.79 (1.47)	—	12.38 (1.25)	18.38 (3.36)
2. Mean FTE Employment, Wave 2	21.05 (0.46)	20.86 (0.48)	20.71 (0.46)	—	24.80 (1.20)	—	—
3. Mean Starting Wage, Wave 1 ($/hr)	4.62 (0.02)	4.62 (0.02)	4.62 (0.02)	4.70 (0.09)	4.59 (0.12)	4.43 (0.12)	4.79 (0.23)
4. Mean Starting Wage, Wave 2 ($/hr)	5.00 (0.01)	5.00 (0.01)	4.99 (0.01)	5.05	5.02 (0.08)	—	—
5. Mean Price Full Meal, Wave 1 ($)	3.29 (0.03)	3.32 (0.04)	3.26 (0.04)	3.01 (0.10)	3.21 (0.15)	2.98 (0.09)	2.95 (0.05)
6. Mean Price Full Meal, Wave 2 ($)	3.34 (0.03)	3.37 (0.04)	3.38 (0.04)	2.99 (0.06)	3.09 (0.13)	—	—
7. Percentage of Restaurants in New Jersey	80.7 (1.9)	81.2 (2.1)	80.8 (2.2)	85.7 (9.4)	83.3 (10.8)	83.3 (15.2)	100.0
8. Percentage KFC Restaurants	19.5 (2.0)	20.7 (2.1)	22.7 (2.4)	0.0	8.3 (8.0)	0.0	0.0
9. Number of Observations in Subsample	410	357	317	14	12	6	4

Note: Standard errors are shown in parentheses. Means are taken over all available observations for the particular variable in the sample. FTE employment denotes full-time-equivalent employment and is equal to the number of full-time workers plus 0.5 times the number of part-time workers. The price of a full meal is the combined price for a main course, a small order of french fries, and a medium-sized soda.

Sample Definitions:

Column 1: Overall sample.

Column 2: Restaurants with nonmissing data on employment and wages in wave 1 and wave 2.

Column 3: Restaurants with nonmissing data on employment, wages, and prices in wave 1 and wave 2.

Column 4: Restaurants with valid employment data in wave 1 and missing employment data in wave 2 (including four temporarily closed restaurants).

Column 5: Restaurants with valid employment data in wave 2 and missing employment data in wave 1.

Column 6: Restaurants that were closed in wave 2.

Column 7: Restaurants that were temporarily closed in wave 2 (one restaurant closed because of highway construction, one closed because of a fire, and two closed for renovations).

Otherwise, both sets of restaurants look similar to the subsamples with valid data for both waves.

Inspection of column 6 shows that restaurants that closed between wave 1 and wave 2 were much smaller than others in our sample—the t-ratio for the difference in wave 1 employment between the subsamples in columns 2 and 6 is 6.4. They also had slightly lower wages than other restaurants ($0.29 per hour lower, with a t-ratio of 1.5). A probit model for the probability of permanent closure suggests that size is the main predictor of closure. Controlling for size, other variables, including ownership status and the level of starting wages in wave 1, have numerically small and statistically insignificant effects on the closure rate.

Finally, a comparison of the data for restaurants that were closed temporarily at the time of our second-wave interview suggests that these restaurants are very similar to the sample of continuing establishments. Wave 1 employment was slightly smaller for the four temporarily closed restaurants, but the wave 1 starting-wage rate was slightly higher.

NOTES

1. In fact, Lester was criticized widely by other economists for interpreting his results as evidence against the competitive labor demand model.

2. Randomized trials are now used frequently by social scientists to study the effects of training programs, income-support programs, and other individual-based interventions in the labor market (see Burtless [1993]).

3. Similar effects can arise in other experimental settings. For example, in a test of a vaccine for a contagious disease, the vaccination of the treatment group might also reduce the infection rate of the control group. Such contamination effects are thought to have plagued early tests of the Salk polio vaccine (see Freedman, Pisani, and Purves [1978, pp. 5–7]).

4. Another often-cited example is the analysis by Schultz (1964) of output levels in different provinces of India after a typhoid epidemic that differentially affected the provinces' populations.

5. Campbell (1957, 1969) describes a list of "threats" to the validity of a natural, or "quasi-," experiment originally in the context of studies of education test scores. See Meyer (1994) for a recent discussion and critique of the methodology of natural experiments.

6. Formally, the validity of the control group can be addressed by the same types of specification tests as those used in the program-evaluation literature (see, for example, Lalonde [1986] and Heckman and Hotz [1989]). The question of the validity of the control group is identical to the question of whether an indicator variable for treatment-group status is econometrically exogenous in a pooled model for the outcomes of the treatment and control groups.

7. See Hamermesh (1993, chapter 3) for a wide-ranging discussion of the identification issue in labor-demand studies.

8. Biases resulting from specification searching are described in Leamer (1978), who is sharply critical of standard econometric practice.

9. The use of evidence from previous interventions to form "model-free" forecasts is sometimes criticized by economists, who argue that the behavioral responses to a particular intervention could change over time or across different situations. For example, responses to a small increase in the minimum wage may not give much useful information on the effect of a large increase in the minimum.

10. The legislative history of the federal minimum-wage bill is described in more detail in chapter 10.

11. See chapter 10, Table 10.1. The share of jobs in the restaurant industry that franchise restaurants account for is based on data in Table 13 of U.S. Department of Commerce (1990a).

12. The average age of workers in Charner and Fraser's sample is 20. They report that 30 percent of fast-food workers are age 21 or older. Our figure is probably higher than theirs because our age group was divided at 20, rather than at 21 and because demographic changes since 1982 have reduced the size of the teenage work force.

13. In a pilot survey for the Texas study, Katz and Krueger (1992) obtained very low response rates from McDonald's restaurants. For this reason, McDonald's restaurants were excluded from both the Texas and New Jersey–Pennsylvania studies.

14. These programs typically offer a bounty of $40–75 for the successful recruitment of a new employee. We excluded other noncash recruiting bonuses (such as "employee of the month" designations) from our tabulations.

15. An alternative possibility is that seasonal factors produce higher employment at fast-food restaurants in February and March than in November and December. An analysis of national employment data for food preparation and service workers, however, shows higher average employment in the fourth quarter than in the first quarter.

16. To investigate the cyclicality of fast-food-restaurant sales, we regressed the year-to-year change in U.S. sales of the McDonald's restaurant chain from 1976–1991 on the corresponding change in the average unemployment rate. The regression results show that a one percentage point increase in the unemployment rate reduces sales by $257 million, with a t-statistic of 3.0.

17. In a regression model without other controls, the expected attenuation of the GAP coefficient due to measurement error is the reliability ratio of the GAP variable (γ_0), which we estimate at 0.70. The expected attenuation factor when region dummies are added to the model is $\gamma_1 = (\gamma_0 - R^2)/(1 - R^2)$, where R^2 is the R-Squared of a regression of GAP on region effects (equal to 0.30). Thus, we expect the estimated GAP coefficient to fall by a factor of $\gamma_1/\gamma_0 = 0.8$ when region dummies are added to the regression model.

18. We cannot use the familiar log specification because some of the res-

taurants have zero employment in wave 2. Instead, we have divided the change in employment by average employment in waves 1 and 2. This results in very similar coefficients but slightly smaller standard errors than the alternative of dividing the change by wave 1 employment. For restaurants with zero employment in wave 2, the proportional change in employment is set to -1.

19. Analysis of the 1991 Current Population Survey (CPS) reveals that part-time workers in the restaurant industry work about 46 percent as many hours as do full-time workers. Katz and Krueger (1992) assume that the ratio of part-time workers' hours to full-time workers' hours in the fast-food industry is 0.57.

20. The interviewer telephoned all restaurants at least two more times, if she failed to obtain an interview on the first call.

21. The 070 three-digit ZIP code area (around Newark) and the 080 three-digit ZIP code area (around Camden) contain the largest numbers of restaurants among three-digit ZIP code areas in New Jersey and, together, account for 36 percent of New Jersey restaurants in our sample.

22. It is likely that some, if not most, of this variability can be traced to idiosyncratic reporting errors. On average, we expect that the reporting errors should be of comparable magnitude in New Jersey and Pennsylvania. Thus, they should cancel out in the comparison.

23. Hamermesh (1993, chapter 3) concludes that a "best guess" of the output-constant elasticity of employment demand is -0.30. The output-constant elasticity is necessarily smaller in absolute value than the elasticity implicit in our analysis, which allows output to vary.

24. In the other 19 percent of restaurants, full-time workers were paid more—typically, 10 percent more.

25. A formal model can be built on these ideas.

26. In wave 1 of our survey, the average time to the "usual first increase" was 18.9 weeks, and the average amount of the first increase was $0.21 per hour.

27. According to the McDonald's Corporation *1991 Annual Report*, payroll and benefits are 31 percent of operating costs at McDonald's restaurants. Because workers affected by the increase in the minimum wage earn lower wages than do other workers, their share of cost is somewhat less than their share of total employment.

28. These predictions follow from the joint assumptions of free entry and constant returns to scale. In this case, price is equal to average cost for firms in each submarket.

29. We used January, February, and March data from the 1992 CPS to derive these figures.

30. We define FTE employment as the sum of managers; assistant managers; full-time, nonmanagerial employees; and 0.57 times the number of part-time, nonmanagerial employees. The 0.57 figure is based on a tabulation of hours for full-time and part-time fast-food workers in a 1982–1983 survey conducted by the National Institute for Work and Learning. See Charner and Fraser (1984) for further description of this data set.

31. If the list of covariates is expanded to include seven region dummies, the coefficient in the model for FTE employment falls slightly but remains marginally significantly different from zero.

32. Direct inquiries to the chains in our sample revealed that, during 1992, Wendy's opened two stores in New Jersey and one store in Pennsylvania. The other chains were unwilling to provide information on new openings.

33. We used the 1986 CPS files to construct the minimum-wage variables. State minimum-wage rates in 1990 were obtained from the Bureau of National Affairs (undated).

CHAPTER 3

Statewide Evidence on the Effect
of the 1988 California Minimum Wage

> It is one of the happy incidents of the federal system that a
> single courageous state may, if its citizens choose, serve as
> a laboratory; and try novel social and economic experiments
> without risk to the rest of the country.
> —Justice Louis D. Brandeis

As WE HAVE SEEN in chapter 2, individual employers do not always respond to an increase in the minimum wage by reducing employment. Although this finding is surprising and important, much of the controversy surrounding the minimum wage concerns aggregate outcomes, such as the employment rate of teenagers. In this chapter, based on Card (1992b), we move from the narrow perspective of individual employers to a broader, market-level study of the July 1, 1988, increase in California's minimum wage. The shift in perspective opens up a new set of questions: How does the minimum wage affect the distribution of wages? Does an increase in the minimum wage reduce the employment rate of teenagers or other low-wage workers? Which industries are most affected by the minimum wage? Despite this change in focus, we continue to use the natural-experiment methodology in our analysis. Specifically, we rely on the labor-market trends in states that did not change their minimum wages in order to infer what would have happened in California in the absence of the new law.

Several features of the California law and the state's economy combine to make the 1988 minimum-wage change especially informative. First, the increase in the minimum wage from $3.35 to 4.25 per hour was relatively large—27 percent—and occurred in one step. Prior to the increase, 11 percent of workers in the state and 50 percent of California teenagers were earning between $3.35 and 4.24 per hour. There is little doubt that the increase had the potential to substantially affect the California labor market. Second, because of the state's size, we can use detailed microdata from the Current Population Survey (CPS) to study the characteristics and labor-market outcomes of individuals affected by the increase. These data, combined with data for a comparison sample drawn from states that did not change their minimum-wage laws, yield relatively precise inferences on the effects of the minimum wage. Third, as a result of an unanticipated legal decision, coverage of the $4.25 per hour minimum wage was extended to employees in the restaurant industry who received tips. This unexpectedly high minimum wage creates an ideal natural experiment for an important sector of the economy. Finally, the timing of the 1988 law coincided with a period of modest inflation and declining unemployment. This type of stable economic environment makes it easier to disentangle the effects of the minimum wage from other shocks to the labor market.

Our analysis of the California experience shows that an increase in the minimum wage has substantial effects on the earnings of low-wage workers. For teenagers, the effects are particularly striking: we estimate that the minimum wage increased average teenage wages in the state by 10 percent. Nevertheless, we find no indication that these wage gains led to employment losses for teenagers or other low-wage workers. To the contrary, we find that the rise in the minimum wage actually may have increased both wages *and* employment rates of teenagers in the state. Even in the retail trade industry, we find little evidence that the increase led to significant employment losses.

A Brief Legislative History

The increase in California's minimum wage in mid-1988 followed a year-long sequence of legislative, administrative, and judicial decisions.[1] In May 1987, the state assembly's Labor and Employment Commission voted to increase the minimum wage from $3.35 to 4.25 per hour effective January 1, 1988, with additional increases in 1989 and 1990. Both houses of the legislature subsequently passed a bill specifying a single increase, to $4.25 per hour, effective January 1, 1988. This bill was vetoed in September 1987 by the governor, who cited a pending decision of the state's Industrial Welfare Commission (IWC). The IWC, which is empowered under California law to set minimum wages for all workers in the state, had begun hearings on a new minimum in 1986. In December 1987, it announced an increase in the minimum wage to $4.25, effective July 1, 1988.

The IWC's ruling also established a subminimum rate of $3.50 per hour for tipped employees. This provision was immediately appealed by the California Labor Federation on the grounds that the subminimum rate violated the California Labor Code. An appellate court ruled against the subminimum in June 1988. The new law therefore took effect on July 1 amid much confusion as to the legal minimum wage for tipped employees. The issue was finally resolved on October 31, 1988, when the state supreme court upheld the lower court and rejected the subminimum provision. By late 1988, the minimum wage was clearly established at $4.25 per hour for all California workers, including tipped employees. The only exemptions applied to individuals younger than 18 years of age (who were subject to a $3.60 subminimum) and certain narrow occupations and industries.

CHARACTERISTICS OF LOW-WAGE WORKERS IN 1987

To understand the effects of the increase in the minimum wage in California, it is important to identify the sectors of the economy and the types of workers affected by the law. Table 3.1 presents the demographic characteristics and industry affiliations of low-wage workers in the state in the year before the increase. The data are taken from merged files of the 12 monthly CPS surveys conducted during 1987.[2] The first column of the table shows characteristics for all workers in the state. The second and third columns present corresponding data for individuals whose hourly wages during the survey week were less than the prevailing minimum of $3.35 per hour, and between $3.35 and 4.24 per hour.

In 1987, 1.3 percent of California workers had an hourly wage below the federal minimum wage. Because California law prescribed a $3.35 minimum rate for most workers who were not covered by the federal statute, some of these individuals presumably were working illegally for noncomplying employers.[3] Others, including some 16- and 17-year-old workers and some live-in household workers, were legally exempt from the federal and state laws. A third group of subminimum-wage earners consists of salaried workers (those paid by the week, month, or year) who misreport their usual weekly earnings or usual weekly hours. Because the hourly wage of salaried workers is constructed by dividing usual weekly earnings by usual weekly hours, individuals who overreport hours (for example, by claiming to work 40 hours per week when they work only 37.5 hours) will be assigned a wage that is too low. Two facts point to the importance of this phenomenon. First, the group earning less than $3.35 per hour reports higher average hours than does the group earning between $3.35 and 4.24 per hour. Second, even though salaried workers have substantially higher average earnings than hourly-rated workers, salaried workers are three times more likely than hourly-rated workers to report subminimum wages.

TABLE 3.1
Characteristics of California Workers, 1987

	All Workers (1)	Workers with Hourly Wage	
		<$3.35 (2)	$3.35–4.24 (3)
1. Average Hourly Wage ($/hr)	10.69	2.64	3.70
	(0.06)	(0.05)	(0.01)
2. Usual Hours per Week	38.5	36.9	30.7
	(0.1)	(1.9)	(0.4)
3. Usual Weekly Earnings ($/wk)	426.3	97.9	114.3
	(2.8)	(5.4)	(1.4)
4. Average Age (years)	35.3	31.9	27.7
5. Percentage Aged 16–19	6.4	26.2	31.0
6. Percentage Aged 20–24	14.1	14.7	23.0
7. Percentage Enrolled (of those aged 16–24)	30.1	41.8	47.0
8. Ethnicity (%)			
a. Hispanic	22.5	36.8	39.0
b. Black Non-Hispanic	6.1	4.1	4.6
c. White Non-Hispanic	62.7	45.2	46.6
9. Percentage Female	45.8	67.2	57.9
10. Percentage in Central City	37.4	47.6	39.4
11. Average Family Income[a] ($/yr)	35,548	24,863	24,338
	(222)	(2,023)	(649)
12. Percentage with Family Income <$15,000 per year	19.0	48.8	44.2
13. Industry Distribution (%)			
a. Agriculture	2.7	5.4	7.4
b. Low-Wage Manufacturing[b]	2.3	9.4	7.3
c. Retail Trade	16.7	21.9	48.0
14. Sample Size	11,591	150	1,220

Source: Data are taken from the 1987 Current Population Survey.
Note: Standard errors are shown in parentheses. Workers are wage and salary earners aged 16–68, excluding self-employed and unpaid workers.
[a]Reported interval values are assigned interval means.
[b]Apparel, textiles, furniture, toys, and sporting goods manufacturing.

In comparison to the subminimum-wage group, a much larger set of individuals—10.8 percent of all California workers—was paid either exactly $3.35 per hour or between $3.36 and 4.24 per hour. For simplicity, we refer to these workers as the "affected group." Assuming that individuals earning between $3.35 and 4.24 per hour were employed in jobs covered by the minimum wage and at firms that complied with the law, workers in the affected group were directly at risk of losing their jobs because of the minimum wage. After July 1, 1988, they either had to receive pay increases or lose their jobs.

Relative to the overall California workforce, the affected group includes disproportionately more women, Hispanics, inner-city residents, and enrolled students. Affected wage earners also work fewer hours per week than either lower- or higher-wage workers. The age distribution of the affected group is highly skewed: slightly less than one-third are teenagers, and another 23 percent are aged 20 to 24. Indeed, 52 percent of California teenagers and 29 percent of 20- to 24-year-old workers earned between $3.35 and 4.24 per hour during 1987. Rows 11 and 12 of Table 3.1 present family-income data, based on incomes in the 12 months preceding the CPS interview. About 44 percent of affected wage earners lived in families with annual incomes of less than $15,000. By comparison, 24 percent of *all* Californians aged 16 to 68 and 19 percent of employed individuals lived in such families in 1987. As we discuss in more detail in chapter 9, the concentration of affected workers in the lower tail of the family-income distribution implies that an increase in the minimum wage has a potentially equalizing effect on the distribution of family income.

Examination of the industry-composition data for the affected group (in rows 13a–13c of the table) shows that nearly one-half were employed in retail trade. Of these, about 35 percent (or close to one-fourth of all affected workers) worked in the restaurant industry. Given this concentration, we devote special attention to the retail trade and restaurant industries in this chapter.

THE EFFECTS OF THE MINIMUM WAGE ON THE OVERALL LABOR
  MARKET

Effects on the Wage Distribution

The first issue of interest is whether the California minimum-wage increase had any effect on the distribution of wages in the state. As shown in Figure 3.1, the answer is clearly "Yes." The upper panel of this figure shows the percentages of California workers earning less than $3.35 per hour, between $3.35 and 4.24 per hour, and exactly $4.25 per hour during each quarter between the first quarter of 1987 and the fourth quarter of 1989. For comparison, the lower panel of the figure shows the corresponding fractions of workers in a group of southern and western states that did not change their minimum wage laws during the 1987–1989 period. The "control-group" sample includes workers in Arizona; Florida; Georgia; New Mexico; and

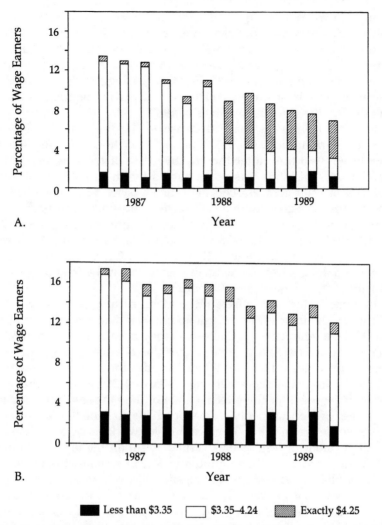

Figure 3.1 Percentage of workers earning $4.25 per hour or less. A. California. B. Comparison areas.

Dallas–Fort Worth, Texas. Although we might have preferred to use a different set of states in the comparison sample—such as those that are closer to California—the states of Nevada, Oregon, and Washington all raised their minimum wage rates during late 1988 or 1989. Therefore, we chose to include Florida, Georgia, and Dallas–Fort Worth in the control-group sample, along with Arizona and New Mexico.[4]

In the appendix to this chapter, we compare the characteristics of workers in California and the comparison areas. During 1987, individuals in the two groups had very similar labor-force participation rates, employment–population rates, and unemployment rates. The two samples also had comparable age and education distributions, although the fraction of Hispanic workers was higher in California than in the comparison areas. Perhaps the biggest difference is in the average level of wages, which were 22 percent higher in California than in the comparison areas in 1987.

Figure 3.1 shows a sharp decrease in the fraction of California workers earning between $3.35 and 4.24 per hour after the second quarter of 1988 (i.e., after the effective date of the new minimum-wage law). This shift was accompanied by an increase in the percentage of California workers reporting exactly $4.25 per hour. In the comparison-area sample the fractions of workers in each wage range were fairly stable. A comparison of annual averages for 1987 and 1989 shows that the relative reduction in the fraction of workers earning between $3.35 and 4.24 per hour in California was 5.2 percentage points, whereas the relative increase in the fraction earning exactly $4.25 per hour was 3.5 percent.

In contrast to these effects on workers earning more than $3.35 per hour, the increase in the minimum wage had virtually no effect on the relative fraction of California workers earning less than $3.35 per hour. This stability implies that the relative size of the sub-minimum-wage work force (which includes those earning less than $3.35 per hour *and* those earning $3.35 to 4.24 per hour after July 1988) increased after the effective date of the new law. We used the measure of noncompliance developed by Ashenfelter and Smith (1979) to determine that 31 percent of all workers who had earned $3.35 per hour or less in 1987 earned less than the legal minimum. With the increase in the minimum to $4.25 per hour, the measured noncompliance rate rose to 46 percent.

One potential explanation for this increase in noncompliance is provided by the California law, which permits a lower minimum wage ($3.60 per hour) for individuals younger than 18 years of age and for apprentices and job learners during their first 160 hours of employment. To investigate this explanation, we computed the fraction of California teenagers earning between $3.59 and 3.62 per hour. During the six quarters between July 1, 1988 and December 31, 1989, only 1 California teenager (out of a sample of 877) reported a wage in this interval. As we note in chapter 5, a wide body of other evidence confirms that firms rarely make use of subminimum-wage provisions. In our opinion, a more likely explanation for the increase in measured noncompliance is a combination of true non-compliance behavior and measurement errors in wages, earnings, and hours.

To summarize, a comparison of pre-July 1988 and post-July 1988 wage distributions suggests that the increase in the California minimum wage reduced the fraction of California workers earning $3.35 to 4.24 per hour by about 5 percentage points, with little or no effect on the fraction earning less than $3.35 per hour. Judging by the size of the "spike" in the wage distribution at exactly $4.25 per hour, two-thirds of affected workers who remained employed moved to the new minimum-wage level. Some workers who would have been expected to earn between $3.35 and 4.24 per hour may have been pushed *above* the new minimum, and others may have lost their jobs. To investigate the latter possibility, we turn to evidence on employment rates.

Effects on Employment

We obtain a first indication of the employment effects of the increase in the minimum wage by comparing employment and unemployment trends in California and in the United States as a whole. Between 1987 and 1989, the unemployment rate in California fell from 5.8 to 5.1 percent, and the national rate fell from 6.2 to 5.3 percent. These trends suggest that economic growth in California was similar to or slightly slower than growth elsewhere in the United States. The same conclusion emerges from an analysis of the overall employment–population rate, which increased 1.1 percentage points in California between 1987 and 1989, compared with an increase of 1.5 percentage points nationwide.

For California teenagers, however, the pattern was quite different. Between 1987 and 1989, teenage unemployment rates in California decreased 3 percentage points (from 16.9 to 13.9 percent), whereas the average U.S. rate fell only 1.9 percentage points (from 16.9 to 15.0 percent). An even stronger relative trend is indicated by the teenage employment–population rate, which increased 4.1 percentage points in California (from 43.0 to 47.1 percent), and 2 percentage points nationwide (from 45.5 to 47.5 percent). Because teenagers are heavily overrepresented in the population of workers affected by a minimum-wage increase, these trends are inconsistent with significant job losses caused by an increase in the minimum wage.

To analyze the employment effects of the minimum wage more carefully, we used published Bureau of Labor Statistics data to compare changes in the employment–population rate of California workers relative to workers in our comparison sample.[5] Data for 1985–1990 are presented in Table 3.2. The pre-1987 data can be used to check the validity of the comparison sample. If the comparison areas form a legitimate control group, then differences in employ-

TABLE 3.2
Employment–Population Rates for Teenagers and All Workers,
California Versus Comparison Areas: 1985–1990

	Employment–Population Rate (Percent)					
	1985 (1)	1986 (2)	1987 (3)	1988 (4)	1989 (5)	1990 (6)
All Workers, Aged 16+						
1. California	61.3	62.0	63.1	63.8	64.2	63.1
	(0.4)	(0.4)	(0.4)	(0.4)	(0.4)	(0.4)
2. Comparison Areas	59.9	60.9	61.7	62.4	62.2	62.2
	(0.3)	(0.3)	(0.3)	(0.3)	(0.3)	(0.3)
3. California –	1.4	1.1	1.4	1.4	2.0	0.9
Comparison Areas	(0.5)	(0.5)	(0.5)	(0.5)	(0.5)	(0.5)
Teenagers						
4. California	41.0	41.2	43.0	47.1	47.1	41.4
	(1.3)	(1.3)	(1.3)	(1.3)	(1.3)	(1.3)
5. Comparison Areas	45.7	47.0	47.0	46.5	47.0	45.2
	(1.2)	(1.2)	(1.2)	(1.2)	(1.2)	(1.2)
6. California –	−4.7	−5.8	−4.0	0.6	0.1	−3.8
Comparison Areas	(1.8)	(1.8)	(1.8)	(1.8)	(1.8)	(1.8)

Source: Employment–population rates are taken from U.S. Department of Labor, *Geographic Profiles of Employment and Unemployment*, 1985–1990 editions.

Note: Standard errors are shown in parentheses and are based on published sampling errors for 1989. Data for comparison areas represent a weighted average of data for Arizona; Florida; Georgia; New Mexico; and Dallas–Fort Worth, Texas, using 1988 population counts as weights.

ment rates between California and the comparison areas should be relatively stable throughout the 1985–1987 period. This specification test is clearly satisfied for both the overall employment rate and the teenage employment rate.[6] Relative to the comparison-area sample, the overall employment–population rate in California increased by 0.6 percentage points between 1987 and 1989, potentially accounting for as much as 1 percentage point of higher teenage employment growth in California.[7] The actual relative increase in teenage employment from 1987 to 1989 was 4.1 percentage points, however, suggesting a sizable unexplained gain in teenage employment after the rise in the minimum wage.[8] The data for 1990 show a return to the earlier pattern, although 1990 marked the onset of a recession (which was particularly severe in California, as shown by the drop in the overall employment–population rate relative to the comparison areas) and an increase in the federal minimum wage to $3.80 per hour (on April 1, 1990).

Effects for Specific Demographic Groups

Although the employment rates in Table 3.2 suggest that the increase in California's minimum wage had no adverse employment effect on teenagers, it is useful to extend the comparison to other low-wage workers. The entries in Table 3.3, derived from CPS microdata, show the changes in wages, employment, and unemployment for 18 narrowly defined age-ethnic-education groups between 1987 and 1989. The groups have been selected to yield at least 400 observations per year in California. The first column of the table gives the fraction of workers in each group earning between $3.35 and 4.24 per hour in 1987. This measure of the potential impact of the increase in the minimum ranges from 1 percent for white college graduates to 52 percent for the two teenage groups (white non-Hispanics and Hispanics). The next three columns contain the means of selected labor-market outcomes in 1987: average hourly earnings, the employment–population rate, and the unemployment rate. The last three columns give the changes in these outcomes between 1987 and 1989 in California *relative to* the corresponding changes for the same groups in the comparison areas.[9] These simple differences-in-differences measure the excess changes that occurred in California during the period as a result of the increase in the minimum wage or of other unspecified factors.

On average, wages in California fell slightly relative to the comparison sample between 1987 and 1989 (see the last row of the table). However, for 3 of the 15 groups—white teenagers, Hispanic teenagers, and 20- to 24-year-old Hispanics—wages rose significantly faster in California. Interestingly, all three groups show a relative increase in employment. Among the other groups in the table, the pattern of relative changes in wages, employment, and unemployment varies. Although none of these changes is statistically significant, one can ask whether there is any systematic correlation between the fraction of a group that earned $3.35 to 4.24 per hour in 1987 and the relative changes in the labor-market outcomes for that group. The answer with respect to wages is "Yes": a simple (unweighted) regression of the difference-in-differences of wages on the fraction of workers in the group earning $3.35 to 4.24 per hour in 1987 yields a coefficient of 0.32, with a standard error of 0.10. In contrast, groups with a higher fraction of low-wage workers do not

TABLE 3.3
Wages, Employment, and Unemployment Rates for Various Groups: California 1987 and California – Comparisons 1987–1989

	Percent $3.35–4.24 (1)	California, 1987			Difference-in-Differences[a]		
		Mean Wage (2)	Employment Rate (3)	Unemployment Rate (4)	Mean Wage (5)	Employment Rate (6)	Unemployment Rate (7)
White Non-Hispanic							
1. Aged 16–19	52.1	4.69 (0.10)	48.2 (1.5)	13.9 (1.4)	9.6 (4.3)	5.9 (3.1)	0.2 (2.6)
2. Aged 20–24 and Education ≤12	13.8	7.65 (0.19)	73.5 (1.6)	7.9 (1.1)	1.3 (5.8)	-0.9 (3.2)	-0.7 (2.2)
3. Aged 20–24 and Education >12	14.0	7.53 (0.16)	77.0 (1.6)	5.0 (0.9)	0.7 (4.8)	2.0 (3.1)	-0.6 (1.8)
4. Aged 25+, Education <12	14.6	9.17 (0.28)	46.3 (1.5)	9.3 (1.2)	9.5 (7.0)	-2.3 (2.8)	-3.7 (1.9)
5. Aged 25+, Education = 12	4.5	10.77 (0.13)	65.7 (0.8)	4.2 (0.4)	-2.3 (2.4)	1.4 (1.4)	-0.3 (0.7)
6. Aged 25+, Some College	3.2	12.35 (0.14)	75.1 (0.8)	3.3 (0.4)	-0.3 (2.5)	-0.4 (1.5)	-0.3 (0.7)
7. Ages 25+, Education ≥16	1.0	16.45 (0.18)	83.4 (0.6)	2.3 (0.3)	0.5 (2.4)	0.5 (1.2)	-0.8 (0.5)
Black Non-Hispanic							
8. Aged 16–24	27.0	6.93 (0.37)	46.9 (2.6)	21.7 (2.8)	-8.6 (8.4)	-0.8 (5.0)	1.5 (5.4)
9. Aged 25+, Education ≤12	6.8	9.53 (0.29)	53.5 (2.1)	10.1 (1.6)	-2.9 (5.1)	4.5 (3.5)	-1.2 (2.6)

10. Aged 25+, Education >12	1.4	12.35 (0.33)	79.4 (1.7)	6.4 (1.1)	2.7 (6.1)	5.7 (3.1)	−2.5 (1.9)
Hispanic							
11. Aged 16–19	52.6	4.36 (0.11)	37.7 (2.1)	21.4 (2.6)	23.1 (8.6)	5.8 (4.8)	−4.9 (5.4)
12. Aged 20–24	26.2	5.87 (0.12)	69.8 (1.8)	10.3 (1.3)	12.4 (5.3)	1.2 (3.9)	1.4 (2.9)
13. Aged 25+, Education <12	22.9	6.49 (0.11)	61.3 (1.2)	8.5 (0.8)	3.3 (5.5)	−0.1 (2.8)	−0.7 (2.1)
14. Aged 25+, Education = 12	7.8	8.67 (0.18)	71.7 (1.5)	6.1 (0.9)	4.1 (4.8)	3.5 (3.1)	−1.8 (1.9)
15. Aged 25+, Education >12	3.5	12.20 (0.30)	82.6 (1.5)	4.2 (0.8)	−7.0 (5.3)	3.6 (2.9)	−1.8 (1.6)
Other Non-Hispanic							
16. Aged 16–24	23.7	6.10 (0.23)	48.8 (2.3)	10.5 (1.9)	—	—	—
17. Aged 25+, Education ≤12	21.1	7.44 (0.24)	58.6 (1.9)	4.9 (1.1)	—	—	—
18. Aged 25+, Education >12	3.1	13.04 (0.28)	81.2 (1.2)	3.2 (0.6)	—	—	—
All							
19. Aged 16–68	10.8	10.69 (0.06)	68.4 (0.3)	5.8 (0.2)	−1.8 (1.2)	0.8 (0.6)	−0.6 (0.4)

Note: Standard errors are shown in parentheses. Other Non-Hispanic includes Asians and Native Americans.
[a]Change between 1987 and 1989 for outcome in California minus corresponding change for outcome in comparison areas.

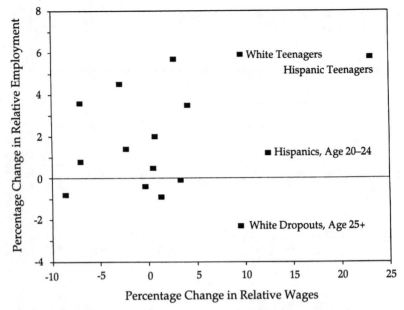

Figure 3.2   Relative changes in wages and employment rates, by group.

appear to have suffered any relative losses in employment. Indeed, the correlation between the difference-in-differences in employment rates and the fraction of workers earning $3.35 to 4.24 per hour in 1987 is 0.30. As a result, the correlation across groups between the relative change in employment and the relative change in wages is positive (0.29). This pattern is illustrated in Figure 3.2, in which we highlight several of the important demographic groups, including the two teenage groups and the 20- to 24-year-old Hispanic group. On the basis of the positive correlation between employment and wage changes across groups, we conclude that the increase in California's minimum wage had no adverse effect on the relative employment rate of low-wage workers in the state.

EFFECTS OF THE CALIFORNIA MINIMUM WAGE ON TEENAGERS

In light of the findings in Tables 3.2 and 3.3, we turn to a more detailed analysis of the experiences of teenage workers after the increase in California's minimum wage. Figure 3.3 presents hourly-wage distributions for teenage workers in California and the comparison sample in 1987 and 1989. The 1987 wage distributions are remarkably similar in the two samples, with modes at the federal

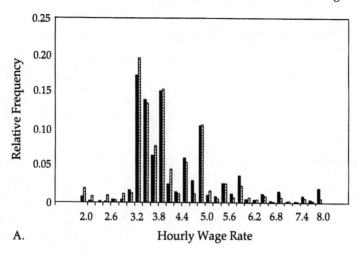

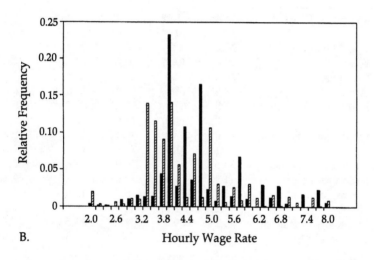

■ California Teenagers   ▨ Comparison Teenagers

Figure 3.3   Teenagers' wage distributions. A. 1987. B. 1989.

minimum wage and significant spikes at $3.50, 4.00, and 5.00 per hour. In 1989, however, the distributions are quite different. Many teenagers in the comparison sample continue to earn $3.35, 3.50, or 4.00 per hour, whereas most of the lower tail of the California wage distribution has been pushed up to the new $4.25 minimum.

These visual impressions are confirmed by the data in Table 3.4.

TABLE 3.4

Characteristics of Teenagers in California and Comparison Areas, 1987 and 1989

	California		Comparison Areas		Difference-in-
	1987 (1)	1989 (2)	1987 (3)	1989 (4)	Differences[a] (5)
Percentage with					
1. Hourly Wage = $3.35	15.5 (1.3)	0.7 (0.3)	16.1 (1.2)	11.3 (1.0)	−10.1 (2.1)
2. Hourly Wage Between $3.35 and 4.24	52.0 (1.8)	8.5 (1.1)	55.3 (1.6)	48.1 (1.6)	−36.5 (3.1)
3. Hourly Wage = $4.25	1.6 (0.5)	22.5 (1.7)	3.3 (0.6)	4.4 (0.7)	19.8 (1.9)
Other Characteristics					
4. Mean Log Wage	1.46 (0.01)	1.62 (0.01)	1.40 (0.01)	1.46 (0.01)	0.10 (0.02)
5. Usual Hours per Week	26.2 (0.4)	26.7 (0.5)	27.9 (0.4)	28.1 (0.4)	0.3 (0.8)
6. Usual Earnings per Week ($)	125.6 (3.5)	149.8 (4.3)	121.3 (2.4)	132.1 (2.6)	13.4 (6.6)
7. Enrollment Rate (%)	66.5 (1.0)	63.1 (1.3)	57.2 (1.0)	59.2 (1.0)	−5.4 (2.2)
8. Employment Rate (%)	42.0 (1.1)	47.4 (1.3)	46.4 (1.0)	46.1 (1.1)	5.6 (2.3)
9. Labor-Force Participation Rate (%)	50.5 (1.1)	54.2 (1.3)	56.9 (1.0)	54.8 (1.1)	5.9 (2.3)
10. Unemployment Rate (%)	16.7 (1.2)	12.6 (1.2)	18.5 (1.1)	15.9 (1.1)	−1.5 (2.3)
11. Employment Rate of Enrollees[b] (%)	34.2 (1.3)	39.2 (1.6)	37.0 (1.3)	36.5 (1.3)	5.5 (2.8)
12. Sample Size	2,032	1,381	2,354	2,206	—

Note: Standard errors are shown in parentheses. The samples include all individuals aged 16–19.

[a]Change in outcome between 1989 and 1987 for California teenagers minus corresponding change for comparison-area teenagers.

[b]Employment rate among teenagers enrolled in school.

During 1987, 52 percent of teenagers in California and 55 percent of those in the comparison sample earned between $3.35 and 4.24 per hour. During 1989, the fraction of comparison-sample teenagers in that wage interval was 48 percent, whereas the fraction of California teenagers decreased to 9 percent, suggesting that compliance with the minimum wage was fairly high (80 percent or higher). The difference-in-differences, in the fifth column of the table, is 36 percentage points. This relative shift was associated with a 20 percent relative increase in the fraction of teenagers earning exactly $4.25 per hour, and a 10 percent relative increase in the mean wage of California teenagers. As indicated in Table 3.2, however, no offsetting decline in teenage employment occurred. Hours per week of employed teenagers increased slightly in California relative to the comparison group, and the relative employment–population rate rose 5.6 percent. Most of the additional employment resulted from net additions to the labor force: the unemployment rate of California teens registered only a small net decline.

Figure 3.4 provides a broader perspective on the increase in the rate of teenage employment in California. This figure plots the 1989 teenage employment–population rates for all 50 states (and Washington, DC) against their corresponding 1987 rates. We highlight both the California data and the data for the other 13 states that increased their minimum wage rates between 1987 and 1989. We also show the fitted regression line obtained by regressing the 1989 teenage employment rate on the 1987 rate for the same state. During the 1987–1989 period, the teenage employment–population rate increased by 2 percentage points nationwide, compared with an increase of 4.1 percent in California, and with a negligible change in the comparison areas. This broader comparison suggests that the relative increase in the teenage employment rate in California may be overstated by the comparison with teenagers in our control-group sample. Relative to the fitted regression line in the figure, for example, the employment rate of California teenagers was 1.7 percent higher than predicted (with a standard error of 3.4 percent). We have also fit models that predict the teenage employment rate in 1989 using the teenage employment rate in 1987 and the change in the overall employment rate between 1987 and 1989. In this model, the employment rate of California teenagers in 1989 was 2.2 percent higher than predicted (with a standard error of 3.1 percent). Whatever the comparison method, however, no measurable decrease in employment among California teenagers is found.

A long-standing issue in the minimum-wage literature is whether changes in the minimum wage affect patterns of teenagers' school enrollment (see, for example, Ehrenberg and Marcus [1980]). The data in Table 3.4 suggest that enrollment rates fell in California relative to the comparison areas after the minimum-wage increase occurred. Interestingly, these enrollment drops were not associated directly with the relative increase in California employment. Indeed,

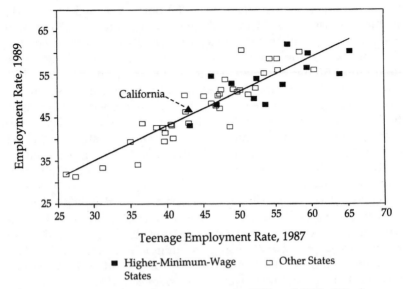

Figure 3.4 Teenagers' employment rates, in 1987 and 1989. Fitted regression line shown.

as shown in the second-to-last row of the table, the relative increase in employment among enrolled students was about as large as the increase for all teenagers.

The enrollment measures in Table 3.4 are based on averages over all 12 months of the year and therefore combine enrollment in traditional schools, summer schools, and other programs. A more conventional enrollment measure is based on data for the fall months. The difference-in-differences of enrollment rates from September to December shows a smaller relative decline in California (−3.8 percent, with a standard error of 4.0 percent). Although imprecisely estimated, this effect is still relatively large. To check the accuracy of the enrollment change, we collected administrative data on 1987–1989 high school and college enrollment in California and in the comparison areas. Combined data on public high school enrollment and undergraduate enrollment in all types of higher education shows that, between fall 1987 and fall 1989, the number of California students decreased by 2 percentage points, whereas the number of comparison-area students increased by 1.3 percentage points.[10] This divergence is roughly consistent with the patterns shown in Table 3.4.

The simple means and differences-in-differences in Table 3.4 make no adjustment for the demographic characteristics of the teenagers actually sampled in the CPS. In principle, the weighted CPS sample should be representative of the population; it is possible, however, that adjustments for measured characteristics, such as age, sex, and ethnicity, could lead to more stable and precise estimates of the relative changes between California and the comparison areas. It is easy to make these adjustments in a regression framework by pooling the samples for California and the comparison areas in the two years, and by including various control variables, as well as indicators for the four underlying samples (1987 California, 1989 California, 1987 comparisons, and 1989 comparisons). Using this procedure, we estimated the relative changes in employment rates, wages, and enrollment rates between 1987 and 1989, controlling for age (four age categories), gender, ethnicity (four categories), the month in which the individual was interviewed, and location (indicators for four major cities in California and the individual states in the comparison sample). After controlling for these characteristics, we find that the relative changes in the employment rate and the mean log wage rate are essentially identical to the unadjusted differences-in-differences presented in Table 3.4. The standard errors of the regression-adjusted differences are also very similar to the standard errors in the table. The relative change in the regression-adjusted enrollment rate is −3.1 percent, which is slightly smaller than the unadjusted difference-in-differences and is comparable to the relative change in fall enrollments.

On balance, the addition of control variables does not alter our conclusions about the effect of the minimum wage on teenagers. Relative to the comparison sample, teenage employment rates in California increased between 1987 and 1989 by 4.1 percent (using the published data in Table 3.2) or by 5.6 percent (using the microdata estimate in Table 3.4). Relative to predictions based on the pattern of teenage employment changes across *all* states between 1987 and 1989, teenage employment rates in California were 1.7 to 2.2 percent higher than expected in 1989. These estimates are not sufficiently precise to rule out the hypothesis that the minimum wage had no effect on teenage employment, but they do rule out the hypothesis of a significant reduction in employment. For example, if the elasticity of teenage employment with respect to the minimum wage is 0.10, as suggested in the time-series literature (see chapter 6), the 27 percent increase in California's minimum wage should have reduced teenage employment by 2.7 percentage points. The data do not support an effect this large.

EFFECTS ON RETAIL TRADE

In 1987, one-half of the California workers who earned a wage rate between the old federal minimum and the new state minimum were employed in retail trade. The experiences of the retail-trade industry following the increase in the minimum are especially interesting because the Industrial Welfare Commission, which established the new minimum wage, intended to set a subminimum rate for tipped employees in the restaurant industry. This provision was later overruled by the state supreme court, leaving the state with a 20-percent higher-than-expected minimum wage for a large sector of the retail-trade industry. One might expect the effects of an unintended wage floor to be larger than the effects of a deliberately chosen rate.

Table 3.5 describes the wage and demographic characteristics of retail-trade employees in California and the comparison areas in 1987 and 1989. There was a substantial relative reduction in the fraction of California workers earning between $3.35 and 4.24 per hour after the new minimum wage took effect. This change was associated with a relative increase in hourly and weekly earnings in the retail-trade industry of 5 to 7 percent. Perhaps surprisingly, no significant changes in weekly hours or in the age or gender composition of the retail workforce occurred. The one significant relative demographic change was an increase in the fraction of Hispanic workers in California. Contrary to conventional predictions, none of these comparisons suggest a substitution away from younger or less-skilled workers.

We have also computed the same relative comparisons for restaurants employees. These workers constituted 30 percent of all employees in retail trade in California in 1987, and more than one-fourth of those who earned between $3.35 and 4.24 per hour. The main comparisons are summarized in Table 3.6. After the increase in the minimum wage, 32 percent of restaurant employees in California reported being paid the new minimum wage. The increase in the minimum wage was associated with an 8-percent relative increase in log wages, but no significant change in hours per week or in the fraction of young workers in the industry. As for the retail-trade industry as a whole, there is no indication of "skill upgrading" in the restaurant industry after the minimum-wage hike took effect.

The CPS microdata show significant relative wage gains for retail-trade and restaurant workers between 1987 and 1989. To measure the potential employment effects of the minimum wage, we have assembled industry-level data from *County Business Patterns* (CBP) in Table 3.7 (see p. 99). CBP employment counts are derived from tax-record data and pertain to March 31 of the calendar year. One minor difficulty associated with using this data source is the absence of separate data for the Dallas–Fort Worth metropolitan area. Therefore, we used the entire state of Texas in defining the comparison group. For

TABLE 3.5

Characteristics of Workers in the Retail-Trade Industry, California and Comparison Areas, 1987 and 1989

	California		Comparison Areas		Difference-in-Differences[a]
	1987 (1)	1989 (2)	1987 (3)	1989 (4)	(5)
Percentage with					
1. Hourly Wage <$3.35	1.7 (0.3)	1.2 (0.3)	7.1 (0.5)	6.6 (0.5)	−0.1 (0.8)
2. Hourly Wage = $3.35	10.6 (0.7)	0.7 (0.2)	7.1 (0.5)	4.7 (0.4)	−7.6 (1.0)
3. Hourly Wage Between $3.35 and 4.24	30.8 (1.1)	4.7 (0.5)	30.1 (0.9)	24.2 (0.8)	−20.2 (1.7)
4. Hourly Wage = $4.25	0.8 (0.2)	14.7 (0.9)	1.7 (0.3)	2.8 (0.3)	12.7 (1.0)
Other Characteristics					
5. Mean Log Wage	1.80 (0.01)	1.90 (0.01)	1.67 (0.01)	1.72 (0.01)	0.05 (0.02)
6. Usual Hours per Week	34.9 (0.2)	35.0 (0.3)	36.7 (0.2)	36.8 (0.2)	0.1 (0.5)
7. Usual Earnings per Week ($)	261.1 (5.0)	291.2 (6.3)	241.5 (4.0)	252.4 (3.7)	19.2 (9.8)
8. Aged 16–19 (%)	16.7 (0.7)	16.4 (0.9)	15.7 (0.6)	16.1 (0.6)	−0.7 (1.4)
9. Aged 20–24 (%)	19.6 (0.8)	19.0 (0.9)	18.1 (0.7)	17.4 (0.6)	0.1 (1.5)
10. Aged 16–24 and in School (%)	14.9 (0.7)	15.7 (0.8)	12.7 (0.6)	12.5 (0.6)	1.0 (1.4)
11. Female (%)	49.2 (1.0)	46.4 (1.1)	51.0 (0.9)	49.9 (0.9)	−1.6 (1.9)
12. Hispanic (%)	20.6 (0.8)	24.9 (1.0)	11.9 (0.6)	11.6 (0.6)	4.5 (1.5)
13. Sample Size	2,521	1,889	3,394	3,388	—

Note: Standard errors are shown in parentheses. The samples include individuals aged 16–68 employed in the retail-trade industry.

[a]Change in outcome between 1989 and 1987 for California workers minus corresponding change for comparison-area workers.

retail trade as a whole, the CBP data show slightly faster post-1987 employment growth in California than in the rest of the United States (defined as the U.S. total minus California) or in the comparison areas. For the restaurant industry, CBP data show almost identical relative employment growth from 1987 to 1989 in all three areas.

These relative employment trends are illustrated in Figure 3.5. The top panel presents data for the entire retail-trade sector, and the bottom panel shows the data for the restaurant industry. One trend that stands out in the lower panel is the relative surge in employment in California's restaurant industry between March 1987 and March 1988, followed by a relative decrease between March 1988 and March 1989. Because the minimum wage rose in July 1988, we

TABLE 3.6

Characteristics of Workers in the Restaurant Industry,
California and Comparison Areas, 1987 and 1989

	California		Comparison Areas		Difference-in-Differences[a]
	1987 (1)	1989 (2)	1987 (3)	1989 (4)	(5)
Percentage with					
1. Hourly Wage <$3.35	3.2 (0.7)	2.0 (0.6)	18.3 (1.3)	18.2 (1.3)	−1.1 (2.1)
2. Hourly Wage Between $3.35 and 4.24	54.6 (2.0)	7.7 (1.2)	39.0 (1.7)	34.7 (1.6)	−41.6 (3.2)
3. Hourly Wage = $4.25	1.2 (0.4)	32.1 (2.1)	1.7 (0.4)	1.9 (0.4)	30.7 (2.2)
Other Characteristics					
4. Mean Log Wage	1.52 (0.02)	1.66 (0.02)	1.42 (0.02)	1.47 (0.02)	0.08 (0.03)
5. Usual Hours per Week	32.3 (0.5)	32.0 (0.5)	34.6 (0.4)	35.0 (0.4)	−0.6 (0.9)
6. Aged 16–19 (%)	23.7 (1.6)	23.3 (1.7)	23.2 (1.3)	22.2 (1.3)	0.6 (3.0)
7. Aged 20–24 (%)	44.1 (1.8)	45.0 (2.1)	47.2 (1.6)	42.5 (1.3)	5.6 (3.5)
8. Hispanic (%)	26.0 (1.6)	34.2 (2.0)	12.8 (1.1)	12.1 (1.0)	8.9 (2.9)

Note: Standard errors are shown in parentheses. The samples include individuals aged 16–68 employed in the restaurant (i.e., eating and drinking) industry.

[a]Change in outcome between 1989 and 1987 for California workers minus corresponding change for comparison-area workers.

TABLE 3.7
Employment in Retail-Trade and Restaurant Industries

| | | | | | Employment Index Relative to 1987 = 100 | | | |
	1983 (1)	1984 (2)	1985 (3)	1986 (4)	1987 (5)	1988 (6)	1989 (7)	1990 (8)
All Retail Trade								
1. California	82.73	87.55	91.00	95.73	100.00	102.95	105.50	108.91
2. Comparison Areas	81.11	87.35	92.66	96.21	100.00	101.40	104.24	107.63
3. United States, Excluding California	82.70	87.29	91.57	95.24	100.00	101.98	104.92	107.43
Restaurant Industry								
4. California	80.70	86.21	89.25	93.95	100.00	103.66	105.60	108.56
5. Comparison Areas	76.76	82.43	88.54	94.87	100.00	101.71	105.56	109.47
6. United States, Excluding California	79.83	84.55	88.88	93.48	100.00	102.07	105.44	108.33

Source: Data are taken from *County Business Pattérns*, 1983–1990 editions.
Note: In this table only, the comparison areas are Arizona, Florida, Georgia, New Mexico, and Texas.

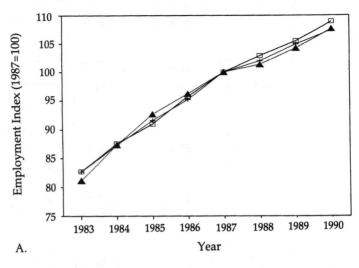

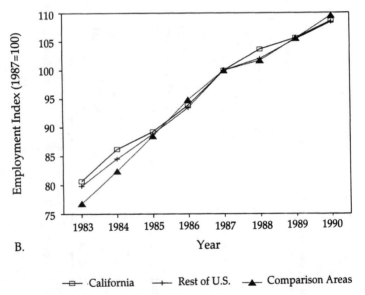

—□— California   —+— Rest of U.S.   —▲— Comparison Areas

Figure 3.5   Employment in the retail-trade and restaurant industries. A. All retail-trade industries. B. Restaurant industry.

could have used 1988 as a baseline for evaluating the effect of the minimum wage. This choice indicates a *decrease* of 1.3 to 1.9 percent in restaurant-industry employment in California after the increase in the minimum wage took effect. It is difficult to know whether the relative upsurge in restaurant employment in California between

1987 and 1988 would have continued in the absence of the minimum-wage increase. We conclude that the employment effect on the restaurant industry could have been zero (using 1987 as a baseline) or between −1 and −2 percent (using 1988 as a baseline).

FURTHER ANALYSIS OF INTERINDUSTRY PATTERNS OF EMPLOYMENT GROWTH

Our conclusion that the increase in the California minimum wage had little or no effect on employment growth in the state has not gone unchallenged. In a recent paper, Kim and Taylor (1994) present a series of models fit to CBP employment data for detailed sectors of the California retail-trade industry. Contrary to our conclusions, Kim and Taylor argue that the increase in California's minimum wage had a substantial negative effect on employment growth in the state. Their estimates imply that the $4.25 minimum wage reduced retail-trade employment in the state by 5 percent, and restaurant employment by 8 percent.[11] Given that no obvious employment losses in retail trade as a whole are shown in Table 3.7 and Figure 3.5, these estimates are surprising. Kim and Taylor argue, however, that unobserved demand shocks in California's retail-trade sector offset the employment losses generated by the minimum wage.

In this section, we present an analysis and discussion of Kim and Taylor's estimation methods and findings. To preview the results, we conclude that their findings are driven mainly by weaknesses in the CBP data. A fundamental difficulty with CBP data is the absence of wage information. *County Business Patterns* reports total industry employment (as of March of each year) and total industry payroll (for the first quarter of the year). Pay rates must be estimated by dividing total payroll by employment—a procedure that introduces a mechanical correlation between employment and measured "wages." A second, related difficulty is the presence of large, random fluctuations in industry employment. These fluctuations mean that inferences about the minimum wage are highly sensitive to the choice of sample period and estimation method. Table 3.8 illustrates this sensitivity by showing the relative growth rates in payroll per worker and employment for seven sectors of retail trade between California and the country as a whole. The table follows the format used by Kim and Taylor in their Table 3.1. Columns 1 and 2 present the relative growth rates from 1988 (just before the increase in the minimum wage) to 1989 (just after the increase). Note that industries with faster growth in payroll per worker between 1988 and 1989 had slower employment growth. Kim and Taylor interpret this correlation as evidence of the effect of the minimum wage: industries that

TABLE 3.8
Relative Growth Rates in Pay per Employee and Total Employment,
by Industry, California − United States as a Whole

	Change, 1988–1989		Change, 1987–1989	
	Pay per Worker (1)	Employment (2)	Pay per Worker (3)	Employment (4)
1. General Merchandise	6.86	−6.16	5.97	2.06
2. Restaurants	4.63	−1.25	3.61	0.14
3. Food Stores	2.36	−0.37	−3.28	0.81
4. Apparel, Accessories	2.31	1.20	6.28	−0.28
5. Building Supplies	0.77	3.15	5.48	−0.17
6. Furniture	0.04	3.87	1.44	7.81
7. Auto Dealers and Service Stations	−1.56	2.02	−0.18	−2.75

Source: Entries are calculated using published data from U.S. Department of Commerce, *County Business Patterns.*

Note: The relative changes in columns 1 and 2 are from March 1988 to March 1989. The relative changes in columns 3 and 4 are from March 1987 to March 1989. The correlation of the entries in columns 1 and 2 is −0.90. The correlation of the entries in columns 3 and 4 is −0.03.

had to raise wages between 1988 and 1989 to comply with the law had commensurate employment losses. Columns 3 and 4 show relative growth rates in employment and payroll per worker from 1987 to 1989. Over this longer period, *no* correlation between wage and employment growth across industries is found. It is difficult to understand why the change in baseline should matter if the wage and employment changes between 1988 and 1989 actually are driven by the minimum wage. As we show, a similar set of specification tests calls into question the estimates in Kim and Taylor's analysis.

Another type of evidence also points toward small effects of the minimum wage, at least on the restaurant industry. City-specific price indexes for the cost of food eaten away from home, and for the price of a fast-food restaurant hamburger, show about the same rate of price increases in California as elsewhere in the country.[12] This similarity is inconsistent with the view that the minimum wage had a large, adverse employment effect on the restaurant industry that was offset by an unobserved positive demand shock, and is more consistent with the evidence presented in Table 3.7 and Figure 3.5. The evidence in the table and figure suggests that total employment in California's restaurant industry was either unaffected by the increase in the minimum wage (using 1987 as a baseline), or was reduced by 1 to 2 percent (using 1988 as a baseline).

Methods

Kim and Taylor use annual CBP data for approximately 60 four-digit industries within the retail-trade sector. Their basic estimating equation expresses the relative change in employment in a given industry between California and the rest of the United States as a function of the corresponding relative change in the industry's wage:

$$\Delta E_{cit} - \Delta E_{Rit} = a + b\,(\Delta W_{cit} - \Delta W_{Rit}) + v_{it}, \qquad (3.1)$$

where ΔE_{cit} refers to the proportional change in employment in California for industry i between year $t - 1$ and t, ΔE_{Rit} refers to the proportional change in employment for the same industry in the rest of the United States, ΔW_{cit} refers to the proportional change in wages (payroll per worker) in California for industry i between $t - 1$ and t, ΔW_{Rit} refers to the proportional change in wages for the industry in the rest of the United States, and v_{it} is an industry- and year-specific shock. Kim and Taylor interpret this equation as a structural-demand equation, and the coefficient, b, as the elasticity of employment demand with respect to wages.

Because CBP data contain no information on hourly wages, Kim and Taylor measure the "wage" by the ratio of total payroll in the industry in the first quarter of a year to total employment as of March 31. Any error in the measured growth rate of employment arising from changes in the industry classification of particular establishments or any other source automatically generates an equal and opposite proportional error in the growth rate of wages. To see this, notice that the logarithm of the measured "wage" in industry i in California is simply the difference in the logarithms of total payroll and employment:

$$W_{cit} = P_{cit} - E_{cit}.$$

Suppose that the log of measured employment, E_{cit}, differs from the log of true employment, E^{*}_{cit}, by a measurement error:

$$E_{cit} = E^{*}_{cit} + u_{cit}.$$

Then the growth rate in measured employment is

$$\Delta E_{cit} = \Delta E^{*}_{cit} + \Delta u_{cit},$$

where the second term represents the difference in the measurement errors. The growth rate in measured wages is

$$\Delta W_{cit} = (\Delta P_{cit} - \Delta E^*_{cit}) - \Delta u_{cit}.$$

Notice that measured wage growth differs from true wage growth (the term in parentheses) by the negative of the change in the measurement error in employment. Any spurious change in employment leads to an offsetting change in the measured wage.

The strong negative correlation between employment and wage growth is illustrated in Figure 3.6, where we plot the relative changes in employment between 1988 and 1989 for each four-digit industry against the corresponding relative change in wages. The data are not far off a line with slope of -1 (shown in the figure), which would be expected if *all* the variance in the relative wage growth is attributable to random measurement errors in employment. (The unweighted ordinary least squares [OLS] regression coefficient is -0.89, with a standard error of 0.09.) The figure also shows the very large dispersion in industry-specific growth rates in the CBP data. Wage growth in California relative to the rest of the United States ranges from -22 to $+11$ percent. Relative employment growth ranges from -11 to $+40$ percent. The magnitudes of

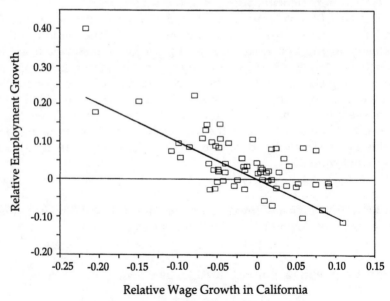

Figure 3.6 Plot of relative employment growth and relative wage growth, 1988–1989. The line in the figure has slope of -1.0.

some of these relative changes suggest significant measurement errors.[13]

Because of the mechanical correlation between CBP-based estimates of employment and wages, OLS estimates of the coefficient, b, in equation (3.1) are biased toward −1. Kim and Taylor are concerned about this problem and implement an instrumental variables (IV) estimation procedure to overcome this bias, and to eliminate any possible correlation between the demand shock, v_{it}, and relative wage growth. As instruments for the relative change in wages, they use the logarithm of average wages in the industry in an earlier period and the logarithm of average establishment size in the industry in an earlier period. To estimate the wage elasticity, the IV technique uses only the part of the measured change in wages that is "explained" by the instruments. Therefore, in evaluating the IV estimates, it is important to consider the nature of this "explained" variation.

The rationale for the use of the lagged wage as an instrumental variable for wage growth is straightforward: industries with lower wages prior to the rise in the minimum wage should have larger wage gains resulting from the law. Thus, the lagged level of wages in California should be negatively correlated with the change in relative wages between 1988 and 1989. Unfortunately, any measurement error in employment again creates a mechanical correlation between the wage in period $t - 1$ and employment growth between $t - 1$ and t. To avoid this problem, a simple strategy is to use the wage in California in period $t - 2$ as an instrument for the wage change induced by the minimum wage. This variable is unaffected by measurement errors in employment in either $t - 1$ or t. On the other hand, the average level of wages in an industry in 1987 should give a good indication of the impact of the minimum-wage law on wage growth between 1988 and 1989, as the pattern of wage differentials across industries is highly stable over time.

The rationale for Kim and Taylor's other instrumental variable— average establishment size—is less clear. Because smaller establishments have lower average wages (Brown and Medoff [1989]), one might expect a negative correlation across industries between relative wage growth and average establishment size. As it happens, however, relative wage growth in the CBP data between 1988 and 1989 is positively correlated with average establishment size. Kim and Taylor argue that this positive correlation reflects noncompliance behavior. They conjecture that larger establishments are more likely to comply with the minimum wage law, leading to a larger effect of the law on industries with larger average establishment sizes. What is relevant for the impact of the minimum wage, however, is the fraction of workers in the industry whose employers comply with the law *and* who previously were earning less than the new minimum wage. Given the much greater incidence of low wages at smaller establishments, we suspect that the effect of the minimum wage is actually greater in industries with smaller average establishment size.

Because of the large component of measurement error in employment fluctuations at the four-digit industry level, the issue of instrument choice is particularly important in the estimation of equation (3.1). By construction, employment and wage changes are negatively correlated in the CBP data, leading to a negative bias in OLS estimates of equation (3.1). Moreover, in the absence of a valid instrumental variable, IV estimates are biased toward the OLS estimates (Nagar [1959], Buse [1992], and Angrist and Krueger [1994]). Thus, the use of an instrument that is only spuriously correlated with relative wage changes will lead to IV estimates that are large and negative.

Estimates of the Employment Effect of the 1988 Minimum-Wage Law

Kim and Taylor generously provided us with their data set, and we have merged it with additional data for 1990 in order to compute the estimates of equation (3.1) reported in Table 3.9. The top panel of this table presents estimates using a one-year difference in employment and wages, and the bottom panel reports estimates over two-year intervals. In principle, the choice of a shorter or longer differencing interval should lead to similar estimates, as long as the interval includes July 1988—the effective date of the minimum-wage increase. Thus, a comparison of the upper and lower panels provides a specification check on the interpretation of the estimates. We report OLS estimates and estimates using two alternative instruments: (1) the second lag of industry wages in California; and (2) the logarithm of average establishment size in California in 1987.[14] All the models are estimated by weighted least squares, using as a weight the relative size of the industry in the United States as a whole in either year $t - 2$ (for the first-differenced models) or year $t - 1$ (for the second-differenced models). For reference, we have highlighted in bold the first-differenced specification for 1988–1989 (the main specification in the paper by Kim and Taylor) and the two-year differences from 1987–1989 and 1988–1990. All three differences span the July 1, 1988, date.

TABLE 3.9
Estimated Models for Relative Employment Growth Over Various
Time Intervals

| | | Instrumental Variables | |
	OLS (1)	Instrument: Lagged Wage (2)	Instrument: Log Size (3)
First-Differenced Specifications			
1. 1987–1988	−0.20	0.21	−1.88
	(0.22)	(0.85)	(1.13)
2. **1988–1989**	**−0.90**	**−0.38**	**−1.29**
	(0.08)	**(0.36)**	**(0.20)**
3. 1989–1990	−0.81	−0.62	−0.59
	(0.10)	(0.45)	(0.24)
Second-Differenced Specifications			
4. 1986–1988	−0.10	−1.79	−0.22
	(0.10)	(3.51)	(0.38)
5. **1987–1989**	**0.23**	**−0.10**	**0.33**
	(0.23)	**(0.53)**	**(2.27)**
6. **1988–1990**	**−0.80**	**−0.29**	**−4.01**
	(0.12)	**(0.89)**	**(5.07)**

Notes: Standard errors are shown in parentheses. The dependent variable in all specifications is the change in log employment in California minus the change in log employment in the rest of the United States. The explanatory variable is the relative change in the log of payroll per worker. All models include a constant. The models are estimated on samples of 52–56 industries. All estimates are weighted. In the first-differenced specifications, the weight is the second lag of employment in the industry in the United States as a whole. In the second-differenced specifications, the weight is the lagged value of employment in the industry in the United States as a whole.

As shown in the first column of Table 3.9, OLS estimates of the first-differenced version of equation (3.1) are negative, and the estimates for 1988–1989 and 1989–1990 are large in absolute value and highly significant. OLS estimates of the second-differenced specification vary in sign—the estimate for the 1987–1989 change is weakly positive, whereas the estimate for the 1988–1990 change is large and negative. When the lagged industry wage is used as an instrument (column 2), none of the estimated coefficients is statistically significant. The IV estimate for the critical 1988–1989 change is −0.38, with a t-ratio of about 1. Examination of the first-stage equation for this estimate shows that, as expected, lagged wages are significantly negatively correlated with wage growth between 1988 and 1989. By comparison, the first-stage equations for the 1987–1988 and 1989–1990 models are not statistically significant, suggesting that industry wage growth is unrelated to the level of wages in the absence of a minimum-wage change.[15]

The second-differenced IV estimates using the lagged California wage as an instrument are also negative, but statistically insignificant. The first-stage equations underlying the 1987–1989 and 1988–1990 IV estimates are statistically significant and show that industry-specific wage growth over the period of the minimum-wage increase was faster in industries with lower average wages. However, the second-stage estimates are too imprecise to be very informative about the effect of the minimum wage.

Instrumental variables estimates using establishment size as an instrument are presented in column 3 of Table 3.9. Notice first the highly significant IV estimate in row 2 for the critical 1988–1989 period. This estimate is even more negative than the corresponding OLS estimate, suggesting that the OLS estimate of equation (3.1) for this period is *positively* biased. Inspection of the first-stage equation shows that industries with larger average establishments had faster wage growth and slower employment growth between 1988 and 1989. As we noted, we do not believe that this pattern reflects the greater impact of the minimum wage on industries with larger establishments. Rather, we suspect that it represents a peculiarity of the 1988 data. As evidence for this interpretation, consider the second-differenced specifications for 1987–1989 and 1988–1990. Because both of these two-year intervals span the July 1988 increase in the minimum wage, both should yield estimates similar to the 1988–1989 specification—if that specification truly reflects the effect of the minimum wage. For the 1987–1989 change, the IV estimate using size as an instrument is positive; for the 1988–1990 change, it is large, but extremely imprecise. Inspection of the associated first-stage equations shows that establishment size is uncorrelated with industry wage growth from either 1987 to 1989 or from 1988 to 1990. If the minimum wage had a larger impact on industries with larger establishment sizes, we would have expected industry wage growth over the 1988–1989, 1987–1989, and 1988–1990 periods to *all* be positively correlated with establishment size. Because this is not the case, we suspect that the positive correlation between establishment size and the rate of wage growth from 1988–1989 is spurious.

Summary

The imposition of a uniform minimum wage should lead to more rapid wage growth in low-wage industries. Consistent with this hypothesis, we find that relative wages grew faster in lower-wage industries over *any interval* spanning the effective date of the California minimum-wage law. This finding suggests that the lagged industry wage can be used as a valid instrumental variable in the estimation of the employment effects of the minimum wage. The results of this procedure lead to estimated employment effects that are negative, but small in magnitude (with elasticities ranging from − .10 to − .38) and relatively imprecise (with standard errors ranging from 0.36 to 0.89).

In their specifications, Kim and Taylor use both lagged wages and average establishment size as predictors of the effect of the minimum wage on industry-wage growth. Instrumental variables estimates for the 1988–1989 period using average establishment size as an instrument are large and negative. This is the critical feature that generates the large, negative employment elasticities reported in their analysis. To test the validity of the establishment-size variable as an instrument, we reestimated the models over the 1987–1989 and 1988–1990 periods. Both intervals span the effective date of the new minimum wage and should yield the same results as the 1988–1989 difference. Over either of these longer time intervals, however, the correlation between establishment size and industry wage growth disappears, casting doubt on the validity of average establishment size as an instrument for wage growth. We conclude that more appropriate specifications, using the level of wages to capture the differential impact of the minimum, show small and statistically insignificant employment effects of the 1988 minimum-wage law.

Conclusions

The 1988 increase in California's minimum wage had a significant effect on wages in the state. We estimate that the 27 percent increase in the minimum wage increased the average wages of teenagers by 10 percent, increased the average wages of employees in the retail-trade industry by 5 percent, and increased the average wages of restaurant workers by 8 percent. Contrary to conventional predictions, but suggestive of the findings presented in chapter 2, we find that the increase in the minimum wage had a slightly positive effect on teenage employment. For the retail-trade sector as a whole, we find that employment trends in California after the increase in the minimum wage were very similar to trends in a group of southern and western comparison states and in the United States as a whole. Even in the restaurant industry, where the increase in the minimum wage for tipped workers resulted from an unexpected legal decision, we find only mixed evidence of employment losses relative to the comparison states or the rest of the country.

Our conclusion that the increase in the minimum wage had little or no adverse employment effect has been challenged recently by analysts who compare employment outcomes in narrowly defined sectors of the retail-trade industry. We have reexamined the evidence underlying this challenge and conclude that it points toward small and statistically insignificant employment effects arising from the minimum wage. Nevertheless, the estimates using this alternative methodology tend to indicate employment losses, rather than the gains that are observed for teenagers. On balance, we believe that the evidence from California shows that the increase in the state minimum wage had a significant impact on wages, but no large or systematic effect on employment.

Appendix

This chapter uses microdata from the 1987–1989 Merged Outgoing Rotation Group monthly files of the Current Population Survey (CPS). The extracts include all individuals aged 16–68 from the states of Arizona, California, Florida, Georgia, and New Mexico, as well as all those identified as living in the Dallas–Fort Worth, Texas, PMSA. Individuals in the extracts who report being paid by the hour on their main job (91 percent of teenagers) are assigned their reported hourly pay as a "wage." Individuals who report being paid by the week, month, or other interval are assigned the ratio of their reported weekly earnings to their reported usual weekly hours as a "wage." In 1987, weekly earnings information is provided in the CPS in two fields: (1) an edited field, which is censored at $999 per week; and (2) an unedited field, which is censored at $1,923 per week. We use the edited earnings data for individuals who are paid by the week, month, or other interval and who report edited weekly earnings of less than $999. We use the unedited earnings data for those whose edited weekly earnings are censored. Individuals with allocated hourly or weekly earnings are assigned a missing wage. Individuals whose reported or constructed hourly wage is less than $1.00 per hour are also assigned a missing wage. The latter procedure affects 2 observations in 1987, and 18 in 1989.

TABLE A.3.1
Characteristics of California and Comparison-Area Samples, 1987

	California (1)	Comparison Areas (2)
1. Mean Age	37.5	38.3
2. Female (%)	50.9	51.5
3. Aged 16–19 (%)	8.7	8.7
4. Average Education (Years)	12.6	12.4
5. College Graduates (%)	21.4	17.7
6. White Non-Hispanic (%)	63.1	70.7
7. Black Non-Hispanic (%)	6.7	15.5
8. Hispanic (%)	21.2	11.7
9. Asian and Other Non-Hispanic (%)	8.9	1.9
10. Married Spouse Present (%)	55.5	58.0
11. Living in Central City (%)	37.0	26.8
12. Union Member (%)	19.5	7.8
13. Government Worker (%)	13.6	13.6
14. Self-Employed (%)	8.5	6.9
15. Mean Wage ($/hr)	10.69	8.77
16. Industry Distribution		
a. Agriculture	3.4	2.7
b. Construction	10.3	12.3
c. Manufacturing	14.4	10.4
d. Transportation/Communication/Utilities	6.6	7.3
e. Trade	23.1	25.2
f. Finance/Insurance/Real Estate	7.2	7.4
g. Services	34.0	32.8

Note: Means are weighted by sample weights in the Current Population Survey earnings supplement.

Table A.3.1 presents selected characteristics of individuals in the 1987 extract from California and the comparison areas.

Notes

1. The information in this section is taken from reports in the Bureau of National Affairs' *Daily Labor Report*, including 1987 DLR 157: A-2, 1987 DLR 246: A-4, 1988 DLR 127: A-2, 1988 DLR 135: A-4, and 1988 DLR 215: A-4.

2. The CPS samples are described in the appendix to this chapter.

3. For example, noncompliance is a likely explanation for the relatively large number of workers in low-wage manufacturing industries who were paid less than $3.35 per hour. Ashenfelter and Smith (1979) describe the extent of noncompliance with federal minimum-wage legislation during the early 1970s.

4. We included only Dallas–Fort Worth, rather than the entire state of Texas, for two reasons. First, during the mid-to-late 1980s, economic conditions in many parts of Texas were affected by the slump in oil prices. Second, by including only Texans living in Dallas and Fort Worth, we increase the relative fraction of urban workers in the comparison sample.

5. An important advantage of the published data is that they are derived from the full CPS sample in each month, rather than the one-quarter sample used in our tabulations in the rest of this chapter.

6. If the comparison sample is expanded to include all of Texas, the gap between the overall employment–population rate in California and the comparison areas shows less stability over the 1985–1990 period, although the gap in teenage employment rates still drops 3 to 4 percentage points after 1987.

7. As noted in chapters 4 and 6, teenage employment rates normally respond to the aggregate employment rate with a coefficient greater than 1.

8. The standard error of the difference in teenage employment rates between California and the comparison sample in any year is approximately 1.8 percent. Thus, the relative rise in teenage employment between 1987 and 1989 (4.1 percent) is not statistically significant at conventional levels ($t = 1.6$).

9. Owing to the low number of Asians outside California, the sample sizes of the "Other non-Hispanic" groups are too small for a meaningful analysis in the comparison sample.

10. The data on public high school enrollment are taken from U.S. Department of Education, *Digest of Education Statistics 1991*, Table 39. Undergraduate enrollment data are from the same source, Table 185.

11. Their preferred specifications give elasticities of employment with respect to wages of -1.0. Given our estimates of the effect of the minimum wage on wages in the retail-trade and restaurant industries (Tables 3.5 and 3.6), Kim and Taylor's elasticity estimates imply employment losses of 5 and 8 percent in these industries.

12. This evidence is reported in Card (1992b).

13. Another way to check the CBP data is to compare them with data assembled annually by the U.S. Department of Labor in *Employment and Wages—Annual Averages*. This publication uses Unemployment Insurance data collected in the so-called ES-202 reports to estimate total employment and average weekly wages, by state and industry. A comparison of employment data for specific retail-trade industries, such as grocery stores, shows large discrepancies between the two sources.

14. In the second-differenced specifications, we use as an instrument the California wage in period $t - 1$, which is orthogonal to any measurement error in employment in period t or period $t - 2$.

15. It is interesting to note that, even though the first-stage equation for the change in wages between 1989 and 1990 is insignificant, the second-stage estimate of the employment equation gives a coefficient of -0.62, with a standard error that is not much larger than the standard error in the 1988–1989 employment equation. This illustrates the potential difficulties that arise in interpreting IV estimates when the first-stage equation is poorly specified.

CHAPTER 4

The Effect of the Federal Minimum Wage on Low-Wage Workers: Evidence from Cross-State Comparisons

> Some hypothesis is a preliminary to every inductive investigation.
>
> —Jacob Viner

THE U.S. LABOR MARKET is characterized by wide differences in the level of wages across states. In 1989, for example, average hourly earnings were 73 percent higher in Alaska (the highest-wage state) than in Mississippi (the lowest-wage state).[1] As a consequence of this diversity, the relative value of the federal minimum wage varies greatly by state. Indeed, critics of the federal minimum wage often point to this fact in arguing against a national wage standard. For purposes of studying the effects of the minimum wage, however, a uniform federal rate is a valuable asset. Any increase in the federal minimum wage affects pay rates of a much larger fraction of workers in some states than in others. This variation creates a simple natural experiment for measuring the effect of the minimum, with a "treatment effect" that varies across states depending on the fraction of workers initially earning less than the new wage floor.

The natural experiment provided by an increase in the federal minimum wage circumvents two of the potential difficulties that arise in the kinds of state-specific experiments studied in chapters 2 and 3. On the one hand, the political process leading to a federal minimum-wage hike presumably is independent of *state-specific* economic conditions. There is no reason to expect that the passage of a federal minimum-wage increase signals a trend in one state's labor market relative to another's. On the other hand, an increase in the federal minimum wage creates 50 different experiments of varying intensities. By analyzing all these experiments simultaneously, we guard against the possibility that the results are biased by a state-specific shock that coincides with the timing of the minimum-wage law.

In this chapter, based on Card (1992a), we use the labor-market experiences of different states after the 1990 and 1991 increases in

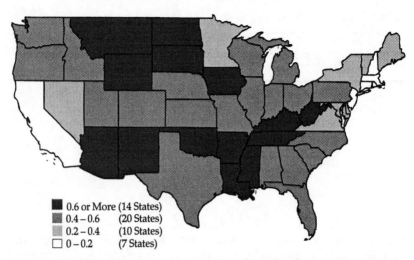

Figure 4.1 Proportion of teenage workers affected by 1990–1991 minimum wage increases. Alaska, Hawaii, and Washington, D.C., not shown.

the federal minimum wage in order to measure the effect of the minimum wage on various groups of low-wage workers, including teenagers and employees in the retail-trade industry. During the 1980s, wage differentials across states were accentuated by the passage of an unprecedented number of state-specific wage laws, which raised state minimum wages above the federal minimum. By 1989, 15 states and the District of Columbia had minimum wage rates that exceeded the federal standard. These laws created wide differences across states in the fraction of low-wage workers affected by the 1990 and 1991 increases in the federal minimum wage. The map in Figure 4.1, for example, shows the fraction of teenagers earning between \$3.35 per hour (the federal minimum wage in 1989) and \$4.25 per hour (the minimum wage as of April 1991) across different states. This fraction ranged from less than 20 percent in states in New England and in California to more than 70 percent in some southern and northcentral states. These differences in the potential "bite" of the 1990 and 1991 increases set the stage for our empirical analysis.

Our findings lend further support to the conclusion that modest increases in the minimum wage have no adverse effect on the employment outcomes of low-wage workers. Although the 1990 and 1991 minimum-wage increases led to significant earnings gains for teenagers and retail-trade workers in many states, these wage increases were not associated with any measurable employment losses. Indeed, teenage employment trends across different states are essentially unrelated to the wage changes induced by the federal minimum wage. We reach a similar conclusion when we examine data for a broader set of workers with low predicted wages, and employees in the retail-trade and restaurant industries.

THE 1990 AND 1991 MINIMUM-WAGE STATUTES

The federal minimum wage rose to $3.35 per hour on January 1, 1981 and remained frozen throughout the remainder of the decade. By 1989, inflation had eroded the purchasing power of the minimum wage to its lowest level since January 1950 (see Figure 1.2). The decline in the real value of the federal minimum prompted state legislatures and wage boards to respond with state-specific minimum rates that exceeded the federal standard. These higher minimums were first passed in the New England states—Maine ($3.45, effective January 1985), Massachusetts and Rhode Island (both $3.55, effective July 1986), New Hampshire ($3.45, effective January 1987), and Connecticut ($3.75, effective October 1987). By 1989, approximately 25 percent of all U.S. workers were covered by a state-specific wage floor above the federal standard.[2]

Political pressure for an increase in the federal minimum wage came to a head in March 1989 with passage of a House resolution to raise the minimum wage to $4.55 over a three-year period. A similar resolution passed the Senate but was vetoed by President Bush. A bill providing for smaller wage increases and a liberalized youth subminimum was finally passed into law in November 1989.[3] The new law raised the minimum wage in two steps—to $3.80 per hour on April 1, 1990, and to $4.25 per hour on April 1, 1991—and established a subminimum equal to 85 percent of the regular minimum wage for employees aged 16 to 19.

Other provisions of the federal minimum wage law were modified only slightly by the November 1989 legislation. The tip credit, which allows employees to credit a portion of their tips toward the minimum, was raised from 40 to 45 percent effective April 1, 1990, and 50 percent effective April 1, 1991. Consequently, the federal minimum wage for tipped employees rose from $2.01 to 2.09 per hour on April 1, 1990, and to $2.12 per hour on April 1, 1991. Exemptions for smaller businesses were also expanded and simplified. Previously, retail and service enterprises with an annual sales volume of less than $250,000 were exempt from coverage. This threshold was raised to $500,000 and extended to all industries.[4]

THE EFFECT OF THE MINIMUM WAGE ON TEENAGERS

An Overview of the Teenage Labor Market

As we noted in chapter 3, teenagers are among the most heavily affected groups of workers whenever the minimum wage is increased. Table 4.1 contains some descriptive information for teenagers taken from the period immediately preceding the 1990 and 1991 increases in the federal minimum wage. To facilitate comparisons with the postincrease periods, the sample includes only observations from April–December 1989. The first column of the table reports data for all teenagers (workers and nonworkers). The remaining columns report similar information for employed teenagers and for those with hourly wages in specified intervals.

A comparison of the first two columns of Table 4.1 shows that females comprise about one-half of all teenagers and all working teenagers. Nonwhites and Hispanics, on the other hand, are underrepresented in the working population relative to their shares in the overall population. Employed teenagers also tend to be older and have more years of completed education than do nonworkers. A majority of teenagers (56.5 percent) report that they are enrolled in high school, college, or university. This fraction must be interpreted carefully, as school attendance rates vary over the year. During 1989, the average fraction of teenagers enrolled in school varied from 77 percent in April to 14 percent in July and August.

The Current Population Survey (CPS) collects hourly wage information for individuals who are paid by the hour (93 percent of teenagers) and collects usual weekly earnings for other workers. The wage measure presented in row 10 of Table 4.1, and which is used to define the columns of the table, represents the reported wage for hourly-rated workers and the ratio of usual weekly earnings to usual weekly hours for other workers. According to this "straight-time" wage measure, teenage workers earned an average of $4.61 per hour during 1989, compared with an average of $10.10 per hour for all workers in the United States. As shown by the percentages in row 2, 7.4 percent of teenagers with valid wage data earned less than the prevailing federal minimum wage of $3.35 per hour, 25.7 percent earned from $3.35 to 3.79 per hour (i.e., as much as or more than the old minimum wage but less than the April 1, 1990, minimum rate), 41.4 percent earned from $3.35 to 4.25 per hour (i.e., as much as or more than the old minimum but less than the April 1, 1991, minimum), and 51.2 percent earned $4.25 per hour or more.[5]

One difficulty with a straight-time wage measure is that some teenagers who report being paid by the hour also receive tips or

TABLE 4.1
Characteristics of Teenagers and Teenage Workers, 1989

	All (1)	All Workers (2)	Hourly Wage Range			
			<$3.35 (3)	$3.35– 3.79 (4)	$3.35– 4.24 (5)	>$4.25 (6)
1. All Teenagers (%)	100.0	49.0	3.6	12.6	20.3	25.1
2. Working Teenagers (%)	—	100.0	7.4	25.7	41.4	51.2
Percentage of Teenagers Who Are						
3. Female	49.7	48.3	61.0	53.4	52.8	43.7
4. Nonwhite	19.0	11.9	10.7	15.1	13.1	11.0
5. Hispanic	9.9	8.1	5.5	6.9	6.5	9.7
6. Aged 16–17	48.2	38.9	52.4	54.3	50.4	27.7
7. Education <12 Years	62.8	53.0	65.2	68.1	64.3	41.9
8. Enrolled	56.5	45.6	51.3	55.8	52.7	39.1
Labor-Market Outcomes						
9. Hours per Week	—	26.6	22.0	22.5	23.6	30.0
10. Wage ($/hr)	—	4.61	2.45	3.49	3.68	5.69
11. Wage with Tips ($/hr)	—	4.77	3.07	3.61	3.80	5.81
12. Percentage with Tips	—	11.6	25.5	12.2	11.2	10.0
Industry						
13. Agriculture	—	4.2	6.0	2.2	2.9	3.2
14. Retail Trade	—	50.1	49.5	68.4	65.0	40.8
15. Services	—	25.0	35.2	21.5	22.3	24.6
16. Sample Size	18,511	9,205	674	2,326	3,716	3,716

Source: Data are taken from 1989 monthly CPS files for April–December.

Note: All Workers includes unpaid and self-employed workers. The four hourly wage ranges exclude unpaid or self-employed workers and all workers with allocated wages. The wage rate in row 10 excludes tips; the wage rate in row 11 includes prorated average weekly tips.

commissions. This practice is especially widespread in retail trade, which employs more than one-half of teenagers (see row 14 of the table). For hourly-rated workers, the CPS also collects usual weekly earnings *including* regular tips and commissions. This information can be used to construct an estimate of average weekly tips and an alternative measure of hourly wages. The average level of wages including prorated tips (in row 11 of Table 4.1) is 3 percent higher than the average based on straight-time earnings, reflecting the addition of tips and commissions for about 12 percent of teenage workers.

The characteristics of teenagers with straight-time earnings less than the minimum wage are presented in the third column of Table 4.1. There are a variety of explanations for subminimum-wage pay, including noncoverage (for tipped employees in retail trade and for full-time students covered under the student subminimum[6]), employer noncompliance, and measurement error. Examination of the wage distribution of teenagers earning less than $3.35 per hour shows a substantial spike (21 percent of workers) near the tipped minimum of $2.01 per hour, suggesting that many subminimum-wage workers are exempt from the $3.35 standard. This possibility is further confirmed by the higher incidence of tip income among subminimum-wage teenagers: 26 percent of subminimum-wage earners report some tip income, versus 12 percent of teenagers overall. When hourly wages are calculated to include tip income, 19 percent of workers with straight-time pay that is less than $3.35 per hour have effective wages above the minimum wage. Even when usual tip income is included in the calculation, however, a substantial number of teenagers reported subminimum wages during 1989.

Employer noncompliance could explain some of these findings. Compared with other teenagers, subminimum-wage workers are more likely to work in agriculture and household services, where noncompliance may be higher. Subminimum-wage workers are also less likely to report that their employers are withholding Social Security taxes, suggesting that a higher fraction of subminimum-wage earners are working "off the books."[7] Another aspect of the subminimum-wage labor force is the relatively high fraction of workers who report being paid by the week or month, rather than by the hour (25 percent versus 7 percent of teenagers as a whole). Some salaried workers are legally exempt from the minimum wage, while others may have overreported their usual weekly hours, leading to a downward bias in their imputed hourly wages.[8]

Column 4 of Table 4.1 presents the characteristics of teenagers who reported wages between $3.35 and 3.79 per hour. As in chapter

3, we refer to individuals in this wage range as workers who were "affected" by the April 1, 1990, federal minimum-wage change. These individuals, who presumably were working at jobs that were in compliance with the minimum wage law, were affected most directly by the increase in the minimum wage to $3.80 per hour.[9] The next column of the table shows the broader group of teenagers who were "affected" by the $4.25 minimum wage effective April 1, 1991. The two groups are fairly similar. Both contain more enrolled students and a higher fraction of retail-trade workers than do groups of either higher-wage or lower-wage teenagers. During 1989, about 10 percent of all teenage workers reported an hourly wage *exactly* equal to $3.35 per hour. These workers comprised 40 percent of the $3.35–3.79 group, and 25 percent of the $3.35–4.24 group.

Aggregate Changes After the Minimum-Wage Increases

Figure 4.2 illustrates the effects of the 1990 and 1991 increases in the federal minimum wage on the wage distribution of teenage workers. This figure shows the quarterly fractions of teenagers earning less than $3.35 per hour, exactly $3.35 per hour, $3.36–3.79 per hour, and $3.80–4.24 per hour from 1989 to 1992. The fraction of teenagers earning less than $3.80 drops sharply in the second quarter of 1990 (i.e., after the April 1 minimum-wage increase). Most of this drop reflects a shift in the distribution of workers from the $3.35–3.79 wage range to the $3.80–4.25 wage range. There is almost no change in the fraction earning less than $3.35 per hour, nor in the trend of the overall fraction earning less than $4.25 per hour.

After the second increase in the federal minimum wage took effect, on April 1, 1991, the fraction of teenagers earning less than $4.25 per hour decreased 20 percentage points. Although not shown in the figure, this drop was accompanied by a dramatic increase in the fraction earning $4.25 per hour (the new minimum wage), and by a modest increase in the fraction earning $4.50 per hour. The latter increase suggests that the rise in the minimum wage had a spillover effect on workers who otherwise would have been expected to earn just above the new minimum wage. To explore this possibility further, we computed the fraction of teenagers earning up to $4.50 per hour, and the fraction earning up to $4.99 per hour. If an increase in the minimum wage simply shifts workers from the affected wage range to the new minimum rate, with no spillover effect for higher-wage workers, then one would expect to observe a decrease in the fraction of workers earning below $4.25 after April 1991, but relative constancy in the fraction earning less than any

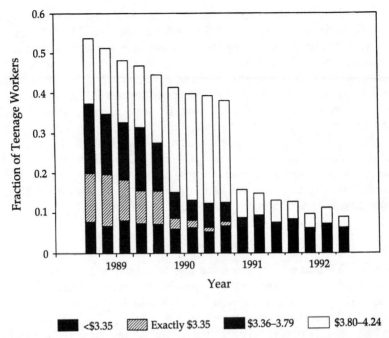

Figure 4.2   Fraction of teenagers earning less than $4.25 per hour, 1989–1992.

higher wage rate.[10] Contrary to this hypothesis, the overall fraction of teenagers earning as much as $4.50 per hour shows a drop of 6 percentage points relative to the trend after April 1991, and the fraction earning as much as $5.00 per hour shows a drop of 2 to 3 percentage points. We conclude that the rise in the minimum wage had a modest spillover effect on wages for higher-wage workers. Further evidence of this effect is analyzed in chapter 5.

An interesting feature of the data in Figure 4.2 is the lag in the response of measured wages to a change in the minimum wage. The fraction of workers reporting exactly $3.35 per hour, for example, drops discretely during the second quarter of 1990 but does not completely disappear for another year. Likewise, the fraction of workers earning $3.35 to 4.24 per hour gradually decreases between the second quarter of 1991 and the end of 1992. These lags may reflect true lags in the adjustment of wages, or lags in the respondents' reporting of recent wage changes to the CPS survey.

The first four rows of Table 4.2 present quantitative estimates of the wage changes that are illustrated in Figure 4.2. The data in this table pertain to April–December of each year from 1989 to 1992.

TABLE 4.2
Labor-Market Outcomes of Teenagers, 1989–1992

	1989 (1)	1990 (2)	1991 (3)	1992 (4)
1. Earning <$3.35 per Hour (%)	7.4	5.9	6.1	5.3
2. Earning $3.35–3.79 per Hour (%)	25.7	7.7	2.6	1.5
3. Earning $3.35–4.24 per Hour (%)	41.4	34.4	8.7	4.9
4. Average Wage ($/hr)	4.61	4.84	4.97	5.04
5. Average Hours/Week	26.6	26.4	25.1	24.9
6. Average Weekly Earnings ($/wk)	134.3	137.8	134.9	134.0
7. Employed (%)	49.0	46.4	43.5	42.4
Comparison Employment Rates				
8. All Individuals Aged 16+	63.0	62.7	61.6	61.4
9. Men Aged 16+	72.5	71.9	70.2	69.7

Note: Data in rows 1–7 are tabulated from monthly CPS files for April–December of each year. Data in rows 8 and 9 pertain to the entire calendar year and are taken from *Economic Report of the President* (1993), Table B–34.

During the period, the fraction of teenagers earning $3.35 to 4.24 per hour fell from 41.4 to 4.9 percent, and the average hourly wage of teenagers rose by about 40 cents (or 9 percent). By comparison, between 1989 and 1992, mean hourly wages of adult male workers rose by about 8 percent.[11] These figures suggest that the minimum wage led to only a small relative increase in average teenage wages. However, one should bear in mind that there has been a secular trend toward declining relative wages of less-skilled workers since the early 1980s, and that during 1990–1992, the country was in a recession. Both factors might have contributed to a decline in relative teenage wages in the absence of a minimum-wage change. Indeed, using comparisons of the effect of the minimum wage across states, we show below that the minimum probably led to an increase of 8 to 10 percent in average teenage wages.

Rows 5–7 of Table 4.2 give an indication of the corresponding changes in hours per week, weekly earnings, and the fraction of employed teenagers. Between 1989 and 1992, average weekly hours of teenager workers fell, offsetting the gains in hourly wages and leading to relative stability in weekly earnings. Even more importantly, the fraction of employed teenagers dropped by 6.5 percentage points.

Part of this decline is clearly attributable to the recession that began in mid-1990. The youth labor market is highly cyclical, and teenage employment rates normally would be expected to fall during a recession. Rows 8 and 9 show the employment–population rates for all workers and for men during the 1989–1992 period. Historically, the teenage employment rate responds to changes in the overall employment–population rate with a coefficient of between 2.0 and 2.5.[12] On the basis of this elasticity, the decline in the aggregate employment–population rate between 1989 and 1992 might have been expected to generate a decrease of 3.2 to 4.0 percentage points in teenage employment rates during the period. The observed decrease of 6.6 percentage points is far larger than this predicted amount.

Although it is tempting to attribute this discrepancy to the effect of the federal minimum wage, recall that the increase in the minimum wage should have had much different effects on teenagers in different labor markets, depending on the level of wages prior to the federal minimum-wage hikes. Thus, a critical "validity check" on the link between the minimum wage and the decline in aggregate teenage employment is a comparison of employment trends across different states. We pursue two complementary approaches to this comparison. The first is to aggregate states into three groups containing similar fractions of affected workers in 1989. This approach generates relatively large sample sizes in each group, permitting a quarterly analysis along the lines shown in Figure 4.2. The second approach uses *annual* data for each of the 50 states (plus the District of Columbia) from before and after the increases in the minimum wage.

A Grouped Analysis

The top panel of Figure 4.3 plots the fraction of workers earning $3.35 to 3.79 per hour, by quarter, for three groups of states: (1) states in which more than 40 percent of teenage workers earned $3.35 to 3.79 per hour during 1989 ("high-impact" states); (2) states in which fewer than 20 percent of teenage workers earned that amount ("low-impact" states); and (3) all other states ("medium-impact" states).[13] The bottom panel of Figure 4.3 shows a similar plot of the fraction of teenagers earning $3.35 to 4.24 per hour, using the same three state groups. The two figures illustrate the very different impacts of the 1990 and 1991 federal minimum-wage laws on the three groups of states. During 1989, the fraction of teenagers earning between $3.35 and 4.24 per hour ranged from 25 percent in the low-impact states to 70 percent in the high-impact states. By late 1991, the fractions were equal in the three groups.

How did teenage employment patterns compare across the three

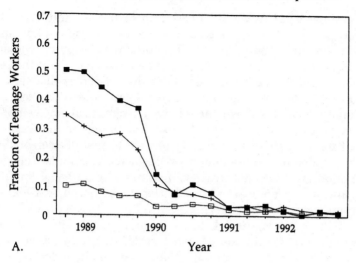

A.

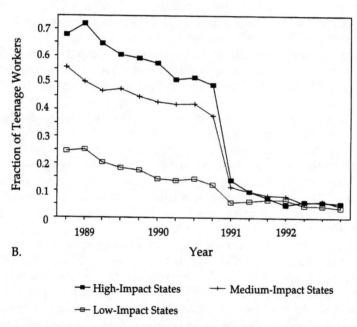

B.

-■- High-Impact States   -+- Medium-Impact States
-□- Low-Impact States

Figure 4.3 Fractions of teenage workers affected by minimum wage increases in three groups of states. A. Fraction earning \$3.35–3.79 per hour. B. Fraction earning \$3.35–4.24 per hour.

state groups? The answer is provided in Figure 4.4 and Table 4.3. The top panel of Figure 4.4 plots teenage employment–population rates in the three state groups. The bottom panel plots the same rates, adjusted for trends in the overall employment rate in the relevant state group. The adjustment procedure assumes that teenage employment rates respond to the aggregate rate with a coefficient of 2.5. Finally, Table 4.3 shows the relative changes in average employment rates in the three groups between a pre-minimum-wage increase baseline period (first quarter of 1989 to first quarter of 1990) and two different post-minimum-wage increase periods: the one-year period after the first increase in the minimum wage (in April 1990); and the seven-quarter period after the second increase in the minimum wage (in April 1991).

As illustrated in Figure 4.4, teenage employment rates are highly seasonal. Even around the seasonal cycle, quarterly employment rates in the three state groups are somewhat erratic, reflecting sampling errors and other unsystematic sources of quarter-to-quarter variation.[14] Nevertheless, the unadjusted employment rates in the upper panel of the figure show a clear pattern of more rapid employment growth in the high- and medium-impact states than in the low-impact states. This visual impression is confirmed by the differences-in-differences of the unadjusted employment rates in rows 1 and 2 of Table 4.3. Relative to rates in the low-impact group, teenage employment rates in the high-impact group were 3.5 percentage points higher after the first increase in the federal minimum wage, and 6.9 percentage points higher after the second. As shown in column 2, employment rates also increased in the high-impact states relative to those in the medium-impact states. The comparison between the medium-impact group and the low-impact group (column 3) is less dramatic, indicating a relative increase of 0.5 percentage points after the first minimum-wage hike, and of 2.3 percentage points after the second.

Much of the relative divergence in employment rates across the three state groups is attributable to the uneven effects of the 1990–1992 recession. Between the first quarter of 1990 and the first quarter of 1992, for example, overall employment rates fell by 1.3 percentage points in the high-impact states, by 1.1 percentage points in the medium-impact states, and by 2.8 percentage points in the low-impact states. Factoring these aggregate changes into the teenage employment rates generates the comparisons in rows 3 and 4 of Table 4.3. Even after accounting for overall labor-market trends, teenage employment rates in the high-impact states increased relative to either the low-impact states or the medium-impact states. On the other

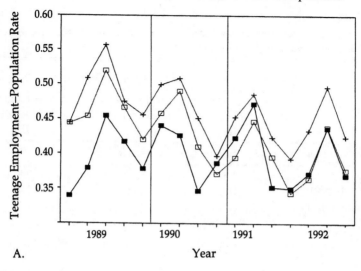

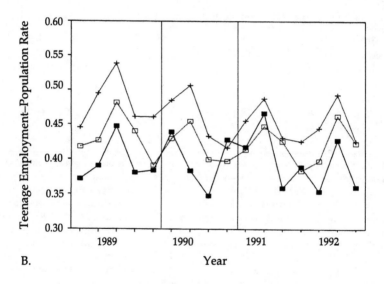

Figure 4.4   Teenagers' employment rates in three groups of states. A. Unadjusted employment rates. B. Adjusted employment rates.

TABLE 4.3
Difference-in-Differences of Teenage Employment Rates, Before and After
1990 and 1991 Minimum-Wage Increases

	Difference-in-Differences		
	High Impact − Low Impact (1)	High Impact − Medium Impact (2)	Medium Impact − Low Impact (3)
Unadjusted Differences in Teenage Employment Rates			
1. April 1990– March 1991 Relative to Base Period	3.5 (1.9)	3.0 (1.9)	0.5 (1.1)
2. April 1991– December 1992 Relative to Base Period	6.9 (1.7)	4.7 (1.7)	2.3 (1.0)
Adjusted Differences in Teenage Employment Rates[a]			
3. April 1990– March 1991 Relative to Base Period	1.6 (2.4)	2.4 (2.2)	−0.9 (1.3)
4. April 1991– December 1992 Relative to Base Period	1.1 (2.1)	3.0 (1.9)	−1.9 (1.1)

Note: Standard errors are shown in parentheses. Entries represent average differences in quarterly teenage employment–population rates (in percents) between the different groups of states indicated in the column headings. The base period for all differences-in-differences is April 1989 to March 1990. The high-impact group includes 13 states with the highest fraction of teenagers earning between \$3.35 and 3.79 per hour in 1989. The low-impact group includes 16 states with the lowest fraction of teenagers earning between \$3.35 and 3.79 per hour in 1989. The medium-impact group includes the remaining 22 states.

[a]The teenage employment rate is adjusted for changes in the overall employment rate in the state group, using a coefficient of 2.5. See text.

hand, adjusted teenage employment in the medium-impact states fell slightly relative to the low-impact states, although the shifts are not statistically significant.

These comparisons show little evidence of systematic employment effects attributable to the federal minimum-wage increase. Relative to other states, teenage employment rates in states with the lowest levels of teenage wages actually *increased* after the 1990 and 1991 minimum-wage increases. Unadjusted teenage employment rates also show a small increase in medium-impact states relative to low-impact states. When overall employment trends are taken into account, however, adjusted teenage employment rates show a slight decline in the medium-impact group relative to the high-impact group. On balance, we conclude that the rise in the minimum wage had no clear effect on relative teenage employment rates in the three groups of states.

An Analysis, by State

An alternative to the grouping strategy is to treat each state as a separate observation, and to correlate changes in employment, wages, and other outcomes with the fraction of workers affected by the minimum wage in the state. A state-level analysis has the advantage of providing far more "degrees of freedom" than does the grouped analysis, permitting a closer examination of the connection between the impact of the minimum wage and the change in teenage employment. In addition, variability in the effect of the minimum wage across all 50 states is greater than across the three aggregate state groups. On the other hand, the number of individual observations for each state in the CPS data files is relatively small. For this reason, we do not attempt to analyze quarterly data, by state. Rather, we examine annual data for each state.

Table 4.4 summarizes our analysis. Each panel of the table presents an analysis of employment and wage changes for teenage workers over a different time horizon. The top panel uses data for April–December 1989 and the corresponding months in 1990. This comparison measures the immediate effect of the April 1990 increase in the minimum wage from $3.35 to 3.80 per hour. The critical explanatory variable is the fraction of affected workers in the state, defined as the fraction of teenage workers who earned between $3.35 and 3.79 per hour during April–December 1989. To control for any aggregate-level labor-market changes, we also include the change in the overall employment–population rate in the state between 1989 and 1990.[15] The models are estimated by weighted least squares, using as weights the sizes of the CPS samples of teenagers in each state in 1989.

The middle panel of Table 4.4 presents a parallel analysis using data for April–December 1989 and April–December 1991. This comparison allows us to measure the combined effects of the April 1990 and April 1991 increases in the minimum wage. Taking into account

TABLE 4.4
Estimated Regression Models for Changes in State Averages of Teenage
Wages and Teenage Employment–Population Rates

	Models for Change in Mean Log Wage		Models for Change in Employment Rate	
	(1)	(2)	(3)	(4)
A. Changes, April–December 1989 to April–December 1990				
1. Fraction of Affected Teenagers[a]	0.15 (0.03)	0.14 (0.04)	0.02 (0.03)	−0.01 (0.03)
2. Change in Overall Employment Rate[b]	—	0.46 (0.60)	—	1.24 (0.60)
3. R-Squared	0.30	0.31	0.01	0.09
B. Changes, April–December 1989 to April–December 1991				
4. Fraction of Affected Teenagers[a]	0.29 (0.04)	0.24 (0.04)	0.13 (0.04)	0.04 (0.04)
5. Change in Overall Employment Rate[b]	—	1.03 (0.41)	—	1.69 (0.44)
6. R-Squared	0.57	0.62	0.15	0.35
C. Changes, January–December 1989 to January–December 1992				
7. Fraction of Affected Teenagers[a]	0.28 (0.04)	0.22 (0.05)	0.13 (0.03)	0.01 (0.03)
8. Change in Overall Employment Rate[b]	—	1.05 (0.51)	—	1.94 (0.31)
9. R-Squared	0.58	0.62	0.31	0.62

Note: Standard errors are shown in parentheses. The models in panels A and B are estimated on 51 state-level observations (including the District of Columbia), using data derived from monthly Current Population Survey (CPS) samples for 1989–1991. The models in panel C are estimated on 50 state-level observations (excluding the District of Columbia), using wage data derived from CPS files for 1989 and 1992 and teenage employment rates taken from U.S. Department of Labor, *Geographic Profiles of Unemployment and Employment*. All models are estimated by weighted least squares, using the number of teenagers in the the state in the 1989 CPS file as a weight.

[a]Fraction of teenagers earning $3.35–3.79 per hour in the state (panel A) or $3.35–4.24 per hour (panels B and C) in 1989. In panels A and B, the fraction affected is estimated using data for April–December only. In panel C, the fraction affected is estimated using data for all 12 months of 1989.

[b]The change in the overall employment–population rate for the state, taken from *Geographic Profiles of Unemployment and Employment*.

both minimum-wage increases, we define the fraction-affected variable in this panel as the fraction of teenagers in the state who earned between $3.35 and 4.24 per hour during April–December 1989. The aggregate-employment variable is defined as the change in the overall employment rate in the state between 1989 and 1991.

Finally, the lower panel repeats the entire analysis over the longer 1989–1992 period. Because the federal minimum wage was constant throughout 1989 (at $3.35), and throughout 1992 (at $4.25), we use published employment data for all 12 months of 1989 and 1992 in this panel and define the fraction of affected workers as the fraction of teenagers who earned between $3.35 and 4.24 per hour during 1989.[16] The aggregate-employment variable is defined as the change in the overall employment rate in the state between 1989 and 1992.

The similarity of the findings in all three panels of the table is striking. The models for teenage wage growth in columns 1 and 2 suggest that teenage wages in lower-wage states were affected substantially by the increase in the federal minimum wage. Between 1989 and 1990, the coefficient of the fraction-affected variable is 0.14 (controlling for aggregate-employment trends), with a t-ratio of more than 3. This coefficient is slightly larger than would be expected if the minimum wage led to a simple "topping up" of wages to the new minimum rate for all workers in the $3.35–3.79 per hour range. Under this hypothesis, the expected coefficient of the fraction-affected variable is approximately 0.10 (reflecting the fact that average wages for workers in the $3.35–3.79 per hour wage range were about 10 percent below the new minimum wage—see Table 4.1). Between 1989 and 1991 or 1992, the correlation between state-specific wage growth and the fraction-affected variable is even stronger. Again, the coefficient of the fraction-affected variable (0.22 to 0.24) is slightly larger than would be expected if the minimum wage led to a "topping up" of wages for affected workers (the expected coefficient is 0.15, based on an average wage of $3.68 per hour for workers in the affected wage range). This larger coefficient is consistent with our previous finding of a spillover effect of the minimum wage on higher-wage workers and suggests that the increase in the minimum wage raised average teenage wages in the United States as a whole by about 8 percent.

The correlation between the fraction-affected measure and teenage wage growth from 1989 to 1992 is illustrated in the top panel of Figure 4.5. The state-level observations lie on a relatively tight line. In contrast, the correlation between the fraction-affected variable and changes in teenage employment is far weaker (see the bottom panel of the figure). As suggested by the grouped analysis in the

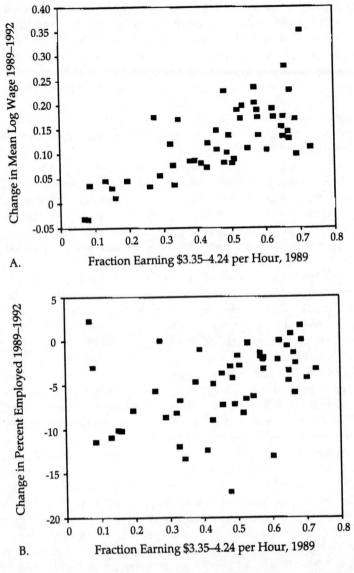

Figure 4.5 Interstate patterns of wage and employment growth, 1989–1992. A. Change in teenage wage rates. B. Change in teenage employment rates.

previous section, employment changes occurring after the 1990 and 1991 increases in the federal minimum wage took effect are actually positively correlated with the fraction of teenagers in the affected wage ranges. This correlation is shown by the simple regression models in column 3 of Table 4.4. After the differential patterns of aggregate-employment growth are taken into consideration, however, the fraction-affected variable is essentially unrelated to the teenage employment rate (see column 4), and the estimated standard error is relatively precise.

We investigated a variety of alternative specifications to probe the robustness of this conclusion. Some of these alternatives are presented in Table 4.5. All the models presented in this table pertain to the change in teenage employment between 1989 and 1992. The first column repeats the basic specification from the fourth column of the bottom panel of Table 4.4. The second column presents a model that includes as an additional control variable the change in the mean log wage of adult men (aged 25 and older) between 1989 and 1992. Although this variable has a modest effect on teenage wage growth, it has no effect on teenage employment growth or on the estimate of the fraction-affected variable.[17] Another specification test is reported in column 3. The model presented here includes a set of region dummies (representing the northeastern, northcentral, southern, and western regions). As shown in Figure 4.1, the effect of the 1990 and 1991 minimum-wage increases was concentrated in the southern and northcentral states, creating a potential concern about the influence of region-specific shocks. The estimated region dummies in the expanded model are jointly insignificant, however, and the estimated coefficients of the fraction-affected variable are almost identical to those reported in column 1. The models in columns 4–6 of Table 4.5 present more general specifications for the lagged effects of the overall employment–population rate, and for the lagged effect of pre-1989 teenage employment outcomes. The model in column 4 adds six variables representing the overall employment rate in the state for each year from 1987 to 1992. The pre-1989 employment variables and the 1990 and 1991 employment rates are jointly insignificant, and their addition has little effect on the coefficient of the fraction-affected variable. To test the validity of the first-differenced specification for the dependent variable, the model in column 5 adds the level of teenage employment in 1989. The estimated coefficient of this variable is very close to zero, suggesting that the first-differenced specification is appropriate. Finally, the model in column 6 adds lagged values of the overall employment rate for 1987–1992, and lagged values of the teenage employment rate for 1987–1989. The addition of these variables leads to a marginal improvement in fit relative to the base specification in column 1 (the probability value for their joint significance is 13 percent), but no significant change in the estimated coefficient of the fraction-affected variable. We also estimated models that include the overall unemployment rate, rather than (or in addition to) the overall employment–population

TABLE 4.5
Alternative Regression Models for the Change in State-Average Teenage Employment–Population Rates, 1989–1992

	(1)	(2)	(3)	(4)	(5)	(6)	(7)	(8)
				Dependent Variable: Change in Teenage Employment Rate, 1989–1992				
1. Fraction of Affected Teenagers[a]	0.01	0.01	0.01	0.02	0.01	0.05	0.03	0.01
	(0.03)	(0.03)	(0.03)	(0.03)	(0.03)	(0.03)	(0.03)	(0.03)
2. Change in Overall Employment Rate[b]	1.94	1.94	1.97	—	1.94	—	1.90	1.91
	(0.31)	(0.32)	(0.33)		(0.32)		(0.31)	(0.31)
3. Change in Wage of Adult Men[c]	—	−0.01	—	—	—	—	—	—
		(0.17)						
4. Levels of Overall Employment Rate								
a. 1992	—	—	—	2.41	—	2.18	—	—
				(0.60)		(0.60)		
b. 1991	—	—	—	−0.51	—	−0.23	—	—
				(0.76)		(0.79)		
c. 1990	—	—	—	−0.21	—	−0.66	—	—
				(0.82)		(0.80)		
d. 1989	—	—	—	−1.89	—	−0.85	—	—
				(0.74)		(0.77)		
e. 1988	—	—	—	−0.39	—	−0.73	—	—
				(0.79)		(0.78)		
f. 1987	—	—	—	0.69	—	0.56	—	—
				(0.64)		(0.64)		

5. Lagged Teenage Employment Rate								
a. 1989	—	—	—	—	0.01 (0.06)	−0.57 (0.17)	—	—
b. 1988	—	—	—	—	—	0.34 (0.18)	—	—
c. 1987	—	—	—	—	—	0.07 (0.15)	—	—
6. Excess State Vote for H.R. 2 (1989)[d]	—	—	—	—	—	—	0.03 (0.02)	0.04 (0.02)
7. Interaction of Fraction Affected and Low Vote for H.R. 2[e]	—	—	—	—	—	—	—	0.01 (0.02)
8. Region Dummies	No	No	Yes	No	No	No	No	No
9. R-Squared	0.62	0.62	0.62	0.65	0.62	0.72	0.64	0.64

Note: Standard errors are shown in parentheses. The models are estimated on 50 state-level observations (excluding the District of Columbia), using 1989 and 1992 teenage employment rates taken from U.S. Department of Labor, *Geographic Profiles of Unemployment and Employment*. All models are estimated by weighted least squares, using the number of teenagers in the state in the 1989 Current Population Survey (CPS) file as a weight.

[a]The fraction of the teenagers earning $3.35–4.24 per hour in the state in 1989, estimated using CPS files for all 12 months of 1989.

[b]The change in the overall employment–population rate for the state, taken from *Geographic Profiles of Unemployment and Employment*.

[c]The change in the mean log wage of men aged 25 and older in the state from 1989 to 1992, estimated using CPS files for all 12 months of 1989 and 1992.

[d]The fraction of members of the House of Representatives from the state who voted in favor of H.R. 2 (a March 1989 resolution to increase the federal minimum wage from $3.35 per hour to $4.55 per hour), adjusted for the fraction of members of the House of Representatives from the Democrat party. See text.

[e]The interaction of the fraction of teenagers affected by the minimum wage and an indicator for states in which the adjusted fraction of members of the House of Representatives who voted for H.R. 2 was in the lowest 25 percent of all states. See text.

rate.[18] These models give estimates that are very similar to the ones in the table. For example, a model similar to the one in column 6, but including values of the state *unemployment* rate during 1987–1991, yields an estimated coefficient for the fraction-affected variable of 0.01, with a standard error of 0.04.

In another set of specifications (not shown in the table), we introduced controls for changes in the fraction of teenagers enrolled in school. Although we believe that enrollment should be modeled as jointly determined with employment (rather than as an "exogenous" determinant of employment), it is interesting to consider the effect of controlling for enrollment, because this has been done in some of the previous literature (see chapter 7). The addition of the change in state-specific enrollment rates to the employment models in Tables 4.4 and 4.5 leads to no change in the coefficient of the fraction-affected variable (see also Card, Katz, and Krueger [1994], Table 3). Finally, we reestimated the models using different weights for the state-level observations. In particular, we compared the weighted estimates in Tables 4.4 and 4.5 (which use the number of teenagers in the CPS sample as a weight) with both unweighted estimates and weighted estimates using the population of teenagers in the state as a weight. All three sets of estimates are similar and yield estimated coefficients for the fraction-affected variable that are very close to zero.

We emphasize that the effect of the federal minimum wage varies greatly across states, depending on the overall level of wages and the presence of state-specific minimum-wage floors. This diverse impact is potentially reflected in the level of political support for a federal minimum-wage increase. Politicians from states in which an increase in the minimum wage is expected to have a strong effect on wages or employment opportunities might oppose the increase, whereas those from states in which the expected effect is smaller might support it. This suggests that we can use the level of support for the federal minimum-wage increase as a proxy for otherwise unobservable factors in a state that might be related to impact of the law.

To pursue this idea, we collected voting data on House Resolution 2 (H.R. 2) of the 1989 session of Congress—a bill introduced in March 1989 to raise the federal minimum wage to $4.55 per hour.[19] We found that the vote was split along party lines, with 87 percent of Democrats and 13 percent of Republicans voting in favor of the resolution. This finding is consistent with findings in earlier studies of voting on the minimum wage (Bloch [1980, 1989]). We therefore constructed a "party-adjusted" measure of political support for the minimum wage for each state, based on the *excess fraction* of representatives from the state who voted for an increase in the minimum wage, controlling for party affiliation.[20] The model in column 7 of Table 4.5 includes this adjusted measure of political support as an additional control variable. Teenage employment growth between 1989 and 1992 was slightly stronger in states in which congressmen tended to support the minimum-wage hike. However, the addition of this variable has no effect on the estimated coefficient of the fraction affected variable. We reach a similar conclusion when we use the unadjusted fraction of congressmen who voted in support of H.R. 2 in the state, with or without a variable measuring the fraction of Democrats in the state's congressional delegation.

We also used the adjusted measure of political support to define a set of states in which the opposition to the minimum wage was strongest. In the model in column 8 of Table 4.5, we include both the adjusted political-support variable and an interaction of the fraction-affected variable with an indicator for the 13 "most-strongly opposed" states. The interaction term is small but *positive*, providing no evidence that the minimum wage had a stronger adverse-employment effect in states in which it was most strongly opposed.

A final set of specification checks is presented in Table 4.6. In the top panel, we regress changes in teenage wages and employment from 1986 to 1989—i.e., during the three-year period before the increase in the federal minimum wage—on the fraction of teenagers in the state earning \$3.35 to 4.24 per hour during 1989. If our interpretation of the fraction-affected variable in models for the changes from 1989 to 1992 is correct, then there is no reason for state-specific employment trends in the period *before* the minimum-wage increase to be correlated with the potential impact of the 1990 and 1991 increases.[21] If the fraction-affected variable is spuriously correlated with underlying labor-market trends in the state, however, then we might expect it to have a positive effect on employment trends prior to the increase in the minimum wage.

As shown in columns 1 and 2, the fraction-affected variable is negatively correlated with teenage wage growth from 1986 to 1989. This correlation reflects the strong inverse correlation between the average level of teenage wages in a state during 1989 and the fraction of teenagers earning \$3.35 to 4.24 per hour during that year. More importantly, the fraction-affected variable is unrelated to the change in teenage employment rates between 1986 and 1989. The absence of a correlation suggests that our findings for the post-1989 period are unlikely to be biased by unobserved state-specific trends in teenage employment.

TABLE 4.6

Estimated Regression Models for Changes in State Averages of Teenage Wages and Teenage Employment–Population Rates, 1986–1989

	Models for Change in Mean Log Wage		Models for Change in Employment Rate	
	(1)	(2)	(3)	(4)
A. Using Fraction of Teenagers Earning $3.35–4.24 per hour in 1989				
1. Fraction of Affected Teenagers in 1989[a]	−0.25 (0.04)	−0.26 (0.04)	0.02 (0.03)	0.01 (0.03)
2. Change in Overall Employment Rate[b]	—	1.11 (0.59)	—	1.36 (0.45)
3. R-Squared	0.50	0.53	0.01	0.17
B. Using Fraction of Teenagers Earning $3.35–4.24 per hour in 1986				
4. Fraction of Affected Teenagers in 1986[c]	−0.16 (0.10)	−0.16 (0.10)	0.08 (0.06)	0.07 (0.06)
5. Change in Overall Employment Rate[b]	—	0.36 (0.82)	—	1.35 (0.43)
6. R-Squared	0.05	0.05	0.04	0.19

Note: Standard errors are shown in parentheses. The models are estimated on 51 state-level observations (including the District of Columbia), using wage data derived from Current Population Survey (CPS) files for 1986 and 1989 and teenage employment rates taken from U.S. Department of Labor, *Geographic Profiles of Unemployment and Employment.* All models are estimated by weighted least squares, using the number of teenagers in the the state in the 1989 CPS file as a weight.

[a]The fraction of teenagers earning $3.35–4.24 per hour in the state in 1989, estimated using CPS files for all 12 months of 1989.

[b]The change in the overall employment–population rate for the state from 1986 to 1989, taken from *Geographic Profiles of Unemployment and Employment.*

[c]The fraction of teenagers earning $3.35–4.24 per hour in the state in 1986, estimated using CPS files for all 12 months of 1986.

In the bottom panel of the table, we regress the 1986–1989 wage and employment changes on the fraction of teenagers in the state earning $3.35 to 4.24 per hour during *1986*. The idea of these specifications is to further check our methodology by incorrectly applying it to a period during which the fraction-affected variable should have no causal relation to wage or employment trends. As shown by the regression results, the fraction of teenagers earning $3.35 to 4.24 per hour during 1986 is not significantly correlated with either wage growth or employment changes over the next three years. These results give added credence to our findings for the 1989–1992 period, during which the fraction-affected variable is highly correlated with wage growth, but unrelated to employment changes.

To summarize, our estimates suggest that interstate differences in teenage employment growth occurring after the 1990 and 1991 minimum-wage increases took effect were unrelated to the state-specific wage effect of these laws. This finding is robust to changes in specification, including the addition of region-specific effects, the use of alternative cyclical indicators, and the addition of controls for trends in adult wages and changes in teenagers' school enrollment. Given the imprecision of our estimates, however, we cannot rule out the possibility that the increase in the minimum wage had a small, negative employment effect on teenagers. Estimates in the literature (Brown, Gilroy, and Kohen [1982]) suggest that the 27 percent increase in the minimum wage would lower overall teenage employment rates by 1.3 to 4.0 percentage points between 1989 and 1992. Because the overall fraction of teenagers earning $3.35 to 4.24 per hour during 1989 was 41 percent, our basic model (in column 1 of Table 4.5) implies that the rise in the minimum wage increased teenage employment by 0.4 percentage points, with a standard error of 1.2 percentage points. This estimate is inconsistent with the upper range of the employment effects predicted by the previous literature but does not rule out employment losses of 1 to 2 percentage points.

Effect of the Minimum Wage on a Broader Group of Low-Wage Workers

The methodology presented in the previous section can be extended easily in order to study the effect of the minimum wage on other groups of low-wage workers. In this section, we briefly summarize the results of one such extension, based on the wage and employment outcomes of workers who were most "at risk" of being affected by the 1990 and 1991 increases in the federal minimum wage. As we have noted, workers who are most likely to be affected by an increase in the minimum wage are those who work at firms that comply with minimum-wage laws (and who therefore earn at least as much as the existing minimum wage), but who earn less than the new minimum rate. This group does not consist solely of teenagers. Indeed, of the 8.7 percent of the U.S. work force earning between $3.35 and 4.24 per hour during 1989, only one-third were teenagers.

The others were a mix of young adults, less-educated workers, and minority and female workers (see chapter 9).

To capture this diverse population of directly affected workers, we first fit a simple linear-probability model in which the dependent variable was a dummy variable indicating whether an individual earned between \$3.35 and 4.24 per hour during 1989. We fit this model to the entire sample of workers in the 1989 CPS sample, including as explanatory variables a set of four race/gender interactions for 16- to 19-year-old workers, and another set of race/gender interactions for 20- to 25-year-old workers. We also included a high-school-dropout dummy variable; measures of education, potential labor-market experience (a third-order polynomial), race, gender, Hispanic ethnicity; and interactions of the education and experience variables with gender. We then used this estimated model to predict the probability that a given individual would be affected by the 1990 and 1991 minimum-wage changes, and stratified the entire adult population of the 1989–1992 CPS samples into three groups: (1) a group whose predicted probability of earning \$3.35 to 4.24 per hour during 1989 is in the top 10 percent of all workers; (2) a group whose predicted probability is in the lower half of all workers; and (3) all remaining individuals. For simplicity, we refer to the first group as those with a high probability of being affected by the 1990 and 1991 minimum-wage changes, and the second group as those with a low probability of being affected by the changes.

Examination of the high-probability group of workers shows that it is made up of approximately 60 percent teenagers, with another 12 percent between the ages of 20 and 25. The group is two-thirds female, and 21 percent African American, and has an average education of 10.3 years (compared with an average of 13 years among all workers in 1989). By comparison, low-probability workers are *all* older than 25 years of age, and have an average of 14.4 years of education. This group is disproportionately composed of white males (70 percent male; 94 percent white).

We followed the same methods used to analyze teenage labor-market outcomes across different states to estimate the fraction of high-probability workers who earned between \$3.35 and 4.24 per hour in each state during 1989, and the mean log wages and employment–population rates for these individuals in each state during 1989 and 1992. We then regressed the change in mean log wages and the change in the employment rate for high-probability individuals across each state on the fraction of these workers in the affected wage range in 1989, and on the overall change in the employment–population rate in the state. The estimates are presented in Table 4.7 (the format is the same as that used in the tabulations for teenagers).

TABLE 4.7

Estimated Regression Models for Changes in State Averages of Wages and Employment–Population Rates for Individuals with High Probability of Being Affected by 1990 and 1991 Minimum-Wage Increases

	Models for Change in Mean Log Wage			Models for Change in Employment Rate		
	(1)	(2)	(3)	(4)	(5)	(6)
1. Fraction of Affected Workers in 1989[a]	0.22 (0.03)	0.19 (0.05)	0.19 (0.05)	0.11 (0.02)	0.03 (0.03)	0.03 (0.03)
2. Change in Overall Employment Rate[b]	—	0.46 (0.51)	0.38 (0.51)	—	1.05 (0.30)	1.03 (0.30)
3. Change in Wage of Individuals with Low Probability of Being Affected[c]	—	—	0.41 (0.28)	—	—	0.09 (0.17)
4. R-Squared	0.46	0.47	0.50	0.31	0.45	0.46

Note: Standard errors are shown in parentheses. The models are estimated on 50 state-level observations (excluding the District of Columbia), using employment and wage data derived from Current Population Survey (CPS) files for 1989 and 1992. The dependent variables are the change in mean log wages (columns 1–3) and the change in the employment–population rate (columns 4–6) for individuals in the CPS files whose predicted probability of earning between $3.35 and 4.24 per hour in 1989 is in the top 10 percent of the population. Predictors include age, sex, education, and race, and interactions—see text. All models are estimated by weighted least squares, using the number of teenagers in the state in the 1989 CPS file as a weight.

[a]The fraction of individuals with a high probability of being affected by the 1990 and 1991 minimum-wage increases who actually earned between $3.35 and 4.24 per hour in the state in 1989.

[b]The change in the overall employment–population rate for the state from 1989 to 1992, taken from U.S. Department of Labor, *Geographic Profiles of Unemployment and Employment*.

[c]The change in the mean log wage of workers whose predicted probability of earning between $3.35 and 4.24 per hour is in the lowest 50 percent of the population.

The estimation results for this broader group of "high risk" workers are very similar to our results for teenagers. In the wage-growth models, the estimated coefficient of the variable that measures the fraction of high-risk workers who earned between $3.34 and 4.24 per hour during 1989 is about 0.2, with a relatively small standard error. The estimated coefficient of the fraction-affected variable in models for the change in the employment rate of these individuals is small and positive, but not significantly different from zero. Columns 3 and 6 of Table 4.7 present models that also include the mean wage growth of workers with a low probability of being affected by the minimum wage. As we found for teenagers, the addition of a measure of overall wage trends in the state has very little effect on either the wage or employment outcomes of workers most directly affected by the federal minimum-wage changes.

These results suggest two important conclusions. First, our findings for teenagers are representative of the effects of the 1990 and 1991 minimum-wage increases on a wider range of low-wage workers. Second, even though the minimum-wage increases were associated with substantial wage gains for low-wage workers in many states, these gains did not lead to reduced employment opportunities.

EFFECTS ON THE RETAIL-TRADE AND RESTAURANT INDUSTRIES

Overview

Retail trade is the industry that is most heavily affected by minimum wages. During 1989, 25 percent of all employees in the retail-trade industry earned between $3.35 and 4.24 per hour. The impact of the minimum wage is even more pronounced in the restaurant industry. During 1989, 35 percent of restaurant workers earned hourly wages between $3.35 and 4.24. The retail-trade industry as a whole, and the restaurant industry in particular, are also major sources of low-wage jobs in the U.S. economy. Forty-seven percent of all workers earning between $3.35 and 4.24 per hour during 1989 were employed in retail trade, and slightly more than 20 percent were employed in restaurants. These statistics suggest that restaurants and other retail-trade employers play a critical role in the minimum-wage labor market.

In this section, we combine CPS wage data for workers in the retail trade and restaurant industries with establishment-based employment data in order to estimate the effects of the 1990 and 1991 minimum-wage increases. To preview the results, our findings are very similar to our results with respect to teenagers. The 1990 and 1991 minimum-wage hikes led to sizable pay increases for retail trade and restaurant workers, but we find no evidence of offsetting employment losses. Using a different source of state-level employment data, Lang (1994) reached similar conclusions with respect to the restaurant industry.

We begin our analysis by presenting an overview in Table 4.8 of the characteristics of workers in the retail trade and restaurant industries in 1989 and 1992. Relative to the work force as a whole (i.e., columns 1 and 4) retail-trade workers are more likely to be younger, less-educated, and female. These relative contrasts are even more

TABLE 4.8

Characteristics of Retail Trade and Restaurant Workers, 1989 and 1992

	1989			1992		
	All (1)	Retail Trade (2)	Restaurant (3)	All (4)	Retail Trade (5)	Restaurant (6)
1. Earning $3.35–4.24 per Hour (%)	8.7	24.6	34.5	1.4	2.9	5.0
2. Earning $4.25 per Hour (%)	1.3	3.8	6.1	2.9	8.6	14.7
Percentage of Workers Who Are						
3. Female	47.0	53.1	57.2	47.8	52.5	55.1
4. African American	11.0	9.5	11.4	11.0	9.2	12.2
5. Hispanic	7.7	8.4	11.2	8.0	9.0	12.2
6. Aged 16–19	6.5	20.2	27.8	5.1	16.3	23.8
7. Aged 20–24	12.3	19.7	22.4	11.3	19.6	23.1
8. High School Dropouts	15.7	24.3	34.5	13.6	21.0	31.5
Other Labor-Market Outcomes						
9. Hours per Week	38.6	34.6	32.0	38.4	34.3	31.8
10. Wage ($/hr)	10.14	6.54	4.95	11.31	7.37	5.65
11. Wage with Tips ($/hr)	10.34	6.90	5.61	11.53	7.70	6.33
12. Percentage with Tips	10.1	15.7	25.7	9.6	15.6	25.2
13. Percentage Earning $3.35–4.24 per Hour, Including Tips	8.1	22.7	31.6	1.3	2.8	4.8
Industry						
14. Retail Trade	16.7	—	—	16.9	—	—
15. Restaurant	5.1	30.5	—	5.2	31.1	—
16. Sample Size	168,398	28,238	8,575	171,241	28,865	8,995

Note: Data are taken from 1989 and 1992 monthly Current Population Survey files for all 12 months. The sample excludes unpaid and self-employed workers, and all paid workers with allocated wages. The wage rate in row 10 excludes tips; the wage rate in row 11 includes prorated average weekly tips. The percentages in rows 1 and 2 exclude tips.

pronounced with respect to the restaurant industry. During 1989, the average wage in retail trade was about 65 percent of the economy-wide average wage. Average "straight-time" wages in the restaurant industry were approximately one-half the overall average. When tips are included in the calculation, however, the average wage in the restaurant industry rises to about 55 percent of the average for all industries.

The effect of the 1990 and 1991 minimum-wage increases is illustrated in the first two rows of the table. Between 1989 and 1992, the fraction of employees in retail trade earning from $3.35 to 4.24 per hour decreased from 25 to 3 percent. The decline in the restaurant industry—from 35 percent to 5 percent—was even more dramatic. Nevertheless, these changes were associated with only modest increases in average hourly wages relative to all industries. Hourly wages in retail trade rose 1.2 percent faster than in the labor market as a whole between 1989 and 1992. Hourly wages in the restaurant industry rose 2.6 percent faster than in the labor market as a whole. As with the similar comparisons for teenagers, these relative wage changes must be interpreted carefully. The secular trend of falling real wages for younger and less-educated workers, together with the effects of the 1990–1991 recession, could have contributed to a decline in relative wages for retail-trade and restaurant workers in the absence of a minimum-wage hike.

Cross-State Evidence on the Effects of the Minimum Wage

As in our cross-state analysis of labor-market outcomes for teenagers, a potentially better way to measure the effect of the minimum wage on wages is to compare wage trends between 1989 and 1992 with the fraction of workers who originally were earning between $3.35 and 4.24 per hour. This analysis is conducted in columns 1–4 of Table 4.9. The top panel of the table reports results for all retail-trade industries; the bottom panel gives results for the restaurant industry. We used CPS microdata for 1989 to compute the fraction of workers in the retail-trade and restaurant industries in each state who earned between $3.35 and 4.24 per hour (excluding tips). We then regressed the changes in average wages (computed from CPS microdata for 1989 and 1992) on the industry-specific estimate of the fraction-affected variable and other covariates. The estimation results are very similar to the results for teenagers and other low-wage workers. The estimated coefficient of the fraction-affected variable ranges between 0.13 and 0.25, with t-statistics of three or higher. The estimate is not too different when a measure of wage growth for adult men is included in the model (see column 4). Assuming that the fraction-affected coefficient is 0.22, these estimates imply that the federal minimum-wage increases raised average wages in the retail trade and restaurant industries by 4.8 and 6.5 percent, respectively.[22] Of course, the effect in many lower-wage states was substantially larger than this.

To measure the effects of the minimum wage on employment in

the retail-trade and restaurant industries, we collected annual data on state employment totals from the U.S. Department of Labor, Bureau of Labor Statistics publication, *Employment and Wages—Annual Averages*. In principle, these data represent complete counts of employment for nongovernmental workers covered by the Unemployment Insurance system in each state.[23] The regression models in columns 5–8 of Table 4.9 have as their dependent variable the change in the log of total employment in each state from 1989 to 1992 for either the entire retail-trade industry (top panel) or the restaurant industry (bottom panel).

Without controls for different cyclical patterns across states (column 5), the estimated coefficient of the fraction-affected variable is large and positive. The coefficient falls slightly when we introduce a control for the change in the state's employment–population rate (column 6) and falls even further when we measure cyclical conditions by the change in the state's unemployment rate (column 7). In column 8, we include the changes in both the employment–population rate and the unemployment rate, as well as the change in mean log wages for adult men in the state and a set of three region dummies. This expanded specification continues to show estimates of the fraction-affected coefficient that are positive and, in the case of the restaurant industry, different from zero at conventional significance levels.[24] We also estimated more general models that include unrestricted lags of the cyclical variables, and that relax the first-differenced specification of the dependent variable. These alternative models yield estimates of the fraction-affected coefficient that are very similar to the ones presented in the table.

The Effect of the Minimum Wage on Restaurant Prices

As we noted in chapter 2, one of the implications of conventional economic models is that an increase in the minimum wage will lead to an increase in the prices of products that minimum-wage workers produce. Given the importance of low-wage labor inputs to the restaurant industry, it is natural to ask whether the wage increases created by the rise in the federal minimum wage lead to measurable changes in restaurant prices. To study this question, we assembled two sources of price data. The first is the Bureau of Labor Statistics' Consumer Price Index (CPI) for food eaten away from home. City-specific CPIs are available for 29 major urban areas, ranging from New York City to Anchorage, Alaska. The second data source is the American Chamber of Commerce Research Association (ACCRA), which publishes quarterly data on prices for 59 standard items in

TABLE 4.9
Estimated Regression Models for Changes in State Averages of Wages and Employment in Retail-Trade and Restaurant Industries, 1989–1992

	Models for Change in Mean Log Wage				Models for Change in Log Employment			
	(1)	(2)	(3)	(4)	(5)	(6)	(7)	(8)
A. All Retail-Trade Industries								
1. Fraction of Affected Workers in 1989[a]	0.23 (0.04)	0.21 (0.05)	0.25 (0.06)	0.23 (0.07)	0.36 (0.07)	0.29 (0.07)	0.03 (0.07)	0.08 (0.05)
2. Change in State Employment Rate[b]	—	0.19 (0.36)	—	0.66 (0.45)	—	0.83 (0.54)	—	−0.39 (0.34)
3. Change in State Unemployment Rate[c]	—	—	0.27 (0.54)	1.37 (0.76)	—	—	−3.54 (0.63)	−2.64 (0.59)
4. Change in Log Wage of Adult Males[d]	—	—	—	0.13 (0.20)	—	—	—	0.33 (0.15)
5. Region Effects	No	No	No	Yes	No	No	No	Yes
6. R-Squared	0.40	0.41	0.41	0.49	0.42	0.45	0.65	0.87

B. Restaurants Only

7. Fraction of Affected Workers in 1989[e]	0.17	0.13	0.21	0.22	0.29	0.27	0.13	0.09
	(0.04)	(0.05)	(0.07)	(0.07)	(0.04)	(0.04)	(0.05)	(0.04)
8. Change in State Employment Rate[b]	—	0.80	—	1.65	—	0.25	—	-0.55
		(0.53)		(0.66)		(0.43)		(0.34)
9. Change in State Unemployment Rate[c]	—	—	0.54	2.10	—	—	-2.34	-2.44
			(0.85)	(1.15)			(0.59)	(0.60)
10. Change in Log Wage of Adult Males[d]	—	—	—	-0.39	—	—	—	0.38
				(0.29)				(0.15)
11. Region Effects	No	No	No	Yes	No	No	No	Yes
12. R-Squared	0.25	0.28	0.25	0.38	0.58	0.58	0.69	0.85

Note: Standard errors are shown in parentheses. The models are estimated on 50 state-level observations (excluding the District of Columbia), using wage data derived from Current Population Survey (CPS) files for 1989 and 1992 and employment data from *Employment and Wages— Annual Averages*. All models are estimated by ordinary least squares.

[a]The fraction of workers in the state's retail-trade industry in 1989 who earned between $3.35 and 4.24 per hour.

[b]The change in the overall employment–population rate for the state from 1989 to 1992, taken from U.S. Department of Labor, *Geographic Profiles of Unemployment and Employment.*

[c]The change in the overall unemployment rate for the state from 1989 to 1992, taken from *Geographic Profiles of Unemployment and Employment.*

[d]The change in the mean log wage of men aged 25 and older in the state from 1989 to 1992, estimated using CPS files for all 12 months of 1989 and 1992.

[e]The fraction of workers in the state's restaurant industry in 1989 who earned between $3.35 and 4.24 per hour.

approximately 300 cities. Among the items sampled by ACCRA is the price of a quarter-pound hamburger, obtained from McDonald's, where available. By linking hamburger prices for the same city over time, ACCRA price data can be used to measure city- or state-specific price changes in the fast-food industry.

Table 4.10 reports the results of our analysis of these two, alternative sources of restaurant price data. To analyze the effect of the minimum wage on the price of food eaten away from home, we used CPS data to compute the fraction of restaurant industry employees in each city who earned between $3.35 and 4.24 per hour during 1989, as well as the mean log wage of restaurant workers in

TABLE 4.10

Estimated Regression Models for Changes in City or State Averages of Prices and Wages in Restaurant Industry, 1989–1992

	Models for Change in Log Prices			Models for Change in Mean Log Wages		
	(1)	(2)	(3)	(4)	(5)	(6)
A. Estimated for 29 Cities with Price Index for Food Eaten Away from Home						
1. Fraction of Affected Workers in 1989[a]	0.11 (0.03)	0.13 (0.04)	0.06 (0.04)	0.30 (0.11)	0.28 (0.14)	0.18 (0.14)
2. Change in City Employment Rate[b]	—	−0.29 (0.33)	—	—	0.28 (1.07)	—
3. Change in City Unemployment Rate[c]	—	—	−0.69 (0.47)	—	—	−2.02 (1.52)
4. R-Squared	0.28	0.30	0.34	0.23	0.23	0.28
B. Estimated for 39 States with ACCRA Data for Quarter-Pound Hamburger						
5. Fraction of Affected Workers in 1989[d]	0.09 (0.03)	0.04 (0.03)	0.04 (0.04)	0.21 (0.07)	0.08 (0.09)	0.16 (0.12)
6. Change in State Employment Rate[e]	—	0.55 (0.22)	—	—	1.56 (0.61)	—
7. Change in State Unemployment Rate[f]	—	—	−0.60 (0.40)	—	—	−0.71 (1.18)
8. R-Squared	0.24	0.36	0.29	0.18	0.30	0.19

TABLE 4.10
(continued)

Note: Standard errors are shown in parentheses. The models in Panel A are estimated on 28 city observations, using Consumer Price Index price data for food eaten away from home and wage data derived for the city from Current Population Survey (CPS) files. The models in Panel B are estimated on 39 state observations, using price data for the cost of a quarter-pound hamburger from the American Chamber of Commerce Research Association (ACCRA), *Cost of Living Index: Comparative Data for 291 Urban Areas*, and wage data derived from CPS files. The models in Panel A are estimated by ordinary least squares. The models in Panel B are estimated by weighted least squares, using the number of price-change observations for the state as a weight.

[a]The fraction of workers in the city's retail-trade industry in 1989 who earned between $3.35 and 4.24 per hour.

[b]The change in the overall employment–population rate for the city from 1989 to 1992, taken from U.S. Department of Labor, *Geographic Profiles of Unemployment and Employment*. Data for Anchorage and Honolulu are based on state averages.

[c]The change in the overall unemployment rate for the city from 1989 to 1992, taken from *Geographic Profiles of Unemployment and Employment*. Data for Anchorage and Honolulu are based on state averages.

[d]The fraction of workers in the state's restaurant industry in 1989 who earned between $3.35 and 4.24 per hour.

[e]The change in the overall employment–population rate for the state from 1989 to 1992, taken from *Geographic Profiles of Unemployment and Employment*.

[f]The change in the overall unemployment rate for the state from 1989 to 1992, taken from *Geographic Profiles of Unemployment and Employment*.

each city during 1989 and 1992. We also obtained city-specific employment–population and unemployment rates from *Geographic Profiles of Unemployment and Employment*.[25] We then regressed the change in the log of the price index for food eaten away from home between 1989 and 1992 on the fraction of affected restaurant workers in the city in 1989 and on the labor-market indicators. For comparison purposes, we fit similar models to the change in mean log wages of restaurant workers in the 29 cities.

The estimation results are somewhat imprecise but suggest that the cost of food eaten away from home rose more quickly in cities containing higher fractions of restaurant workers affected by the federal minimum-wage increase. A comparison of the magnitude of the coefficient of the fraction-affected variable in the models for prices and wages is revealing. According to standard economic models, an increase in wages should lead to an increase in prices in proportion to the share of minimum-wage labor in total product cost. The estimates in Table 4.10 (row 1, columns 3 and 6) suggest that low-wage labor's share of cost is about one-third—not too different from the actual share of labor costs in the fast-food industry. It is also reassuring that the estimated coefficients of the fraction-affected variable in the wage-change models are similar to the coefficients that we obtained in Table 4.9.

To analyze the ACCRA hamburger-price data, we first identified the set of cities that reported hamburger prices in both the first quarter of 1990 and the first quarter of 1992.[26] We then constructed state averages of the city-specific changes in hamburger prices. Because the ACCRA reporting system is voluntary, some states are not represented in the data base.[27] Only 39 states had at least one city with data for the first quarter of both 1990 and 1992. We regressed the average change in hamburger prices for each state on the fraction of restaurant workers in the state who earned $3.35 to 4.24 per hour during 1989, and on measures of the change in overall employment or unemployment in the state between 1989 and 1992. Again, we fit a parallel set of models for the change in mean log wages of restaurant workers in the state over the same time interval.

Like the estimates based on the city-specific CPI, estimates based on the ACCRA data are imprecise but point toward a pattern of more-rapid price increases in states in which the federal minimum-wage hikes had the largest effect on wages. The ratio of the coefficients of the fraction-affected variable in the price and wage models is between 0.25 and 0.50.

On the basis of the results for these two, independent sources of price data, we conclude that restaurant prices probably increased faster in cities or states in which the 1990 and 1991 minimum-wage increases led to larger wage gains for restaurant workers. The relative rate of increase in restaurant prices as compared with restaurant workers' wages is roughly equal to the share of labor cost in the fast-food industry. Unfortunately, the results from both data sources are too imprecise to reach a more confident assessment about the effects of the minimum wage on restaurant prices.

CONCLUSIONS

The imposition of a national wage standard sets up a very useful natural experiment in which the "treatment effect" in any particular state depends on the fraction of workers initially earning less than the new minimum. By the end of the 1980s, interstate dispersion in the level of wages among teenagers and other less-skilled workers was remarkable. Many states had already passed state-specific minimum wages above the prevailing federal rate. As a result of these laws and the inherent variation in wage levels across the United States, the fraction of low-wage workers potentially affected by the

1990 and 1991 increases in the federal minimum wage ranged from less than 20 percent in some New England states and California to more than 60 percent in some southern states.

The 1990 and 1991 increases raised the minimum wage by 27 percent. Estimates in the literature suggest that this increase would lower teenage-employment rates by 3 to 8 percentage points. More importantly, however, these employment losses should have been concentrated in low-wage states, providing a test that the changes are attributable to the minimum wage. Analysis of grouped and individual-level state data confirms that the increase in the minimum wage raised average teenage wages more in states with higher fractions of affected workers than in states with lower fractions. The wage gains were as large as or slightly larger than the increases predicted by assuming that individuals earning less than the new minimum rate had their wages "topped up" to the new standard. On the other hand, there is no evidence that the increase in the minimum wage significantly lowered teenage employment rates in more highly affected states. We reach the same conclusion when we expand the analysis to include a broader set of workers, whose age, education, and other characteristics make it likely that they were affected by the increase in the minimum wage.

We use a similar methodology to examine the effect of the minimum wage on employment and wages in the retail-trade industry, and in the restaurant sector of the retail-trade industry. Again, we find a consistent pattern of wage gains associated with the increase in the federal minimum wage, but no indication of any offsetting employment losses. Indeed, our estimates for the restaurant industry suggest that employment actually increased *more rapidly* in states in which the federal minimum-wage hike generated the largest pay increases. Finally, we examine two sources of regional price data for the restaurant industry and find some tentative indication that restaurant prices rose faster in states in which wages were pushed up further by the minimum wage.

NOTES

1. The average hourly wage in Alaska was $13.53; the average in Mississippi was $7.81. These figures are based on tabulations of monthly files from the 1989 Current Population Survey (CPS).

2. The widespread setting of state minimum wages above the federal rate was unprecedented. Cullen (1961) observed, for example, that the federal minimum wage had served as a *ceiling* for state-specific minimum rates during the period from 1940 to 1960.

3. In chapter 10, we present a detailed chronology of the political process that led to the 1990–1991 increases.

4. See Bureau of National Affairs (undated, pp. 1415–22).

5. Five percent of working teenagers were self-employed, worked without pay, or failed to report earnings information. We have excluded them from the wage-interval tabulations.

6. Under the pre-1989 law, employers in retail trade, agriculture, and higher education were permitted to pay full-time students a subminimum wage 15 percent below the regular rate. The available evidence suggests that usage of this exemption was relatively low (see chapter 5).

7. This comparison is based on data from the April 1993 CPS.

8. It is also possible that some salaried workers report their net weekly wage, rather than their pretax salary.

9. We exclude from the affected group teenagers who were earning the tipped subminimum ($2.01 per hour), because the 1990 and 1991 increases in the federal minimum wage had only a minor effect on the tipped minimum.

10. This prediction ignores any employment effects of the minimum wage. As we shall show, however, no loss of employment seems to have occurred after the increases in the minimum wage.

11. This figure is based on tabulations of log hourly wages for men aged 25 and older in the 1989 and 1992 CPS files.

12. For example, a regression of the teenage employment rate on the overall employment rate and on a linear trend, estimated with data for 1975–1989, gives the following equation:

$$\text{Teenage Employment} = \text{Constant} - 0.86 \times \text{Trend} + 2.17 \times \text{Overall Employment Rate}.$$

The R-Squared of the model is 0.99.

13. The low-impact group includes 15 states plus the District of Columbia, most of which had passed state-specific minimum wages above $3.35 per hour: Alaska, California, Delaware, District of Columbia, Hawaii, Maryland, Minnesota, Nevada, all the New England states, New Jersey, New York, and Washington. The high-impact group contains a mix of southern, mountain, and northcentral states: Arkansas, Kentucky, Louisiana, Mississippi, Montana, New Mexico, North Dakota, Oklahoma, South Carolina, South Dakota, Tennessee, West Virginia, and Wyoming. The medium-impact group includes the remaining 22 states.

14. The typical sampling errors of the quarterly employment rates in the three state groups are as follows: for the high-impact group, 1.5 percentage points; for the medium-impact group, 0.9 percentage points; and for the low-impact group, 1.1 percentage points.

15. This aggregate variable is taken from *Geographic Profiles of Unemployment and Employment,* published by the U.S. Department of Labor, Bureau of Labor Statistics, rather than from the CPS files.

16. The published employment data, taken from *Geographic Profiles of Employment and Unemployment*, are based on the full CPS sample in each month, rather than on the one-quarter sample available on the microdata files that we use.

17. A model for the change in mean log wages of teenagers yields a coefficient for the adult male wage of 0.35, with a standard error of 0.28. The estimated coefficients of the fraction-affected variable and the overall employment–population rate are essentially the same as the coefficients reported in column 2, panel C, of Table 4.4.

18. When both the overall employment–population rate and the overall unemployment rate are included as cyclical indicators, the unemployment-rate variables are jointly insignificant and have generally small estimated coefficients, whereas the employment–population variables retain their statistical significance.

19. See chapter 10 for a detailed discussion of the various federal minimum-wage bills that were introduced during the late 1980s. This bill was passed by the House and Senate but was vetoed by the President.

20. To construct this measure, we estimated a linear probability model for the vote on H.R. 2 as a simple function of party affiliation, and then used the average residual from this model, by state.

21. This statement is not quite true, as one might expect state-specific minimum-wage increases to be more likely in states with stronger teenage employment growth. In this case, employment growth from 1986 to 1989 may be correlated with the presence of a state wage floor above $3.35 per hour in 1989, and with the fraction-affected variable.

22. To obtain these estimates, we multiplied 0.22 times the change in the fraction of workers in the affected wage range from 1989 to 1992, from the top row of Table 4.8.

23. See, for example, U.S. Department of Labor, Bureau of Labor Statistics, *Employment and Wages—Annual Averages*, 1990 edition, page 1. The Unemployment Insurance reports are also known as ES-202 reports.

24. The fraction-affected variable has a probability value of 12 percent in the retail-trade model, and 3 percent in the restaurant-industry model.

25. These rates are available for all but 2 of the 29 cities for which Consumer Price Index data are available. For Honolulu and Anchorage, we used employment and unemployment data for Hawaii and Alaska, respectively.

26. A total of 208 cities have data for both 1990-I and 1992-I.

27. Personal communication with Mr. Edward Sturgeon, of ACCRA, November 1991.

CHAPTER 5

Additional Employment Outcomes

> Everything should be made as simple as possible, but not
> simpler.
>
> —Albert Einstein

IN ADDITION TO its implications for employment, the standard economic model of the labor market makes a number of predictions about the impact of a binding minimum wage on other outcomes. For example, firms that are compelled by the minimum to increase wages are expected to respond by reducing fringe benefits, charging uniform fees, and using other means to evade the law's effect. When permitted, *any* firm that previously hired eligible workers at a wage that was less than the minimum wage is expected to use a subminimum wage. In addition, a binding minimum wage should lead firms to reduce investments in worker training. Finally, some firms are expected to respond to the minimum wage by moving to the "underground" sector and not complying with the law. The research discussed in this chapter investigates the effect of the minimum on several employment-related outcomes. We begin by examining the impact of the minimum wage on the distribution of wages, and then discuss the subminimum wage. Next, we examine whether firms cut fringe benefits and training in response to a minimum wage. Finally, we examine whether the minimum wage influences the rate of applications for jobs and turnover.

To preview the chapter's main conclusions, we document several anomalous findings from the standpoint of the standard model of the low-wage labor market. First, substantial wage dispersion for seemingly identical workers and jobs exists that cannot be explained easily in the context of the conventional model. Second, a sizable spike in the wage distribution occurs at the minimum wage. Brown (1988) noted that this spike is an indication that people with presumably different ability levels earn the same wage—a phenomenon that is at variance with the assumptions of the standard model. Perhaps even more puzzling, a spike in the wage distribution occurs at the minimum wage even for firms that are exempt from the minimum wage. Third, an increase in the minimum wage has a spillover effect in some firms, causing workers earning above the minimum to receive raises. The spillover effect probably does not extend very far up the wage distribution, however. Fourth, several studies have found that youth subminimum wages are hardly ever used by employers in the United States. For example, only a small percentage of fast-food restaurants took advantage of the youth subminimum wage when it was available during 1990–1993, even though they paid teenagers less than the subminimum before the minimum wage was increased. Finally, firms do not appear to offset increases in the minimum wage with reductions in fringe benefits or in employer-provided on-the-job training.

Each of these findings is puzzling from the standpoint of the simplest version of the conventional model, and, taken together, they further lead one to question the applicability of that model to the low-wage segment of the labor market. The alternative models discussed in chapter 11 are capable of explaining some of these anomalous findings, although some of the findings are anomalies in the context of the alternative models as well.

Effects on the Distribution of Wages

The Law of One Price and the Minimum-Wage Spike

The "law of one price" asserts that identical commodities should trade for the same price. In the labor market, it implies that workers with equal skills should be paid the same compensation (where compensation is broadly construed to reflect pay, fringe benefits, and working conditions). The law of one price has a strong intuitive appeal in the impersonal commodity and financial markets, in which identical bundles of goods are traded continuously to agents whose sole interest is private financial gain. Under these conditions, any difference in prices between identical goods would quickly be arbitraged away. In the labor market, however, a variety of factors might prevent the law of one price from operating. For example, if workers' motivation and work effort depend on whether they believe that they are paid adequately or treated fairly, then it may be in a firm's interest to set wages with an eye toward motivating workers, rather than simply paying the minimum salary necessary.

Economists have long debated whether equally skilled workers receive equal compensation in different sectors of the labor market. Beginning with Slichter (1950), economists have documented large and persistent wage differentials for workers in different industries. For example, auto companies consistently pay a higher wage for janitors than do service companies. Moreover, larger firms tend to pay higher wages than do smaller firms (see Brown and Medoff [1989]). Wage variability that apparently violates the law of one price also has been documented across firms in specific occupations and industries. For example, airline pilots who fly the same type of aircraft receive dramatically different pay rates at different airlines (Card [1989]). Revisionist economists such as Richard Lester interpreted wage variability for seemingly identical workers as an indication that the neoclassical model is incomplete, and that the simple marginalist interpretation of the minimum wage may not apply.

One difficulty with this line of research, however, is that it is not clear whether the differentials represent compensation for differences in the average level of skills possessed by workers in different firms. Studies have tried two main approaches to control for differences in workers' skills that may justify wage premiums. First, many studies have explicitly held constant workers' characteristics, including occupation, level of educational attainment, and work experience. Second, several studies have used longitudinal data to estimate wage differentials for the same workers as they move from industry to industry, or from small firms to large firms.[1] Although the interindustry and firm-size wage differentials appear to be robust in these statistical approaches, it is nonetheless possible that the differentials are the result of unobserved differences in workers' skills or unmeasured aspects of working conditions.

The significance of wage variability for identical workers is as follows: If identical workers at different firms are offered different compensation for performing the same tasks, then the wage structure is in part determined by forces outside the standard model. Moreover, the fact that wages differ across firms for seemingly identical workers is consistent with the notion that employers have some degree of flexibility to set wages in order to accomplish a variety of aims, such as motivating workers, facilitating recruitment, reducing turnover, or creating loyalty. As we shall see in chapter 11, economic models predict that a modest increase in the minimum wage may lead to increased employment if firms set their pay levels for reasons other than simply meeting a uniform market-wage rate.

In view of the literature on interfirm wage variability, it is probably not surprising that wage variability also exists across employers in the low-wage segment of the labor market. In chapter 2, we documented the existence of differences in entry-level wages across fast-food restaurants (see Figure 2.2). For example, the coefficient of variation of entry-level wages across restaurants was 7 percent before the New Jersey state minimum increased in 1992, and the extent of wage dispersion may have been reduced already by the federal minimum, which was paid to new hires by one-third of all restaurants. Although it is possible that much of this wage variability is the result of regional differences in labor-market conditions, we find considerable wage variability even within labor markets defined by the three-digit ZIP code of the restaurants. Three-digit ZIP-code locations account for only 17 percent of inter-restaurant wage variability. In other words, even restaurants that are located near each other pay different starting wages.

An increase in the minimum wage compresses wage dispersion. Most visibly, an increase in the minimum wage produces a spike in the distribution of wage rates at the minimum. This phenomenon is apparent for starting wages of the fast-food restaurants discussed in chapter 2 (see Figure 2.2). When the minimum wage in New Jersey was increased to $5.05 per hour, the coefficient of variation of starting wages among fast-food restaurants in the state fell from 7 percent to less than 2 percent. Furthermore, wage data on fast-food restaurants in Texas show exactly the same pattern over the period during which the federal minimum wage rose from $3.35 to 4.25 per hour: a decrease in the coefficient of variation of wages from 7 percent prior to April 1990 to 2 percent in August 1991.

A spike in the overall wage distribution at the minimum wage is also evident in Figures 5.1.A–C. These figures show the proportion of teenage workers whose wages fell within each 5-cent interval between $3.00 and 7.00 per hour, with the intervals containing $3.35, 3.80, and 4.25 per hour highlighted.[2] The wage data pertain to the months of April through August of 1989, 1990, and 1991. During 1989, the minimum wage was $3.35 per hour, and, in Figure 5.1.A, a sizable spike in the wage distribution is apparent at $3.35. After the minimum wage increased to $3.80 per hour on April 1, 1990, the spike at $3.35 decreased, and a new spike arose at $3.80.[3] The spike at $3.80 is especially significant in view of the fact that very few workers were paid $3.80 per hour prior to the increase in the minimum. Between 1989 and 1990, the share of workers earning within 5 cents of $3.35 per hour (i.e., from $3.30 to 3.40 per hour) fell from 17.4 to 4.1 percent, while the share earning within 5 cents of $3.80 per hour increased from 5.6 to 15.9 percent. Figure 5.1.C shows that the spike in the wage distribution moved again, to $4.25 per hour in 1991, after the minimum wage was increased to that level on April 1, 1991. Indeed, with 24 percent of teenagers paid exactly $4.25 per hour, the minimum wage became the modal wage rate for teenage workers.

The spike in the wage distribution at the minimum wage is one of the most persistent and distinctive features of observed wage distri-

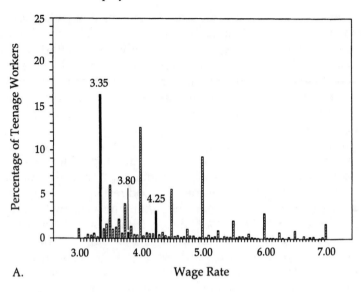

A.

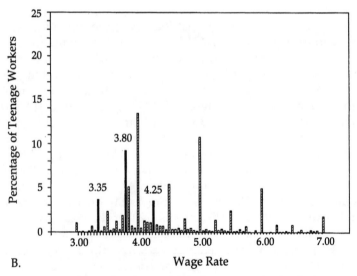

B.

Figure 5.1 Histogram of teenagers' hourly wages. A. April–August 1989.
B. April–August 1990.

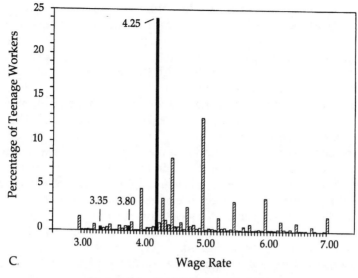

Figure 5.1 C. April–August 1991.

butions. In the context of the law of one price, the spike should come as a major surprise: if, prior to the increase in the minimum wage, all workers were paid a wage that equalled their productivity level, then the existence of the spike implies that workers with different productivity levels are paid the same wage after the rise in the minimum. Indeed, before large data sets containing microdata on wage rates became available, many economists predicted that the wage distribution in the covered sector simply would be truncated at the minimum wage; that is, the minimum wage would simply take a "bite" out of the part of the wage distribution that was below the minimum. For example, in his classic article, Stigler (1946) hypothesized that, ". . . workers whose services are worth less than the minimum wage are discharged." Contrary to this expectation, Figure 5.1 indicates that many workers who had been paid less than the new minimum wage prior to the increase are moved up to the new minimum wage.

Of course, it is possible that, when the minimum wage increases, firms reduce nonwage compensation or increase the pace of work for employees who had been paid less than the minimum. These actions would generate a "smooth" distribution of total compensation costs, even though wages display a spike at the minimum. For example, fringe benefits could be reduced by 90 cents per hour for a worker who originally was paid $3.35 per hour, enabling the employer to pay $4.25 per hour when the minimum increased to that level. We address the issue of nonwage offsets later in this chapter. For now, suffice it to say that the finding of a spike at the minimum wage is consistent with the view that the law of one price did not hold to begin with, so employees with the same productive capacity originally were paid differently.

Another curious aspect of the spike in the wage distribution at the minimum wage is that it appears to exist even for firms that are *not covered* by the minimum wage, albeit to a lesser extent than for covered firms. In a two-sector model of the labor market in which firms in one sector are covered by the minimum wage and firms in the other sector are uncovered by the minimum (or choose not to comply with the minimum), we would expect workers who lose their jobs in the covered sector to seek work in the uncovered sector, thereby depressing wages of low-skilled workers already in the uncovered sector (see chapter 11 for discussion of this model). Thus, one would not expect to find many workers earning the minimum wage in the uncovered sector, because the sector has an excess supply of low-skilled workers. In a study prepared for the Minimum Wage Study Commission, however, Fritsch (1981) found that many retail establishments that were uncovered by the law because their sales volumes were too low tended to pay the minimum wage anyway. Indeed, a noticeable spike in the wage distribution occurs at the minimum wage for firms that are exempt from the wage floor.

We find a related phenomenon for individuals who work at firms that do not pay Social Security taxes. Our analysis is based on the Employee Benefits Supplement of the April 1993 Current Population Survey (CPS), which asked workers, among other questions, whether their employers deducted Social Security taxes from their earnings. In the CPS, about 8 percent of workers reported that their employers did not do so. Both the mean and standard deviation of wages are higher for workers in firms that did not deduct Social Security taxes than for those in firms that did.[4] Ten percent of workers in firms that failed to deduct Social Security taxes were paid less than the minimum wage, compared with 2 percent of workers in firms that did deduct these taxes. Most employers who fail to deduct Social Security taxes probably are exempt from the Fair Labor Standards Act (FLSA) or would not feel compelled to comply with the minimum wage even if they were covered.[5] Using the April 1993 data set, we estimate that 2.3 percent of workers whose employers contribute Social Security taxes are paid exactly the minimum wage ($4.25 per hour), and that 1.5 percent of those whose employers do not pay Social Security taxes are paid exactly the minimum wage. Thus, the concentration of workers at the minimum for firms that do not pay Social Security taxes is almost two-thirds as large as it is for firms that comply with the Social Security law. This finding provides additional confirmation that many firms that do not have to pay the minimum wage pay it anyway.[6]

Although the conventional two-sector model has difficulty explaining the spike in the wage distribution at the minimum for firms that are not required to comply with the law, an alternative explanation is that the minimum wage becomes a focal point, representing the going, or acceptable, wage. Employers who are not compelled to pay the minimum wage might choose to pay it because workers perceive the minimum wage as the "fair" wage. In this way, the minimum wage might influence workers' reservation wages. Moreover, if there is an element of arbitrariness or indeterminacy in the wage distribution prior to the imposition of a minimum, then many employers might believe that paying the minimum wage is no less arbitrary than is paying some other amount, and that it might have the added benefit of engendering greater employee loyalty.

Another result of a minimum-wage hike is the attenuation of existing wage differentials associated with employer or employee characteristics. For example, Katz and Krueger (1992) found that, before the federal minimum-wage increase in April 1990, company-owned fast-food restaurants and restaurants located in low-unemployment-rate counties in Texas paid significantly higher wages than did other restaurants in the state.[7] Indeed, before the rise in the minimum wage, company ownership status and local unemployment rates accounted for 28 percent of the variability in the starting wage rate. By August 1991—after the minimum had increased from $3.35 to 4.25 per hour—the wage differentials associated with company-ownership and the local unemployment rate were statistically insignificant, and these explanatory variables accounted for only 5 percent of the variability in starting wages.

Finally, we note that evidence on the existence of discrimination in labor markets violates the law of one price. By definition, discrimination means that equally productive workers are paid differently because of personal characteristics. Several studies have documented the existence of wage differentials that apparently result from racial or gender discrimination in the U.S. labor market.[8] In addition, Hamermesh and Biddle (1994) and Sargent and Blanchflower (1994) found that employees with more attractive appearances earn higher wages, even within occupations.[9] We emphasize that allegations of discrimination are not confined to high-wage employers; for example, the Wendy's, Denny's, Shoney's, and Taco Bell fast-food chains have all been sued recently for racial discrimination against employees and customers.[10]

If low-wage employers are able to discriminate against some employees on the basis of personal characteristics that are unrelated to productivity, then it seems that the low-wage labor market is not as competitive as is assumed in the textbook model, and that the sharp predictions of the textbook model on the effect of a minimum wage may not apply. Lester (1994), for example, noted that in the 1940s and 1950s many southern textile employers paid higher wages to white workers than black workers performing the same jobs. Starting from this situation, it is possible that employers would not lay off black workers if their wages were raised by the minimum wage, contrary to the predictions of the standard model.

Wage Spillover Effects

Casual observation suggests that the minimum wage sometimes has a spillover, or ripple, effect, meaning that when the minimum increases the wages of some workers may rise *above* the new minimum, and the wages of workers who already were earning slightly more than the minimum may increase as well. The existence of a spillover effect poses a problem with respect to some versions of the standard model, because any worker who previously earned a wage that was less than the minimum wage should not be paid more than the minimum as a result of an increase.

Industry experts frequently allude to a ripple effect of minimum wages. For example, Jeffrey Stoller, of the New Jersey Business & Industry Association, has said, "It's not just what happens to minimum-wage earners; its the ripple effect. . . . People earning above minimum expect more once the [wage] goes up because they are upset if someone just starting earns more or as much as they do."[11] Similarly, in its 1992 annual report, SG&A Company reported:

> The only groups of employees directly affected by these increases [in the federal minimum wage] were the Company's part-time sales associates and, beginning with the fiscal 1991 increase, certain employees at the Company's Distribution Center. The direct impact of the increases in the hourly minimum wage rate on the Company in fiscal 1991 and 1990 was to increase SG&A expenses by less than one percent. *The increases in the minimum wage also had a slight ripple effect on the salaries of other groups of store and distribution employees.* (Italics added.)

The first empirical study on whether minimum-wage increases have a spillover effect was conducted by Grossman (1983). For each of seven occupations, Grossman related the change in the average wage to contemporaneous and lagged changes in the minimum wage across 16 SMSAs for the years 1960–1975. Her results indicated that wages became more compressed immediately following a minimum-wage increase, but that the wage structure gradually returned to its original state. Grossman argued that the eventual fanning out of the wage structure after the rise in the minimum is consistent with a spillover effect. One difficulty in interpreting the results, however, is that wages could eventually become less compressed after a minimum-wage increase because inflation has eroded the value of the minimum wage.

The second wave of the survey of Texas fast-food restaurants described in chapter 2 collected direct information on how *within-firm* wage policies responded to the April 1991 increase in the federal minimum wage.[12] In particular, suppose that, before April 1991, a firm paid $3.80 per hour to newly hired workers, and that, after April 1991, it increased its starting hourly wage to $4.25. What did this firm do to the pay of more senior workers who were already earning, say, $4.00 per hour? The survey results presented in row 3 of Table 5.1 indicate that 16 percent of firms in this situation increased the wages of workers earning $4.00 per hour to an amount above the new starting wage, thereby maintaining their wage hierarchies. After the minimum-wage increase took effect, one-third of the restaurants that started workers between $3.80 and 4.25 per hour increased the pay of incumbent workers who were earning more than the entry salary but less than the new minimum to *above* $4.25.

A similar question was asked in the earlier wave of the Texas survey: specifically, what happened to the wages of workers who were earning more than $3.35 per hour, but less than $3.80 per hour, when the federal minimum wage rose from $3.35 to $3.80? The results indicated that 41 percent of restaurants in this situation maintained their relative wage structures. Thus, firms were more likely to preserve wage differentials between new workers and long-service workers after the 1990 increase in the minimum wage than after the 1991 increase. A possible explanation for the apparently lower level of concern for internal equity after the 1991 increase is that, relative to the 1990 minimum wage, the 1991 minimum was farther above the equilibrium wage level.

A related question is whether firms increase the pay of workers who are already earning more than the new minimum wage when the minimum goes up. As shown in row 4 of Table 5.1, restaurants with higher starting wages prior to the April 1991 minimum wage increase were more likely to grant raises to workers who were already earning $4.50 per hour. Among restaurants with the lowest initial starting wages (column 1) only 9 percent granted wage in-

TABLE 5.1

Responses of Texas Fast-Food Restaurants to Change in Minimum Wage, by Starting Wage Before April 1, 1991

	Starting Wage = $3.80 (1)	Starting Wage $3.80–4.25 (2)	Starting Wage ≥$4.25 (3)
1. Average Starting Wage Before April 1, 1991 ($)	3.80	3.93	4.28
2. Increase in Starting Wage from April 1 to December 1991 ($)	0.46	0.37	0.20
3. Proportion Maintaining Wage Hierarchy[a]	0.16	0.33	—
4. Proportion with Spillovers to Workers Earning $4.50 per Hour[b]	0.09	0.29	0.60
5. Proportion Decreasing Amount of First Pay Raise	0.05	0.03	0.00
6. Proportion Increasing Time to First Pay Raise	0.03	0.05	0.00
7. Proportion Using the Youth Subminimum	0.06	0.03	0.06
8. Proportion that Cut Fringe Benefits	0.04	0.04	0.06
9. Sample Size	174	122	17

Source: Based on Katz and Krueger (1992), Table 3.

[a]The "proportion maintaining wage hierarchy" is the fraction of restaurants that, after April 1, 1991, paid a wage above the restaurant's new starting wage to workers who had been earning between the restaurant's starting wage and $4.25 per hour before April 1, 1991.

[b]The "proportion with spillovers to workers earning $4.50 per hour" is the fraction of restaurants that, after the minimum-wage increase took effect, increased the pay of workers who had been earning $4.50 per hour.

creases to workers earning $4.50 per hour when the minimum rose to $4.25. Among restaurants with higher starting wages rates (column 2 and 3), the corresponding fractions are higher. Thus, there is some evidence of wage spillovers for workers who were earning more than the new minimum wage, but mainly at firms where the starting wage was already relatively high.

We also examined whether, in response to an increase in the minimum wage, firms delayed the time until workers received their first

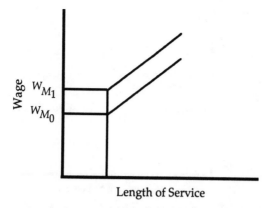

Figure 5.2 The tenure-earnings profile before and after an increase in the minimum wage, assuming no change in the amount or timing of seniority raises. W_{M_0} represents the minimum wage before the increase, W_{M_1} represents the wage after the increase.

pay raise, or reduced the amount of the first raise. Rows 5 and 6 of Table 5.1 provide some information on this issue. Although restaurants that were forced by the minimum-wage increase to raise their starting wage are more likely to delay the first raise they give to workers, and to reduce the amount of the first raise, only a small proportion of firms took these actions. For the majority of firms that did not delay pay raises or reduce the amount of raises, the tenure-earnings profiles before and after the minimum-wage increase correspond to those presented in Figure 5.2. In the long run, a lack of adjustment of pay raises will lead to a spillover effect, because the entire wage structure will ratchet up. For firms that did alter the timing or amount of raises, the tenure-earnings profiles correspond to those presented in Figure 5.3.A or 5.3.B.

Figures 5.4.A and 5.4.B shed some light on the importance of spillover effects more generally. These figures present the fraction of teenage workers earning less than $4.50 per hour and less than $5.00 per hour during each quarter from 1989 to 1992.[13] Following the approach used in chapter 4, we classified the states into three groups depending on whether the fraction of teenagers directly affected by the minimum-wage increase was high, medium, or low. In chapter 4, we found that, if anything, total teenage employment increased more in the states with a higher fraction of teenagers affected by the minimum-wage hikes. Given this finding, if there were no spillover effects beyond $4.50 per hour, then we would expect the fractions of

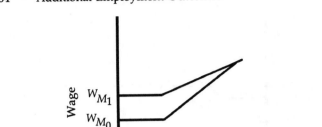

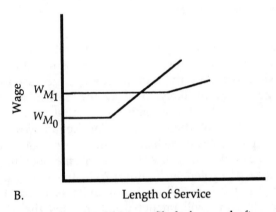

Figure 5.3   A. The tenure-earnings profile before and after an increase in the minimum wage. W_{M_0} represents the minimum wage before the increase, W_{M_1} represents the minimum wage after the increase. A. Firms reduce the amount of seniority increases, leading to spillover effects. B. Firms defer seniority increases, leading to a cross-over of the tenure-earning profiles.

workers paid less than $4.50 and less than $5.00 to be unchanged in the high-impact states relative to the low-impact states. If spillover effects extended beyond $4.50 but not beyond $5.00, then we would expect the fraction of workers paid less than $5.00 per hour to follow the same trend in high-impact and low-impact states, but we would expect a relative reduction in the fraction of workers paid less than $4.50 per hour in the high-impact states.

The figures provide some support for the existence of spillover

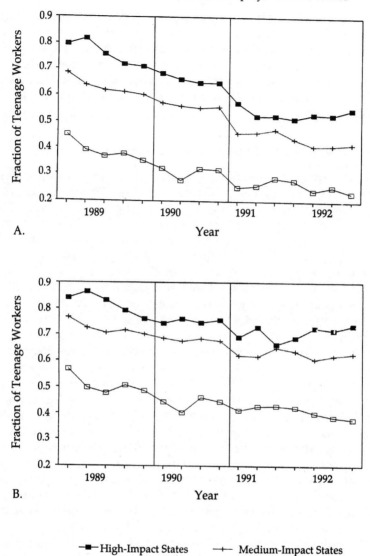

Figure 5.4 Fractions of teenagers earning less than $4.50 and 5.00 per hour, 1989–1992. A. Fraction earning less than $4.50 per hour. B. Fraction earning less than $5.00 per hour.

effects up to $4.50 per hour, but little evidence of spillovers beyond $4.50. In high-impact states, for example, the fraction of workers earning less than $4.50 per hour fell from 80 percent in early 1989 to 50 percent after the April 1991 minimum-wage increase. In the low-impact states, the fraction paid less than $4.50 per hour decreased as well, but the decrease was not as sharp nor as large as in the low- or medium-impact states.

The Curiously Low Utilization of Subminimum Wages

In some circumstances, the FLSA permits employers to pay designated groups of workers a subminimum wage. Expanding coverage of the subminimum wage was an important component of the Bush administration's minimum-wage policy. Indeed, in June 1989, President Bush vetoed the Kennedy-Hawkins amendments to the FLSA, explaining, "I made it clear that I could accept an increase [in the minimum wage] only if it were a modest one, and only if it were accompanied by a meaningful training wage for new employees of a firm, to help offset the job loss" (Bureau of National Affairs [1989]). Amendments to the FLSA that were passed during 1989 enabled employers to pay newly hired teenage workers a subminimum wage that was 15 percent less than the minimum, for as long as six months. The youth subminimum was enacted for a three-year trial period. Although the FLSA had permitted payment of a subminimum wage to full-time students since 1961, the new legislation expanded coverage of the subminimum to all teenagers and made it easier for firms to obtain a subminimum exemption. Essentially, employers could pay a subminimum wage to teenage employees for as long as 90 days without providing additional training or filing any special paperwork. An employer could continue to pay a subminimum wage for an additional 90 days if a suitable training plan was filed with the Department of Labor, but no employee could be paid a subminimum wage for longer than 180 days.[14]

The rationale for the subminimum wage is to allow employers to hire inexperienced workers who otherwise would be unemployable, because their productivity is below the level of the minimum wage. This logic is inescapable in the standard model. Indeed, the standard model predicts that *every* employer who paid a worker less than the new minimum wage prior to an increase in the minimum would take advantage of the subminimum-wage provision, if permitted. A wealth of experience now indicates, however, that employers very rarely take advantage of youth subminimum wages.

Freeman, Gray, and Ichniowski (1981) found that, during the late

1970s, only 3 percent of students' work hours were paid the sub-minimum wage that applied to full-time students. On the basis of the survey of Texas fast-food restaurants described in chapter 2, Katz and Krueger (1992) concluded that fewer than 4.8 percent of fast-food restaurants used the youth subminimum wage during 1991 (see row 7 of Table 5.1). In a similar survey, Spriggs, Swinton, and Simmons (1992) found that fewer than 2 percent of fast-food restaurants in Mississippi and North Carolina used the subminimum. Moreover, in a nonrandom survey of restaurants conducted by the National Restaurant Association, only 8 percent of restaurants were found to have used the youth subminimum.[15] Katz and Krueger (1990) found that the introduction of the youth subminimum in 1990 had no discernable effect on teenage workers' wages. Additional confirmation that firms rarely use the subminimum wage is presented in Figure 5.1.C: no spike is evident in the interval of the wage distribution that contains $3.62 (the 1991 subminimum wage). Finally, and perhaps most definitively, a 1993 Department of Labor study based on the Wage and Hour Survey found that only 1 percent of all employers used the federal subminimum wage, and that only 2 percent of employers who paid at least one worker the minimum did so.[16]

Why don't more employers use the subminimum wage? In some cases, employers offer their workers a starting wage that is higher than the minimum wage. In others, they do not hire teenage workers and therefore do not have an opportunity to use the youth subminimum. But this is not the case for most fast-food restaurants. The fast-food industry has lobbied against increases in the minimum wage and has been a staunch supporter of a subminimum wage for youths (Bureau of National Affairs [1985]). Just before the minimum wage increased to $4.25 per hour, 95 percent of Texas fast-food restaurants were offering new workers an hourly wage rate that was less than $4.25. Furthermore, the fast-food industry has an extremely high turnover rate—estimated to be as high as 300 percent per year (Bureau of National Affairs [1985]). This fact, combined with the fact that the industry hires many first-time workers, makes it highly likely that fast-food restaurants can take advantage of the youth subminimum.[17]

In the second wave of the Texas fast-food restaurant survey, Katz and Krueger (1992) examined reasons for the low utilization of the subminimum wage. In 1991, 62 percent of restaurant managers who were not using the subminimum wage believed they could not "attract *qualified* teenage workers at a subminimum wage" (italics added). This finding is remarkable, because the vast majority of these restaurants were hiring workers at less than \$4.25 per hour prior to the increase in the minimum wage. One explanation for the finding is that, after the increase in the minimum wage, restaurants could no longer attract enough workers at the former wage because the rise in the minimum wage increased potential applicants' reservation wages. Managers might also believe that relative pay is important to workers, and that young workers will not accept jobs, or will shirk, if they are paid less than older workers for the same work.

The survey also found that about 20 percent of managers at firms that did not use a subminimum wage believed that it is not "fair" to do so. About one-half of responding managers believed that their restaurants would use the subminimum wage if it could be paid to all workers, not just to teenage workers. Twenty-three percent responded that the difficulty of applying for the subminimum wage was at least one of the reasons why their restaurants did not offer it. Finally, about one-third stated that their restaurants would use the subminimum wage if it were easier to administer (for example, if the time limitation or training requirement were eliminated). Although one could argue that bureaucratic red tape discouraged employers from using the subminimum wage, the level of administrative effort required to use it was relatively light. If such a small administrative burden did discourage its usage, the perceived benefits of the subminimum wage must have been slight.

Given the limited use of the subminimum wage, it is probably not surprising that Congress did not renew it in 1993. Moreover, there was hardly any notice paid in the popular press when the subminimum wage expired. There is a wide consensus that the subminimum wage did not generate additional job training or expand employment.

NONWAGE OFFSETS

Fringe Benefits

The textbook model of a minimum wage typically ignores fringe benefits and other nonwage compensation, yet even workers in low-wage firms receive some fringe benefits. A natural response by firms to a legislated minimum wage increase is to reduce nonwage compensation. Several economists have argued that the *rents* created for workers by a minimum-wage hike are partially or even totally offset by reductions in nonwage benefits. The reason for this prediction is that, in a competitive labor market, an increase in the minimum will produce a queue of workers for minimum-wage jobs. Employers would therefore be able to cut nonwage compensation yet continue to recruit a sufficient number of workers.

There are several reasons why employers may not want to—or may not be able to—reduce nonwage benefits by enough to offset the rise in the minimum wage.[18] First, employers might gain by providing some rents to workers. For example, a wage premium might reduce turnover, enhance recruiting, or reduce shirking. Second, some nonwage benefits cannot be cut exclusively for minimum-wage workers.[19] For example, fast-food restaurants cannot eliminate air conditioning for their lowest-wage workers without affecting working conditions for other employees and the environment for their customers. Finally, some employers may be bound by non-negativity constraints—they simply do not offer enough fringe benefits that a reduction in fringes can offset a significant rise in the minimum wage.

The quantitative importance of nonwage offsets in response to a minimum-wage increase is an open question. Certainly, minimum-wage workers are less likely than higher-wage workers to receive employer-provided health insurance and other fringe benefits, but this disparity might occur simply because fringe benefits are a "normal good"—higher-wage workers "use" some of their compensation to purchase nonwage benefits. There is also a tax incentive that encourages higher-wage workers to desire greater fringe benefits, because the benefits are not treated as taxable income.

Several studies have directly examined the extent to which minimum-wage increases are offset by reductions in fringe benefits. Wessels (1980) found that fewer than 1 percent of retail stores reported reducing year-end bonuses, paid vacations, sick leave, or store discount privileges in response to New York State's minimum-wage increase in 1957. Alpert (1986) found evidence that, during the 1970s, the restaurant industry responded to large increases in the minimum wage with modest reductions in fringe benefits. At best, the literature supports a conclusion that reductions in fringe benefits only partially offset the higher compensation costs of a minimum-wage hike.

We pursued the issue of fringe benefits in our New Jersey–Pennsylvania survey of fast-food restaurants. Perhaps surprisingly, 91 percent of restaurants offered at least some fringe benefits to workers. The most common fringe benefit was free or low-priced meals. We found no evidence that New Jersey restaurants reduced fringe benefits after the increase in the New Jersey minimum wage took effect. As discussed in chapter 2, restaurants that were affected directly by the increase were no more likely than restaurants in Pennsylvania or than high-wage restaurants in New Jersey to cut back on free meals. Similarly, row 8 of Table 5.1 indicates that Texas fast-food restaurants that were forced by the 1991 federal minimum-wage increase to raise pay the most were no more likely to cut fringe benefits than were higher-wage fast-food restaurants in the state. With respect to observable fringe benefits, the evidence suggests small offsets in response to minimum wage hikes, at most. We return to this issue later in this chapter, in our examination of job queues and turnover.

Training

Because the human-capital model predicts that employees partially pay for training by accepting a lower initial wage, a minimum-wage increase might affect the ability of firms to provide training. Rather than directly examining the provision of on-the-job training before and after minimum-wage changes, however, tests of this hypothesis primarily have been based on evidence on wage profiles. In the human-capital model, workers' wages are expected to rise as a result of job training. Therefore, a reduction in the rate of wage growth after a minimum-wage hike would provide indirect evidence that training is reduced. Leighton and Mincer (1981) and Hashimoto (1982) examined the impact of a higher minimum wage on wage growth rates and found that a higher minimum wage is associated with lower wage growth. They interpreted this finding as evidence that training is reduced in response to a higher minimum wage. By contrast, Lazear and Miller (1981) found that extending the minimum wage to newly covered industries does not seem to alter the rate of wage growth in these industries. Lazear and Miller (p. 348) interpreted their finding as evidence that, "industries selected for new coverage are those least likely to suffer any ill effects."

There are two principal problems with an indirect test of job-training-offsets based on the rate of wage growth.[20] First, wages can grow over time as a result of factors other than job training. One hypothesis is that steep wage profiles provide a disincentive against shirking (see Becker and Stigler [1974] and Lazear [1981]). If an increase in the minimum wage creates rents for workers, then workers will value their jobs more and will be less likely to shirk. Following a rise in the minimum wage, employers would be able to flatten the wage profile, since they do not have to offer as much of an incentive to prevent shirking. Second, the training-offset hypothesis implies that the total amount of training accumulated by more senior workers will be lower after an increase in the minimum wage. Thus, one would expect a rise in the minimum wage to lead to an experience–earnings profile that actually *crosses* the previous profile, as shown in Figure 5.3.B. Tests of the training-offset hypothesis have not focused directly on whether the profiles cross, but have only investigated whether the wage profile is flatter when the minimum wage is higher. It is entirely possible that a rise in the minimum wage increases the entry level wage and lowers the slope of the experience profile, but that workers of *all* experience levels earn higher wages when the minimum is higher (as in Figure 5.3.A). In this case, one could not presume that job training was reduced, since the more-senior workers are not earning lower wages. Our finding that fast-food restaurants do not delay the time until a pay raise or reduce the amount of the raises is consistent with the view that wages are higher at all levels of seniority after a minimum-wage increase.

We provide additional evidence on this issue in Figure 5.5. This figure shows the age–earnings profiles in California and in five comparison areas in 1987 and 1989, before and after the July 1988 increase in the California minimum wage. Each point represents the mean log wage of workers in the specified age range. As one would expect, the age–earnings profiles are upward sloping. In 1987, the geometric average wage of 16- and 17-year-old workers in both California and the comparison areas was \$3.67 per hour (= exp[1.3]). The California minimum wage increased to \$4.25 per hour during

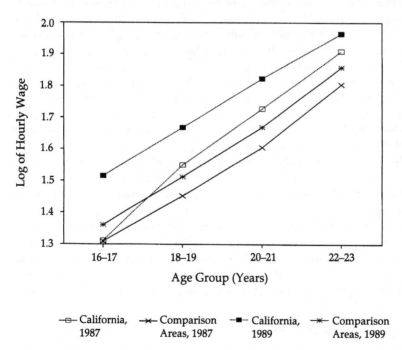

Figure 5.5 Wage profiles for young workers, California and comparison areas, 1987–1989.

1988, and the mean wage of the workers in the state shifted up considerably, whereas the mean wage of 16- to 17-year-old workers in the comparison areas increased only slightly. The figure shows that the age–earnings profile became relatively flatter for California workers than for workers in the comparison areas after the increase in the minimum wage but that the profiles do not cross. Indeed, the age–earnings profile in California looks more like the profile in the comparison areas *after* the increase in the minimum wage than before. It is certainly difficult to infer from this figure that training was reduced by the rise in the minimum wage.

In a recent paper, Grossberg and Sicilian (1994) attempted to measure the impact of the minimum wage on job training directly by comparing the extent of job training provided in jobs with starting wages equal to the minimum wage, less than the minimum, and above the minimum. (Employers that pay a subminimum starting wage are either exempt from the minimum wage or not complying with the law.) Of course, it is difficult to measure activities that constitute on-the-job training. Grossberg and Sicilian analyzed data from the Employment Opportunity Pilot Project (EOPP), which contains information on the number of hours of on-the-job training provided for the last worker hired by a sample of low-wage employers. They estimated a training-intensity equation, with the key explanatory variables being dummy variables for whether the starting pay for the job equalled the minimum or was less than the minimum; the base group comprised those who started above the minimum. The results are mixed. For women, they found that jobs starting workers at the minimum wage actually provided more training than did subminimum-wage or above-minimum-wage jobs, although the differentials are statistically insignificant. For men, they found that minimum-wage jobs provided less training than did below-minimum-wage jobs or above-minimum-wage jobs, but the differential between the below-minimum and minimum-wage jobs is statistically insignificant. It is possible that the result for men is merely a reflection of the fact that companies provide less training for lower-paid workers, rather than a discrete effect of the minimum wage. Moreover, the finding of possibly higher training rates for female workers who start at the minimum wage is notable, because women constitute a majority of minimum-wage workers.

JOB QUEUES AND TURNOVER

If the minimum wage confers rents on workers who hold minimum-wage jobs, then one would expect minimum-wage jobs to attract a long queue of job seekers, and to have relatively low turnover. By contrast, if the extra compensation generated by a minimum wage is offset fully by reduced fringe benefits and changes in working conditions, then minimum-wage jobs would not have lower turnover or longer queues of job seekers.

If we confine our attention to jobs that can be filled by workers who possess a homogeneous set of skills, it is easy to see why the queue of applicants would be longer for jobs that offer the minimum wage than for jobs that offer *more* or *less* than the minimum (assuming that there are incomplete nonwage offsets). In this situation, the theory of equalizing differences predicts that, compared with jobs paying a higher wage, subminimum-wage jobs must offer better working conditions or better nonwage benefits: otherwise, subminimum employers would not be able to fill their job openings. Likewise, the theory of equalizing differences predicts that jobs that pay more than the minimum wage must offer undesirable working conditions or low nonwage benefits. In equilibrium, all jobs that can be filled by homogeneous workers should have the same number of job seekers. If the minimum wage disrupts this equilibrium and is not offset by nonwage reductions, however, then minimum-wage jobs would have more applicants than would jobs that pay either above or below the minimum.

Holzer, Katz, and Krueger (1991) used the EOPP data set to estimate whether minimum-wage jobs attract a longer queue of applicants than do either subminimum-wage jobs or above-minimum-wage jobs. The length of the applicant queue was measured by the number of people who applied for the last job opening at the sampled firms. Holzer, Katz, and Krueger found that jobs offering starting wages that were equal to the minimum wage attracted 36 percent more applicants than did those paying a subminimum wage, and 21 percent more applicants than did those paying more than the minimum wage but less than $5.00 per hour. When they restricted the sample to new jobs that paid *within* 25 cents of the minimum wage, Holzer, Katz, and Krueger found that minimum-wage jobs attracted an average of 11.5 applicants per job opening, compared with 6.7 applicants per opening for subminimum-wage jobs, and 10.9 applicants per opening for above-minimum-wage jobs. The differential between minimum-wage jobs and above-minimum wage jobs is statistically significant, whereas the differential between minimum-wage jobs and subminimum-wage jobs is not. The apparent spike in the job-application differential holds after several variables are held constant in a regression model, including occupation, industry, the log of the wage rate, demographic variables, firm size, and union status.

In economic theory, the length of the queue of job seekers for a position provides a genuine indication of the desirability of the job. In practice, however, job queues are difficult to measure. Most importantly, data on job applications are not necessarily comparable across firms, and some potential applicants might not apply for jobs because they do not expect to be selected. Moreover, the test of higher application rates for minimum-wage jobs would be stronger if it were based on a comparison of application rates before and after an increase in the minimum wage. Nonetheless, the comparatively longer queue of job applicants for minimum-wage jobs is consistent with the view that minimum-wage jobs are more highly prized by low-skilled workers than are jobs that pay slightly more or slightly less than the minimum wage.

Turnover

Much research has documented a negative association between labor turnover and wage rates (see, for example, Parker and Burton [1967] and Pencavel [1970]). Researchers also have found that turnover is lower in larger firms than small firms, and lower for unionized workers than for nonunion workers. If the minimum wage forces total compensation to rise above the competitive level, then one would expect voluntary turnover to be lower in minimum-wage jobs than it would be in the absence of a minimum wage.

Wessels (1980) and Sicilian and Grossberg (1993) examined the relationship between job turnover and the minimum wage. Wessels estimated log quit rate regressions for 14 manufacturing industries, using monthly time-series data. The key explanatory variable was the percentage change in the minimum wage, lagged four months.[21] The results indicate that minimum-wage increases have a negative association with turnover in low-wage industries, but a positive association in high-wage industries.

Sicilian and Grossberg (1993) used the EOPP data set to examine the relationship between the quit rate and the starting wage rate for the last position filled by sampled firms. The key explanatory variables were dummy variables indicating whether the starting pay for the job equalled the minimum or was less than the minimum; the base group comprised those who started above the minimum. Sicilian and Grossberg included as an explanatory variable the worker's tenure on the job. One difficulty with this variable is that some jobs were filled several years previously, whereas others were filled more recently. Thus, job tenure arguably is endogenous. The results are also difficult to interpret because tenure was interacted with the minimum-wage dummy variable, but not with the subminimum-wage dummy variable. Another problem with using the EOPP data for this purpose is that the EEOP sample design over-represents high-turnover jobs by asking about the job most recently filled by the firm. Paul Sicilian provided us with simple tabulations from the EEOP of the quit rate for all workers hired during the last year.[22] The quit rate for minimum-wage jobs was 22 percent, which differed little from the 21 percent rate for subminimum-wage jobs, but was greater than the 15 percent rate for above-minimum-wage jobs. It is unclear, however, whether the higher turnover rate for minimum-wage jobs than for above-minimum-wage jobs is simply a reflection of the general finding that turnover tends to be lower in higher-wage jobs.

CONCLUSION

This chapter has documented a number of anomalies in the low-wage labor market. First, there is considerable wage variability even for identical low-skill jobs (such as hamburger flippers), suggesting that workers with the same skills are paid different wages. Second, the minimum wage compresses wage variability. Third, a large spike in the wage distribution occurs at the minimum wage; during 1991, one-fourth of teenage workers in states without their own minimum-wage laws were paid a wage exactly equal to the federal minimum. The spike at the minimum wage suggests that workers with different abilities are paid the same wage. Fourth, there is a spike at the minimum even for workers who are not covered by the minimum wage. Fifth, an increase in the minimum wage creates a small ripple effect, causing employers to raise pay for workers who were earning slightly more than the new minimum. Sixth, employers are extremely reluctant to use the youth subminimum wage, perhaps because they are concerned about equity. Seventh, an increase in the minimum wage reduces wage growth by raising entry-level wages, not by lowering wages for workers with higher seniority. Eighth, fringe benefits and training do not appear to be offset substantially when the minimum wage increases. Finally, tentative evidence suggests that minimum-wage jobs attract relatively more job seekers and are subject to lower turnover than would be expected in the absence of a minimum wage.

In isolation, it might be possible to dismiss any one of these findings. Taken as a whole, however, they suggest that the low-wage labor market does not operate in accordance with the predictions of the standard economic model. Moreover, combined with our findings in chapters 2–4 of negligible or positive employment effects of recent minimum-wage increases, these anomalies pose a challenge to the conventional model. The main support for the conventional model has been the presumed adverse employment effect of a minimum wage. In the next three chapters, we reexamine the literature that has provided the basis for this presumption.

NOTES

1. See Krueger and Summers (1987), Gibbons and Katz (1992), Murphy and Topel (1987), and Brown and Medoff (1989).

2. These figures are based on data from the Current Population Survey (CPS). We restricted the sample to workers who live in the 25 states that did not have a state minimum wage exceeding $3.35 per hour on April 1, 1990. The 25 states are: Alabama, Arizona, Arkansas, Colorado, Florida, Georgia, Indiana, Kansas, Kentucky, Louisiana, Michigan, Mississippi, Missouri, Nebraska, Nevada, New Jersey, New Mexico, North Carolina, Ohio, South Carolina, Tennessee, Texas, Virginia, West Virginia, and Wyoming.

3. It is unlikely that the remaining spike at $3.35 per hour reflects use of the subminimum wage, because the data also show a spike at $3.35 for 20- to 21-year-old workers, who were not eligible for the subminimum (see Katz and Krueger [1990]).

4. The average wage for employees in firms that do not deduct Social Security taxes is $12.30 per hour, and the standard deviation of wages is $8.39. By contrast, the average wage for employees in firms that deduct Social Security taxes is $11.77 per hour, and the standard deviation is $7.12.

5. For first-time offenders, the penalty for failing to comply with the Social Security Act is much greater than the penalty for failing to comply with the Fair Labor Standards Act.

6. Of course, it is possible that part of the spike at the minimum for uncovered firms represents classification errors. In other words, some of the workers classified by Fritsch (1981) as employed by uncovered firms might actually have been employed by covered firms. In this case, it would not be surprising to find a spike. This explanation seems less likely with respect to workers who voluntarily reported that their employers did not pay Social Security taxes.

7. See Krueger (1991) for a discussion of why company-owned fast-food restaurants pay higher wages.

8. See, for example, Freeman (1981), Heckman and Paynor (1989), and Ashenfelter and Hannan (1986).

9. Sargent and Blanchflower's finding that weight is negatively associated with wages for women, but not for men, suggests that these wage differentials result from discrimination, rather than from unobserved personal characteristics.

10. The Wendy's restaurant chain recently was sued for discrimination in a class action suit covering 700 stores (see Bureau of National Affairs [1994]). Denny's recently agreed to a $54 million settlement in two federal class-

action suits alleging customer discrimination based on race (see *New York Times*, May 29, 1994, p. 4) and has been sued for employment discrimination based on race (see *The Plain Dealer*, June 16, 1993). Shoney's reportedly made $105 million available for employees who alleged racial discrimination (see *Wall Street Journal*, November 4, 1992). Taco Bell paid a $140,000 settlement for allegedly firing a manager for hiring "too many" black employees (see *Star Tribune*, July 17, 1993).

11. Quoted in *Crain's New York Business*, September 27, 1993, p. 33.

12. This material draws from Katz and Krueger (1992).

13. These figures are based on CPS data. The data are described in chapter 4.

14. In addition, the subminimum wage could not be applied to more than 25 percent of an employers' work-force hours, and could not be paid if an employee was laid off to make room for new subminimum-wage workers.

15. See Bureau of National Affairs (1993).

16. The same study found that only 4.7 percent of retailers used the subminimum—a figure that is very close to Katz and Krueger's (1992) estimate. Results from the Department of Labor study were reported in Bureau of National Affairs (1993).

17. Indeed, Love (1986) estimated that 1 in 15 workers obtained their first job from McDonald's. Although we are uncertain whether this estimate is accurate, many young workers undoubtedly obtained their first jobs in the fast-food industry.

18. For an elaboration of these issues, see Holzer, Katz, and Krueger (1991) and Wessels (1980).

19. A related point is that firms are required by law to offer some fringe benefits to all their workers, if they offer them to any worker.

20. See Grossberg and Sicilian (1994) for a critical evaluation of tests using wage growth to infer the extent of job-training offsets.

21. The regressions also included the log vacancy rate, the log hourly wage of production workers in manufacturing establishments, month dummies, and a quadratic time trend. One might question the inclusion of the vacancy rate, because any reduction in turnover caused by the minimum wage is likely to reduce vacancies.

22. Personal correspondence, June 24, 1994. We are grateful to Paul Sicilian for giving us this information.

CHAPTER 6

Evaluation of Time-Series Evidence

When I get new information, I use it.
—attributed to John Maynard Keynes

How can the evidence presented in chapters 2–4 showing that minimum-wage increases have not harmed employment be so much at odds with the previous literature? The main evidence usually cited to support the claim of adverse employment effects of the minimum wage is based on time-series analysis—typically, of aggregate teenage employment rates. Time-series studies relate the employment rate of workers in a particular year to a measure of the minimum wage in that year. The goal of the analysis is to determine whether employment is lower (or higher) when the "coverage-adjusted minimum wage" is at a relatively high (or low) level. In this chapter, we update and evaluate previous time-series studies.

We reach three major conclusions that lead us to question the view that the time-series evidence shows an adverse employment effect of the minimum wage. First, the time-series evidence is based on shaky methodological ground. Second, a "meta-analysis" suggests that the published time-series studies have been affected by "publication bias" or "specification searching," leading to a tendency toward finding statistically significant effects of the minimum wage. Third, an update of the time-series models through the 1980s indicates that whatever historical relationship might have existed between the minimum wage and teenage employment rates is weakened when data covering the past 10 to 15 years are included in the analysis.

Methodology and Review

Since 1970, researchers have conducted more than 30 time-series studies of the effect of the minimum wage in the United States. A typical study relates the employment–population rate of teenagers to a variable indicating the importance of the minimum wage. More formally, the canonical estimating equation in the literature is of the form:

$$Y_t = g(MW_t, X_{t1} \ldots X_{tk}) + \epsilon_t, \tag{6.1}$$

where Y_t represents a measure of employment or unemployment in year t, $g(\cdot)$ is a function of a set of explanatory variables, and ϵ_t represents a stochastic error term. Most studies have focused on employment, rather than on unemployment, because a two-sector model leads to ambiguous predictions about the effect of the minimum wage on unemployment (see, for example, Mincer [1976]). The main explanatory variable is MW_t, which is a measure of the minimum wage in period t.

A key issue concerns the other explanatory variables (denoted X_1 $\ldots X_k$) to be included in the equation. Most studies have included some measure of aggregate demand, such as the adult male unemployment rate. Often, the specifications in the literature include some supply-side variables, such as the fraction of teenagers in training programs, the fraction in the armed forces, or, less frequently, the fraction enrolled in school. The X variables might also include secular trend terms, such as linear or quadratic functions of time. The model typically is estimated with the dependent variable in logarithms, although some studies use a linear specification. The function, $g(\cdot)$, is almost always assumed to be a simple linear function of the explanatory variables (either in levels or logarithms). Most studies have used quarterly data, although some have used monthly or annual data. The sample sizes have ranged from 40 to 140 quarters of data. About one-half of the studies have corrected for an autoregressive component in the residuals. Although two-thirds of minimum-wage earners are adults, the time-series literature has focused primarily on teenagers. The reason for this is that most adult workers earn substantially more than the minimum wage, whereas 15 to 30 percent of teenage workers earn the minimum wage, depending on the year.

The minimum-wage variable most often specified in the time-series literature is the so-called Kaitz index. This index was developed by Hyman Kaitz during the 1970s, when wage data for teenagers and other low-wage workers were far more limited than they are today. The Kaitz index is defined as

$$MW_t = \Sigma_i f_{it}(m_t/w_{it})c_{it}, \tag{6.2}$$

where f_{it} is the fraction of teenage employment in industry i in year t, m_t is the minimum wage in year t, w_{it} is the average hourly wage in industry i in year t, and c_{it} is the fraction of workers in industry i covered by the minimum wage in year t.[1] In words, the Kaitz index is the coverage-weighted minimum wage relative to the average wage in the industry. The Kaitz index summarizes several aspects of the minimum wage: the extent of coverage, the level of the minimum wage relative to average wages, and the industry distribution of teenage employment.

About one-half of the time-series studies relate the employment rate to the contemporaneous Kaitz index, and about one-half include some lags of the Kaitz index. In their survey of the time-series literature, Brown, Gilroy, and Kohen (1982, p. 507) observed "few differences between those studies which assume that the effect of the minimum wage is instantaneous and those which assume a lagged response." Note that studies of quarterly or monthly data that include the contemporaneous Kaitz index or only a few lags allow less time for the minimum wage to affect employment than do our case studies of the fast-food industry, described in chapter 2.

Summary of Aggregate Time-Series Estimates

Brown, Gilroy, and Kohen (1982) thoroughly summarized the available time-series studies of the effect of the minimum wage up to the early 1980s. Table 6.1 is adapted from their literature review. The table reports the percentage change in employment for a 10 percent increase in the minimum wage implied by the estimates in each time-series study in the literature. Brown, Gilroy, and Kohen (p. 508) summarized this literature as follows:

> In summary, our survey indicates a reduction of between one and three percent in teenage employment as a result of a 10 percent increase in the federal minimum wage. We regard the lower part of this range as most plausible because this is what most studies, which include the experience of the 1970s and deal carefully with minimum-wage coverage, tend to find.

The prediction of a 1 to 3 percent reduction in teenage employment for a 10 percent increase in the minimum wage has become widely ingrained in people's thinking and is often cited in the halls of Congress and academia in discussions on the minimum wage.[2] Because teenage employment rates average about 50 percent, a 1 to 3 percent reduction corresponds to a reduction of 0.5 to 1.5 *percentage points* in the teenage employment–population rate.

Brown, Gilroy, and Kohen's other conclusions have received less attention. First, they concluded that the minimum wage has had a smaller effect on the teenage unemployment rate than on the teenage employment rate. Another important conclusion that they reached from their literature review is that, "While it is often asserted that blacks are more adversely affected than whites by the

TABLE 6.1

Estimated Impact of a 10 Percent Increase in the Minimum Wage
on Employment of 16- to 19-Year-Olds: Early Studies

Study	Percent Change in Employment (1)	Period (2)
1. Kaitz (1970)	−0.98*	1954–1968
2. Kosters and Welch (1972)	−2.96[a]	1954–1968
3. Kelly (1975)	−1.20[a]	1954–1968
4. Kelly (1976)	−0.66[a]	1954–1974
5. Gramlich (1976)	−0.94[a]	1948–1975
6. Hashimoto and Mincer (1970) and Mincer (1976)	−2.31[a]	1954–1969
7. Welch 1976	−1.78*	1954–1968
8. Ragan (1977)	−0.65[a]	1963–1972
9. Mattila (1978)	−0.84[a]	1947–1976
10. Freeman (1979)	−2.46[a]	1948–1977
11. Wachter and Kim (1979)	−2.52[a]	1962–1978
12. Iden (1980)	−2.26[a]	1954–1979
13. Ragan (1981)	−0.52[a]	1963–1978
14. Abowd and Killingsworth (1981)	−2.13	1954–1979
15. Betsey and Dunson (1981)	−1.39[a]	1954–1979
16. Boschen and Grossman (1981)	−1.50	1948–1979
17. Brown, Gilroy, and Kohen (1983)	−0.96	1954–1979
18. Hamermesh (1981)	−1.21	1954–1978
19. Average	**−1.52**	

Source: Brown, Gilroy, and Kohen (1982), Tables 1 and 3.

*Statistically significant at the 0.10 level.

[a]No significance tests are available because reported coefficients were derived from disaggregated data.

minimum wage, previous studies provide conflicting evidence on the issue. . . . such an assertion must rest on theoretical rather than empirical grounds" (p. 508). They further concluded that the effect of the minimum wage on young adults (aged 20 to 24) is smaller than its effect on teenagers.

In Table 6.2, we extend the review of the time-series studies of U.S. employment through to the present.[3] In each case, we report the estimate that the author highlighted as a preferred estimate for all teenagers. These three recent studies found a smaller impact of the minimum wage on employment than did the studies reported in Brown, Gilroy, and Kohen. In the three studies, on average, a 10 percent increase in the minimum wage was associated with a 0.7 percent decrease in employment. The study that used the most re-

TABLE 6.2
Estimated Impact of a 10 Percent Increase in the Minimum Wage
on Employment of 16- to 19-Year-Olds: Recent Studies

Study	Percent Change in Employment (1)	Period (2)
1. Solon (1985)	−0.99*	1954–1979
2. Wellington (1991)	−0.60	1954–1986
3. Klerman (1992)	−0.52*	1954–1988
4. Average	−0.70	

*Statistically significant at the 0.10 level.

cent data (Klerman [1992]) found the smallest effect. Wellington (1991, p. 45) summarized her findings as follows: "The results suggest that a 1 percent decline in the employment of teens may be an overestimate of teen employment losses—the estimates of this study indicate approximately a 0.60 percentage point decline. In addition, I found no evidence that an increase in the minimum wage has any effect on the employment status of young adults." Wellington also found that the employment effects of the minimum wage were smaller for nonwhite and female teenagers than for all teenagers, even though these two groups are far more likely than white and male teenagers to be paid the minimum wage. Moreover, she found that "the change in the unemployment rate of teens due to an increase in the minimum wage index is approximately zero" (p. 42).

In his influential book, *Labor Demand*, Daniel Hamermesh (1993, p. 188) argued that the explanation for the smaller minimum wage effects in the recent time-series studies is that, "During the 1980s the effective minimum moved far into the left tail of the [wage distribution], so that changes in it could not have had a very large effect on teenage employment." This may be true, but it misses the point that the variable used in most of the time-series studies is the Kaitz index. The Kaitz index actually reached a higher level during the 1980s than during the 1950s and 1960s because coverage had increased substantially (see Figure 6.3). Thus, a dramatically lower Kaitz index cannot explain why the more recent studies found smaller effects. Moreover, the Kaitz index is normed relative to the average wage, so that a lower effective minimum *is* reflected in the Kaitz index. If one believes that the Kaitz index is a valid measure of the minimum wage, then one must conclude from the most recent studies that the minimum wage now has a much smaller effect on employment than indicated by the earlier studies.

Methodological Issues in the Time-Series Approach

Often, policymakers are concerned about the effect of the federal minimum wage on national employment, rather than on any particular industry or region. The main advantage of the time-series approach is that the dependent variable—aggregate employment—measures employment in all sectors of the economy. Under the time-series approach, if the minimum wage causes some workers to move from the covered to the uncovered sector, they continue to be counted as employed. Another advantage of aggregate time-series studies is that, unlike the the case with cross-state studies, jobs that move across state lines are not counted as employment changes.

The time-series approach has major disadvantages, as well. First and foremost, the counterfactual is not clear. The aggregate time-series approach implicitly compares employment in years during which the minimum wage is relatively high with employment in years during which it is relatively low. Many things change over time, however. The problem is that it is difficult to distinguish the effect of the minimum wage on employment from the many other factors that are occurring simultaneously. Although time-series studies attempt to control for the effect of changes in some exogenous variables (for example, the state of the business cycle), one can never be certain whether the controls are adequate. The implicit assumption is that, controlling for the other explanatory variables, employment would be the same over time if the minimum wage were constant. Unfortunately, there is no way to test this assumption, because the aggregate time-series studies do not try to identify groups that are unaffected by the minimum wage.

A related concern is that the government might choose the timing of minimum-wage increases in response to changes in the economy. For example, the government might find it easier to enact an increase in the minimum wage when employment is expanding. By the time the minimum-wage increase is phased in, however, the economy might have weakened, inducing a spurious relationship between the minimum wage and employment. In other words, it is unclear whether employment conditions affected the minimum-wage increase, or whether the minimum-wage increase affected employment conditions. Without a clear understanding of how the government adjusts the minimum wage, the endogeneity of minimum wages can bias the aggregate time-series studies in any direction.

Second, according to economic theory, the proper specification of the employment-demand function includes the wages of the relevant groups of workers. Exogenous movements in wages, such as those induced by changes in the minimum wage, can be used to identify the demand elasticity. But changes in the minimum wage or coverage rate *only* affect employment through their effect on wages. In the time-series literature, the Kaitz index is used as a proxy for the teenage wage, probably because wage data on teenagers were unavailable until the mid-1970s. The expectation was that the average teenage wage would be highly correlated with the Kaitz index, so that the Kaitz index could be used in the employment-demand equation in lieu of a direct measure of wages. In econometric parlance, the standard specification of the employment–population rate as a function of the Kaitz index is a "reduced-form" approach.

Under the static theory of factor demand, the employment-demand function depends on the price of inputs and the price of output. For example, if the factors of production are teenage labor, adult labor, and capital, with unit prices W^T, W^A, and r, respectively, and the price of output is p, then the demand function for teenage labor, L^T, would be specified as

$$L^T = D(W^T, W^A, r, p). \qquad (6.3)$$

According to the standard theory, the demand function is homogeneous of degree zero, which implies that all prices can be divided by one of the other prices without altering the relationship.[4] For example, this feature enables one to normalize prices relative to the wage of adults, as follows:

$$L^T = D(W^T/W^A, 1, r/W^A, p/W^A). \qquad (6.4)$$

Alternatively, the normalization could be based on the price of output, giving the following specification:

$$L^T = D(W^T/p, W^A/p, r/p, 1). \qquad (6.5)$$

To understand the relevance of this issue, suppose that all industries are fully covered by the minimum wage, that all teenagers earn the minimum wage, and that teenage employment is entirely demand determined. In this situation, observed employment will depend on the minimum wage relative to the wage of adults, as well as on the cost of capital relative to adult wages, and the price of output relative to adult wages. (In this example, because coverage is assumed to be 100 percent, the minimum wage relative to the adult wage is the Kaitz index.) Studies in the literature generally do not control for variables measuring output prices or the cost of capital. The specification of equation (6.4) or (6.5) implies that *one* price—the one used to normalize the other prices—can be omitted from the employment model. In the standard specification, however, the teenage wage is divided by the adult wage, implying that the adult wage is used as a normalizing factor. Under this normalization, the price of capital relative to the average adult wage and the price of output relative to the average adult wage should also be included in the teenage employment model.[5]

To correct this problem, one could include the minimum wage and the adult wage as separate explanatory variables. This is easily illustrated in a specification in which the Kaitz index is measured in log units and in which we ignore capital, as is common in the literature. Assuming that coverage is 100 percent, define $\log(Kaitz) = \log(W^M/W^A)$. A properly specified semilog employment equation is then

$$
\begin{aligned}
L^T &= \beta_1\log(W^M/p) + \beta_2\log(W^A/p) \\
&= \beta_1\log(Kaitz) + (\beta_2 - \beta_1)\log(W^A/p),
\end{aligned}
\tag{6.6}
$$

where the βs are coefficients. Viewed in this light, the equations that typically have been estimated in the literature omit a potentially important explanatory variable, the log of the adult wage divided by the output price.

Notice also that the appropriate dependent variable for theoretical models of labor demand is the number of hours that a specified group has worked, perhaps adjusted for the effort expended per hour worked. The time-series studies have not made any attempt to adjust for the number of hours of work; instead, they treat part-time employment and full-time employment as equivalent.

As we have mentioned, a final difficulty with the existing literature involves the choice of control variables in the estimating equation. This problem is a serious one in the time-series minimum-wage studies; in principle, employment of workers who are paid more than the minimum wage is determined by the interaction of demand-side factors and supply-side factors. The employment equations in the literature typically have been interpreted as demand equations. Nevertheless, many studies include as explanatory variables supply-side variables, such as the size of a cohort, the fraction of the cohort enrolled in school, or the fraction of the cohort that participates in training programs.

One could argue that *exogenous* supply-side variables, such as the fraction of teenagers in the overall population, should be included in the aggregate employment equation because the minimum wage may be more or less binding when labor-supply conditions change. It is much more difficult, however, to justify holding constant supply-side variables, such as school enrollment, that potentially are affected by the minimum wage.[6] If a minimum-wage increase causes students to leave school because work is more attractive, or to remain in school longer because work is more difficult to find, then the school enrollment rate is not a legitimate explanatory variable in these equations. Indeed, many studies have sought to determine how the minimum wage influences school enrollment. It is therefore troubling that many time-series studies have included supply-side variables that may be influenced directly by the minimum wage.

PUBLICATION BIAS

Another problem associated with the existing literature on the minimum wage is that academic journals may tend to publish papers that offer "statistically significant" results. Statistical significance typically is judged by whether the study finds a t-ratio—the ratio of the regression coefficient on the minimum-wage variable to its standard error—that is greater than 2 in absolute value. Because a statistical study is deemed more decisive if the null hypothesis of zero (i.e., that the minimum wage has no effect) is rejected, reviewers and editors have a natural proclivity to look favorably on studies that report statistically significant results.

Furthermore, with respect to the minimum wage, economists have a strong theoretical presumption that an increase in the minimum wage should reduce employment. This thinking might lead editors and referees to be more likely to publish results that accord with theoretical expectations. Unfortunately, as we have explained, there is no clear guide for the proper specification of the employment equation in the aggregate time-series studies. Researchers have much discretion over the explanatory variables that they include, the functional form that they impose, the age group on which they focus, the sample that they analyze, and the estimation technique that they use. Researchers may be induced to choose among specifications in part by whether the specifications produce negative and statistically significant employment effects, and reviewers and editors may be induced to publish these studies more often than those containing specifications that produce insignificant effects.[7]

Fortunately, statistical methods known as meta-analysis techniques have been developed to assess the likelihood of publication bias.[8] In the context of the time-series studies, a natural test results from the fact that more recent studies generally use more data. The first time-series studies were conducted during the early 1970s, when the available time series were relatively short, typically going back only to 1954. More recent studies have been able to enlarge their samples by incorporating several decades of additional data.[9]

Studies that were conducted during the late 1980s have more than twice as many observations as did the early studies. Standard results in the theory of sampling imply a strong relationship between the sample size, the standard error, and the t-ratio. All else being equal, if additional data are independent of the initial data, then a doubling of the sample size should result in an increase in the absolute t-ratio of about 40 percent. More generally, the absolute value of the t-ratio is expected to increase proportionally with the square root of the number of degrees of freedom, and a regression of the log of the t-ratio on the log of the square root of the degrees of freedom should yield a coefficient of one.

Time-series data are unlikely to be independent. However, many time-series studies correct their estimates for serially correlated errors, which, in principle, adjusts for the dependence in the data. Because studies that do not make this adjustment implicitly assume that the data are independent, the relationship between the t-statistic and sample size still provides a valid test of publication bias.[10]

What might prevent the t-ratio from increasing with the sample size? One obvious possibility is publication bias. If only studies that achieve t-ratios of 2 or more are published, and if researchers choose their specifications in part to achieve statistically significant results, then the early studies will tend to have high t-ratios even though their samples are small. Another possibility is that structural change has altered the statistical model. In this case, the t-ratio might rise or fall with the sample size. If the effect of the minimum wage has weakened over time, for example, then the t-ratio could fall or remain constant as the sample size increases.

To explore the possibility of publication bias in the time-series literature on minimum wages and employment, we relate the t-ratio found in the studies in Tables 6.1 and 6.2 to their sample size and other characteristics. We limit our analysis to 15 studies that used quarterly data. For studies that estimated a log specification, we have selected the t-ratio on the minimum-wage variable in what we judge to be the author's preferred specification.[11] For studies that estimated only a linear specification, we have selected the t-ratio from the author's preferred linear specification. Because functional form is one aspect over which researchers have discretion, it is appropriate to combine t-ratios based on different functional forms. Nevertheless, we have experimented with limiting the sample to the subset of studies that use a log specification, and our conclusions are unchanged.

Figure 6.1 displays a graph of the relationship between the absolute value of the t-ratio from each study and the square root of the degrees of freedom in the study.[12] Each point on the graph repre-

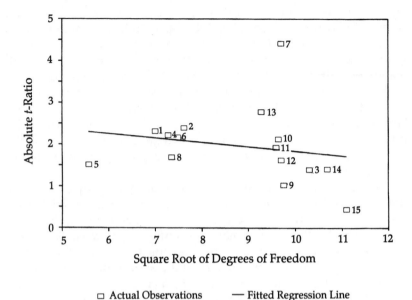

Figure 6.1 *t*-Ratio versus square root of degrees of freedom. The number beside each point refers to the study number.

sents one study; the number beside each point corresponds to the study number in Table 6.3. The ordinary least squares (OLS) fitted line is also displayed on the graph. The figure reveals a striking pattern: *Contrary to the expected upward-sloping relationship between t-ratios and sample size predicted by statistical sampling theory, the graph displays a downward-sloping pattern.* Study 7, which finds a *t*-ratio of 4, clearly is an outlier. The other studies cluster fairly closely around a negatively-sloped line.

To control for other characteristics of the studies, we estimated a set of descriptive multiple regressions with the data illustrated in Figure 6.1. The dependent variable in these regressions is the log of the *t*-ratio from the 15 studies. The key independent variable is the log of the square root of the degrees of freedom, which sampling theory predicts will have a coefficient of one. In addition, we hold constant a dummy variable that equals one if the specification was logarithmic, a dummy variable that equals one if the sample consisted of all teenagers (as opposed to a subset of teenagers), a dummy variable that equals one if an autoregressive correction was included in the estimation approach, and a variable indicating the number of covariates included in the original model. Table 6.4 summarizes these regression estimates.

TABLE 6.3
Authors of Studies in Figure 6.1 and Figure 6.2

Study Number	Author(s)
1	Kaitz (1970)
2	Mincer (1976)
3	Gramlich (1976)
4	Welch (1976)
5	Ragan (1977)
6	Wachter and Kim (1979)
7	Iden (1980)
8	Ragan (1981)
9	Abowd and Killingsworth (1981)
10	Betsey and Dunson (1981)
11	Brown, Gilroy, and Kohen (1983)
12	Hamermesh (1981)
13	Solon (1985)
14	Wellington (1991)
15	Klerman (1992)

The regression results indicate a negative relationship between the studies' t-ratios and their degrees of freedom. The coefficient on the square root of the degrees of freedom is quite far from one, its theoretical expectation.[13] Inclusion of additional explanatory variables does not change the sign of the coefficient or reduce its effect. Surprisingly, however, the explanatory variables do not account for much of the variance in the t-ratios estimated in the various studies. All the study characteristics that we identify are jointly statistically insignificant when a conventional F-test is performed.

We also calculated these regressions for three subsets of studies. First, we eliminated the three studies published after 1985. When we focus on the pre-1985 literature, we continue to find a negative or flat relationship between the studies' t-ratios and their degrees of freedom. Second, we performed the regression analysis after omitting the outlying study, study 7 (see Figure 6.1). When this subsample is analyzed, the negative relationship between the t-ratio and the degrees of freedom becomes statistically significant. Finally, we performed the analysis using only the 11 studies that estimated a log specification. For this sample, we continue to find a negative relationship between the t-ratio and degrees of freedom.

Another type of meta-analysis relates the size of the coefficient estimate in each study to its standard error. If the employment func-

TABLE 6.4
Meta-Analysis of *t*-Statistics from Time-Series Studies

	Estimated Regression Models		
	(1)	(2)	(3)
1. Log Square Root of Degrees of Freedom	−0.81	−0.86	−0.98
	(0.70)	(0.77)	(0.86)
2. Autoregression Correction (1 = Yes)	—	0.02	−0.02
		(0.35)	(0.39)
3. Subsample of Teenagers (1 = Yes)	—	0.28	0.37
		(0.40)	(0.49)
4. Logarithmic Specification (1 = Yes)	—	−0.37	−0.30
		(0.45)	(0.51)
5. Number of Explanatory Variables	—	—	0.02
			(0.04)
6. Intercept	2.87	2.87	3.02
	(1.36)	(1.65)	(1.76)
7. Adjusted *R*-Squared	0.02	0.10	0.01
8. *P*-Value for Joint Test of Coefficients	0.27	0.31	0.45

Note: Standard errors are shown in parentheses. The dependent variable in all models is the log of the absolute value of the *t*-ratio for the minimum-wage variable. The sample size is 15. See text for further explanation.

tion is stable, one would expect to find *no* relationship between the coefficient estimates and the standard errors, because the estimated coefficients are unbiased estimates of the true parameter, regardless of the size of the standard error. If publication bias induces a tendency toward the reporting of *t*-ratios that exceed 2 in absolute value, however, then we would expect to find a positive relationship between the magnitude of estimated coefficients and their standard errors. For example, suppose journals follow a rule of publishing only studies with *t*-ratios that exceed 2. If researchers are aware of this rule, they might be tempted to adjust their specification until they obtain a *t*-ratio of 2 for the minimum-wage coefficient. Because the *t*-ratio is given by $t = b/se$, where b is the coefficient and se is the standard error, this process would imply that $b = 2 \times se$. This proposition can be easily tested.

One difficulty with examining the relationship between coefficients and standard errors, however, is that different studies estimate different functional forms, so that the coefficients are not directly comparable. To overcome this problem, we take Brown, Gilroy, and Kohen's estimates of the percentage change in employment for a 10 percent change in the minimum-wage variable for each of

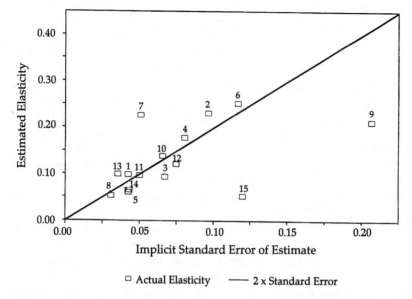

Figure 6.2 Plot of elasticity versus standard error. The number above each point refers to the study number.

the 15 studies. We derive the implicit standard error for these estimated elasticities on the basis of the reported t-ratios for the underlying estimates. Figure 6.2 presents a scatter diagram of the absolute value of the minimum-wage elasticities against their standard errors. The figure also shows a line corresponding to two times the standard error. The line fits the data rather well.[14] Study 9, by Abowd and Killingsworth (1981), and study 15, by Klerman (1992), lie noticeably below the line; and study 7 by Iden (1980), is noticeably above it. The others cluster fairly closely to the line. In contrast to what one would predict from classical hypothesis testing in a model with stable parameters, the estimated elasticity of employment with respect to the Kaitz index in the literature generally is close to two times its standard error.

What might explain the combination of decreasing t-ratios with sample size, and the tendency for studies to report specifications with t-ratios close to 2 irrespective of the magnitude of the coefficient? Structural change is one possibility. The true effect of the minimum wage might have decreased over time, and it might have done so at a faster rate than the decrease in its standard error. If structural changes have occurred, however, the validity of the time-series approach is called into question. The studies in the literature have not allowed for a break in the structure; instead, they assume it is constant. Moreover, if there was true structural change, then one would probably conclude that the minimum wage has an insignificant effect on employment in the most recent data (see Wellington [1991], Klerman [1992], and the next section).

Instead of structural change, however, we think a more likely explanation for these results is that the early literature was affected by specification searching and publication biases induced by the economics profession's tendency to prefer studies that find negative, statistically significant effects of the minimum wage on employment. As Edward Leamer (1978) stresses, nonexperimental econometric studies are particularly prone to specification searching and data mining. We conjecture that, in the early studies, certain combinations of control variables, sample definitions, and functional forms were found to produce a negative, statistically significant effect of the minimum-wage variable. These specifications were selected by the early researchers, who were guided, in part, by the criterion of achieving a t-ratio greater than 2, the critical value for statistical significance. Later researchers tended to replicate the specifications and data constructs used in the earlier literature. Because the statistical significance of the minimum wage effect was overstated in the early studies, however, the later studies discovered weaker effects of the minimum wage.

An example of this phenomenon is provided by a series of articles on the minimum wage authored by Finis Welch (1974, 1976, and 1977). In his 1974 article, Welch estimated that a 10 percent increase in the minimum wage reduced employment of 14- to 19-year-olds by 2 to 3 percent. He concluded, "The evidence is of a statistically significant reduction in the teenage/adult employment ratio associated with increased minimum wage level or coverage." While attempting to replicate Welch's analysis, Fred Siskind (1977) subsequently discovered that Welch had made an error in assembling the data from unpublished Bureau of Labor Statistics sources. The mistake (which Welch acknowledged) arose because Welch's employment series inadvertently spliced together employment data for 16- to 19-year-olds with data for 14- to 19-year-olds. The dependent variable in Welch's study was the log of the ratio of employment of 14- to 19-year-olds to that of adults. For the last three years of his sample (1966–1968), however, Welch used employment data for 16- to 19-year-olds. For those years, the number of employed teenagers naturally was much lower than in the earlier years. The last three years also coincided with the 1967 and 1968 increases in the federal minimum wage.

When Siskind reestimated Welch's exact specification with the corrected data series for 14- to 19-year-olds (the sample Welch had intended to use) he discovered that the estimates of the impact of the minimum wage were much smaller—a 10 percent increase in the minimum reduced employment by only 0.3 to 0.8 percent. Even more importantly, the minimum-wage effect was statistically indistinguishable from zero (the t-ratios ranged from 0.44 to 0.74).

In two subsequent articles, Welch (1976 and 1977) reestimated time-series models using published data that differed from his original unpublished data.[15] In addition, he added a new series to his analysis—employment levels of 16- to 19-year-olds relative to those of adults. Using the corrected data for 14- to 19-year-olds, Welch's estimates of the minimum wage effect were small and statistically insignificant, as Siskind had found. However, Welch found that estimates for the 16- to 19-year-olds were negative and marginally statistically significant. Contrary to expectations, the estimates implied that the minimum wage had a larger impact on the employment of older teenagers than that of younger teenagers. Welch chose to restrict his interpretation of the results to the 16- to 19-year-olds, even though his original work was based on data for 14- to 19-year-olds. The reason Welch (1976, p. 27) gives for this decision is as follows:

> There are only two possible interpretations of such an anomalous result. One is that increased minima increase employment of the youngest teenagers. The other is simply that the CPS employment data for 14- to 15-year-olds are unreliable. Since virtually any model of effects would predict that employment of those 14 to 15 would fall relative to those 16 to 19, I prefer the second interpretation. For this reason, my comments are restricted to Panel B—employment of teenagers 16 to 19 years old.

Similarly, in his reply to Siskind, Welch (1977) speculated that sampling errors in the data on 14- to 15-year-olds were responsible for the insignificant estimates for the 14- to 19-year-olds. Sampling errors for the 14- to 19-year-olds and 16- to 19-year-olds arise naturally, because the employment data are estimated from samples of the population. Sampling errors alone cannot explain the results, however, because the mismeasured variable (teenage/adult employment) is the dependent variable, and sampling errors simply would increase the residual standard error, leaving the coefficient estimates unbiased (see Maddala 1977, pp. 292–293). Furthermore, the standard errors were actually smaller, and the R-squared coefficients higher, in the regressions for the 14- to 19-year-olds than in the regressions for the 16- to 19-year-olds, suggesting that sampling errors were a greater problem with respect to the sample of 16- to 19-year-olds.

In many areas of economics, we suspect that publication bias and specification searching are not serious problems. In the time-series minimum-wage literature, however, our findings that t-ratios decrease as the sample size increases, and that elasticities are positively correlated with their standard errors, suggest that previous studies have been biased in the direction of finding statistically significant results. An alternative explanation is that there has been a structural shift in the economy, so that the statistical models developed during the early 1970s no longer fit as well as they once did. We turn to this issue in the next section. In either scenario, however, the time-series evidence does not strongly support the conventional wisdom.

FURTHER EXPLORATION AND UPDATE OF THE TIME-SERIES LITERATURE

To estimate the effect of the minimum wage with time-series data, we have obtained and updated the data used by Allison Wellington in her 1991 *Journal of Human Resources* time-series study of the impact of the minimum wage. The starting point of Wellington's data was Brown, Gilroy, and Kohen's (1983) data. We extend the time-series literature by analyzing the data through the last quarter of 1993. This analysis has the advantage of incorporating the effects of the 1990 and 1991 increases in the federal minimum wage.

To ensure that we were using the data correctly, we first used the data to replicate Wellington's and Brown, Gilroy, and Kohen's (1983) analyses of the minimum wage. We replicated Brown, Gilroy and Kohen's results exactly. We could not quite relicate Wellington's estimates, probably because we used a different computer program to estimate the autoregression correction. Nevertheless, our estimates are extremely close to hers.[16]

We extended Wellington's data through the end of 1993.[17] Figure 6.3 illustrates the level of the Kaitz index in each quarter from 1954 to 1993. The index shows a jagged pattern, reflecting periodic increases in the minimum wage and extensions of the Fair Labor Standards Act to newly covered industries. Despite occasional declines, the Kaitz index generally drifted upward from 1954 until 1980. The index shows a gradual decline during the 1980s, because the nominal value of the minimum wage was fixed at $3.35 per hour between 1981 and 1990. The Kaitz index increased sharply in 1990 and 1991, as the federal minimum wage increased in April of those years. The decline in the Kaitz index during the 1980s and its subsequent increase during the early 1990s provide additional time-series variability to estimate the employment effect of minimum wages.

Figure 6.4 shows the employment–population rate of 16- to 19-

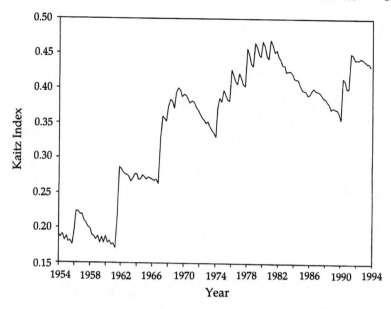

Figure 6.3 Kaitz index, 1954–1993.

year-olds in each quarter from 1954 to 1993. The dotted line indicates the seasonally unadjusted employment–population rate. A strong seasonal pattern is evident in these data; not surprisingly, teenage employment peaks during the summer. The large seasonal fluctuations suggest that employers are able to adjust teenage employment relatively quickly. Notice also that the teenage employment rate is procyclical, with large declines occurring during the recessions of the early 1980s and 1990s. The raw correlation between the Kaitz index and the employment rate is 0.27. Because other factors might also change over time, one would naturally want to adjust for these factors in examining the relationship between the Kaitz index and teenage employment.

We use the updated data to estimate employment equations for various time periods. Our empirical specification is identical to Wellington's, with one exception. We omit a variable measuring the extent of public sector training because it was not readily available after 1986.[18] Table 6.5.A presents estimates of the impact of the minimum wage with a log-log specification, and Table 6.5.B contains estimates for the same time periods with a linear specification. In all specifications, we correct for first-order serial correlation, using the Beach-MacKinnon procedure. There are several interesting results. First, in the linear specification, the Kaitz index is never statistically significant at the 0.05 level. Second, in the log-log specification, the

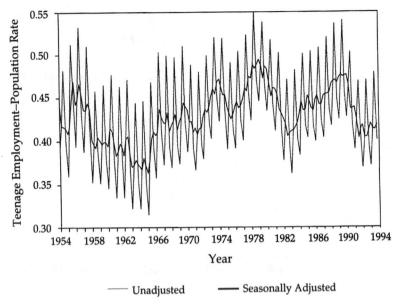

Figure 6.4 Quarterly employment–population rate of 16- to 19-year-olds, 1954–1993.

Kaitz index is statistically significant in the early periods, but not in the later periods. Indeed, the t-ratio falls from 2.15, when the model is estimated over 1954–1972, to 1.72, when it is estimated over 1954–1993. Third, when we update the model through 1993, the estimated minimum-wage effect is slightly larger than that found by Wellington, but still smaller than the bottom of the accepted range. Fourth, the degree of first-order serial correlation increases as additional years of data are added to the sample. This fact may partially account for the failure of the standard errors to decrease as additional time-series observations are added over time.

In Table 6.6 (see p. 199), we explore the sensitivity of the estimated coefficient on the log Kaitz index to alternative corrections for serial correlation. We focus on the log-log specification in column 4 of Table 6.5.A. The first row of Table 6.6 shows the OLS estimate and its unadjusted standard error. In the presence of serial correlation, the OLS estimate will be unbiased, but inefficient. The unadjusted OLS standard error will also be biased, usually downward. The OLS coefficient is smaller than the coefficients that are estimated if generalized least-squares (GLS) corrections for serial correlation are implemented. Surprisingly, we find that the unadjusted OLS standard error is greater than the standard error that arises from GLS estimates that make an explicit AR(1) correction.

TABLE 6.5.A

Time-Series Estimates of Employment Models for Selected Time Periods,
Log Specification

	1954–1972 (1)	1954–1979 (2)	1954–1986 (3)	1954–1993 (4)
1. Log Kaitz Index	−0.088 (0.041)	−0.086 (0.040)	−0.064 (0.046)	−0.072 (0.042)
2. Log Unemployment Rate of Adult Males	−0.116 (0.019)	−0.102 (0.017)	−0.097 (0.020)	−0.091 (0.019)
3. Fraction of 16- to 19-Year-Olds Who Are Aged 16–17	−1.129 (0.306)	−1.139 (0.384)	−1.169 (0.507)	−1.161 (0.464)
4. Fraction of 16- to 19-Year-Olds in Armed Forces	0.328 (0.919)	0.925 (0.969)	1.521 (1.186)	0.958 (1.100)
5. Log of Fraction of Population Aged 16–19	−0.580 (0.227)	−0.153 (0.261)	0.296 (0.376)	0.006 (0.345)
6. Quarter 2 (1 = Yes)	0.084 (0.015)	0.100 (0.013)	0.114 (0.013)	0.111 (0.011)
7. Quarter 3 (1 = Yes)	0.213 (0.019)	0.240 (0.016)	0.277 (0.016)	0.288 (0.014)
8. Quarter 4 (1 = Yes)	0.061 (0.018)	0.086 (0.015)	0.093 (0.014)	0.093 (0.013)
9. Time, Time-Squared, Time and Time-Squared Interacted with Three Season Dummies	Yes	Yes	Yes	Yes
10. R-Squared	0.98	0.98	0.97	0.97
11. Durbin-Watson Statistic	1.83	1.97	2.14	2.22
12. First-Order Autocorrelation (ρ)	0.57 (0.11)	0.72 (0.08)	0.90 (0.04)	0.93 (0.03)
13. Number of Observations	76	104	132	160

Note: Standard errors are shown in parentheses. The dependent variable in all models is the log employment–population rate of teenagers, seasonally unadjusted.

The Durbin-Watson statistic for the equation estimated by OLS is 0.19, indicating the presence of positive serial correlation. This strongly suggests that the unadjusted OLS standard errors are inappropriate. The Newey-West procedure provides consistent standard errors for OLS estimates even in the presence of serial correlation of

TABLE 6.5.B
Time-Series Estimates of Employment Models for Selected Time Periods,
Linear Specification

	1954–1972 (1)	1954–1979 (2)	1954–1986 (3)	1954–1993 (4)
1. Kaitz Index	−0.080	−0.101	−0.070	−0.076
	(0.074)	(0.060)	(0.059)	(0.053)
2. Unemployment	−1.076	−1.006	−0.942	−0.870
Rate of Adult Males	(0.252)	(0.179)	(0.165)	(0.155)
3. Fraction of 16- to	−0.503	−0.482	−0.486	−0.483
19-Year-Olds Who	(0.153)	(0.161)	(0.186)	(0.175)
Are Aged 16–17				
4. Fraction of 16- to	0.346	0.516	0.619	0.347
19-Year-Olds in	(0.415)	(0.382)	(0.424)	(0.407)
Armed Forces				
5. Fraction of Popula-	−1.464	−0.001	1.707	0.281
tion Aged 16–19	(1.180)	(1.073)	(1.429)	(1.368)
6. Quarter 2	0.365	0.039	0.041	0.040
(1 = Yes)	(0.007)	(0.005)	(0.005)	(0.004)
7. Quarter 3	0.103	0.106	0.115	0.119
(1 = Yes)	(0.008)	(0.007)	(0.006)	(0.005)
8. Quarter 4	0.029	0.032	0.033	0.034
(1 = Yes)	(0.008)	(0.006)	(0.005)	(0.005)
9. Time, Time-	Yes	Yes	Yes	Yes
Squared, Time and				
Time-Squared In-				
teracted with Three				
Season Dummies				
10. R-Squared	0.98	0.98	0.98	0.98
11. Durbin-Watson Sta-	1.74	1.85	2.07	2.13
tistic				
12. First-Order Auto-	0.65	0.74	0.90	0.94
correlation (ρ)	(0.10)	(0.08)	(0.04)	(0.03)
13. Number of Obser-	76	104	132	160
vations				

Note: Standard errors are shown in parentheses. The dependent variable in all models is the employment–population rate of teenagers, seasonally unadjusted.

unknown form. The Newey-West standard error is much larger than the unadjusted OLS standard error, and the implied t-ratio is 0.80. The Beach-MacKinnon, maximum likelihood (grid search) estimate (MLE), and first-differenced estimators all yield similar estimates of the coefficient on the Kaitz index and its standard error; the t-ratios range from 1.74 to 1.84. The Cochrane-Orcutt and Hildreth-Lu procedures yield somewhat larger coefficient estimates and slightly

TABLE 6.6
Estimated Minimum-Wage Effects OLS and Various AR(1) Corrections

	Coefficient (1)	Standard Error (2)	t-Ratio (3)	Sample Size (4)
1. OLS	−0.050	0.048	−1.040	160
2. Newey-West	−0.050	0.063	−0.796	160
3. Beach-MacKinnon	−0.072	0.042	−1.740	160
4. MLE (grid search)	−0.072	0.042	−1.740	160
5. First-Difference	−0.077	0.042	−1.835	159
6. Cochrane-Orcutt	−0.087	0.041	−2.097	159
7. Hildreth-Lu	−0.087	0.041	−2.097	159

Note: Estimates are based on the log-log specification in column 4 of Table 6.5.A.

smaller standard errors.[19] We conclude that the coefficient and standard error estimates from the Beach-MacKinnon procedure are about in the middle of the range of estimates. A conservative estimate of the t-ratio based on the Newey-West procedure would not allow one to reject a chance relationship, whereas the t-ratio from the Hildreth-Lu procedure is statistically significant.

In Table 6.7, we explore the robustness of the estimates to the inclusion of two additional explanatory variables: (1) the employment–population rate of adult males (aged 25 and older); and (2) the average wage of employees in manufacturing. For ease of comparison, the first column of Table 6.7 replicates estimates from the specification in column 4 of Table 6.5.A. In column 2 we add the log of the adult male employment–population rate. The adult employment rate has a large, positive effect on teenage employment (t-ratio = 3.66). Interestingly, the coefficient on the unemployment rate falls considerably after this variable is added. In addition, the coefficient on the Kaitz index falls by about 25 percent—to 0.055—when the adult male employment rate is added to the model. Moreover, the t-ratio on the Kaitz index falls to 1.36. Finally, in column 3 we add the log of the manufacturing wage, as an approximation to the specification suggested by equation (6.6). This variable is statistically insignificant, however, and its inclusion does not change the (statistically insignificant) coefficient on the Kaitz index.

Figure 6.5 depicts a partial-regression plot of the teenage employment rate against the Kaitz index. We created the figure by calculating residuals of the log teenage employment rate and the log Kaitz index from regressions on the other explanatory variables in the model in column 2 of Table 6.7 (excluding the Kaitz index). Figure 6.6 contains the same information, with the points arrayed in chro-

TABLE 6.7

Time-Series Estimates of Employment Models, with Additional Variables

	(1)	(2)	(3)
1. Log Kaitz Index	−0.072	−0.055	−0.055
	(0.042)	(0.041)	(0.041)
2. Log Unemployment Rate of Adult Males	−0.091	−0.020	−0.011
	(0.019)	(0.027)	(0.028)
3. Fraction of 16- to 19-Year-Olds Who Are Aged 16–17	−1.161	−1.177	−1.227
	(0.464)	(0.447)	(0.450)
4. Fraction of 16- to 19-Year-Olds in Armed Forces	0.958	0.754	0.798
	(1.100)	(1.058)	(1.059)
5. Log of Fraction of Population Aged 16–19	0.006	0.039	0.054
	(0.345)	(0.341)	(0.338)
6. Quarter 2 (1 = Yes)	0.111	0.097	0.099
	(0.011)	(0.011)	(0.012)
7. Quarter 3 (1 = Yes)	0.288	0.275	0.281
	(0.014)	(0.014)	(0.015)
8. Quarter 4 (1 = Yes)	0.093	0.085	0.088
	(0.013)	(0.012)	(0.013)
9. Log Employment–Population Rate, Adult Males	—	1.904	1.932
		(0.518)	(0.520)
10. Log of Average Manufacturing Wage	—	—	0.276
			(0.302)
11. Time, Time-Squared, Time and Time-Squared Interacted with Three Season Dummies	Yes	Yes	Yes
12. R-Squared	0.97	0.97	0.97
13. Durbin-Watson Statistic	2.22	2.12	2.12
14. First-Order Autocorrelation (ρ)	0.93	0.94	0.94
	(0.03)	(0.03)	(0.03)
15. Number of Observations	160	160	160

Note: Standard errors are shown in parentheses. The dependent variable in all models is the log employment–population rate of teenagers, seasonally unadjusted. All specifications adjust for an AR(1) error term using the Beach-MacKinnon procedure.

nological order. Teenage employment fell during the recession in the early 1980s, increased during the mid-1980s, and began to fall again during the late 1980s. Throughout the 1980s, the employment rate exhibits no secular trend, even though the Kaitz index fell considerably—a pattern which explains why the Kaitz index has a smaller coefficient in Wellington's and Klerman's analyses than in earlier ones. The increase in the Kaitz index in the early 1990s was accompanied by a decline in employment, but the decline began several quarters prior to the increase in the Kaitz index.[20] This result

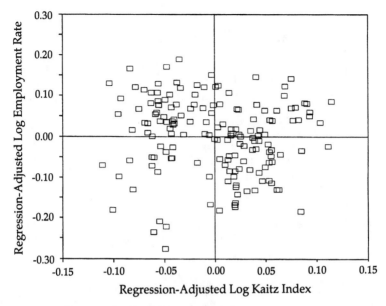

Figure 6.5   Partial regression plot.

is consistent with the finding that the coefficient on the Kaitz index is slightly larger when the data are extended through 1993. Nevertheless, the figures provide evidence of, at most, a weak relationship between teenage employment and the Kaitz index.

We have also estimated models with several different specifications of the minimum-wage variable, including the same control variables as the model in column 4 of Table 6.5.A. Table 6.8 summarizes results from these alternative estimates. The first specification includes a quadratic of the log Kaitz index. This specification allows the minimum-wage index to have a different effect on employment at different levels. Both the linear and squared terms are positive, which suggests that higher levels of the Kaitz index are associated with greater teenage employment. The two minimum-wage variables are jointly insignificant in this specification; however, the results do not provide support for the view that the minimum wage has a detrimental impact on employment when the coverage-adjusted minimum is at a relatively high level. In the second specification, we include as separate explanatory variables the log of the minimum wage, the log of the coverage rate, and the log of the average manufacturing wage. Here, the minimum wage has a negative association with employment ($t = 1.75$), and expanding coverage is associated with an *increase* in employment.[21] When it is entered sep-

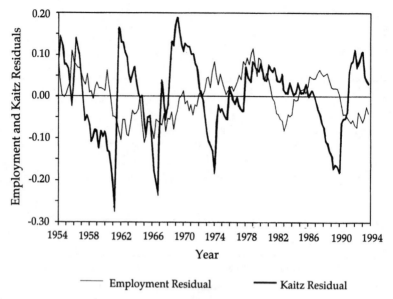

Figure 6.6 Regression-adjusted teenage log employment rate and log Kaitz index.

arately, the manufacturing wage has a positive, but statistically insignificant, association with teenage employment in all specifications.

The third specification corresponds to the model estimated by Gramlich (1976): the coverage rate is multiplied by the log of the real minimum wage. This specification yields a small and statistically insignificant negative coefficient for the minimum-wage variable. The fourth specification multiplies the square of the coverage rate by the log of the minimum wage. Again, we find a small and statistically insignificant effect of the minimum-wage variable. These alternative specifications do not provide strong evidence of an adverse effect of the minimum wage on employment.

As a final estimation strategy, we applied an instrumental variables (IV) approach, using the minimum wage as an instrument for the Kaitz index. The reason for this estimation approach is that, in the basic model, the variability in the Kaitz index stems from four sources: (1) changes in the statutory minimum; (2) changes in the extent of coverage; (3) changes in the industry distribution of teenage employment; and (4) changes in the average wages of workers in different industries. Using the minimum wage as an instrument yields estimates of the effect of the Kaitz index that rely exclusively

TABLE 6.8
Alternative Specifications of Minimum-Wage Variable

Specification	Coefficients
1. Log (Kaitz Index)	0.022
	(0.197)
[Log (Kaitz Index)]^2	0.036
	(0.074)
2. Log (Minimum Wage)	−0.088
	(0.050)
Log (Coverage)	0.025
	(0.067)
Log (Manufacturing Wage)	0.280
	(0.317)
3. Coverage × Log (Minimum Wage)	−0.042
	(0.051)
Log (Manufacturing Wage)	0.229
	(0.318)
4. (Coverage)^2 × Log (Minimum Wage)	−0.012
	(0.054)
Log (Manufacturing Wage)	0.216
	(0.318)

Note: Standard errors are shown in parentheses. The dependent variable is the log employment rate of teenagers. Coverage is the average fraction of workers covered by the minimum wage weighted by teenage industry employment shares. In addition to the variables listed in this table, the other included explanatory variables are the same as those in Table 6.5.A. All specifications adjust for an AR(1) error term using the Beach-MacKinnon procedure.

on changes in the statutory minimum wage. Specifically, we estimate the log-log model in first differences, which provides appropriate standard errors, and we use the change in the log of the minimum wage as our excluded instrumental variable. The IV estimate of the coefficient for the Kaitz index in a first-differenced specification similar to the one in column 4 of Table 6.5.A is −0.107, with a standard error of 0.072. Although the coefficient is somewhat larger than the OLS estimate of a first-differenced model, the IV estimate falls short of the typical margin of statistical significance (with a *t*-ratio of 1.48).

Separate Estimates, by Race and Gender

Table 6.8 reports estimates of the coefficient on the log Kaitz index from employment models fitted separately for whites and non-

TABLE 6.9
Estimated Effect of Log Kaitz Index on Teenage Employment Rate,
by Race and Gender, 1956–1993

Group	Coefficient of Kaitz Index
1. All	−0.055
	(0.041)
2. Whites	−0.055
	(0.042)
3. Nonwhites	−0.093
	(0.079)
4. Males	−0.069
	(0.045)
5. Females	−0.033
	(0.050)

Note: Standard errors are shown in parentheses. Estimates are based on the log-log specification. The specification is the same as that shown in column 2 of Table 6.7, except that the fraction of 16- to 19-year-olds who are aged 16–17 is specific to the race or gender group. All specifications adjust for an AR(1) error term using the Beach-MacKinnon procedure.

whites, and for males and females. The specification and control variables correspond exactly to the log-log model in column 2 of Table 6.9, except that the variable measuring the fraction of 16- to 19-year-olds who are aged 16–17 is specific to each race or gender group. None of the estimated effects for any of the four groups achieves statistical significance at conventional levels, although each of the estimates is negative.

The estimated employment effect is larger for nonwhites than for whites. Given sampling variability, however, one could not reject that the coefficients are the same. Wellington's (1991) estimates for the period 1954–1986 showed a slightly smaller coefficient for nonwhites than for whites (−0.062 versus −0.064). Finally, as Wellington found, the estimated effect is larger in absolute value for males than for females. Indeed, the estimated coefficient for females is quite small. Because females comprise more than 60 percent of all minimum-wage workers, the fact that the smallest effect is found for this group is noteworthy.

SUMMARY

The material in this chapter raises doubt as to whether the time-series literature strongly supports the conventional view that the minimum wage reduces teenage employment. First, it discusses a number of methodological issues regarding the aggregate time-series approach. Second, the negative relationship between the *t*-ratios and the sample sizes of previous studies suggests that publication bias, specification searching, or structural change has had an important effect on the results. Third, estimates of time-series models based on more-recent data that incorporate the experiences of the 1980s and early 1990s conflict with the previous literature. As we and others have found, if one estimates exactly the same time-series models that have been estimated in the past but includes more recent data, then the minimum wage has a numerically smaller and statistically insignificant effect on employment.

How should one interpret the time-series evidence in light of these new findings? First, note that the earlier time-series evidence is cited widely as the most compelling support for the conventional view of the minimum wage.[22] This is in sharp contrast with most other areas of labor economics, where time-series evidence has lost favor during the last two decades (see Stafford [1986]). Nevertheless, many economists and policy analysts continue to cite the prediction based on the earlier time-series literature that a 10 percent increase in the minimum wage will reduce employment by 1 to 3 percent. We draw two main conclusions from our review and update of this literature. On the one hand, the more up-to-date time-series estimates should lead one to lower the predicted range of employment effects. On the other hand, we believe that the methodological problems of the time-series approach, which we and others have identified, should lead to a reconsideration of whether this approach provides the best means of estimating the employment effects of minimum-wage increases.

NOTES

1. This description is simplified somewhat. Many researchers also adjust the Kaitz index for the minimum-wage rate that was applicable to newly covered workers in 1980 and earlier years. After 1980, the minimum wage for newly covered workers applied only to a trivial fraction of covered workers.

2. For example, Murray Weidenbaum (1993), chairman of the Council of Economic Advisors during the Reagan administration, recently claimed that, "the Minimum Wage Study Commission concluded in 1981 that a 10 percent increase in the minimum wage generates a 1–3 percent increase in the unemployment among those holding minimum wage jobs, mainly teenagers."

3. We omit Adams (1989) from this table because it is unclear whether his estimate pertains to teenagers or to all workers, and because his sample period was not reported.

4. The output-constant demand curve also is homogeneous of degree zero in factor prices.

5. Fisher (1973) and Hamermesh (1980) also raised related criticisms.

6. A classic example of this type of problem was noted by Cochran (1957). Cochran described an agricultural experiment in which oat fields were randomly selected for fumigation to reduce eelworms and thereby increase yields. There were two outcome variables in this experiment: (1) the crop yield; and (2) the number of eelworms remaining. Cochran warned against controlling for the number of eelworms in trying to estimate the effect of the fumigation treatment on crop yields.

7. De Long and Lang (1992) provide evidence of publication bias in economics articles. Concern about publication bias is by no means unique to studies in economics. The problem seems to be especially important in medical studies of cancer treatments (see Berlin, Begg, and Louis 1989).

8. See Begg and Berlin (1988). One factor that Begg and Berlin examined in their study of publication bias is the relationship between sample size and statistical significance. They interpreted the absence of an association between sample size and statistical significance in clinical trials of cancer treatments as evidence of publication bias.

9. Not all studies begin with 1954 data. Thus, the date of publication is not perfectly correlated with the sample size.

10. Notice also that, even with dependent observations, the t-ratio is expected to increase as the sample size increases.

11. Ragan (1977 and 1981) reported t-ratios only for disaggregated groups of teenagers. In this case, we used the average t-ratio. Mincer (1976) does not report a t-ratio, but did report that the minimum-wage effect for white teenagers was significant at the 0.01 level. In this case, we used 2.39, the critical t-value for a two-sided test of a null hypothesis at the 0.01 level.

12. The degrees of freedom are equal to the sample size minus the number of explanatory variables.

13. The standard errors reported in Table 6.1 assume that the errors from the regression equation are independent. This assumption is incorrect, because the underlying studies use overlapping data sets. The standard errors should not be interpreted literally.

14. A regression of the elasticity on the standard error (without a constant) yields a coefficient of 1.51 and a standard error of 0.21.

15. Welch also discovered that he had made a similar mistake in his analysis of the industrial distribution of teenage employment relative to adult employment. When he corrected the sample to consistently represent 14- to 19-year-olds, he found that, contrary to his original results, the minimum wage had a much larger impact on the manufacturing sector than on the retail-trade and service sectors. The corrected results are puzzling, because a much higher fraction of workers are paid the minimum wage in services and retail trade than in manufacturing.

16. Wellington reported using a "Cochrane-Orcutt type" procedure that uses the first data point to adjust for serial correlation. We were unable to exactly replicate her estimates with the Beach-MacKinnon procedure in RATS. We also attempted to replicate her results with a Cochrane-Orcutt procedure that does not use the first observation in two computer packages, TSP and RATS. Even with the same data, the two programs produced a

small discrepancy, which was roughly on the order of magnitude of the difference between our estimates and Wellington's. We doubt that the small difference between our estimates and Wellington's is of any substantive importance.

17. To confirm the comparability of the series, we calculated the Kaitz index from 1983 forward as a means of ensuring that our estimate was the same as Wellington's in the years in which they overlapped.

18. When we omit this variable, estimates of the coefficient on the Kaitz index for Wellington's sample period changed very little.

19. The discrepancy between the coefficient estimates with the various estimators is not due to the influence of the first observation. If we drop the observation for the first quarter of 1954, the Beach-MacKinnon and maximum likelihood coefficient estimates both fall to 0.065, with a standard error of 0.041.

20. Recall that, in chapter 4, we found the decline in teenage employment during the late 1980s and early 1990s to be greatest in the states in which the minimum wage had the least impact on the wage distribution.

21. The coverage rate is calculated as the weighted average of industry-specific coverage rates, where the weights are the employment shares of teenagers in the industry.

22. Some economists never put much stock in the time-series analyses of the minimum wage. For example, in their research for the Minimum Wage Study Commission, Heckman and Sedlacek (1981) sharply criticized the time-series approach.

CHAPTER 7

Evaluation of Cross-Section
and Panel-Data Evidence

It's not what you don't know that's the problem. It's what
you think you know that ain't so.

—attributed to Will Rogers

MOST OF THE EVIDENCE that is cited in academic debates and congressional hearings on the minimum wage is based on the analysis
of time-series data, but some is based on cross-section and panel-
data. Cross-section studies use variation in the minimum wage at a
point in time to identify the effect of the minimum wage; panel-data
studies follow the experiences of states or individuals over time. Unlike time-series studies, the cross-sectional and panel-data studies do
not have to rely on movements in the national minimum wage for
their estimation results.

The cross-section and panel studies generally are considered to
provide less-definitive evidence on the impact of the minimum wage
than the time-series evidence. For example, Brown, Gilroy, and Kohen (1982, p. 512) observed, "On the basis of the cross-section studies
alone, one is able to say little with confidence." Nevertheless, interest in using the cross-section approach to analyze the minimum
wage has been increasing. We expect that, as traditional time-series
regressions fail to produce statistically significant disemployment
effects, interest in cross-section methods in this area will increase
further.

In this chapter, we evaluate previous cross-section and panel-data
approaches to studying the employment impact of the minimum
wage. We focus on recent studies, because the earlier studies have
been carefully surveyed elsewhere, and because the recent studies
have received a great deal of attention in the popular press and
among economists. Three basic approaches have been used in this
literature.[1] In the first approach, data on a sample of states are followed over time. The employment–population rate of young
workers for a particular state in a given year is related to a measure
of the minimum wage. Variation in the minimum-wage variable
arises from changes in state-specific laws, variability in prevailing

wages across states, or changes in the federal laws that affect all states. In the second approach, the employment histories of low-wage workers are compared with those of high-wage workers over time. The pay rates of many low-wage workers are affected directly by the minimum wage, possibly leading employers to lay them off after a minimum-wage increase. Thus, researchers have attempted to measure whether low-wage workers are less likely to be reemployed in the year after a minimum-wage increase is imposed. In the third approach, an assumption is made about the distribution of wage rates in the absence of the minimum wage; for example, the distribution may be log-normal. Discrepancies between the actual and assumed distributions are then used to estimate the fraction of jobs that are eliminated as a result of the minimum wage.

Studies that analyze microdata have three main advantages over aggregate time-series studies. First, the unit of observation (e.g., workers and firms) in microstudies typically is the unit that corresponds to the decisionmakers in economic theory, enabling one to make a stronger connection between theory and empirical work. Second, in cross-section studies, unlike time-series studies, multiple factors are not changing over time. Third, and most importantly, it is possible in microstudies to specify a control group that can be compared with the group that is affected by the policy variable. In evaluating the previous microdata studies, we devote special attention to the four questions that need to be answered by any study that purports to show the effect of the minimum wage:

1. *Was there a program?* In other words, does one have evidence that the variable measuring the impact of the minimum wage is positively correlated with the wages of affected workers? The answer to this question may seem obvious, and not worth examining. The answer is critical in any program evaluation, however, because many government programs are not implemented or well-enforced, and because the variables may not be measured correctly. Determining whether the program variable is correlated with the program outcome of interest may indicate problems with the specification, and may help to answer the next question.

2. *What is the source of variation in the key explanatory variables, after holding constant the other variables in the model?* In chapters 2–4, we emphasized the importance of selecting credible control groups. Knowing why the program variable (e.g., the minimum-wage variable) differs across observations in the sample is critical for interpreting the empirical results, and for evaluating whether the comparison group is credible.

3. *How plausible is the control group?* Sometimes we can use *a priori* infor-

mation to judge the plausibility of a control group, such as when random assignment is used to determine members of the treatment and control groups. Whenever possible, however, the plausibility of the control group should be tested. For example, in our study of New Jersey and Pennsylvania fast-food restaurants, we compared employment trends in two control groups: New Jersey restaurants that paid more than the new, state minimum wage, and Pennsylvania restaurants that were unaffected by it. In addition, in some situations, one can test whether the program variable affects the outcome of interest in the control group. For example, in chapter 2 we found that the *GAP* variable had no effect on employment growth in the Pennsylvania restaurants. If the treatment variable has an effect on the control group, then it probably is reflecting a spurious factor. In a well-designed experiment, the treatment variable should not have an effect on the control group. Thus, this check sometimes is called the "do it wrong" check.

4. *How robust are the empirical results to plausible changes in the specification?* Many variables that are held constant in empirical work could be endogenous to the process being studied. For example, one could argue that the minimum wage affects school enrollment. If this is the case, then it is important to know how robust the results are to including or excluding the possibly endogenous variables. Similarly, one may be interested in knowing how robust the results are to including region or state dummies, or estimating the equations in first-differences form. To the extent that empirical results are qualitatively similar under different specifications and estimation strategies, the conclusions of the study are strengthened.

CROSS-STATE STUDIES

In the cross-state approach, employment is related to a measure of the minimum wage and other explanatory variables. The data typically consist of a sample of the 50 states pooled over several years. The employment equation that is estimated is of the form:

$$E_{it} = \alpha_0 + MW_{it}\beta + X_{it}\gamma + T_t\tau + S_i\delta + \epsilon_{it}, \qquad (7.1)$$

where E_{it} is the teenage employment–population rate in state i and year t; MW_{it} is a minimum-wage index (often a state-level variant of the Kaitz index); X_{it} is a set of explanatory variables, possibly including the school enrollment rate; T_t is a set of year dummy variables; and S_i is a set of state or regional dummy variables. The estimation error is represented by ϵ_{it}; the other Greek letters denote parameters that are estimated, usually by ordinary least squares (OLS) regression. The coefficient on the minimum-wage variable, β, is the key parameter estimate of interest. In some specifications, the dependent variable and the minimum-wage variable are measured in natural logarithms, in which case β is interpreted as the elasticity of employment with respect to the minimum wage.

We illustrate and evaluate this approach by considering two recent articles that provide cross-state analyses of the minimum wage. These articles have figured prominently in the recent debate of whether to increase the U.S. minimum wage.

Neumark and Wascher (1992)[2]

Neumark and Wascher (1992) used state-level data covering the years 1973 through 1989 to estimate equation (7.1).[3] They derived most of their data directly from May Current Population Survey (CPS) files. Their minimum-wage variable (*MW*) is a state-level version of the Kaitz index, which we describe in detail in chapter 6. The variable equals the maximum of the state or federal minimum-wage rate relevant for a given state-year observation, divided by the average wage of adults in the state, and multiplied by the overall Fair Labor Standards Act (FLSA) coverage rate in the state. Neumark and Wascher provided separate estimates for the employment–population rate of 16- to 19-year-olds and of 16- to 24-year-olds. We focus primarily on their estimates for 16- to 19-year-olds for two reasons. First, one would expect to find the greatest employment effects of the minimum wage in this population. Second, this population is the one that most of the literature has examined. Neumark and Wascher have kindly provided us with their data. The first two columns of Table 7.1 reproduce their main estimates of equation (7.1) for 16- to 19-year-olds. In comparing the two columns, notice that the negative effect of the minimum-wage variable hinges critically on whether a variable that Neumark and Wascher referred to as "the proportion of the age group enrolled in school" is also included as a regressor in the model.[4] If this variable is excluded (column 1), the minimum-wage index has a statistically insignificant and *positive* contemporaneous effect on teenage employment; if this variable is included (column 2), the minimum-wage index has a statistically significant, negative effect on employment. Thus, the interpretation of their estimates depends on the specification of the employment equation.

The variable that Neumark and Wascher labeled the "proportion of age group in school" is calculated in such a way as to treat anyone who is enrolled in school *and* either working or seeking work as *not* in school.[5] In other words, this variable measures the proportion of

TABLE 7.1
Reanalysis of Neumark and Wascher's (1992) Cross-State Data

| | Dependent Variable | | | | | | | | | |
| | Teenage Employment–Population Rate | | | | | | Log of Average Teenage Wage Rate | | | |
Explanatory Variable	(1)	(2)	(3)	(4)	(5)	(6)	(7)	(8)	(9)	(10)
1. Coverage-Adjusted Relative State Minimum Wage[a]	0.07 (0.10)	-0.17 (0.07)	—	—	—	—	-0.88 (0.22)	-0.10 (0.35)	—	—
2. Log of State Minimum Wage[b]	—	—	0.16 (0.08)	0.04 (0.05)	0.17 (0.08)	0.03 (0.61)	—	—	0.63 (0.18)	0.52 (0.18)
3. Fraction of Teenagers in School and Not Working[c]	—	-0.75 (0.03)	—	-0.74 (0.03)	—	-0.75 (0.03)	—	—	—	—
4. Log of Average Adult Wage	—	—	—	—	-0.03 (0.04)	0.03 (0.03)	—	0.41 (0.15)	—	0.41 (0.09)
5. Proportion of Teenagers in State Population	-0.19 (0.22)	-0.11 (0.15)	-0.16 (0.22)	-0.14 (0.15)	-0.19 (0.22)	-0.11 (0.15)	-0.54 (0.49)	-0.34 (0.49)	-0.65 (0.49)	-0.31 (0.49)
6. Prime-Age Male Unemployment Rate	-0.54 (0.10)	-0.31 (0.07)	-0.52 (0.11)	-0.32 (0.07)	-0.54 (0.11)	-0.31 (0.07)	-0.80 (0.24)	-0.69 (0.24)	-0.80 (0.24)	-0.66 (0.24)
7. State and Year Effects	Yes	Yes	Yes	Yes	Yes	Yes	Yes	Yes	Yes	Yes
8. R-Squared	0.72	0.87	0.72	0.87	0.72	0.87	0.77	0.78	0.77	0.78

Note: Standard errors are shown in parentheses. All models are fit to a sample of 751 state-year observations. The dependent variable in columns 1–4 is the employment–population rate for teenagers in the state in May of the year. The mean and standard deviation of the dependent variable are 0.432 and 0.090, respectively. The dependent variable in columns 5–8 is the log of the average hourly wage of teenagers in the state in May of the year. The mean and standard deviation of the dependent variable are 1.267 and 0.225, respectively.

[a] Maximum of the state-specific or federal minimum wage, divided by the average wage of adults in the state, and multiplied by the estimated fraction of workers in the state covered by the federal minimum wage.

[b] Log of the maximum of the state-specific or federal minimum wage.

[c] Fraction of teenagers in the state not working (during the May CPS survey week) and in school.

the age group not working and not looking for work, but enrolled in school. In fact, *most* teenagers who work (or who are looking for work) are also enrolled in school. The systematic exclusion of students who are working or are looking for work from the population of enrolled students led Neumark and Wascher to underestimate enrollment significantly. Their estimated enrollment rates for 16- to 19-year-olds average 40 percent. In contrast, we calculate that, during May 1986, the school enrollment rate for 16- to 19-year-olds was about 75 percent. The true enrollment rate is only slightly lower for teenagers in the labor force. Fully 65 percent of teenagers who work are also enrolled in school.

Neumark and Wascher's peculiar definition of the enrollment rate creates a serious statistical problem: the dependent variable (the employment–population rate) and a key independent variable (the enrollment rate) are mechanically related by construction. If relatively more students work in any state, then, by definition, the enrollment rate will be lower in that state. Furthermore, the decrease in the enrollment rate will be in proportion to the increase in the employment rate. Any variability in the state-specific teenage employment rate (including sampling variability) automatically enters into the enrollment measure with an equal and opposite effect. This statistical link will cause the coefficient on their enrollment variable to be biased toward -1. Indeed, Neumark and Wascher's regression estimates indicate that an increase in school enrollment has a large, negative effect on employment, with a t-statistic of more than 25. By contrast, the next-highest t-ratio for any variable in this regression is barely over 4. The high t-ratio is a symptom of a mechanical relationship between the dependent variable and the enrollment rate. As we shall see, another cross-state study that derived its school enrollment data from administrative school records found that the school enrollment rate has a much smaller, and statistically insignificant, effect on teenage employment.[6] In subsequent research, Neumark and Wascher (1994) used another definition of the enrollment rate. They used the same May CPS files as they had used in their 1992 study to calculate the fraction of teenagers who reported their *major activity* during the survey week as "going to school." When this variable is used in lieu of their initial "enrollment" variable, the minimum-wage variable in their estimated employment model was negative, but statistically insignificant. In addition, the coefficient and t-ratio on the new enrollment-rate variable were about one-half as large as in the previous study. Although their new enrollment variable is an improvement over the previous one, it continues to suffer from many of the same weaknesses. Most importantly, if a student reports that his or her major activity is "working," then he or she is not asked about school enrollment. Consequently, the teenage employment rate and Neumark and Wascher's alternative estimate of enrollment *are still mechanically correlated*, although to a lesser extent than in their original specification.

A second and related problem arises because Neumark and Wascher's estimates of the enrollment rate and employment rate were calculated from the same sample of teenagers. Consequently, the estimated enrollment and employment rates share a common component of sampling error. The sampling variability in state-level estimates from one month's CPS is quite large.[7] As we noted, students who report their major activity in the survey week as "working" *cannot* be counted as enrolled in school by Neumark and Wascher's measure. If, due to sampling variability, the May CPS sample of teenagers in one state contains an unusually high fraction of students who work, the sample will necessarily contain a low fraction of enrolled students, inducing a negative correlation between employment and the enrollment rate.

Independent of these statistical problems, an important conceptual issue is whether an endogenous variable, such as the enrollment rate, should be included as an explanatory variable in an employment model that seeks to estimate the effect of the minimum wage. As discussed in chapter 6, if one interprets the employment equation (7.1) as a combination of a demand equation for markets that are constrained by the minimum wage and the reduced form of a demand and supply system for markets that are unconstrained by the minimum wage, then exogenous determinants of the supply side of the market can be included legitimately in the employment equation. Clearly, however, one should not hold constant the effects of supply-side variables, such as school enrollment, that are possibly influenced by the minimum wage.

In our opinion, school enrollment should be treated as an outcome measure that is possibly influenced by the minimum wage.[8] The literature reflects this concern: only 4 of the 24 time-series studies surveyed by Brown, Gilroy, and Kohen (1982) include the school enrollment rate as an explanatory variable. There is no reason, aside from the possible effects of the minimum wage on employment opportunities, to believe that school enrollment is higher or lower in states with different levels of the minimum wage—especially if state and year effects are included in the regression model. Consequently, school enrollment can be omitted from the employment model without affecting the estimates. Thus, we believe that the most appropriate specification estimated by Neumark and

Wascher is one that excludes the school enrollment rate.[9] Like the estimates reported in chapter 4, this specification generates estimates that show no significant effect of the minimum wage on teenage employment.

State-Level Kaitz Index

The advantage of analyzing state-level panel data, rather than aggregate time-series data, is that different time-series patterns of the minimum wage across states can be used to estimate the impact of the minimum wage. In particular, by including year and state dummy variables, the identification of the impact of the minimum wage results exclusively from different time paths of the minimum-wage index in each state. Any common variation over time (e.g., as a result of an increase in the federal minimum wage in a particular year) is absorbed by the time dummies. The remaining variability in the relative minimum-wage index is the result of varying state minimum wages, differences in coverage rates, and differences in the average wage in the state. It is therefore important to know which component of the minimum-wage index is driving the estimated relationship.

Recall that the state-level Kaitz index for each state is defined as $MW = C \times M/W$, where C is the fraction of workers of all ages who are covered by the federal minimum wage in the state, M is the maximum of the federal minimum wage and the state minimum wage, and W is the average wage of adults in the state. The state-level Kaitz index has many of the same limitations that we noted in the context of the aggregate time-series models in chapter 6. In particular, the denominator of the Kaitz index is correlated with economic activity and with teenage wages. Factors that lead to an increase in adult wages in a state, such as an upturn in the state economy, will lead to a decline in the Kaitz index and will also tend to lead to an increase in teenage wages. If these factors are the dominant source of variation in the state-level Kaitz index, then the minimum-wage index will be *negatively* correlated with teenage wages.

To examine the relationship between teenage workers' wages and the minimum wage, columns 7–10 of Table 7.1 report regression results using as the dependent variable the log of the average hourly wage rate of 16- to 19-year-olds.[10] Results in column 7 show that increases in the state-level minimum-wage index used by Neumark and Wascher are associated with lower teenage wages, and the *t*-ratio for this relationship is −4. We suspect that this negative correlation is a reflection of the strong positive association between average adult wages and average teenage wages in a state. In any case, the negative effect of the Kaitz index on average teenage wages poses a significant problem for the interpretation of the employment models in columns 1 and 2 of the table, since it suggests that the minimum wage index is a poor proxy for the upward wage pressure exerted by the minimum wage.

In their employment regressions, Neumark and Wascher included as an explanatory variable the Kaitz index, but not the average wage of adults. Even if there are no other factors of production than teenage and adult labor, however, a properly specified employment equation for teenage labor should include both the Kaitz index and the adult wage (see chapter 6). This raises the question of whether teenage wages are positively correlated with the Kaitz index, holding constant average adult wages. As shown in column 8 of Table 7.1, the Kaitz index is still negatively, but insignificantly, related to the wage of teenagers conditional on the adult wage. These results confirm that the Kaitz index is a poor measure of the higher labor costs imposed by a minimum wage.

By contrast, column 9 shows that the logarithm of the actual minimum wage has a positive, and statistically significant, association with teenage wages, as one would expect. Furthermore, after controlling for the adult wage, the minimum wage continues to have a positive, and statistically significant, effect on teenage wages. These results imply that the minimum wage, without any further adjustment, is a more appropriate variable for measuring the impact of a wage floor on labor costs than is the Kaitz index.

Another limitation of the state-level Kaitz index stems from the way in which coverage by the minimum wage is measured. Neumark and Wascher's FLSA coverage rate refers to *all* workers, not just to teenagers. This shortcoming is an important one because teenagers and adults generally are employed in different industries—teenagers are overrepresented in retail trade and services, and underrepresented in manufacturing, finance, and government. Increases in the overall coverage variable may not portend much of an expansion in coverage for teenagers. For example, economy-wide coverage under the FLSA jumped by 13 percent during 1985 because coverage was extended to the public sector. This change is unlikely to have had much effect on teenagers. Another limitation is that the coverage measure makes no allowance for state minimum-wage laws, which greatly expand the coverage of minimum-wage statutes in some states. Finally, the coverage measure does not take into account noncompliance with the law.

In contrast to these problems with the Kaitz index, we emphasize that the minimum wage itself is positively correlated with teenage wages. Because the fraction of teenagers covered by the minimum wage was relatively high and fairly stable during the 1980s, the minimum wage arguably is a more appropriate variable than is the state-level Kaitz index. Furthermore, the level of the minimum wage generally is the variable of direct interest to policymakers. In columns 3–6 of Table 7.1, we include the log of the state minimum wage directly in the employment equation, rather than the minimum-wage index. Columns 5 and 6 also include the average wage of adults as an additional explanatory variable. The results show that a *higher* minimum wage is associated with *higher* teenage employment. Furthermore, this effect is statistically significant in the models in columns 3 and 5, which exclude the mismeasured enrollment rate. Moreover, even if Neumark and Wascher's school enrollment variable is included in the model, increases in the minimum wage are found to have a positive effect on employment.

To sum up, our reinvestigation indicates that the adverse employment effects of the minimum wage in Neumark and Wascher's study are the result of the peculiar way in which the school enrollment rate is measured. Furthermore, the Kaitz index used by Neumark and Wascher to proxy the minimum wage is negatively correlated with the average wage of teenagers. The minimum wage itself, on the other hand, is positively correlated with the teenage wage. When we relate teenage employment directly to the minimum wage, using Neumark and Wascher's data, we find that increases in the minimum wage have, if anything, a positive effect on employment.

Nicolas Williams (1993)

Another recent cross-state analysis was conducted by Nicolas Williams (1993). His sample consisted of annual observations on 50 states, from 1977 to 1989.[11] Williams estimated a model similar to equation (7.1) but included 8 region dummies, rather than 50 state dummy variables. Another feature of Williams' work is that, in some specifications, he allowed the minimum wage to have a different impact on employment in different regions. Our estimates in chapter 4, as well as those of Neumark and Wascher, constrain the minimum wage to have the same effect in all regions of the country.

Williams used two measures of the minimum wage. The first measure was the ratio of the *federal* minimum wage to the average hourly wage in manufacturing for each state. The second measure was the *federal* minimum wage divided by a state-level implicit price deflator. Williams did not adjust either minimum-wage index for the extent of coverage by the FLSA.[12] He also did not make any adjustment for state minimum wages, justifying this procedure by the fact that only 6.6 percent of the states in his sample period had a state minimum wage that differed from the federal minimum. As a result of these simplifications, in any given year the minimum wage was set at the same level for every state.[13]

The first specification that Williams estimated is

$$\log(E_{it}) = \alpha_0 + \log(M_t/W_{it})\beta + X_{it}\gamma + T_t\tau + R_i\delta + \epsilon_{it}, \qquad (7.2)$$

where $\log(E_{it})$ is the natural logarithm of the teenage employment–population rate; $\log(M_t/W_{it})$ is the minimum-wage index (ratio of nominal minimum wage in year t to the average manufacturing wage in the state); X_{it} is a vector of explanatory variables that consists of the adult unemployment rate, the population share of teenagers, and the enrollment rate of teenagers; T_t is a set of year dummy variables; R_i is a set of eight region dummy variables, and ϵ_{it} is a residual.

Notice that, because the minimum-wage index is measured in log units, and because the minimum wage does not vary across states in any given year, equation (7.2) could be rewritten as

$$\log(E_{it}) = \alpha_0 + \log(1/W_{it})\beta + X_{it}\gamma + T_t\tau' + R_i\delta + \epsilon_{it}, \qquad (7.3)$$

where the minimum-wage index is replaced by the inverse of the average wage in manufacturing in the state, and the coefficients on the year dummies are now $\tau'_t = \tau_t + \log(M_t)\beta$. The estimated coefficient, β, which Williams interprets as the effect of the minimum wage, is identical in equation (7.2) and in equation (7.3). In other words, if we set the minimum wage to the number 1 in every year (or any other number), the estimated minimum-wage coefficient in Williams' specification (β) would be the same: because the minimum wage does not vary across states in any year, any variation in the minimum wage is completely absorbed by the year dummies. As a general rule, any variable with only a t subscript will be completely absorbed by the year dummy variables.

To demonstrate this point, in column 1 of Table 7.2, we show Williams' basic set of estimates.[14] In column 2, we replace the minimum-wage index with the log of the inverse of the average manufacturing wage (which is equivalent to setting the minimum wage to $1 every year). Notice that the coefficients in rows 1 and 2 are identical. The minimum-wage itself plays no role in Williams' estimation strategy. All of the identification derives from variation in the manufacturing wage.

Although the statutory minimum wage plays no direct role in

TABLE 7.2

Reanalysis of Williams' (1993) Cross-State Estimates with Relative Minimum-Wage Variable

	(1)	(2)	(3)
1. Log(Minimum Wage/Average Manufacturing Wage)	−0.182 (0.036)	—	—
2. Log(1/Average Manufacturing Wage)	—	−0.182 (0.036)	−0.038 (0.062)
3. Log(Adult Unemployment Rate)	−0.384 (0.015)	−0.384 (0.015)	−0.175 (0.012)
4. Log(Teenage Population Share)	0.042 (0.055)	0.042 (0.055)	−0.150 (0.060)
5. Log(Teenage Enrollment Rate)	0.064 (0.056)	0.064 (0.056)	−0.020 (0.060)
6. Eight Region Dummy Variables	Yes	Yes	No
7. Forty-Nine State Dummy Variables	No	No	Yes
8. Twelve Year Dummy Variables	Yes	Yes	Yes
9. R-Squared	0.727	0.727	0.922

Note: Standard errors are shown in parentheses. The dependent variable in all models is the log employment–population rate of teenagers. See Williams (1993) for a description of data sources. The sample size is 650 state-by-year observations. Each regression also includes an intercept term.

these estimates, one could argue that the estimates nonetheless contain information about the employment effect of raising the minimum wage. In particular, if one believes that the federal minimum wage increases teenage workers' wages relative to adult workers' wages by a greater amount in states with a low manufacturing wage than in states with a high manufacturing wage, then the coefficient on the inverse of the manufacturing wage may reflect the impact of the minimum wage. However, alternative interpretations can explain why the inverse of the manufacturing wage may be correlated with teenage employment in a state. An equally plausible interpretation is that, in states in which economic conditions are strong, the manufacturing wage is high (so the inverse of the manufacturing wage is low), and the employment of teenagers is high, as well. In this scenario, the minimum-wage index does not reflect high labor costs, but rather, a strong state economy.

One way to examine the importance of omitted state-level variables is to estimate a state-fixed-effects regression model.[15] A state-fixed-effects model includes a set of state dummy variables as additional regressors in the employment equation. Unlike Neumark and Wascher (1992), Williams did not include state dummy variables in his specification. He did present estimates with and without the region dummy variables. When these variables were included, the minimum-wage coefficient was cut nearly in half. If there are permanent differences in the economic conditions among the states within a particular region, then it is necessary to include state dummy variables.

In column 3 of Table 7.2, we add 49 state dummy variables to Williams' basic model. These estimates indicate that the log of the inverse of the manufacturing wage has a statistically insignificant and small, negative effect on teenage employment. The point estimate implies that a 10 percent increase in the average manufacturing wage would increase teenage employment by 0.038 percent. The t-ratio for this estimate is only 0.62, however, indicating that the negative estimate could easily have occurred by chance. Furthermore, an F-test shows that, relative to the region dummies, the state dummy variables are statistically significant determinants of the teenage employment rate ($F = 35.5$). As one might suspect given this test statistic, inclusion of the state dummies greatly improves the explanatory power of the model, causing the R-squared coefficient to increase from 73 percent to 92 percent. The augmented model, which includes state fixed effects, provides a substantially better fit and suggests that the level of the manufacturing wage has no effect on the teenage employment–population rate.

Williams also presented estimates in which he interacted the minimum-wage index with region dummy variables, allowing the minimum wage (actually, the inverse of the manufacturing wage) to have a different effect in different regions of the country. The rationale for including these interactions is that the minimum wage might have a greater effect on employment in some regions than in others. In particular, one might expect increases in the minimum wage to have a greater effect on employment in lower-wage regions. Because this expectation is certainly plausible, the strategy of interacting the minimum-wage index with the region dummy variables is a sensible way to explore this issue. However, the interpretation of the estimates is clouded by the fact that the minimum-wage index depends solely on interstate variation in the average manufacturing wage. Moreover, the pattern of the estimated employment effects across regions makes little sense. Williams found that the minimum wage had the largest detrimental effect on employment ($\beta = -0.62$) in the Pacific region, which tends to have high wages. The estimate for the low-wage west-south-central region is statistically insignificant and close to zero. We interpret this pattern as another sign that the equations are not identifying the impact of minimum-wage changes.

Before leaving these estimates, observe that Williams also included an enrollment measure as an additional explanatory variable. Recall that the inclusion of an enrollment variable is pivotal to Neumark and Wascher's finding of adverse employment effects of the minimum wage. We have argued that Neumark and Wascher's enrollment measure, which excludes teenagers who are working, is mechanically related to their dependent variable, leading to biases in their estimates. Williams' enrollment-rate variable is defined as the ratio of the number of students enrolled in high school in the state to the population aged 16–19 in the state. This measure is derived from administrative enrollment data and thus does not suffer from the mechanical correlation problems that affect Neumark and Wascher's enrollment measure. In Table 7.2, estimates using Williams' data indicate that the enrollment rate has a small, positive, but statistically insignificant, effect on teenage employment when region dummies are controlled and a small, negative, but statistically insignificant, effect when state dummies are included.[16] These results contrast sharply with Neumark and Wascher's estimate that the enrollment rate has a t-ratio of 25 and a coefficient of -0.75. We take this contrast as additional evidence that Neumark and Wascher's results are biased due to the use of an enrollment measure that is mechanically (and spuriously) linked to the dependent variable. When enrollment is independently measured, it has little effect on teenage employment or on inferences about the effect of the minimum wage.

Specifications Based on a Price-Deflated Minimum Wage

Williams' second approach was to measure the minimum wage by dividing the federal minimum wage by the implicit price deflator for gross state product (GSP).[17] The specification estimated is

$$\log(E_{it}) = \alpha_0 + \log(M_t/P_{it})\beta_1 + \log(W_{it}/P_{it})\beta_2 + X_{it}\gamma + T_t\tau + R_i\delta + \epsilon_{it}, \quad (7.4)$$

where M_t denotes the federal minimum wage, P_{it} denotes the price deflator, W_{it} is the average wage in manufacturing, and all the other variables are defined as in equation (7.3). The coefficient, β_1, is interpreted as the effect of the "real minimum wage" on teenage employment.

Notice that, as in equation (7.2), the federal minimum is absorbed completely by the year dummies. Thus, the variability in the "real minimum wage" arises exclusively from differences in the price deflator across states and over time, rather than from any legislated changes in the level of the minimum wage.

Table 7.3 presents additional estimates using Williams' data. Col-

TABLE 7.3
Reanalysis of Williams' (1993) Cross-State Estimates with Price-Deflated
Minimum-Wage Variable

	(1)	(2)	(3)
1. Log(Minimum Wage/Price Deflator)	−0.325	—	—
	(0.111)		
2. Log(1/Price Deflator)	—	−0.325	0.042
		(0.111)	(0.089)
3. Log(Average Manufacturing Wage/	0.187	0.187	0.061
Price Deflator)	(0.036)	(0.036)	(0.064)
4. Log(Adult Unemployment Rate)	−0.249	−0.249	−0.178
	(0.015)	(0.015)	(0.012)
5. Log(Teenage Population)	−0.102	−0.102	−0.160
	(0.057)	(0.057)	(0.061)
6. Log(Teenage Enrollment Rate)	0.081	0.081	−0.032
	(0.058)	(0.058)	(0.060)
7. Eight Region Dummy Variables	Yes	Yes	No
8. Forty-Nine State Dummy Variables	No	No	Yes
9. Twelve Year Dummy Variables	Yes	Yes	Yes
10. R-Squared	0.717	0.717	0.922

Note: Standard errors are shown in parentheses. The dependent variable in all models is the log teenage employment rate. See Williams (1993) for a description of data sources. The sample size is 650 state-by-year observations. Each regression also includes an intercept term.

umn 1 replicates his main estimates. The estimate of the real-minimum-wage variable is near the top of the range of the past literature: a 10 percent increase in the "real minimum wage" is associated with a 3 percent decrease in employment. In column 2, we demonstrate that the price deflator is solely responsible for the estimated minimum-wage effect. The estimates show that the log of the inverse price deflator has a negative and statistically significant effect on teenage employment. Why is this? We conjecture that these estimates are merely a reflection of the regional Phillips curve. Prices are higher in states with low unemployment and booming economies. Teenage employment is especially procyclical and is naturally also higher when a state's economy does well.

To probe the results further, in column 3 of Table 7.3, we add state dummy variables to control for omitted state effects. These results show that the real minimum wage has a small, *positive* effect on employment. Again, the state dummy variables are highly statistically significant determinants of the teenage employment rate. One possible objection to including the state effects is that the state dummy variables absorb too much variability in the price index, so that one cannot obtain precise estimates. This objection does not apply here, however, as the standard error for the estimated minimum-wage variable is actually smaller in the model that includes the state dummies than in the model that includes only regional dummies. We conclude that once state effects are taken into account, teenage employment and state prices are insignificantly correlated.

STUDIES OF INDIVIDUALS OVER TIME

A second approach to measuring the effects of the minimum wage that is used in the literature is to follow individual workers before and after a minimum-wage increase is imposed. Workers are first classified by their initial wages or their "predicted" wages on the basis of their characteristics. Workers whose wages initially are less than the new minimum wage are expected to have more difficulty retaining their jobs than are higher-wage workers, because the increase in the minimum wage raises their cost to employers above their marginal productivity level. Peter Linneman's (1982) article in the *Journal of Political Economy* is a well-known application of this approach. Related work by Ashenfelter and Card (1981) and by Currie and Fallick (1994) extends this line of research.

Linneman focused on the increase in the minimum wage between 1973 and 1974. After remaining unchanged for five years, the minimum wage increased from $1.60 per hour in 1973 to $2.00 per hour on April 1, 1974, and to $2.10 per hour on April 1, 1975. Linneman first estimated a wage regression for a sample of adult workers, to identify the characteristics of workers who were earning less than the new minimum. The explanatory variables used to predict wages included education, experience, and other demographic variables. The wage regression was estimated using data for household heads or spouses from the Panel Study of Income Dynamics (PSID) for 1973, before the minimum wage increased. Linneman then predicted a wage rate for each member of his sample in 1974 and 1975. For nonworkers in 1973, the predicted wages for the later years were based on individual characteristics combined with coefficient estimates obtained from the 1973 sample of workers, plus an inflation adjustment. For those working in 1973, the predicted wages for 1974 and 1975 were based on 1973 wages plus an inflation adjustment.

Linneman then calculated the gap between each worker's wage or predicted wage and the minimum wage. The results showed that workers whose wages fell short of the minimum experienced a substantial decline in employment in 1974 and 1975. They also showed that workers with wages that were substantially above the minimum wage experienced a decline in employment, although not quite as large as the subminimum-wage group. We suspect that this decline reflected the downturn in economic conditions associated with the recession that began in late 1974. Linneman did not calculate the overall reduction in adult employment attributable to the minimum-wage increase. However, Brown, Gilroy, and Kohen (1982) pointed out that Linneman's results imply that a 10 percent increase in the minimum wage reduces affected workers' employment by more than 10 percent. This is a much larger effect than has been typically estimated in the literature.

At first glance, Linneman's approach seems plausible and related to our firm-level research discussed in chapter 2. Neoclassical theory predicts that workers whose wages are in the range that is affected directly by the minimum-wage increase would have lower employment rates (at least in the covered sector) after the increase. There is a serious problem in Linneman's analysis, however. Low-wage and low-skilled workers normally have lower employment rates and less stable employment histories than do higher-wage workers, even in years in which the minimum wage does not change. Thus, relative to a sample of higher-wage workers, we would normally expect a sample of lower-wage workers in one year to have lower employment rates in a subsequent year.

A second problem is that Linneman's sample of affected workers is composed of remarkably old workers—on average, the subminimum-wage group was aged 56, whereas the higher-wage group was aged 43. Retirement is likely to be quite prevalent among workers in a sample with an average age of 56. Unfortunately, based on Linneman's results, one cannot tell whether the decline in employment of the subminimum-wage group between 1973 and 1975 was a result of the minimum-wage increase or the fact that low-wage and older workers ordinarily have higher employment-with-drawal rates.[18]

The essential methodological flaw in Linneman's approach is the absence of a credible "counterfactual" for the employment histories of the affected group. High-wage workers provide a poor comparison group for studying the employment histories of low-wage workers. The insight from the "natural-experiments" approach to empirical research is that it is crucial to have a control group representing the experiences that the affected group of workers would have had in the absence of the minimum-wage increase. The high-wage workers who serve as a control group in Linneman's research clearly are an inadequate control group; these workers ordinarily have more stable employment histories than do low-wage workers—a phenomenon that has nothing to do with the rise in the minimum wage.[19]

Ashenfelter and Card (1981) reexamined the same minimum-wage increase that Linneman studied, but with a more plausible control group. Specifically, they used workers whose employment records showed wages of less than $2.10 per hour in 1973, *but who were employed in sectors of the economy that were not covered by the minimum wage*, as a control group for workers earning less than $2.10 per hour but who were employed by firms that were covered by the minimum wage.[20] Workers who are displaced from covered-sector jobs might be able to find new jobs in the uncovered sector eventually. One would expect, however, that their employment rates shortly after the minimum-wage increase would be lower than those of uncovered workers because uncovered jobs tend to be regionally based (e.g., agriculture) and because of adjustment lags. Ashenfelter and Card's choice of control group has the attractive feature that, prior to the increase in the minimum wage, workers in the control group were earning very similar wage rates to workers in the "treatment group." One can also examine employment rates of workers in the two sectors who were earning more than $2.10 per hour in 1973 as a check on whether the sectors experienced different shocks. Ashenfelter and Card based their analysis on three data sets: (1) the PSID, (2) the National Longitudinal Study of Young Women, and (3) the National Longitudinal Study of Young Men.

Table 7.4 summarizes Ashenfelter and Card's estimates for young women.[21] The table shows, for example, that 68.9 percent of women who worked in covered jobs in 1973 and were paid less than $2.10 per hour were still working by 1975—the year during which the minimum wage increased to $2.10 per hour. Almost exactly the same percentage of women who earned less than $2.10 per hour but who started out in the uncovered sector were still working in 1975. (Statistically, the 68.9 percent and 67.8 percent estimates are indistinguishable.) By contrast, 81.9 percent of women who initially earned $2.10 per hour or more in the covered sector were still employed in 1975, compared with 80.0 percent of similarly paid workers in the uncovered sector. Among workers earning less than $2.10 per hour, the initially covered workers were more likely to remain employed in the same sector than were the initially uncovered workers (not shown in the table). If the minimum wage has an effect on covered employment that is as large as Linneman's estimates imply, then the 31 percent increase in the minimum wage between 1973 and 1975 would have reduced employment of covered

TABLE 7.4

Percent of Young Women Employed in 1975, Based on 1973 Wage
and FLSA Coverage

	FLSA Coverage Status in 1973	
	Covered (1)	Uncovered (2)
1. 1973 Wage Less than $2.10 per Hour	68.9 (2.5)	67.8 (2.5)
2. 1973 Wage Greater than or Equal to $2.10 per Hour	81.9 (2.0)	80.0 (2.1)

Note: Standard errors are shown in parentheses. The table entries are 1975 employment rates of young women who were employed in 1973. The estimates are calculated
from Tables 2.6 and 2.9 of Ashenfelter and Card (1981) and are based on the National
Longitudinal Survey of Young Women. The sample size is 1,277 covered workers and 810
uncovered workers.

workers by more than 21 percentage points relative to that of low-
wage uncovered workers. Even with sampling variability, an effect
of that magnitude clearly would have been detectable in Ashenfelter
and Card's data.

If one compares the employment rate of workers who were paid
less than $2.10 per hour with the rate of those who were paid $2.10
or more per hour (as Linneman did), the results indicate that the
lower-wage workers are less likely to remain employed. This finding
almost certainly has nothing to do with the minimum wage, however, because the same pattern can be discerned in the uncovered
sector. Moreover, the fact that the employment rate of those earning
more than $2.10 per hour in 1973 was approximately the same two
years later, regardless of whether the worker initially was employed
in the covered or uncovered sector, suggests that the aggregate employment patterns in the two sectors were similar.

These simple tabulations provide no evidence that the substantial
minimum-wage increases in 1974 and 1975 reduced employment of
young women. Indeed, the results provide support for the interpretation that minimum-wage increases had no effect whatsoever on
employment. We should reiterate that the tabulations in Table 7.4
reflect the same minimum-wage increases as those studied by Linneman. The two studies reached different conclusions because Ashenfelter and Card compared the employment records of low-wage
workers with those of a more plausible control group, namely, other
low-wage workers, who initially were employed in the uncovered
sector.

A possible limitation of the covered versus uncovered comparison is that errors might have occurred when the workers were classified into covered and uncovered sectors. Ashenfelter and Card assigned coverage status on the basis of the workers' initial industry of employment. Random misclassification errors in coverage status would tend to drive the employment rates of the two groups together. During the early 1970s, however, coverage under the FLSA was much less complete than it is today. A large fraction of retail trade workers were excluded from coverage, and the entire sector is treated as uncovered by Ashenfelter and Card. Nevertheless, random classification errors would tend to cause covered and uncovered workers to look alike.

Currie and Fallick (1994) recently conducted another minimum-wage study which is similar in spirit to Linneman's study. Currie and Fallick used National Longitudinal Survey of Youth (NLSY) data to examine the impact of the 1980 and 1981 increases in the federal minimum wage. The minimum increased from $2.90 to 3.10 per hour on January 1, 1980, and to $3.35 per hour on January 1, 1981. Currie and Fallick followed a sample of 11,607 workers over the period 1979–1987. Although the minimum wage did not change between 1981 and 1987, they included observations in these years as well. They created a *GAP* variable, which equalled the shortfall between each worker's wage in the base year and the minimum wage in the following year. For example, if a worker was employed in a covered sector and earned $2.95 per hour in 1979, the *GAP* variable was set equal to 15 cents; if the worker was employed in a covered sector and earned $3.10 per hour in 1980, the variable was set equal to 25 cents. The *GAP* variable was also set equal to zero for any worker who, in the base year, earned less than the existing minimum wage, or earned more than the new minimum wage, or was deemed to be employed in an uncovered sector. By definition, then, the *GAP* equals zero for all workers in every year after 1980, regardless of their initial employment status. Currie and Fallick also defined a dummy variable, *BOUND*, which equalled one if the worker's wage in 1979 or 1980 was between the existing minimum and the new minimum and the worker was employed in a covered job, and equalled zero for all other workers. The *BOUND* variable indicated the workers who were expected to be affected directly by the 1979 or 1980 minimum-wage hike.

The *GAP* variable was intended to measure the amount by which each employee's wage had to be increased to bring him or her up to the new minimum wage. It is therefore critical that the GAP variable be positively correlated with wage growth from one year to the next.

Surprisingly, Currie and Fallick's results provided mixed evidence on this issue. When Currie and Fallick related the change in log wages to the *GAP* variable, they found a statistically insignificant and small relationship. However, when they eliminated 2,595 observations (5 percent of the sample) that had a greater than 100 percent increase in annual earnings, the results indicated a positive and statistically significant effect of the minimum wage on wage growth.

In the mainstay of their analysis, Currie and Fallick related individuals' employment probabilities to the *GAP* and *BOUND* variables. The results indicated that workers with wages in the range directly affected by the ensuing increase in the minimum were less likely to be employed during the following year than were workers in the comparison group. This result is not particularly surprising, however, as 87 percent of individuals in the comparison group were earning more than the new minimum wage.[22] As we discussed, high-wage earners generally have higher employment rates than do low-wage earners. Currie and Fallick were aware of this problem and implemented two different approaches in order to correct for the bias.

The first approach was to net out permanent differences in employment rates by using data on the individuals' employment rates between 1981 and 1987, after the minimum wage had increased. Currie and Fallick estimated a model in which they included individual fixed effects. Intuitively, this estimation strategy identifies the effect of the minimum wage by using the annual deviations of each individual's data about their means, taken over the entire sample period. If some individuals have permanently higher employment rates and others have permanently lower employment rates, the fixed-effects approach would net out the individual heterogeneity that might cause bias. However, there is little reason to believe that, for the NLSY sample, the unobserved individual effects that are correlated with base-year pay are fixed, or even approximately fixed, over time. The average worker in Currie and Fallick's 1979–1980 sample was younger than 18. In such a sample, one would expect productivity, wages, and employment rates to evolve rapidly over time, as workers move in and out of school and shop among jobs.[23]

The second approach that Currie and Fallick pursued was to compare the group that was bound by the minimum wage with three distinct comparison groups: (1) those above the minimum wage; (2) those below the minimum wage; and (3) those with wages that would make them bound by the minimum-wage increase but who were employed in industries that were not covered by it.[24] In our opinion, the latter group provides the best control group on *ex ante* grounds, because wages in this group are very similar to those of the bound group. When Currie and Fallick used regression analysis to compare employment rates between the covered and uncovered groups with wages in the affected range, they found a *greater* decrease in the employment rate of those who were in jobs that initially were *uncovered* by the minimum-wage increase relative to those who were in jobs that were covered by the increase. Furthermore, the decrease in employment of the uncovered group relative to the covered group was large (about 8 percentage points), and statistically significant (t-ratio = 5.3). The addition of individual fixed effects did not change the magnitude or statistical significance of this finding.

Currie and Fallick's regression estimates were based on a sample that tracked individuals for as long as six years after the minimum-wage hikes occurred. One could argue that employment experiences of the affected group at the end of the six-year period would be clouded by other factors that obscure the impact of having been employed in the covered sector much earlier. Table 7.5 presents estimates of workers' employment rates in *the year after* the minimum-wage increase, based on Currie and Fallick's NLSY sample.[25] For the covered and uncovered sector, employment rates are reported for three groups: (1) those whose wages in the previous (base) year

TABLE 7.5

Percent of Young Workers Employed in 1980 and 1981, Based on Wage Rate and FLSA Coverage in Previous Year

	FLSA Coverage Status in Previous Year	
	Covered (1)	Uncovered (2)
1. Wage in Previous Year Less than	71.3	65.4
Minimum Wage in Previous Year	(1.2)	(2.1)
2. Wage in Previous Year Between	74.4	67.3
Minimum Wage in Previous Year	(1.1)	(2.8)
and New Minimum Wage		
3. Wage in Previous Year Greater	83.3	82.1
than New Minimum Wage	(0.6)	(1.9)

Note: Standard errors are shown in parentheses. The table entries are 1980 and 1981 employment rates of workers who were employed in the previous (base) year. Estimates are calculated from unpublished tabulations provided by Janet Currie, and are based on data from the National Longitudinal Survey of Youths. The sample size is 7,621 covered workers and 1,178 uncovered workers.

were below the minimum wage for the previous year; (2) those whose wages in the previous year were between the old minimum-wage rate and the new minimum rate (i.e., directly affected workers); and (3) those whose wages in the previous year were above the new minimum-wage rate. As in Currie and Fallick's regression results, the entries in row 2 of Table 7.5 reveal that the employment rate was higher for covered-sector workers in the affected wage range than for uncovered-sector workers in the same wage range. This difference is inconsistent with the prediction that the rise in the minimum wage would force covered-sector workers in the affected wage range to lose their jobs. Moreover, the difference in employment rates of these two groups is statistically significant (t-ratio = 2.3). The table also shows that above-minimum-wage workers in the covered and uncovered groups had roughly equivalent employment experiences in the ensuing years, whereas sub-minimum-wage workers had a higher employment rate if they initially had been employed in the covered sector. Taken together, these results suggest that workers who were directly affected by the increase in the minimum wage fared no worse, and probably better, than workers who initially were paid about the same but were not employed in jobs that were forced to raise pay by the minimum-wage increase.

For reasons that we do not find compelling, Currie and Fallick dismissed the results of the comparison between the covered and uncovered samples. They observed (p. 14):

> All of the power in the original equations comes from comparing people with different wage rates, not people in covered vs. uncovered industries. This is not too surprising, given the very small number of people in this group, and the fact that not everyone in the industries that we designated as not covered are, in fact, in uncovered jobs. Moreover, what we call covered industries may differ from uncovered industries in ma[n]y ways other than their status under the FLSA, for which we do not control. Apparently, our attempt to identify uncovered industries is just too crude to be informative.

This argument has several shortcomings. First, Currie and Fallick's sample of 256 observations in the affected wage range in the uncovered sector provides a statistically significant estimate of the difference between the covered and uncovered group. One cares about sample size only insofar as the sample is too small to yield sufficiently precise inferences. The t-ratio of 5.3 that they estimate for the difference between the employment rates of the covered and uncovered affected workers could only have arisen by chance about one time in one million, if covered workers were more likely to lose their jobs. Their sample size is large enough to conclude that the lower employment rate of the uncovered group relative to that of the covered group probably did not occur by chance.

Second, as noted, random classification errors in coverage status will tend to make the groups look alike, thereby creating similarities in the groups' employment patterns, as well. The fact that Currie and Fallick found a statistically significant differential in the employment rates between the covered and uncovered groups, however, is evidence that random classification errors do not dominate their results. Moreover, their tabulations suggest that their industrial breakdown *does* distinguish between covered and uncovered workers. In particular, they found that workers who were paid less than the minimum wage were disproportionally employed in the uncovered sector.[26] This finding is exactly what one would expect, because uncovered employers are legally permitted to pay a subminimum wage.

Third, Currie and Fallick could have explicitly tested their assertion that employers or employees in the covered sector differ from those in the uncovered sector in many ways "other than their status under the FLSA." For example, they could have compared the annual employment rates of workers who originally earned more than the new minimum wage, broken down by whether they were employed in the covered or the uncovered sector. Ashenfelter and Card provided such a comparison and showed that the evolution of employment in the covered sector between 1973 and 1975 was quite similar to the evolution of employment in the uncovered sector (see Table 7.4). The tabulations based on Currie and Fallick's data, in Table 7.5, provide mixed support for the use of uncovered workers as a control group. The tabulations show that, on the one hand, workers in the two sectors who were already earning more than the new minimum wage had very similar employment rates following the increase in the minimum wage. On the other hand, the employment rate of workers who were earning subminimum wages is higher for those who started out in the covered sector than for those who were employed in the uncovered sector (see row 1 of Table 7.4). Interestingly, the difference in employment rates between sectors is very similar for subminimum-wage workers (difference = 5.9 percent) and for workers in the affected wage range (difference = 7.1 percent). In any case, there is no evidence that covered-sector workers in the affected wage range had lower employment rates following the rise in the minimum wage, compared to either higher-wage or lower-wage workers.

ESTIMATES BASED ON THE ASSUMED DISTRIBUTION OF WAGES

In a pair of articles, Robert Meyer and David Wise (1983a and 1983b) proposed and implemented a third strategy for estimating the effect of the minimum wage on employment. Their method works as follows. In the absence of a minimum wage, the distribution of wage rates would have some shape. Figure 7.1 provides an example, where the wage distribution is assumed to be log-normally distributed. The figure simply displays the total number of workers who are employed at each possible wage rate.

Now suppose that a minimum wage is imposed on this labor market. The minimum wage could have several possible effects on the number of workers who are employed at certain wage rates. In their model, Meyer and Wise assumed that introducing a minimum wage would influence employment by moving some subminimum-wage workers up to the minimum, and by causing some others to lose their jobs. Specifically, of those who originally earned less than the minimum, Meyer and Wise assumed that a fraction, p_1, would move up to the new minimum wage, a fraction, p_2, would remain below the minimum because of noncompliance or exemptions, and a fraction, $1 - p_1 - p_2$, would lose their jobs. These effects are illustrated in Figure 7.2, in which the dashed lines indicate how the distribution of wages changes from the situation in which there is no minimum wage. Notice that Meyer and Wise have ruled out the possibility that the minimum wage has a "spillover" effect on the wages of some workers who originally earned more than the minimum wage, or that some workers who originally earned less than the minimum are moved above the minimum.

In applying this technique, one does not know with certainty what the distribution of wages would have been in the absence of the minimum wage. This distribution is derived by first making an assumption about the parametric shape of the distribution. In partic-

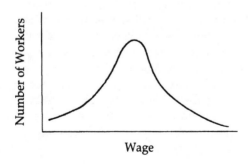

Figure 7.1 Wage distribution in the absence of a minimum wage.

Wage

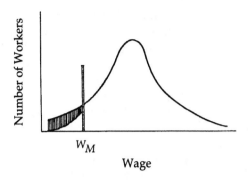

Figure 7.2 Wage distribution with a minimum wage, in the Meyer and Wise model. W_M represents the minimum wage.

ular, Meyer and Wise chose a log-normal earnings distribution. They then estimated the parameters of this distribution with maximum likelihood techniques based on data only for individuals who earned *more* than the minimum wage. In other words, information on the entire shape of the distribution of wages is derived from fitting a log-normal curve to the part of the distribution that is above the minimum wage. After estimating the parameters of the log-normal distribution, Meyer and Wise inferred what the wage distribution would have been for those earning the minimum or less. Discrepancies between the actual and predicted numbers of people earning the minimum or less provide an estimate of the employment effects of the minimum wage.

This is an ingenious method for estimating the difference in employment between a labor market that has a minimum wage and a labor market that does not have a minimum wage. The approach relies on several strong assumptions, however. First, one does not know what the distribution of wage rates would look like in the absence of a minimum wage because the United States has had a federal minimum wage for more than 50 years. The distribution must be imputed, and the statistical assumptions underlying the imputation of the distribution of wages in the absence of the minimum wage are controversial. Most importantly, the assumption that the distribution of wages would be log normal in the absence of a minimum wage is open to question. The assumed shape of the distribution is critical—after the distribution is fit to the right-hand tail of the wage distribution, it is used to "re-engineer" the left-hand tail of the distribution, in order to estimate employment effects. Plausible alternative assumptions about the distribution of earnings in the absence of a minimum wage can result in wildly different estimates.

A second, related issue involves the assumption that imposing a minimum wage does not change the structure of wages for those who originally earn above the minimum wage. As we discussed in chapter 5, evidence indicates that some firms seek to maintain their internal wage hierarchies when the minimum wage increases. For example, when the minimum wage increased to $3.80 per hour in 1990, a sizable fraction of fast-food restaurants in Texas raised the wage they paid to workers who initially earned more than the $3.80 per hour, in order to maintain wage differentials. Furthermore, we noted in chapter 5 that firms seem to maintain their seniority profiles after a rise in the minimum, implying that, ovér time, a minimum wage increase "spills over" to higher wages. The impact of a spillover effect is illustrated in Figure 7.3, in which the darkened segment above the minimum wage results from the spillover. The presence of a spillover effect poses a problem for the Meyer and Wise approach—unless this effect explicitly is taken into account, the distribution of wages above a minimum wage provides a misleading picture of what the wage distribution would be like in the absence of the minimum.

These limitations notwithstanding, Meyer and Wise (1983b) estimated that, had there been no minimum wage, employment of 16- to 19-year-old, out-of-school males in the United States would have been 7 percent higher during 1973–1978 than it actually was. It is difficult to compare this estimate with the others in the literature, because it measures employment in a labor market that is subject to a minimum wage relative to employment in a hypothetical labor market that is not subject to a minimum; the rest of the literature estimates employment changes associated with marginal increments in the minimum wage.

Dickens, Machin, and Manning (1994) applied and tested the Meyer-Wise approach, using data on workers who were employed in the retail-trade sector in Great Britain between 1987 and 1990.

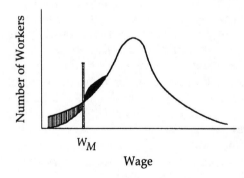

Figure 7.3 Wage distribution with a minimum wage and spillover effect. W_M represents the minimum wage.

They provided a number of extensions to the basic approach. First, they fitted a log-normal distribution to the wages immediately above the minimum in order to impute the shape of the entire wage distribution, as did Meyer and Wise. Second, as an alternative to the log-normal distribution, they fit a more general Singh-Maddala distribution function, which they argued fits the right-hand tail of the wage distribution better than does the log-normal distribution. Third, they varied the wage cutoff used for estimating the parameters of the wage distribution. To derive the shape of the wage distribution, Meyer and Wise used wage data on all individuals who earned at least one penny more than the minimum wage. Dickens, Machin, and Manning pointed out that, if the minimum causes wage spillover effects, and if these spillover effects do not reach very high in the distribution, it is desirable to use a higher wage cutoff point.[27] Specifically, they experimented with using the 10th, 20th, 30th, and 40th percentiles of the wage distribution as cutoff points. Dickens, Machin, and Manning provided a final extension in which, as a specification test, they estimated the Meyer-Wise-type model in the wholesale-trade sector. This sector was not covered by a minimum wage during the period that Dickens, Machin, and Manning investigated. To test the Meyer-Wise approach, they artificially imposed the minimum wage from the retail-trade sector on the wholesale-trade sector. If Meyer and Wise's method is valid, it should not yield estimates of employment losses from such a procedure.

Dickens, Machin, and Manning reported a number of interesting findings. We summarize their results for 1990, although their results generally are similar for earlier years. First, when they fit the log-normal distribution for men, using the 10th percentile of the wage distribution as the cutoff, their estimates imply that the minimum wage caused male employment to fall by 29 percent in the retail-trade sector in 1987, and by 39 percent in the wholesale-trade sector—even though wholesale trade was not covered by a minimum wage. A higher cutoff must be used for women, because the 10th percentile of the wage distribution was below the minimum wage. When Dickens, Machin, and Manning use the 20th percentile as the cutoff, the results imply that the minimum wage reduced female employment by 90 percent in retail trade, and by 47 percent in wholesale trade. The finding of negative employment effects in an uncovered sector raises serious questions about the validity of this technique. Furthermore, the estimates vary greatly when the cutoff point is shifted. Finally, estimates based on the Singh-Maddala wage distribution are quite different from corresponding estimates that presume a log-normal distribution, and some of the estimates with the Singh-Maddala distribution imply that the minimum wage has led to an increase in employment.

Dickens, Machin, and Manning (1994, p. 30) summarized their findings as follows:

> At first glance, the Meyer-Wise approach appears an attractive way of estimating the employment consequences of minimum wages. But, in practice, the fact that the minimum wage seems to affect the distribution of wages among workers paid above the minimum, and the fact that the distribution of wages cannot be adequately explained by a two-parameter model conspire to make estimates of the employment effects derived in this way very dubious.

We would add a final comment to this statement. In the Meyer-Wise approach, the percentage employment reduction created by the minimum wage is represented by $1 - p_1 - p_2$. The probabilities, p_1 and p_2, are constrained to be strictly positive, and to sum to less than one by the maximum likelihood procedure. Thus, the Meyer-Wise approach can find *only* a negative or zero employment effect of the minimum wage. In our view, this is a rather strong restriction to place on the data analysis *a priori*. Dickens, Machin, and Manning relaxed this assumption and sometimes found that the minimum wage led to increased employment.

CONCLUSION

Our intention in this chapter and in the preceding chapter was not to disparage research that has attempted to estimate the employment effects of a minimum wage. Instead, our intention was to probe the robustness of past estimates. We have tried to answer several questions about the literature. Are the estimates internally consistent? Are the results driven by extraneous factors other than the minimum wage? What explains differences among studies? How robust are the estimates to alternative specifications? These critical questions must be addressed if empirical work is to be used to advise policymakers or to guide economic theory.

Under close scrutiny, the bulk of the empirical evidence on the employment effects of the minimum wage is shown to be consistent with our findings in chapters 2–4, which suggest that increases in the minimum wage have had, if anything, a small, positive effect on employment, rather than an adverse effect. In our opinion, the conventional view that increases in the minimum wage necessarily have an adverse effect on employment has very weak empirical foundations. At the very least, we believe that our reanalysis of the literature should encourage economists to keep an open mind about the effect of a minimum wage.

NOTES

1. We do not discuss within-industry impact studies in this chapter, because the topic is covered in chapter 2.

2. Material in this section draws in part from Card, Katz, and Krueger (1994). For additional discussion of these issues, interested readers are referred to the exchange between Card, Katz, and Krueger (1994) and Neumark and Wascher (1994).

3. Neumark and Wascher's sample consists of 751 observations: data for the 50 states and the District of Columbia for 1977–1989, and data for 22 states that are identified individually in the Current Population Survey (CPS) for the years between 1973 and 1976.

4. Neumark and Wascher (1992) also experimented with including lags of the minimum wage, and with instrumenting for the state's minimum-wage index with the minimum wage of neighboring states. In both exercises, they found that, if the school-enrollment variable is omitted from the equation, the minimum wage has a statistically insignificant effect on the employment of 16- to 19-year-olds.

5. The problem stems from the fact that both the employment variable and the school-enrollment rate variable were calculated from the Employment Status Recode (ESR) variable on the CPS files. The ESR variable is designed primarily to measure employment and unemployment. According to the ESR variable, any individual who worked one or more hours during the survey week is coded as employed, regardless of his or her school-enrollment status. For most of the years that Neumark and Wascher examined, the true school-enrollment rate cannot be calculated from May CPS files.

6. Additional evidence that the large effect of the enrollment rate on employment in Neumark and Wascher's analysis is spurious comes from our own analysis of employment data from the Bureau of Labor Statistics publication, *Geographic Profiles of Unemployment and Employment*. The employment data in this series are based on all 12 monthly CPS surveys each year, rather than on one month's CPS. Thus, there is much less mechanical correlation between the employment rate and the May CPS "enrollment" measure. Using this data source, we find that the effect of Neumark and Wascher's "enrollment" rate is only one-fifth as large as in the case in which the data are estimated from the same source (see Card, Katz, and Krueger [1994]).

7. Because of concern about sampling variability, the Bureau of Labor Statistics does not use one month's CPS data to calculate state unemployment rates except for the eight largest states.

8. Indeed, a literature exists examining the effect of the minimum wage on school enrollment (see, for example, Ehrenberg and Marcus [1982] and

Mattilla [1981]). If anything, this literature has found that an increase in the minimum wage is associated with higher school enrollment. Neumark and Wascher's data show the opposite relationship.

9. Neumark and Wascher (1994) offer the following argument in favor of including the school-enrollment variable, "If minimum wages reduce employment, they should do so more for teenagers than for young adults, because a higher proportion of teenagers are minimum wage workers. As it turns out, this result holds in our data only for specifications including the enrollment rate. . . . [W]e interpret this difference as suggesting that the model excluding the enrollment rate is misspecified." Given the *a priori* reasons for excluding the enrollment rate, we do not find this argument compelling.

10. These wage regressions exclude Neumark and Wascher's school-enrollment variable. If included, this variable is statistically insignificant, and all the other coefficients are qualitatively unchanged.

11. We are grateful to Nicolas Williams for providing us with the data used in his article.

12. Williams notes that the minimum wage covered 83.8 percent of workers nationally in 1976, and 87.7 percent in 1989. He argues that the small increase in coverage is unlikely to bias his results. We agree that there probably is little reason for concern about the lack of a coverage adjustment.

13. The federal minimum wage was $2.30 per hour in 1977, $2.65 in 1978, $2.90 in 1979, $3.10 in 1980, and $3.35 from 1981 to 1989.

14. This estimate corresponds to column 2 of table 1 of Williams (1993). The coefficient estimates are identical to Williams'. Williams reports White-corrected standard errors. We have only calculated uncorrected standard errors, which are slightly smaller (about 13 percent smaller for the key coefficients).

15. In his table 3, Williams tries to control for state characteristics by including variables measuring welfare expenditures per capita, gross state product, and the rate of union membership.

16. When Williams omits the region dummies, the enrollment rate has a coefficient of .40 and a *t*-ratio above 6.

17. The implicit gross state product (GSP) price deflator is unpublished. Williams derived the estimator by calculating the ratio between the Bureau of Economic Analysis' nominal GSP and real GSP.

18. Brown, Gilroy, and Kohen (1982, p. 514) note this problem, as well. They observe, "This raises the possibility that his results reflect the fact that low-wage workers are less likely to be employed without convincingly implicating the minimum wage as a cause of this problem."

19. The Linneman study is analogous to a study of the effect of a cancer treatment in which all cancer patients are exposed to a treatment. If, one year later, we discover that those who were initially more sick (lower paid) were more likely to die after the treatment than those who were initially less sick (higher paid), we would not conclude that the cancer treatment had caused their deaths (employment decline). We would conclude that nothing has been learned from this experimental design.

20. The $2.10 cut-off was selected because the minimum wage increased to $2.10 in 1975, and Ashenfelter and Card examined 1973–1975 employment.

21. Although their results are qualitatively similar for men, we focus on the estimates for young women because the employment of this group is most likely to be affected adversely by an increase in the minimum wage.

22. The 87 percent figure is derived from information presented in Currie and Fallick's Table 4.

23. In our opinion, a better use of the 1981–1987 data in their sample would be to *test* their methodology by introducing an artificial minimum wage at some point in the mid-1980s, and to reapply their techniques. Currie and Fallick could create "pseudo" *GAP* and *BOUND* variables, for example, in 1986, that correspond closely to the variables in 1979 and 1980. They could then use these variables to try to predict employment changes between 1986 and 1987. (It would also be desirable to weight the data, so that the age distribution of the sample in this analysis is approximately the same as it was in the 1979–1980 analysis.) If the low-wage workers are found to be less likely to work, their earlier estimates would be called into question. If, on the other hand, they find no disemployment effects in this experiment, their approach would be validated.

24. Workers in the state and local government, agriculture, and domestic service industries are classified as uncovered.

25. The tabulations underlying this table were kindly provided to us by Janet Currie.

26. During 1979 and 1980, 24 percent of those who earned less than the prevailing minimum wage were in the uncovered sector, compared with 14 percent of those between the prevailing minimum and the new minimum, and with 10 percent of those above the new minimum. Most of the covered workers who reported a subminimum wage probably misreported their wage rate or were employed by firms that did not comply with the law.

27. They also noted that using a higher cut-off would not bias the estimates, even in the absence of spillover effects.

CHAPTER 8

International Evidence

> To find a clear employment effect, one needs to examine a
> minimum wage that bites rather than nibbles at the edges
> of the job market.
> —Alida Castillo-Freeman and Richard Freeman

MOST INDUSTRIALIZED COUNTRIES enforce a legal minimum wage. In
some countries, the minimum wage is set on an hourly basis, in
others, on a daily, monthly, or annual basis. In many countries, the
minimum wage varies by sector, age, and gender; in others, the extent of coverage and degree of compliance are far less than 100 percent. Such differences make it difficult to compare the level of minimum wages across countries. With these caveats in mind, however,
Table 8.1 reports the level of the minimum wage in selected countries in 1992. To facilitate comparison, each country's minimum has
been converted to U.S. dollars, using the appropriate exchange rate.
We also report the ratio of the minimum wage to the average wage
of production workers in manufacturing.

A glance down the table shows that the relative level of the minimum wage varies from 17 percent of average manufacturing wages
in Spain to over 40 percent in Australia, New Zealand, Puerto Rico,
and Turkey. By international standards, the relative level of the minimum wage in mainland United States—26.3 percent of average
manufacturing wages—is at a relatively modest level.[1] This observation suggests that there may be much to learn by examining evidence on the effect of the minimum wage in other places, where the
minimum is at a higher relative level or is set by different institutional procedures. In this chapter, we study the effect of the minimum wage in Puerto Rico, Canada, and the United Kingdom. We
devote most of our attention to Puerto Rico, because the minimum
wage there is high relative to prevailing wages by world standards,
and because the minimum wage in Puerto Rico is imposed by
the U.S. federal government. Although some economists consider
Puerto Rico to be an ideal "laboratory" for testing the textbook
model of the minimum wage, we find that Puerto Rico's experiences
provide surprisingly fragile support for the textbook model. As a
result of data limitations and other problems, we conclude that

Table 8.1
Minimum-Wage Rates in Selected Countries, 1992

Country	Minimum Wage (U.S. $) (1)	Minimum Wage/Average Compensation Costs per Hour for Production Workers in Manufacturing (2)
1. Australia	241.00 per week	0.464
2. Austria	12,000.00 per year	0.377
3. Belgium	900.00 per month	0.356
4. Canada (Ontario)	5.26 per hour	0.351
5. Canada (Quebec)	4.72 per hour	0.315
6. France	6.43 per hour[a]	0.381
7. Greece	20.13 per day	0.359
8. Israel	519.00 per month	0.265
9. Japan	32.26–37.56 per day[b]	0.262
10. Mexico	4.01 per day	0.274
11. Netherlands	259.00 per week	0.354
12. New Zealand	3.29 per hour	0.417
13. Puerto Rico	3.75–4.25 per hour[c]	0.493[d]
14. Spain	2.29 per hour	0.171
15. Turkey	210.00 per month	0.463
16. United States	4.25 per hour	0.263

Source: U.S. Department of Labor, Bureau of International Labor Affairs (1992–93) and Employment and Earnings (February 1993).

Note: The minimum wage is calculated by converting national currency figures into U.S. dollars. For Mexico and the Netherlands, data for 1991 were used. The minimum wage relative to average compensation costs per hour for production workers in manufacturing (column 2) was calculated as follows: For Austria, we derived an hourly minimum wage by dividing the yearly minimum by average hours worked per week by all workers times 50 weeks per year. For Belgium, Hungary, Israel, and Turkey, we derived an hourly minimum wage by dividing the monthly minimum by average hours worked per week by all workers times four weeks. The denominator is hourly compensation costs in manufacturing. For Israel, we used the average monthly minimum wage. For Australia and the Netherlands, we derived an hourly minimum wage by dividing the weekly minimum by average hours worked per week. For Australia, average hours per week of males were used. For Japan, Greece, and Mexico, we derived an hourly minimum wage by dividing the daily minimum by average hours worked per week by all workers times five days per week. For Mexico, average hours worked per week pertain to 1990. For France, New Zealand, Puerto Rico, Spain, and the United States, the minimum wage is set on an hourly basis.

[a] Based on 1991 exchange rate.

[b] Pertains to fiscal year starting April 1, 1992.

[c] Phased four-tier system, based on the average wage in the industry.

[d] For Puerto Rico, only the average wage of production workers in manufacturing was available. We inflated the hourly wage by 30 percent to derive hourly compensation costs.

Puerto Rico does not provide as unique or decisive a natural experiment as is widely believed.

The minimum wage in Canada is set at the provincial level, and varies considerably across provinces. The available evidence on possible adverse employment effects of the minimum wage in Canada is mixed. Although studies of provincial data that were conducted during the 1970s and early 1980s found that the minimum wage had a negative employment effect, analysis of more recent data show weaker evidence of such an effect.

Finally, the United Kingdom provides an interesting contrast to countries that impose state- or country-level minimums. Until recently, minimum wages have been set at the industry level by Wage Councils in the United Kingdom. The variation in minimum wages across industries has been used in several recent papers to study the effects of the law.

PUERTO RICO[2]

It often is argued that, if the minimum wage cuts deeply into the wage distribution—if it far exceeds the equilibrium wage for a substantial fraction of the work force—then the adverse employment effects predicted by the textbook model will be readily apparent. The most commonly cited case where it is argued that the minimum wage should, and does, matter is that of Puerto Rico.[3] Reynolds and Gregory (1965) and Castillo-Freeman and Freeman (1992) have analyzed the employment effect of minimum wages in Puerto Rico. Their research is widely cited as evidence that the minimum wage leads to substantial employment losses when it really "bites" (see, for example, Fleisher [1970], Hamermesh and Rees [1993], Ehrenberg and Smith [1994], and Hamermesh [1993]).

We reexamine the evidence on Puerto Rico, beginning with Reynolds and Gregory's classic 1965 study, and following with the more recent study by Castillo-Freeman and Freeman (1992). The main conclusion of our analysis is that the evidence on minimum-wage effects in Puerto Rico is surprisingly fragile. Before turning to this research, however, we present a brief overview of the interesting history of the minimum wage in Puerto Rico.

The History of Minimum Wages in Puerto Rico[4]

The institutions determining Puerto Rico's minimum wage rate are governed by the U.S. Congress. When the Fair Labor Standards Act (FLSA) took effect in 1938, it initially applied to Puerto Rico, as well.

Employers in Puerto Rico were required by law to pay the U.S. minimum wage of 25 cents per hour, which exceeded average wages on the island by perhaps 100 percent. Noncompliance with the minimum wage was widespread, and a number of businesses threatened to close if it was enforced. The Congress, recognizing the problems inherent in enforcing such a high minimum wage in Puerto Rico, passed an amendment to the FLSA in June 1940 that established tripartite industry committees to set separate minimum wages at the industry and occupation level. Between 1940 and 1974, amendments to the FLSA expanded coverage to new industries in Puerto Rico, but industry committees continued to determine minimum wage rates.

The tripartite industry committees were composed of representatives of industry, labor, and the public, drawn from both Puerto Rico and the U.S. mainland. Each committee made recommendations to the Administrator of the Wage and Hours Division of the U.S. Department of Labor, who was authorized to accept the committee's recommendations, or to appoint another committee to rehear the case. The first committees set minimum rates of roughly 20 cents per hour, much lower than the mainland minimum, which by then had risen to 30 cents per hour. Nevertheless, Reynolds and Gregory concluded that the industry minimum-wage rates led to substantial increases in hourly earnings in Puerto Rico.

Union leaders and some mainland employers charged that the Puerto Rican tripartite system did not raise minimum wages rapidly enough. In response to these criticisms, changes in the mid-1950s reduced the Secretary of Labor's authority to interfere with Puerto Rican minimum wages. In particular, tripartite committee recommendations were imposed much more rapidly, weakening employers' ability to appeal minimum-wage increases.

Amendments to the FLSA in 1974 and 1977 introduced a new policy of increasing coverage and enacting automatic increases in Puerto Rico's minimum wages to gradually bring them in line with U.S. levels. By 1983, Puerto Rico effectively had the same minimum wage as the United States.

The minimum wage has had an overwhelming impact on the wage distribution in Puerto Rico. According to Reynolds and Gregory, during 1955, 46 percent of export industries for which data were available employed at least one-half of their workers at exactly the minimum wage, and 75 percent of industries paid more than one-half of their workers within 5 cents of the minimum (see Reynolds and Gregory [1965], Table 2-4, p. 54). In 10 percent of industries, the average wage approximately equalled the minimum wage. Reynolds and Gregory concluded, "There are strong indications that the minimum wage system has been partially responsible for the rapid increase in the real wage level, the diverse movement of wages in individual industries, and the shrinkage of occupational differentials" (p. 80).

Castillo-Freeman and Freeman similarly documented an impressive impact of the minimum wage on the wage structure. In 1979, when about 50 percent of Puerto Rican workers were covered by the U.S. minimum wage of $2.90 per hour, their tabulations of Current Population Survey (CPS) data for Puerto Rico show a large spike at exactly $2.90 per hour. In 1983, after all Puerto Rican industries became covered by the U.S. minimum wage, one-fourth of Puerto Rican workers were paid within 5 cents of the prevailing $3.35 minimum wage. During 1988, 28 percent were paid within 5 cents of $3.35 per hour. By comparison, on the mainland, about one-quarter of teenage workers were paid within 5 cents of the $3.35 minimum hourly rate in the early 1980s, and, by 1989, 17 percent were paid within 5 cents of the minimum (which was still $3.35 per hour).[5] Thus, the minimum wage imposes approximately as much of a constraint on the entire labor market in Puerto Rico as it imposes on the teenage labor market in the United States.

What Did Reynolds and Gregory Actually Find?

As we have noted, Reynolds and Gregory's study of Puerto Rico is often cited as evidence that the minimum wage had dire consequences for Puerto Rican employment. This interpretation is somewhat ironic, because Reynolds and Gregory reached a decidedly mixed conclusion about the impact of the minimum wage in Puerto Rico.

They provided three pieces of evidence on the impact of minimum wages on employment in Puerto Rico—two of which largely have been ignored in the literature. First, they found a positive, but insignificant, correlation between changes in average wages and changes in employment across 36 Puerto Rican manufacturing industries from 1954 to 1958 ($r = 0.151$). Given that Reynolds and Gregory attributed wage growth in Puerto Rico largely to minimum-wage increases, this finding is inconsistent with the expected adverse employment effect of minimum wages. However, Reynolds and Gregory argued that this positive correlation "reflects the fact that the minimum wage setting procedure tends to push wages up fastest in the most profitable industries, which are also those experiencing a rapid rightward shift of demand schedules and, therefore, the largest expansion in employment" (p. 96).

The second piece of evidence presented by Reynolds and Gregory involves the estimation of an employment-demand equation. This evidence might seem primitive by modern econometric standards, but it has proved to be the most influential aspect of their work. Specifically, Reynolds and Gregory estimated the following equation by the ordinary least squares (OLS) method:

$$\frac{dX}{\frac{1}{2}(X_0 + X_1)} - \frac{dN}{\frac{1}{2}(N_0 + N_1)} = \alpha + \beta \frac{dW}{\frac{1}{2}(W_0 + W_1)}, \quad (8.1)$$

where X represents value added in the industry, N represents employment of production workers, and W represents the production worker annual wage bill divided by the number of production workers. The justification for the particular form of the dependent variable is that labor demand may have shifted in some industries. Under the assumption of constant returns to scale, however, one can subtract the growth in output to estimate the pure substitution effect of wage changes, holding output constant. The absolute value of the coefficient, β, is then interpreted as an estimate of the elasticity of substitution between labor and all other factors. The equation is estimated with cross-industry manufacturing data for each of two periods, 1949–1954 and 1954–1958.[6]

Reynolds and Gregory were aware of several conceptual problems with equation (8.1) and warned that their "findings must be interpreted with caution" (p. 101). Importantly, they noted that the assumption of increasing returns might be more appropriate in their sample period than the assumption of constant returns. They also noted that the assumption of a fixed production function excludes technical progress. They were keenly aware that, by holding output constant, they estimated only the substitution effect, although minimum wages could have scale effects, as well.

Reynolds and Gregory overlooked two important statistical limitations of their approach. Most importantly, because physical-output measures were not available for the industries under study, Reynolds and Gregory used value added as a measure of output. By definition, value added equals the total of payroll costs, capital costs, and profits. In the low-technology manufacturing industries in Reynolds and Gregory's sample, value added largely is accounted for by payroll, and changes in value added are driven mainly by changes in payroll. Consequently, because growth in payroll per worker was on the right-hand side of equation (8.1), and growth in value added (approximately payroll) minus growth in employment was on the left-hand side, the coefficient, β, is naturally biased toward 1. The bias will be greater if profits and capital payments are small or are a constant proportion of an industry's payroll over time.

This bias can be seen most easily by considering the logarithmic version of equation (8.1):

$$\log(X_1/X_0) - \log(N_1/N_0) = \alpha + \beta \log(W_1/W_0). \quad (8.2)$$

Recall that X equals payroll (WN) plus profit (denoted π) plus capital payments (denoted r), $X = WN + r + \pi$. Taking a second-order Taylor series expansion of $\log(WN + r + \pi)$ around WN shows that the log of value added approximately equals $\log(WN) + (r + \pi)/WN - (r + \pi)^2/2(WN)^2$. If r and π are small relative to payroll, the left-hand side of equation (8.2) is approximately $\log(W_1/W_0)$. Regressing $\log(W_1/W_0)$ on $\log(W_1/W_0)$ will naturally bias β toward 1. Moreover, if $(r + \pi)/WN$ is constant within industries over time, then first differencing will cancel out this term and its square, inducing a bias toward 1.

Another source of bias in estimating equation (8.1) is that there are likely to be errors in the measurement of employment, so that dividing payroll by employment to derive wages also induces a bias in β toward 1.[7] Current econometric practice would use an instrumental variable for wage growth (either the lagged wage or the change in the minimum wage) in order to overcome these biases.[8]

Reynolds and Gregory's estimate of the labor-demand elasticity is insignificantly different from -1. Their estimated elasticity was -1.1 for 1949–1954, and -0.92 for 1954–1958, with standard errors of 0.13 and 0.21, respectively.[9] Whether these estimates represent an output-constant demand elasticity is open to some question, however. In addition to the likely statistical biases, one could question whether the (output-constant) labor-demand elasticity is as large as -1. First, most of the studies in Hamermesh's (1993) survey of labor demand found the substitution elasticity to be less than -1. Second, a coefficient of -1 implies that, during the 1950s, one-half of manufacturing production workers were displaced as a result of wage increases in Puerto Rico.[10] Because the unemployment rate declined from 15.4 to 14.2 percent between 1950 and 1958, it seems unlikely that the labor market was flooded by a new wave of displaced workers during this time. Our opinion is that Reynolds and Gregory's estimate is significantly biased toward -1, and that the exercise provides little evidence on the impact of the Puerto Rican minimum wage on employment.

The third component of Reynolds and Gregory's evidence consists of a detailed study of the foundation garment industry. They devoted particular attention to the brassiere industry because this industry was large, accounting for one fourth of total U.S. brassiere production, and because brassieres were assembled by low-skill workers and "not as susceptible to wide styling changes."

The minimum wage in the corset, brassiere, and allied garments industry increased from 24 cents per hour in 1950, to 33 cents in 1951, to 55 cents in 1954, to 86 cents in 1960, and to 99 cents in 1961—an increase of more than 400 percent. Average wages in the industry closely tracked the minimum wage, increasing from 29 cents in 1950 to 93 cents in 1960. Remarkably, production worker employment in the industry increased nearly tenfold between 1951 and 1961—from 730 to 7,210. This pattern of employment growth is clearly at variance with an adverse employment effect of the minimum wage. Moreover, it is difficult to argue that a product-demand shock caused employment to increase, because the product price *fell* between 1951 and 1961.[11] A product-demand shock would be expected to affect employment through an increase in the price of output.

How did the industry manage to adjust to such dramatic wage changes? Reynolds and Gregory reported, "The main lines of adjustment have been through a rapid rise in productivity and a decline in profit margins" (p. 105). They documented that dozens of garments shipped per production worker increased by 250 percent in the decade between 1951 and 1961. They also documented that operating profits as a percentage of sales fell from 22 to 11 percent between 1953 and 1961. Thus, their explanation is that of a combination of rapid productivity growth and transfers from firms to workers.

Their careful field study of productivity responses to the minimum wage suggested that, as wages in the industry increased, turnover and absenteeism declined, the screening of job applicants improved, and "managerial effort" improved. Reynolds and Gregory wrote pointedly, "For the most part, these economies have not involved substitution of capital for labor; they have involved mainly a substitution of managerial ingenuity plus a higher level of effort by the supervisors and workers retained in the plant" (p. 193). They also noted that it is possible to increase "standards of expected output" when the minimum wage rises, resulting, in turn, in higher output per worker, "improved work flow and tighter supervision and discipline." On the other hand, their evidence suggests that the sizable productivity enhancements due to the minimum-wage increases were not large enough to offset the decline in profit rates. However, because the industry was earning extra-normal profits at the outset (relative to the mainland), firms continued to operate, and even expanded employment.

Reynolds and Gregory's overall conclusion is decidedly mixed. On the basis of their estimates of equation (8.1), they concluded that there was some capital–labor substitution in response to wage increases, but their direct observations led them to conclude that productivity rose in response to the minimum wage, and that key industries did not shrink, despite dramatic increases in the minimum. Their evidence does not support a purely neoclassical or a purely institutional interpretation of the effect of the minimum wage. In the end, Reynolds and Gregory were quite reluctant to recommend changes in the minimum-wage system in Puerto Rico. They concluded that, "in some Puerto Rican industries it may prove feasible to establish a minimum wage identical with that on the mainland," whereas "in other industries, a lower Puerto Rican minimum may prove desirable" (p. 309).

Modern Analyses of the Puerto Rican Minimum Wage

Castillo-Freeman and Freeman's (1992) analysis of the Puerto Rican minimum wage consists of two components: (1) an aggregate time-series analysis; and (2) an industry-level analysis. We consider each of these in turn.

AGGREGATE TIME-SERIES ANALYSIS

Castillo-Freeman and Freeman analyzed aggregate, annual time-series data for Puerto Rico from 1950–1987.[12] They measured the minimum wage by the Kaitz index, constructed each year as

$$\Sigma \, f_i(m_i/w_i)c_i$$

where f_i is the fraction of employment in industry i, m_i is the minimum wage that applies to industry i, w_i is the average hourly wage in industry i, and c_i is the fraction of workers in industry i who are covered by the minimum wage.[13]

As discussed in chapter 6, the Kaitz index has been widely used in time-series studies of the effect of the minimum wage on the employment of teenagers in the United States. In the chapter, we also discussed a number of problems that are associated with the Kaitz index. With respect to Puerto Rico, we add another concern. The denominator of the Kaitz index is the average wage of all workers in the industry; in the U.S. studies, this is approximately the average wage of workers who are not affected by the minimum wage, because a very small fraction of non-teenagers are paid the minimum. In a labor market such as Puerto Rico's, however, where the minimum wage impinges on a substantial fraction of the work force, the denominator of the Kaitz index (the average wage) is affected by the minimum wage in many industries. As a result, variability in the Kaitz index will be dampened, because an increase in the minimum wage causes the average wage to increase, offsetting the increase in the numerator. In the extreme case in which all workers in every industry are paid the industry minimum, there is *no* measured variability in the Kaitz index. Because of this diminished variability, use of the Kaitz index will tend to overstate the employment effect of the minimum wage in Puerto Rico.

To assess the likely magnitude of the bias caused by the dependence of the denominator of the Kaitz index on the actual minimum wage, we conducted a small-scale simulation experiment. Specifically, we simulated a time series of wage data for an economy with log-normally distributed wages, in which the ratio of the minimum wage to the mean wage in the absence of a minimum wage ranges from 0.7 to 0.9. We then assumed that anyone who earns less than the minimum wage is brought up to the minimum; that is, we censored low wages at the minimum. A realistic value for the standard deviation of log wages (e.g., 0.5) implies that, with these relative values of the minimum wage, 20 to 35 percent of workers will be observed to earn the minimum wage. These are plausible figures for Puerto Rico. In our simulations, the standard deviation of the measured Kaitz index (using the censored wages to compute the denominator of the index) is attenuated by 30 to 40 percent relative to the standard deviation of the index based on uncensored data. This attenuation implies that the estimated coefficient of the measured Kaitz index is *overstated* by a similar percentage (i.e., 30 to 40 percent) in specifications that use the measured Kaitz index as an explanatory variable.

Figure 8.1 uses Castillo-Freeman and Freeman's data to construct a plot of the employment–population rate and the Kaitz minimum-wage index.[14] The figure displays some interesting patterns. Notice that the "coverage-weighted" minimum wage increased sharply during the 1966–1967 period, with no noticeable effect on employment. Furthermore, the 1968–1973 decline in the minimum wage was not accompanied by (or followed by) a corresponding rise in employment. The main support for a negative employment effect of the minimum wage in the figure is the 1974–1975 minimum wage expansion period, which was accompanied by a discrete decline in employment relative to population.[15]

Table 8.2 presents an extension of the time-series regressions presented in Castillo-Freeman and Freeman. Specifically, the log of the employment–population ratio is regressed on the log of the Kaitz index, the log of Puerto Rican gross national product (GNP), the log of U.S. GNP, and a time trend. The estimates are corrected for a first-order autoregressive (AR[1]) term. Column 1 presents a replication of Castillo-Freeman and Freeman's main estimates.[16] The Kaitz

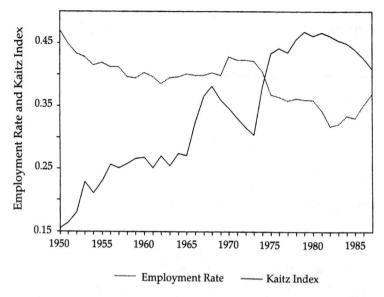

Figure 8.1 Employment and minimum wage trends in Puerto Rico.

index has a negative effect (−0.15) and is statistically significant. We explored several additional variants of this specification: omitting Puerto Rican GNP, including a quadratic time trend, estimating the equation separately for the pre- and post-1973 data, and constructing a minimum-wage index that does not involve coverage. Castillo-Freeman and Freeman tried a number of alternative specifications, as well. In general, the results continue to show a negative effect of the Kaitz index in these alternative specifications, although the size and significance of the coefficient varies.

It is interesting to note that the estimated coefficient of the Kaitz index in column 1 is similar to the estimated coefficients obtained from similar time-series models fit to employment data for teenagers in the U.S. as a whole. Considering that the coefficient of the measured Kaitz index for Puerto Rico probably is biased upward (in absolute value) by 30 to 40 percent, the estimated coefficient of −0.15 is, in fact, well within sampling error of the estimates reported for U.S. teenagers in Table 6.1 of chapter 6.

In light of the process by which minimum wages were set in Puerto Rico, however, one might question the direction of causality of minimum wages in Puerto Rico. Reynolds and Gregory, for example, were concerned that industry minimum wages were increased selectively, in industries in which employment was expected to grow. To explore this issue, we included the contemporaneous mini-

TABLE 8.2

Examination of Minimum-Wage Effects in Puerto Rico, 1951–1987,
Aggregate Time-Series Data

Independent Variable	(1)	(2)	(3)
1. Log(Kaitz) $t - 2$	—	0.03	0.03
		(0.06)	(0.06)
2. Log(Kaitz) $t - 1$	—	−0.05	−0.04
		(0.06)	(0.08)
3. Log(Kaitz) t	−0.15	−0.09	−0.08
	(0.07)	(0.06)	(0.08)
4. Log(Kaitz) $t + 1$	—	−0.03	−0.04
		(0.07)	(0.08)
5. Log(Kaitz) $t + 2$	—	−0.08	−0.09
		(0.07)	(0.07)
6. First-Order Autocorrelation	0.65	0.47	—
	(0.11)	(0.15)	
7. Log(Puerto Rican GNP), Log(U.S. GNP), Time Trend	Yes	Yes	Yes
8. p-Value for Two-Lagged and Contemporaneous Kaitz Variables	—	0.30	0.44
9. p-Value of Two-Leads of Kaitz Variables	—	0.32	0.18
10. Standard Error of Regression	0.026	0.022	0.024
11. R-Squared	0.57	0.87	0.94

Note: Standard errors are shown in parentheses. The dependent variable in all models is the log of the employment–population rate. Column 1 is a replication of Table 6.2 of Castillo-Freeman and Freeman. The sample size is 37 observations in column 1, and 34 observations in columns 2 and 3.

mum-wage index, two lags of the index, and two leads of the index. These results are presented in column 2 of Table 8.2 and column 3 of Table 8.2 (without an autoregressive error correction). The leads of the minimum wage seem to matter as much as do the lagged and contemporaneous values. Because minimum-wage increases took effect soon after they were enacted, it is unlikely that expectations of minimum-wage increases caused employment to adjust in advance. These findings cast some doubt on a causal interpretation of the negative coefficient on the contemporaneous Kaitz index in column 1.

CROSS-INDUSTRY/TIME-SERIES ANALYSES

The mainstay of Castillo-Freeman and Freeman's (1992) analysis is a cross-industry, panel-data analysis of employment. They used pooled cross-industry/time-series data covering 42 industries (37 detailed manufacturing industries and 5 one-digit nonmanufacturing industries) from 1956–1987 to estimate models of the form:

$$\log(EMP_{it}) = a + b \log(c_{it}m_{it}/w_{it}) + T_t\tau + IND_i\delta + \mu_{it} \quad (8.3)$$

where EMP_{it} is employment in industry i in year t, $c_{it}m_{it}/w_{it}$ is the Kaitz index for industry i in year t, T_t is a vector of year effects, IND_i is a vector of industry effects, and μ_{it} is an error term. Because unrestricted year and industry effects are included in this model, the impact of the coverage-adjusted minimum wage is identified by varying patterns in the minimum wage over time within industries. Castillo-Freeman and Freeman considered their industry-level analysis "a stronger test of the hypothesis that the minimum affected employment than thirty-one time-series observations" (p. 187).

Column 1 of Table 8.3 exactly replicates Castillo-Freeman and Freeman's basic estimates for the post-1974 period. This specification shows a large, negative impact of the minimum-wage index on employment, with a t-ratio of -4.2. Castillo-Freeman and Freeman suggested that the -0.54 elasticity is likely to overstate the impact of the minimum on total employment because workers will shift from industries with large minimum-wage increases to those with low increases.

Notice that the standard error of the regression in column 1 is quite large for industry-level data (0.48), suggesting a substantial amount of sampling variability in the dependent variable. Inspection of the data for selected industries reveals enormous variability from year to year, which probably is attributable to noise in the data. To explore the importance of errors in the data, we compared the change in log employment for 25 manufacturing industries from Castillo-Freeman and Freeman's sample (based on the Annual Survey of Manufactures) with data from the Puerto Rican Census of Manufactures. The Census of Manufactures is conducted every five years and, in principle, collects data from every manufacturing company. We find that, between 1967 and 1972, the correlation in the change in log employment between these two data sources is 0.60, and that, between 1972 and 1977, the correlation is 0.63. Both estimates suggest the presence of a considerable amount of noise relative to the signal in the within-industry analysis.[17]

A problem with estimating equation (8.3) by unweighted OLS is that unweighted estimation gives very small industries, with relatively noisier employment data, a great deal of influence on the estimates.[18] Another, possibly more serious, problem is that the unweighted OLS estimates give far too much weight to manufacturing

TABLE 8.3
Examination of Minimum-Wage Effects in Puerto Rico, 1956–1987, Pooled Detailed-Industry/Time-Series Data

	Employment Models			Wage Models	
Independent Variables	Log(Emp) Unweighted (1)	Log(Emp) Weighted (2)	Employment Unweighted (3)	Log(Wage) Unweighted (4)	Log(Wage) Weighted (5)
1. Log(Minimum × Coverage/Average Wage)	−0.54	0.07	8,177	−0.29	0.14
	(0.13)	(0.06)	(1,359)	(0.02)	(0.02)
2. Forty-One Industry Dummies	Yes	Yes	Yes	Yes	Yes
3. Year Dummies	Yes	Yes	Yes	Yes	Yes
4. Standard Error of Regression	0.48	0.31	5,918	0.08	0.09
5. R-Squared	0.87	0.96	0.95	0.98	0.98

Note: Standard errors are shown in parentheses. Column 1 is a replication of the specification in column 1 of Table 6.4 of Castillo-Freeman and Freeman (1992). The weights for columns 2 and 5 are average industry employment, 1956–1987. The sample size is 1,302 observations. Data for 1982 are excluded from the analysis because the Survey of Manufactures was not conducted that year.

industries. Castillo-Freeman and Freeman's sample consists of 37 detailed manufacturing industries and 5 one-digit nonmanufacturing industries. During 1980, manufacturing accounted for only 19.7 percent of Puerto Rican employment.[19] For these reasons, we tried three obvious alternative estimation strategies. First, we estimated equation (8.3) by weighted least squares, using as weights the average industry employment over the period 1956–1987. Second, we estimated equation (8.3) with the dependent variable in levels, rather than in logs. Third, we aggregated the manufacturing employment and Kaitz index to the one-digit level and reestimated the industry-level equations.

The results of these exercises are dramatically different from the base specification in column 1. Columns 2 and 3 of Table 8.3 report weighted estimates and estimates with the dependent variable in levels rather than in logs. The minimum-wage coefficient rises to a positive 0.07 if weighted least squares is used, with a t-ratio of 1.1.[20] Furthermore, when estimated in levels, the employment effect of the minimum wage is again positive, with a t-ratio of 6 (see column 3). It is not clear which specification is to be preferred, but the disparate implications with respect to the minimum-wage variable are troubling.

To illustrate the importance of weighting the industries, Figures 8.2 and 8.3 present partial regression plots of the relationship between employment and the Kaitz index. Specifically, we regressed the log of employment on a set of industry dummies and year dummies. We also regressed the log of the Kaitz index on the same industry dummies and year dummies. Residuals from each of these two regressions are plotted against each other. In Figure 8.2, the size of the point used to plot the residuals is proportional to the average level of employment in the industry. Figure 8.3 contains a plot of the same residuals, with all the points scaled to the same size. The figures suggest three conclusions. First, the equally-weighted residuals in Figure 8.3 are noisy, but the mass of the points tend to lie in a downward-sloping direction. Second, Figure 8.2 shows that the points that lie away from the body of the graph tend to represent smaller industries. Third, Figure 8.2 shows that residuals for the larger industries tend, if anything, to form an upward-sloping relationship.

One way to assess whether weighted or unweighted estimates are more sensible is to compare the effects of the minimum-wage variable on the industry *wage*. In columns 4 and 5 of Table 8.3, we present log wage regressions with the industry-level data. The model in column 4 is estimated by unweighted OLS, and the model in col-

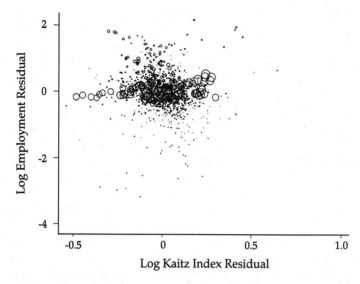

Figure 8.2 Partial regression plot. The size of the point is proportional to industry size.

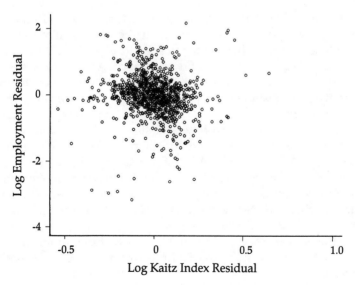

Figure 8.3 Partial regression plot. The size of the point is equal for all industries.

umn 5 is estimated by weighted least squares, where again, the weights are the average employment in the industry. The unweighted estimates in column 4 indicate that the minimum-wage index has a *negative* association with the wage rate ($t = 15.5$), whereas the weighted estimates in column 5 indicate a positive association ($t = 7$), as one would expect. A literal interpretation of the unweighted wage and employment equations implies that an increase in an industry's minimum-wage index is associated with a decline in the mean wage in the industry rate, and a decrease in its employment. By contrast, the weighted results indicate that wages tend to rise with the minimum-wage index, but that employment is not significantly related to the minimum-wage index.

Random measurement errors in the wage data would induce a negative bias in the coefficient of the minimum-wage index in the wage equation. If the measurement errors tend to be smaller in larger industries (e.g., because of greater sampling variability in the smaller industries), then the weighted estimates would have less bias, possibly explaining the positive weighted estimate of the wage effect. In any event, the greater plausibility of the weighted *wage regressions* over the unweighted wage regressions lends additional support to using the weighted specification of the employment equation.

Castillo-Freeman and Freeman reported separate estimates for the pre-1973 and post-1973 periods. They put greater emphasis on the post-1973 period because, beginning in 1974, the Puerto Rican minimum-wage was more closely linked to the U.S. minimum wage. Weighted and unweighted estimates for the post-1973 period are presented in Table 8.4. Castillo-Freeman and Freeman's unweighted specification in column 1 shows a larger negative effect of the minimum wage in this subperiod. When the log-log specification is estimated by weighted least squares, however, the minimum-wage coefficient becomes slightly positive and statistically insignificant. The corresponding weighted estimate for the pre-1974 period is also 0.03 (SE = 0.06). When the model is estimated with employment measured in levels, the log of the Kaitz index has a negative effect that is less than one-half as large as its standard error ($t = 0.47$). Bear in mind, too, that the standard errors reported here and in Table 8.3 probably are underestimated because we have made no attempt to adjust for serial correlation in employment within industries. These results do little to overturn the findings for the full sample reported in Table 8.3.

As a further specification check, we aggregated employment in the 37 detailed manufacturing industries into a single industry, in

TABLE 8.4

Examination of Minimum-Wage Effects in Puerto Rico, 1974–1987, Pooled Detailed-Industry/Time-Series Data

	Dependent Variable and Model		
Independent Variable	Log(Emp) Unweighted (1)	Log(Emp) Weighted (2)	Employment Unweighted (3)
1. Log(Minimum × Coverage / Average Wage)	−0.91 (0.24)	0.03 (0.19)	−1,148 (2,445)
2. Forty-One Industry Dummies	Yes	Yes	Yes
3. Year Dummies	Yes	Yes	Yes
4. Standard Error of Regression	0.37	0.20	3,739
5. R-Squared	0.95	0.98	0.99

Note: Standard errors are shown in parentheses. Column 1 is a replication of the specification in column 3 of Table 6.4 of Castillo-Freeman and Freeman (1992). The weights for column 2 are average industry employment, 1956–1987. The sample size is 546 observations. Data for 1982 are excluded from the analysis because the Survey of Manufactures was not conducted that year.

order to place manufacturing on an equal footing with the other major industries. In Table 8.5, we present (unweighted) cross-industry regressions with the pooled data on six major industries for the years 1954–1987. As before, we include year and industry dummies. The results for the full period indicate a small, but statistically, significant, negative effect of the Kaitz index on employment. Interestingly, the estimated effect of the minimum-wage index is positive for the 1974–1987 subsample, which is arguably the period during which the minimum wage was more nearly exogenous in Puerto Rico. Nevertheless, these results suggest a small, negative effect of the minimum wage on industry employment. We also note that the standard error of the regression with major industry-level data is less than 0.03, much closer to what one would expect with industry-level data.

Finally, we used Castillo-Freeman and Freeman's data to examine changes in industry employment during the period in which the Puerto Rican minimum wage became linked to the U.S. level. Specifically, we split the industries into three groups, depending on whether the industry-specific Kaitz index in 1973 was in the lowest 25 percent among all industries, in the middle 50 percent, or in the highest 25 percent. Industries with the lowest Kaitz indexes in 1973 were the ones most affected by post-1974 changes in the Puerto Ri-

TABLE 8.5
Examination of Minimum-Wage Effects in Puerto Rico, 1954–1987,
Pooled One-Digit Industry/Time-Series Data

	Time Period		
Independent Variable	1954–1987 (1)	1954–1973 (2)	1974–1987 (3)
1. Log(Minimum × Coverage / Average Wage)	−0.057 (0.014)	−0.066 (0.024)	0.003 (0.044)
2. Five Industry Dummies	Yes	Yes	Yes
3. Year Dummies	Yes	Yes	Yes
4. Standard Error of Regression	0.028	0.025	0.018
5. R-Squared	0.97	0.98	0.98

Note: Standard errors are shown in parentheses. The dependent variable is the log of one-digit industry employment (using the sum of employment in the separate manufacturing industries in Castillo-Freeman and Freeman's original sample). All models are estimated by unweighted OLS. The sample size is 186 in column 1, 108 in column 2, and 78 in column 3.

can minimum wage. We then computed the mean and median percentage changes in employment between 1974 and 1983 for industries in the three groups. For industries with Kaitz indexes in the lowest 25 percent, middle 50 percent, and highest 25 percent, we estimated that the mean percentage increases in employment were −6 percent, 6 percent, and −36 percent, respectively, while the median percentage increases were −22 percent, −18 percent, and −24 percent, respectively.

If anything, average employment declined most rapidly in the industries that should have been *least* affected by the increase in the Puerto Rican minimum wage during the 1974–1983 period, when the minimum was linked to the U.S. level. Notice, however, the large differences between the median and the mean growth rates of industry employment. This disparity is most likely a symptom of large sampling errors in the data. In any case, these results provide little support for the conventional demand model.

A CONCEPTUAL PROBLEM WITH THE CROSS-INDUSTRY APPROACH

How convincing is a cross-industry analysis of the minimum wage? Here, we want to point out a problem that arises in the cross-industry analysis if all industries do not have the same elasticity of labor demand.[21] Suppose that there are two industries, denoted A and B. Industry A has an elasticity of demand for labor of −1, and industry B has an elasticity of demand of −0.5. Suppose that industry A is a higher-wage industry than industry B. Now consider the effect of a general minimum-wage hike that increases wages by 5 percent in industry A, and by 10 percent in industry B (because industry A is higher wage). The estimated effect of a minimum-wage increase on employment in this case would be zero—industry A and industry B would both shrink by 5 percent, even though they had different wage changes in response to the minimum wage. Of course, this is only a contrived example, and one could work out an example in which the employment effect of the minimum wage is larger than the elasticity of demand in either sector (by simply reversing the elasticities of demand for industries A and B).

Our point is that the cross-industry studies rely heavily on the assumption that the elasticity of demand is constant across sectors. In the standard competitive model, the elasticity of demand for labor is expected to vary across industries, because industries differ with respect to their substitution possibilities between labor and nonlabor inputs, and with respect to their product-demand elasticities. Indeed, the fact that different schemes for weighting the industries produce dramatically different estimates in Tables 8.3 and 8.4 suggests that the elasticity of demand varies across industries. We provide additional evidence on this issue in Table 8.6. This table presents estimates of the effect of the log Kaitz index on log employment for each of 42 industries.[22] Although more of the estimates are negative than positive, we find a disturbingly high number of positive estimates (18 of 42). Moreover, the estimated coefficients vary widely across industries, with little obvious pattern. For example, men's and boy's clothing has a positive and statistically significant coefficient, whereas women's outerwear has a negative and statistically significant coefficient. In view of these findings, there is little reason for presuming a constant elasticity of demand for labor across industries, which calls into question the cross-industry approach.

The assumption of a constant elasticity of demand across establishments is far more likely to hold across establishments within the same industry. Thus, on methodological grounds, we think that there is a strong argument for the within-industry analyses discussed in chapter 2. In the future, it may prove useful to conduct such studies with data on Puerto Rico.

EMPLOYMENT AND WAGE GROWTH IN GARMENTS AND RELATED PRODUCTS
INDUSTRIES: A U.S.–PUERTO RICO COMPARISON

The effect of linking Puerto Rico's minimum wage to that of the mainland level has been of special interest in the apparel industry.

TABLE 8.6
Estimated Minimum-Wage Effects, by Industry

Industry	Estimated Elasticity	Industry	Estimated Elasticity
Footwear	−0.92 (1.30)	Chemicals	−1.27 (0.39)
Leather Gloves	1.04 (0.37)	Transportation	−0.23 (0.14)
Metal Products	−0.10 (0.40)	Construction	−1.51 (0.43)
Electrical Machinery and Equipment	0.59 (0.37)	Services	0.03 (0.07)
Women's and Children's Underwear	0.20 (0.49)	Food	−0.15 (0.15)
Children's Outerwear	0.12 (1.08)	Household Furniture	−0.61 (0.32)
Corsets and Brassieres	0.30 (0.39)	Other Furniture	−2.40 (0.96)
Men's and Boy's Clothing	1.74 (0.76)	Saw Mills	−0.57 (0.39)
Leather Handbags	−1.96 (1.54)	Paper and Allied Products	0.09 (0.11)
Women's Outerwear	−1.92 (0.58)	Cement	−0.96 (0.27)
Miscellaneous Apparel	1.67 (0.71)	Cut Stone and Asbestos	0.71 (0.60)
Miscellaneous Fabricated Textiles	−0.48 (0.84)	Pottery	0.17 (0.22)
Toys and Athletic Goods	−1.36 (1.60)	Glass	0.37 (0.39)
Jewels and Jewelry	−0.26 (0.44)	Sugar	−0.81 (0.41)
Costume Jewelry	−1.92 (1.07)	Textile Mill Products	−0.18 (0.88)
Office and Art Supplies	−1.04 (0.55)	Plastics	0.02 (0.42)
Alcoholic Beverages	0.62 (0.22)	Rubber Footwear	1.63 (0.91)
Cigars	0.28 (0.23)	Machinery and Transport Equipment	1.03 (0.59)
Tobacco	−0.73 (0.48)	Professional Instruments	−0.54 (0.44)
Drugs	−0.61 (0.36)	Trade	−0.04 (0.07)
Petroleum	0.19 (0.28)	Finance	−0.30 (0.16)

Note: Standard errors are shown in parentheses. Elasticities were estimated from 42 unweighted regressions of log employment on the log of the Kaitz index, year, and year squared.

In terms of employment, the apparel industry was, and still is, Puerto Rico's largest manufacturing industry, so that any impact of the minimum wage on this industry would be of great importance to the island. Reynolds and Gregory devoted particular attention to the low-wage garment industry. We present a brief comparative analysis of employment and wage trends in the textile, apparel, and leather industries in Puerto Rico and the United States.

Table 8.7.A presents data on employment in the textiles, wearing apparel, leather, and footwear industries in Puerto Rico in 1973, 1984, and 1992. Table 8.7.B contains wage data for the same period. For comparison, the tables also present mainland U.S. employment and wages in these industries.[23] The U.S. minimum wage was $2.00 per hour in 1973.

Employment trends in these low-wage industries provide superficial support for the conventional wisdom with respect to Puerto Rico. Between 1973 and 1984, employment declined by 66 percent in the textile industry, by 19 percent in the wearing apparel industry, and by 41 percent in the leather industry. The combined employment in the four industries fell by 13,140 jobs between 1973 and 1984, which amounts to 25 percent of the initial level. However, in these industries, a similar pattern of employment decline occurred in the United States. Between 1973 and 1984, for example, the combined employment in these industries on the mainland fell by 600,000 jobs, or 22 percent of the initial level. Wage growth was 20 percent greater in Puerto Rico than that on the mainland, and employment growth was merely 3 percent lower. Assuming that the differential in wage growth is a result of more rapid growth in the minimum wage in Puerto Rico than on the mainland, one would have expected a relative decline in employment of 10.8 to 18.2 percent, based on Castillo-Freeman and Freeman's elasticity estimates of -0.54 and -0.91. Observe also that, between 1984 and 1992, employment declined by 11 percent more in the United States than in Puerto Rico. Wage growth was 15 percent greater in the U.S. than in Puerto Rico during this time. It is unclear whether the more rapid wage growth was related to the minimum wage, because the minimum increased in both Puerto Rico and the mainland in the early 1990s. Nevertheless, the greater decline in employment in the mainland is consistent with a movement along a downward-sloping relative industry demand curve.

The interindustry *pattern* of employment and wage growth among the four industries provides little support for the conventional view. The lowest-wage, three-digit manufacturing industry in Puerto Rico in 1973 was the leather industry, closely followed by the footwear

TABLE 8.7.A
Employment in the Textile, Wearing Apparel, Leather,
and Footwear Industries

	Industry Code (1)	Employment (1,000s)			Percentage Change		
		1973 (2)	1984 (3)	1992 (4)	1973–1984 (5)	1984–1992 (6)	1973–1992 (7)
Puerto Rico							
1. Textiles	321	7.04	2.41	3.23	−65.8	34.0	−54.1
2. Wearing Apparel	322	38.44	31.08	28.76	−19.1	−7.5	−25.2
3. Leather	323	2.64	1.57	1.79	−40.5	14.0	−32.2
4. Footwear	324	3.64	3.56	3.70	−2.2	3.9	1.6
5. Total		51.76	38.62	37.48	−25.4	−3.0	−27.6
United States							
6. Textiles	321	1,010	746	678	−26.1	−9.1	−32.9
7. Wearing Apparel	322	1,438	1,185	1,018	−17.6	−14.1	−29.2
8. Leather	323	101	66	52	−34.7	−21.2	−48.5
9. Footwear	324	183	124	71	−32.2	−42.7	−61.2
10. Total		2,732	2,121	1,819	−22.4	−14.2	−33.4

Source: International Labor Organization [1983, 1993], Tables 5 and 17.

industry. These industries experienced the greatest wage growth between 1973 and 1984 (both absolutely and relative to the mainland), probably in large part as a result of the linkage to the U.S. minimum wage. Nevertheless, the decrease in employment was much greater in the textile industry than in these two low-wage industries, and employment in the footwear industry actually declined more on the mainland than in Puerto Rico.

The minimum wage could have played a role in the evolution of employment in these industries. However, the natural evolution of industrial employment that occurs during the course of development, with low-wage manufacturing jobs declining as a nation grows in wealth, is probably more important. The most obvious explanation for the pattern of employment shown in Table 8.7.A is that Puerto Rico was undergoing rapid economic development during the 1970s and 1980s, and that the development process naturally led to shifts in employment away from low-wage manufacturing.

LONG-RUN EVIDENCE ON PUERTO RICAN GROWTH

It is sometimes claimed that the high level of the minimum wage has stymied growth in Puerto Rico and has led to substantial distortions in the economy. A broader look at the remarkable growth rate of the Puerto Rican economy during the past four decades, how-

TABLE 8.7.
Hourly Wages in the Textile, Wearing Apparel, Leather,
and Footwear Industries

	Industry Code (1)	Average Wage Rate			Percentage Change		
		1973 (2)	1984 (3)	1992 (4)	1973–1984 (5)	1984–1992 (6)	1973–1992 (7)
Puerto Rico							
1. Textiles	321	1.94	4.31	5.04	122.2	16.9	159.8
2. Wearing Apparel	322	1.83	3.93	4.41	114.8	12.2	141.0
3. Leather	323	1.66	4.02	4.44	142.2	10.4	167.5
4. Footwear	324	1.71	3.97	4.73	132.2	19.1	176.6
5. Average		1.79	4.06	4.66	127.3	14.7	160.8
United States							
6. Textiles	321	2.95	6.46	8.60	119.0	33.1	191.5
7. Wearing Apparel	322	2.76	5.55	6.95	101.1	25.2	151.8
8. Leather	323	2.79	5.71	7.40	104.7	29.6	165.2
9. Footwear	324	2.79	5.71	7.40	104.7	29.6	165.2
10. Average		2.82	5.86	7.59	107.5	29.5	168.8

Source: International Labor Organization, *Yearbook of Labor Statistics* [1983, 1993], Tables 5 and 17.

Note: For the United States, wages are available only for leather and footwear combined. Industry code is the international standard industrial code (ISIC).

ever, suggests that the minimum wage may *not* have been a major stumbling block. Baumol and Wolff (1993) noted that, "in the period since World War II Puerto Rico appears from the available data to have achieved economic progress that places it among the forefront of the world's performers." Table 8.8 reproduces Baumol and Wolff's estimates of real gross domestic product (GDP) growth for 33 countries. Puerto Rico's annual real GDP growth rate of 4.03 percent trails only Japan's and Taiwan's. Bear in mind, however, that international comparisons of GDP growth are plagued by problems of data comparability. These problems may be especially severe in the case of Puerto Rico, since it is not an independent country. Some of Puerto Rico's impressive growth may be attributable to transfers from the mainland. Net direct transfers to Puerto Rico from the U.S. government equalled 15.9 percent of Puerto Rico's GDP in 1950 and 21.3 percent in 1988.[24] In addition, exemptions from federal corporate taxation that were enacted in 1976 resulted in tax expenditures on the order of 10 percent of Puerto Rico's GDP in 1988.[25] We can get a crude estimate of the importance of these transfers by subtracting them from the figures in Table 8.8 and recalculating Puerto Rico's GDP growth rate. After these adjustments, the real GDP growth rate was 3.47 percent per year, which still puts it among the top 10 countries in the table, well ahead of Mexico, Colombia, Chile, and other Central American countries.

TABLE 8.8
Growth Rates and Real GDP Levels, 1950–1988, 33 Countries

| Country | Real GDP Per Capita | | Real GDP Growth Rate |
	1988 (1)	1950 (2)	(3)
1. Japan	$12,209	$1,275	5.95%
2. Taiwan	5,708	630	5.80
3. Puerto Rico	6,973	1,506	4.03
4. Italy	11,741	2,548	4.02
5. Austria	11,201	2,533	3.91
6. Spain	7,406	1,823	3.69
7. West Germany	12,604	3,128	3.67
8. Finland	12,360	3,152	3.60
9. Norway	14,976	4,263	3.31
10. France	12,190	3,692	3.14
11. Turkey	3,598	1,097	3.13
12. Netherlands	11,468	4,002	2.77
13. Belgium	11,495	4,151	2.68
14. Denmark	12,089	4,512	2.59
15. Sweden	12,991	4,967	2.53
16. Switzerland	16,155	6,668	2.33
17. United Kingdom	11,982	4,973	2.31
18. Ireland	6,239	2,599	2.30
19. Canada	16,272	6,913	2.25
20. Costa Rica	3,800	1,643	2.21
21. Dominican Republic	2,209	983	2.13
22. Australia	13,321	5,929	2.13
23. Mexico	4,996	2,224	2.13
24. Trinidad & Tobago	5,674	2,589	2.06
25. Colombia	3,568	1,653	2.02
26. United States	18,339	8,665	1.97
27. New Zealand	9,864	5,608	1.49
28. Peru	2,847	1,642	1.45
29. Chile	4,099	2,623	1.17
30. El Salvador	1,705	1,102	1.15
31. Honduras	1,346	881	1.12
32. Guatemala	2,228	1,540	0.97
33. Argentina	4,030	3,066	0.72

Source: Baumol and Wolff (1993).
Note: Real GDP per capita is measured in U.S. dollars.

CONCLUDING OBSERVATIONS ON PUERTO RICO

Many economists have argued that the experiences of Puerto Rico provide decisive evidence on the employment effects of a high minimum wage. In light of our reinvestigation, however, we consider the evidence surprisingly fragile. The strongest evidence of a negative employment effect arises from an aggregate time-series analysis. Far weaker evidence comes from the arguably better experiment posed by the interindustry patterns of employment and wage growth. Research based on low-wage sectors and teenagers in the United States may in fact provide better evidence on the effect of the minimum wage than is obtainable from Puerto Rico. During the early 1980s, there was a *larger* spike at the minimum in the distribution of wages for teenage workers than in the wage distribution for all Puerto Rican workers. Furthermore, there is considerable variation over time in the relative level of the minimum wage on the mainland, and in the effect of the minimum wage on diverse groups like women, nonwhites, and restaurant workers. Perhaps more importantly, Puerto Rico has a relatively small work force—about the size of Arkansas'. There are nine times more teenage workers in the United States than employees of all ages in Puerto Rico. A related difficulty is that employment and unemployment data for Puerto Rico are based on relatively small samples and are of questionable validity (see Flaim, undated). Finally, because the minimum wage has such a pervasive effect on the entire wage structure in Puerto Rico, it is very difficult to obtain a good *relative* measure of its effect.

Our reading of the evidence from Puerto Rico is that it is remarkably *indecisive* on the question of whether higher minimum wages have a large negative effect on employment. Future research may well demonstrate that high minimum wages have reduced Puerto Rican employment. We suspect that, at sufficiently high levels, the minimum wage probably does reduce employment. Determining the threshold level at which this effect occurs has proved very difficult, however. Perhaps as a result of data limitations, Puerto Rico's experiences do not provide as decisive evidence on the minimum wage as is widely believed.

CANADA

Canada's minimum wage statutes are set by the individual provinces. During the 1950s and 1960s, most provinces set different minimum wage rates for urban and rural areas, and for men and women. In some provinces, separate minimums for male and female workers continued to exist until the early 1970s. The variation in minimum wages by province and gender introduces the possibility of some interesting and potentially informative natural-experiment-type evaluations in Canada.[26] Perhaps surprisingly, however, the main literature on the minimum wage in Canada has tended to follow the pattern set by the U.S. time-series literature, focusing on the correlation between teenage employment–population rates and a Kaitz-index measure of the minimum wage. In this section, we review some recent work by Gilles Grenier and Marc Séguin (1991), which replicates and extends an earlier study by Swidinsky (1980).[27] The main conclusion from this research is that, although the minimum wage is estimated to have had an adverse effect on teenage employment in Canada prior to 1975, its effect has been far weaker in recent decades.

Grenier and Séguin calculated a coverage-weighted minimum-wage index, by gender, separately for each province. This index multiples the appropriate minimum wage by an estimated coverage rate, and divides it by the average provincial wage in manufacturing. Figure 8.4 reproduces Grenier and Séguin's time-series plot of the national average coverage-weighted relative minimum-wage index for males and females aged 15 to 19.[28] The figure shows a sharp rise in the minimum for male teenagers during the early 1960s, and

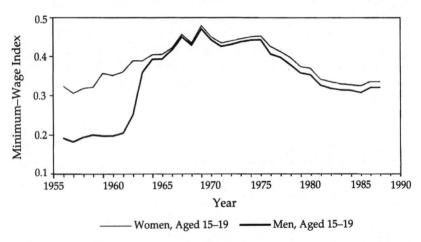

Figure 8.4 Minimum-wage index for Canada, 1956–1988. Reprinted with the authors' permission from Gilles Grenier and Marc Séguin, "L'Incidence du Salaire Minimum sur le Marché du Travail des Adolescents au Canada: Une Reconsidération des Résultats Empiriques," *L'Actualité Économique,* 1991.

a more modest rise for female teenagers between 1955 and 1965. The jump in the minimum for men is primarily due to the introduction of a $1.00 per hour minimum wage rate for men in Ontario in 1963. The relative minimum has declined for both males and females since the early 1970s.

Figure 8.5 reproduces Grenier and Séguin's time-series plot of the employment–population rate of 15- to 19-year-old Canadian teenagers. Despite cyclical peaks and valleys, the employment–population rate shows an upward trend that began during the early 1960s. Before 1980, the employment rate of females was lower than that of males; since 1980, the two rates have been roughly equal. The general movements in the employment trends are roughly parallel for male and female teenagers, even during the early 1960s, when the coverage-weighted minimum increased considerably more for male teenagers.

Following Swidinsky (1980), Grenier and Séguin grouped their province-level data into five regions and calculated regionally aggregated data. They then regressed the employment–population rate of teenagers on the minimum-wage index, four region dummies, the unemployment rate of 25- to 44-year-old males, and a quadratic time trend.[29] In their specification, the variability in the minimum-wage index results from within-region deviations from the nationwide

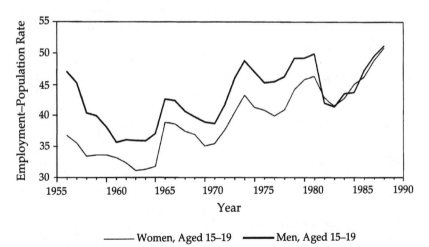

Figure 8.5   Employment–population rate in Canada, 1956–1988. Reprinted with the authors' permission from Gilles Grenier and Marc Séguin, "L'Incidence du Salaire Minimum sur le Marché du Travail des Adolescents au Canada: Une Reconsidération des Résultats Empiriques," *L'Actualité Économique*, 1991.

quadratic time trend. They presented separate estimates for men and women. Furthermore, because of a break in the data series, they presented separate estimates for the 1956–1975 period, and for the 1976–1988 period.

Table 8.9 summarizes their main estimates. Grenier and Séguin's estimates for the 1956–1975 period are qualitatively similar to Swidinsky's earlier findings for the same period and show a somewhat larger negative effect of the minimum. For the 1976–1988 period, however, they found that the minimum wage had a statistically insignificant effect for male and female teenagers, and the estimated effect is positive for females. The positive estimate for young women in the 1976–1988 period is rather surprising, because the estimated adverse effect is so large for this group in the 1956–1975 period. Moreover, the difference is not simply the result of sampling variability, as the change in the estimated minimum-wage effect for women between the two periods is statistically significant.

Grenier and Séguin attribute their puzzling findings for the

TABLE 8.9

Time-Series/Cross-Region Estimates of the Effect of the Minimum Wage on Teenage Employment in Canada, 1956–1975 and 1976–1988

	1956–1975		1976–1988	
Independent Variable	Males (1)	Females (2)	Males (3)	Females (4)
1. Minimum Wage Index	−0.146	−0.357	−0.232	0.118
	(0.040)	(0.109)	(0.138)	(0.108)
2. Atlantic Provinces	0.424	0.376	0.573	0.325
	(0.029)	(0.043)	(0.065)	(0.052)
3. Quebec	0.489	0.463	0.606	0.328
	(0.026)	(0.046)	(0.070)	(0.057)
4. Ontario	0.479	0.454	0.633	0.439
	(0.017)	(0.038)	(0.059)	(0.048)
5. Prairie Provinces	0.562	0.435	0.690	0.437
	(0.019)	(0.040)	(0.061)	(0.049)
6. British Columbia	0.493	0.426	0.649	0.463
	(0.022)	(0.035)	(0.051)	(0.041)
7. Unemployment Rate of Males Aged 25–44	−1.070	−0.550	−1.970	−1.390
	(0.240)	(0.230)	(0.130)	(0.100)
8. R-Squared	0.82	0.66	0.96	0.97

Source: Adapted from Grenier and Séguin (1991), Tables 1 and 2.

Note: Standard errors are shown in parentheses. The dependent variable in all models is the log employment–population rate of teenagers. Regressions also include time and time-squared. The sample size for columns 1 and 2 is 100, and for columns 3 and 4 is 65.

post-1975 period to the "loi de Murphy des économistes," which translates to "Murphy's law for economists." It seems that Murphy's law of the minimum wage is ubiquitous. Indeed, the deteriorating relationship between teenage employment and the minimum wage over time in Canada is reminiscent of the findings from the time-series estimates for the United States, discussed in chapter 6.

WAGE COUNCILS IN THE UNITED KINGDOM

Between 1909 and 1993, minimum wages in the United Kingdom were set at the industry level by Wage Councils. These Councils consisted of an equal number of representatives from business and labor, with as many as three additional members appointed by the government. As of 1990, 26 councils covered roughly 2.5 million low-wage workers. During the campaign for the April 1992 election, the British Labour Party proposed introducing a national minimum wage, rekindling debate on the effect of minimum wages. The Conservative Government, which won the election, abolished the Wage Council system in its 1993 Trade Union Reform and Employment Rights Bill. Unfortunately, it is too early to tell what effect this action has had on employment and wages. Nevertheless, the 1992 election campaign inspired researchers to investigate the impact of adjustments in the Wage Councils' rates on industrial employment.

Steven Machin and Alan Manning (1994) have examined the impact of the Wage Councils on wage dispersion and employment. They collected annual data from 1979 to 1990 on Wage Councils covering several large industries.[30] Machin and Manning defined a "toughness" measure of the minimum wage, which is the ratio of the minimum wage to the average wage of workers covered by the councils. They focused on workers aged 21 and older because legislation in 1986 removed workers younger than age 21 from coverage by the Wage Councils.[31] After 1986, a single minimum was set for each council; before then, the minimum varied across workers within councils. For the pre-1986 period, Machin and Manning defined the minimum wage to equal the lowest adult minimum wage rate set by the councils. In the earlier part of their sample period, the industry minimums were set at fairly high levels relative to average wages. For example, between 1978 and 1982, the minimum wage for women in the dressmaking industry averaged 80 percent of the mean wage in the industry. During the 1980s, under the Conservative government, the minimum wage in most industries decreased relative to the average wage. However, the variation in the rate of change in minimum rates across industries was considerable. Machin and Manning exploited this variation in order to estimate the impact of the industry minimums on wage dispersion and employment.

Given the tripartite nature of the Wage Councils, there is some controversy over whether they effectively raised wages. Machin and Manning first documented that council rates affected wage dispersion within industries. Unless the minimum wage is set below the lowest wage paid in an industry (or employers fail to comply with Wage Councils), one would expect an increase in an industry's minimum-wage rate to be associated with a decrease in wage dispersion in that industry. Machin and Manning tested this proposition by relating the standard deviation of wages in an industry to the log of the minimum wage relative to the average wage for that industry. Their sample consisted of 122 observations on ten industries between 1979 and 1990. Their regression model controlled for several variables, including industry dummies and a time trend. The results indicated that an increase in an industry's minimum wage relative to the average wage in the industry is associated with a decrease in wage dispersion, as expected. Dickens, Machin, and Manning (1994) further documented that minimum-wage increases are associated with greater wage growth in the lowest-paid deciles of the earnings distribution. We interpret these findings as tentative support for the view that Wage Council rates imposed a binding constraint on some jobs.

Machin and Manning then related employment growth in an industry to the change in the relative minimum-wage rate. Their OLS-regression results showed a positive—not negative—effect of relative minimum wages on employment, but the estimate fell short of statistical significance ($t = 1.45$).[32] Because they were concerned that the variation in the relative-minimum-wage variable might have been due to average wages, which were in the denominator, they also presented estimates in which they instrumented the ratio of the minimum to the average wage, using the Wage Council minimum rate. This instrumental-variables approach ensures that the variability in the relative minimum wage arises exclusively from changes in an industry's minimum rate over time. Results from this exercise continued to show a positive effect of changes in the minimum wage on an industry's employment.[33] Machin and Manning (p. 324) concluded, "The negative effect predicted by competitive models of the labor market is not observed in these data; indeed, we can formally reject the hypothesis that the coefficient is in the -0.1 to -0.2 range, which is the conventional wisdom in the U.S. time series studies."

Although Machin and Manning conducted a thorough study, we are left with two lingering concerns. First, the Wage Councils might have set rates strategically, raising them in industries that were expected to grow, and lowering them in industries that were expected to shrink.[34] If this is the case, then the relationship between employment growth and relative-minimum-wage growth would be biased in a positive direction. The fact that political factors in the United Kingdom led to a possibly exogenous shift in the behavior of the Wage Councils during Machin and Manning's sample period might partially allay this concern. Our second concern involves heterogenous industry responses to the minimum wage. As we discussed in the context of Castillo-Freeman and Freeman's work on Puerto Rico, cross-industry studies lean very heavily on the assumption that the elasticity of labor demand is the same among industries. If this assumption is not met, then, in a cross-industry study, the estimated minimum-wage elasticity may be biased in either a positive or negative direction. These concerns aside, it is difficult to find support for the conventional model from the United Kingdom's experience with Wage Councils during the last decade.

CONCLUSION

We have reviewed international evidence on the employment effects of the minimum wage for Puerto Rico, Canada, and the United Kingdom. The international evidence provides a useful complement to U.S.-based studies because, relative to average wages, many countries set their minimum-wage rates well above the U.S. level. In addition, in several countries, the minimum wage varies across industries or regions, affording industry-level or regional-level analyses.

Our review of the evidence on the employment effects of minimum wages for these three economies does not provide unambiguous support for the textbook model of the minimum wage. Puerto Rico has long been considered the ideal laboratory for testing the impact of the minimum wage because its minimum is high relative to prevailing wages. Furthermore, during the past two decades Puerto Rico's minimum has been imposed by the mainland U.S. government, which helps to avoid endogeneity problems in estimation. The evidence on employment effects of the minimum wage in Puerto Rico is surprisingly fragile, however. First, Reynolds and Gregory's (1965) classic study provided mixed results, with case studies suggesting that the minimum wage did not hurt employment, and their own estimates of cross-industry employment equations suggesting that it did. In all likelihood, because of data limitations, Gregory and Reynold's cross-industry regressions were significantly biased in the direction of finding negative effects. Second, Castillo-Freeman and Freeman's (1992) interindustry study is extremely sensitive to the weights applied to the industries. Their sample greatly overstates the importance of small manufacturing industries. If their estimates are recomputed, allowing industry weights to vary according to average employment shares, then increases in the minimum wage are associated with employment gains, rather than employment losses. Although the minimum wage might have caused employment to decline in Puerto Rico, it is very difficult to find robust evidence of this effect.

The pooled time-series/cross-section studies of province-level data for Canada yield strikingly similar results to the U.S. time-series studies. Before 1975, the coverage-weighted relative minimum wage was associated with lower employment of teenagers in Canada, and the elasticity estimates were similar to those from U.S. studies of teenagers in the same time period. When the same models are estimated with more recent data, however, the minimum wage is found to have a statistically insignificant effect on employment. Furthermore, the point estimates indicate that increases in the minimum are associated with employment gains for female teenagers. Thus, as the negative effect of the minimum wage in U.S. time-series models began to erode during the 1980s, the Canadian estimates underwent a similar transformation.

Finally, the United Kingdom provides an interesting contrast because, until recently, minimum wages were set at the industry level by Wage Councils. Machin and Manning found that increases in industry minimum wages were not associated with slower employment growth. Indeed, they found that larger minimum-wage increases were associated with faster employment growth, although this effect is not quite statistically significant.

These conclusions imply that our puzzling empirical findings with respect to the U.S. minimum wage are not isolated incidents. In the United States, the debate over the minimum wage has shifted from the question of whether minimum-wage increases cause small or large job losses to the question of whether minimum-wage increases cause any loss of jobs at all. The international evidence in the chapter suggests that the focus of the debate should shift worldwide. The consistent finding of weak or negligible employment effects in both the United States and elsewhere suggests that the problem may lie with the textbook model, rather than with the evidence.

Notes

1. Some economists have drawn a link between the minimum wage and unemployment on the basis of the casual observation that unemployment in many European countries has risen relative to that in the United States since the mid-1970s, and that European minimum-wage rates are high relative to average wages there. This conclusion is difficult to square with the fact that the unemployment rate has trended upward for low-skilled workers in the United States and in several European nations at about the same pace (see Fitoussi [1994]).

2. Material in this section draws heavily from Krueger (1995).

3. For example, Castillo-Freeman and Freeman (1990, p. 244) commented, "The extension of the U.S. federal minimum to Puerto Rico in the 1970s provides as good a case of a minimum with genuine economic bite as one could imagine."

4. This material borrows heavily from Reynolds and Gregory (1965) and Castillo-Freeman and Freeman (1992).

5. These figures are based on tabulations of the Current Population Survey Outgoing Rotation Group files.

6. Thirty-seven industries were included in the earlier period, and 50 in the latter.

7. Employment appears on the left-hand side. Thus, any omitted variables will induce a bias toward 1, because employment is in the denominator of the right-hand side. Again, this can be seen most readily with the log approximation to equation (8.1).

8. As noted in chapter 3, a similar issue arises in Kim and Taylor's (1994) study of the California minimum wage. They attempted to address this problem by instrumenting for the change in wages with the lagged wage and with firm size.

9. The estimates of the intercept, α, are close to zero, and not statistically significant.

10. Moreover, this is an underestimate, because it ignores the scale effect.

11. The price per dozen units of garments shipped in Puerto Rico fell from $8.48 in 1951 to $7.23 in 1961 (see Reynolds and Gregory, 1965, Table 3A–1).

12. Santiago (1989) also presents an aggregate time-series analysis of the minimum wage in Puerto Rico.

13. Castillo-Freeman and Freeman also used another measure of the minimum wage—the average minimum wage divided by average hourly earnings times an economy-wide coverage measure. Both minimum-wage measures have a negative effect on employment; the effect using the Kaitz index tends to be larger in magnitude.

14. Castillo-Freeman and Freeman reported two series of the employment–population rate. Throughout this book, we use series A. Figure 8.1 is quite similar when series B is used.

15. Notice, however, that this period also coincided with the first OPEC oil price shocks, and with a sizable recession in the mainland.

16. Using the data published in Appendix A of Castillo-Freeman and Freeman, we have been able to replicate exactly the minimum-wage elasticity that they reported in Table 6.3, column 1. However, some of the other coefficients are slightly different, and the R-Squared in column 1 is quite different. We estimated the models with the Cochrane-Orcutt procedure in STATA on a Unix-based computer.

17. The cigar industry provides an example of the discrepancy between the data sources. Castillo-Freeman and Freeman's data set shows only 68 workers in the cigar industry in 1987. In contrast, the 1987 Census of Manufactures reported that one of the ten cigar establishments in the Census employed more than 500 workers, and that two others employed between 100 and 499 workers (U.S. Department of Commerce [1990b], p. 63). Total employment was not reported in the Census of Manufactures, for reasons of confidentiality. The total far exceeds 68, however.

18. The residuals from equation (8.2) are highly heteroskedastic. For example, a White test can be calculated by regressing the squared residuals from equation (8.2) on the right-hand-side variables. The test strongly rejects the null hypothesis of homoskedasticity, with a value of 631.

19. See U.S. Department of Commerce (1984, Table 126).

20. In estimates not reported here, we used an alternative set of weights. Specifically, equation (8.3) was first estimated by OLS. The squared residuals from the estimated OLS equation were then regressed on the explanatory variables. The square root of the fitted values from this auxiliary regression provided the weights for equation (8.3). In this case, the coefficient of the log Kaitz index became 1.9 with a t-ratio of 8.1.

21. Note that this problem arises in other cross-industry studies, as well, including those of Reynolds and Gregory.

22. The reported coefficients were estimated from regressions, fitted separately for each industry, of the log of employment on the minimum-wage index and a quadratic in time.

23. The data are drawn from the International Labor Organization *Yearbook of Labor Statistics.*

24. These figures are derived from *Informe Económico al Gobernador,* published by the Puerto Rico Office of the Governor, Planning Board, various years.

25. An estimate of the tax expenditures in Puerto Rico from Section 936 of the Internal Revenue Code is provided by the Joint Committee on Taxation (CIS 92:S362-15).

26. One such evaluation is the interesting study by Zaidi (1970) of the introduction of the $1.00 per hour minimum wage for male workers in Ontario.

27. We focus mainly on Grenier and Séguin's work, rather than on Swidinsky's, because it covers a longer period, and because it reaches qualitatively similar conclusions for the period in which the studies overlap (1956–1975). We note major differences between the studies. See, also, Schaafsma and Walsh (1983) for a pooled time-series/cross-section study with Canadian provincial data for the years 1975–1979. West and McKee (1980) provide a thorough overview of the earlier Canadian literature.

28. The province-level indexes were weighted by labor-force size to construct the figure.

29. They also presented additional regression estimates, in which the dependent variables were the labor-force activity rate and the unemployment rate. Because the textbook model makes unambiguous predictions about the impact of the minimum wage on employment, but not on these other variables, we focus on the employment equations.

30. The industries that the Wage Councils covered are: catering, clothing manufacturing, hairdressing, nonfood retail trade, food retail trade, dressmaking, tailoring, and textiles. Some of the Wage Councils set separate rates for men and women.

31. Interestingly, Machin and Manning found that very few workers younger than age 21 were paid less than the Wage Council rate, a finding that is similar to our own for the U.S. subminimum wage (see chapter 5).

32. The fact that the denominator of the relative-minimum-wage variable increases with the minimum wage is likely to bias the estimated coefficient upward in absolute value, as we conjectured in the case of Puerto Rico.

33. Machin and Manning performed a number of other statistical checks on their data. For example, they estimated models that also included the first lag of the minimum-wage variable, included industry fixed effects in the employment-change equations, and allowed the minimum-wage coefficient to vary across industries. None of these alternatives qualitatively changed their results.

34. Reynolds and Gregory had the same concern about the industry councils in Puerto Rico.

CHAPTER 9

How the Minimum Wage Affects the Distribution of Wages, the Distribution of Family Earnings, and Poverty

> The manipulation of individual prices [is] neither an efficient nor an equitable device for changing the distribution of income.
>
> —George J. Stigler

> . . . as long as minimum wages are kept low relative to other wages, they are not terribly harmful and in fact have slightly beneficial effects both on low-wage workers and on the overall distribution of income.
>
> —Edward M. Gramlich

MOST ECONOMIC DISCUSSIONS of public policy are concerned with questions of efficiency; in other words, whether a particular policy generates more benefits than costs. Within the broader policy arena, however, questions of distribution—who gains and who loses—are often paramount. Not surprisingly, most economic research on the minimum wage concentrates on the efficiency aspects of a legislated wage floor. Standard economic theory asserts that, by reducing employment, an increase in the minimum wage creates more costs than benefits. As we have seen, it is remarkably difficult to find support for this prediction in the contemporary labor market. Some of the new evidence presented in chapters 2–4 suggests that an increase in the minimum wage might actually *increase* employment and, perhaps, raise efficiency. Even the results in the literature, however, imply that the efficiency costs of a modest increase in the minimum wage are small. In our view, then, the minimum wage is mainly a distributional issue—at least in the range of the current U.S. minimum wage.

In this chapter, we study the distributional impact of the wage increases generated by an increase in the minimum wage. We analyze the personal and family characteristics of workers whose pay rises with the minimum wage and measure the effects of the 1990 and 1991 increases in the federal minimum wage on the distribution of hourly wages, the distribution of family earnings, and the poverty rate. Following a long tradition in labor economics (see, for example, Lewis [1963, 1986], Gramlich [1976], and Freeman and Medoff [1984]), we make no attempt to adjust wages or earnings for such potentially important factors as taxes, income-contingent transfers, or changes in the conditions of work. We also ignore the potential effects of an increase in the minimum wage on the cost of living. We study an important aspect of the *cost* side of a higher minimum wage—its effect on firms' profitability—in chapter 10.

To keep these chapters in perspective, however, one should recognize that a typical increase in the minimum wage generates only a 10 to 15 percent wage increase for fewer than 10 percent of the lowest-paid workers in the economy. The distributional effects of such a policy are necessarily limited. Ignoring employment effects and any wage spillovers, the most recent round of increases in the federal minimum wage, for example, transferred approximately 5.5 billion dollars per year to low-wage workers—only about 0.2 percent of total annual earnings.[1] Even if all these transfers were received by families at the bottom of the income distribution (which they were not), the minimum wage would have only limited effects on the distribution of income.

We begin the chapter with a statistical portrait of workers who are affected by an increase in the minimum wage. A widely held stereotype is that minimum-wage earners are teenagers from middle-class families who work after school for discretionary income.[2] In fact, more than 70 percent of workers affected by recent increases in the minimum wage are adults—predominantly women and minorities. Thirty percent of those affected by a minimum-wage increase are the sole wage-earner in their family, and, on average, minimum-wage earners account for one-half of their family's total earnings. Relative to other workers, those whose wages are affected by an increase in the minimum wage are three times more likely to live in poverty.

In the second part of the chapter, we examine the effect of the minimum wage on the overall distribution of wages. As is well known, wage inequality widened significantly during the past decade. For example, Figures 9.1.A and 9.1.B show two measures of hourly wage inequality for female and male workers from 1973 to 1992.[3] Both the standard deviation of log wages and the difference between the 90th and 10th percentiles of wages rose sharply after 1979. Several authors, including Blackburn, Bloom, and Freeman (1990) and DiNardo, Fortin, and Lemieux (1994), have suggested that part of this increase in wage dispersion was driven by the decline in the real value of the minimum wage (see Figure 1.2). Al-

though the increase in wage inequality during the 1980s clearly coincided with a downward trend in the real minimum wage, a more direct test of the effect of the minimum wage is provided by comparing the relative changes in wage inequality across states after the 1990 and 1991 increases in the federal minimum wage. In the United States as a whole, about 7 percent of workers were directly affected by the 1990 and 1991 minimum-wage hikes. Across different states, however, this fraction ranged from less than 2 percent (in such states as Alaska and California) to more than 20 percent (in Mississippi). These interstate differences allow us to measure directly the effects of the minimum wage on the lower tail of the wage distribution. We find that the increase in the federal minimum wage led to a reversal in the trend toward rising wage inequality that has dominated the U.S. labor market since the early 1980s. On the basis of our own findings and recent research by DiNardo, Fortin, and Lemieux, we conclude that the increase in the minimum wage from $3.35 to 4.25 per hour rolled back a significant fraction of the cumulative rise in wage dispersion from 1979 to 1989.

Although a higher minimum wage directly affects only the *individual earnings* of low-wage workers, it could affect *family incomes* throughout the entire range of incomes, depending on the distribution of affected workers across families. In the third section of the chapter, we analyze the effects of the 1990 and 1991 increases in the federal minimum wage on the distribution of family earnings. As in our analysis of the distribution of wages, we make use of the natural experiment afforded by differences across states in the fraction of workers affected by the federal minimum-wage hikes. On the basis of the family earnings characteristics of minimum-wage workers before the increase in the minimum, about one-third of the overall pay increases associated with the 1990 and 1991 minimum-wage hikes went to families in the lowest decile of the family earnings distribution.[4] Consistent with this prediction, our analysis of the actual changes in family earnings from 1989 to 1991 shows that the hike in the minimum wage led to significant increases in the 10th percentile of family earnings, and to a narrowing of the gap between the 90th and 10th percentiles of family earnings. An important feature of our analysis is that we actually *measure* the effect of the minimum wage on family earnings (by comparing changes in the earnings distributions in different states), rather than merely *simulating* its effect.

Finally, the fourth section of the chapter examines the connection between minimum wages and poverty. As other researchers have noted, the connection is fuzzy: only one-third of adults who are classified as "poor" actually work; and only a fraction of the working poor earn sufficiently low wages to be affected by an increase in the minimum wage. Nevertheless, 30 percent of all workers affected by the minimum wage are poor or near-poor, so that a minimum-wage increase could be expected to lead to some reduction in the fraction of working poor. Following the methods established in the earlier sections of the chapter, we examine interstate differences in poverty trends after the 1990 and 1991 rises in the federal minimum wage. The effect of the minimum wage on the *overall* poverty rate of adults is statistically undetectable. However, we find a modest effect on the poverty rate among workers, leading us to conclude that the minimum wage might have a small effect on poverty outcomes for adults who have some attachment to the labor market.

WHO IS AFFECTED BY THE MINIMUM WAGE?

In chapters 3 and 4, we noted that an increase in the minimum wage has a direct effect on two types of workers: (1) those who were previously earning the former minimum wage; and (2) those who were earning more than the former minimum but less than the new minimum. When California's minimum wage increased from $3.35 to 4.25 per hour, for example, the main group of affected workers included anyone in the state whose wage just before the increase was between $3.35 and 4.25 per hour. Some workers who previously earned above $4.25 per hour might have benefited from a "ripple effect," although our estimates in chapter 5 suggest that these effects are confined to a relatively narrow range above the new minimum. In addition, some of the workers who previously were earning *less* than the old minimum wage may be affected by a minimum wage change. Again, evidence in chapters 3 and 4 suggests that the relative size of this group is roughly constant following a rise in the minimum wage. Thus, the main group of workers who were directly affected by the 1990 and 1991 increases in the federal minimum wage consists of those who were earning between $3.35 and 4.24 per hour in early 1990.[5]

How do these workers compare with other workers in terms of their personal and family characteristics? To answer this question, we drew a sample of wage and salary earners from the January–March 1990 Current Population Survey (CPS).[6] This data set provides us with a "snapshot" of the work force immediately preceding the most recent increases in the federal minimum wage. On April 1, 1990, the federal minimum rose from $3.35 to 3.80 per hour. One year later, it rose again, to $4.25 per hour (its value as of this writing). Thus, we identified three groups of workers in our snapshot sample: (1) subminimum-wage workers, with hourly wages below $3.35 per hour; (2) affected workers, with hourly wages between $3.35 and 4.24 per hour; and (3) all other workers. A more complete description of the samples is provided in the Appendix to this chapter.

Table 9.1 presents descriptive information on workers in the different wage categories. Most of the information pertains to the survey week of the CPS, although the family income, program participation, and poverty status information in rows 10–15 and 24–25 pertains to the previous calendar year. The first column of the table reports the average characteristics of all wage and salary workers in the labor force. Slightly fewer than one-half (47.6 percent) of workers are women, roughly 14 percent are nonwhite (i.e., black, Asian, or "other"), and about 8 percent are of Hispanic origin. Teenagers, whose employment patterns figure so prominently in the minimum wage literature, comprise less than 6 percent of total employment. Forty-one percent of all workers are the sole wage earner in their families, either because they live alone, or because they live with other family members who do not work.[7] As shown in row 23, a typical wage earner accounts for 68 percent of his or her family's total weekly earnings.

In addition to information on labor-force activities during the survey week, the March CPS provides information on income in the previous year. The average family income of workers in March 1990 was $38,000. One and one-half percent of workers lived in families that reported receiving some public assistance or welfare payments in the previous year, while 3 percent lived in households that received food stamps. As Table 9.1 shows, 5 percent of all workers in March 1990 were classified as living in poverty (based on their family income last year), and another 6 percent were classified as near-poor (with family incomes between 100 percent and 150 percent of the appropriate poverty line, adjusted for family size and composition). These relatively low poverty rates reflect the exclusion of nonworkers from our sample. The poverty rate for all adults (workers *and* nonworkers) in 1989 was approximately twice as high as the rate for workers—10.6 percent.

A comparison of the second and third columns of Table 9.1 with the first column shows how subminimum-wage workers and workers who were affected by the increase in the minimum wage differ from the overall work force. Focus for the moment on affected workers (column 3). This group contains proportionally more women and nonwhites than does the population as a whole, and a much larger fraction of young workers. Slightly fewer than one-third of affected

TABLE 9.1

Characteristics of Wage and Salary Workers Just Before the April 1990 Increase in the Minimum Wage

	All Workers (1)	Subminimum-Wage Workers (2)	Workers Affected by Minimum (3)
Individual Characteristics			
1. Female (percent)	47.6	63.2	62.1
2. Nonwhite (percent)	14.4	14.4	20.6
3. Hispanic (percent)	7.7	7.9	9.6
4. Aged 16–19 (percent)	5.8	18.4	29.4
5. Aged 20–24 (percent)	11.5	20.2	19.8
6. Enrolled/Aged 16–24 (percent)	6.5	22.3	30.7
7. <12 Years Education (percent)	15.2	36.6	38.1
Family Characteristics			
8. Living Alone (percent)	18.8	25.3	15.4
9. Only Wage Earner (percent)	41.5	46.5	35.9
10. Family Income Last Year (dollars)	38,067	32,064	29,543
11. Family Received Welfare Last Year (percent)	1.5	2.7	4.4
12. Family Received Food Stamps Last Year (percent)	3.0	7.8	9.5
13. Family Poor (percent)	5.1	14.7	19.7
14. Family Near-Poor (percent)	6.1	13.7	13.4
15. Poverty Gap (dollars)	209.5	625.4	1,073.6
Labor Market Characteristics			
16. Employed in Retail Trade (percent)	16.6	42.0	46.7
17. Average Hourly Wage (dollars)	10.52	2.42	3.77
18. Affected by Minimum (percent)	7.4	0.0	100.0
19. Affected by Minimum, Accounting for Tips (percent)	6.9	4.1	92.5
20. Subminimum Wage (percent)	2.6	100.0	0.0
21. Average Weekly Hours	38.2	30.6	28.1
22. Average Weekly Earnings (dollars)	427.0	112.0	114.4
23. Share of Total Weekly Family Earnings	0.68	0.58	0.51

TABLE 9.1
(*continued*)

	All Workers (1)	Subminimum- Wage Workers (2)	Workers Affected by Minimum (3)
24. Average Earnings Last Year (dollars)	21,255	6,950	5,774
25. Share of Total Family Earnings Last Year	0.65	0.51	0.45

Note: Derived from tabulations of the January–March 1990 Current Population Surveys. Entries in rows 10–15 and 24–25 are derived from the March survey only. Subminimum-wage workers are those whose hourly wage is above $1.00 per hour and below $3.35 per hour. Affected workers are those whose hourly wage is between $3.35 and 4.24 per hour.

workers are 16- to 24-year-olds who are enrolled in school. The stereotype of minimum-wage workers as youngsters who are working after school is therefore *partially* correct. Nevertheless, nearly one-half of all workers affected by the minimum wage are older than age 24, and nearly 70 percent are older than age 20.

The family circumstances of affected workers also differ from those of other workers. Family incomes of affected workers are about 25 percent lower than average ($29,500 per year versus $38,100), and the percentage of those living in poverty is over three times higher (19.7 percent versus 5.1 percent). The poverty gap (i.e., the average income per family needed to move the family out of poverty) is substantially higher for the families of workers who were earning between $3.35 and 4.24 per hour in March 1990. Affected workers are also about three times more likely to live in families that received welfare payments or food stamps in the year preceding the survey.

Compared with other workers, affected workers are slightly less likely to live alone, and are also less likely to be the sole wage earner in the family. When we examine their labor-market outcomes more closely, we see that affected earners work fewer hours than do most other workers. They also earn substantially less per week ($114 per week versus $427 per week for all workers). Perhaps surprisingly, however, affected workers contribute a sizable fraction of their family's current weekly earnings (51 percent, on average), and account for slightly less than one-half of the family's previous year's total earnings (see row 25). Evidently, the earnings of workers who are affected by the minimum wage are important for many families.

Workers earning less than $3.35 per hour present an interesting contrast to those earning between $3.35 and 4.24 per hour. Subminimum-wage earners are older, less likely to be nonwhite or Hispanic, and less likely to be enrolled in school. They also have slightly higher family incomes, lower poverty rates, and higher previous-year earnings. It is possible that these differences are partially the result of misclassification errors. Labor-market data are sometimes misreported to the CPS, leading to inadvertent errors in the classification of subminimum-wage workers. Indeed, examination of individual records in the CPS suggests that a significant number of subminimum-wage workers are actually higher-wage workers who have misreported their hours or earnings.[8] In any case, the economic circumstances of workers affected by the minimum wage are likely to be slightly *overstated* if subminimum-wage workers inadvertently are included in the group of affected workers. Because our analyses in chapters 3 and 4 show that most subminimum-wage workers are unlikely to receive a wage boost when the minimum wage increases, we believe that they should be treated separately from the affected group.

The Distribution of Affected Workers, by Income Class

The data in Table 9.1 show that workers who were affected by the recent increases in the federal minimum wage lived in lower-income families and were more likely to be classified as poor than were other workers. A more complete picture of the family-income distribution of affected workers is presented in Table 9.2. In constructing this table, we have divided all individuals aged 16 and older, including workers and nonworkers, into 10 equally sized groups on the basis of total family income.[9] Within each decile, we calculate the fraction of individuals classified as poor (column 1), the fraction classified as near-poor (column 2), the fraction working at the time of the CPS survey (column 3), and the share of workers in the decile with hourly wages in the $3.35–4.24 range (column 4). Finally, in column 5, we show the percentage of all affected workers in the corresponding family income decile.

These simple distributional data illustrate two important points. First, the fraction of workers affected by a rise in the minimum wage declines sharply across the income deciles: from 29 percent of workers in the first (lowest) decile, to 3 percent in the tenth (highest) decile. Second, even though relatively fewer people in the lower-income deciles participate in the labor market, the bulk of workers affected by a rise in the minimum wage are in these deciles. Indeed,

TABLE 9.2

Distribution of Workers Affected by the April 1990 Minimum-Wage Increase, by Family-Income Decile

	Status of Individuals in Family-Income Decile			Percentage of Workers in Decile Affected by Minimum-Wage Increase	Percentage Distribution of Affected Workers
	Percentage Poor (1)	Percentage Near-Poor (2)	Percentage Working (3)	(4)	(5)
Family-Income Decile					
All	10.6	8.6	62.4	7.1	100.0
1	81.1	16.5	28.3	28.8	17.4
2	21.0	39.7	42.9	13.1	12.7
3	3.8	18.3	53.4	10.5	12.7
4	0.1	9.3	59.9	7.2	9.8
5	0.0	1.5	66.1	6.5	9.9
6	0.0	0.0	68.6	4.6	7.3
7	0.0	0.0	73.8	5.4	9.2
8	0.0	0.0	75.2	4.8	8.1
9	0.0	0.0	78.4	4.7	8.4
10	0.0	0.0	77.5	2.7	4.4

Note: Derived from tabulation of the March 1990 Current Population Survey. Family-income deciles are constructed so that 10 percent of all individuals aged 16 and older are in each decile. Poor individuals are those who live in families with total family income below the appropriate poverty line (taking into account family size). Near-poor individuals are those who live in families with family incomes between 100 and 150 percent of the poverty line. Affected workers are those whose hourly wage is between $3.35 and 4.24 per hour.

43 percent of all affected workers come from the bottom three income deciles. These patterns suggest that lower-income families received a disproportionate share of the earnings gains arising from the 1990 and 1991 increases in the minimum wage. Nevertheless, many affected workers live in upper-income families. The minimum wage is evidently a "blunt instrument" for redistributing income to the poorest families.

Our finding that minimum-wage earners are disproportionately drawn from lower-income families is consistent with many earlier studies of the issue, including those by Gramlich (1976) and by Kohen and Gilroy (1982). However, as shown in Figure 9.2, the income disparity between wage earners who are affected by an increase in the minimum wage and other workers has widened during the past two decades. In this figure, we plot the percentage of affected workers with family incomes below a given cutoff against the percent of

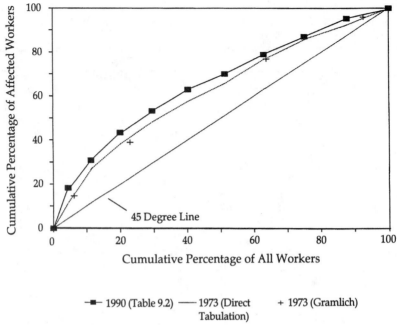

Figure 9.2 Comparison of relative distributions of affected workers, 1973 versus 1990.

all workers whose family incomes are below the same cutoff, using three different data sources: (1) 1990 data from Table 9.2; (2) 1973 data derived directly from CPS files; and (3) 1973 data reported by Gramlich (also derived from the 1973 CPS). As a benchmark, we also plot the 45 degree line in the figure: if affected workers were distributed across family-income categories with the same probabilities as other workers, then all the points in Figure 9.2 would lie along this line.[10]

As suggested by the results in Table 9.2, the 1990 relative distribution is well above the 45 degree line, indicating that workers who were affected by the 1990 and 1991 increases in the federal minimum wage were from poorer families than other workers.[11] To derive a comparison for the 1974 increase in the minimum wage (from $1.60 to 2.00 per hour), we used a matched sample of observations from the March and May 1973 CPS to assign family incomes (from the March file) to workers (in the May file). We defined the affected workers in 1973 as those who earned between $1.60 and 1.99 per hour in May 1973. We then sorted workers in the matched 1973 file into family income groups, choosing the income ranges to include the same relative fractions of all workers as the income ranges in our

1990 sample. Finally, as a check on our tabulations, we computed the relative fractions of affected workers and all workers across five broad income categories, using the 1973 data reported in Gramlich (1976, Tables 10 and 11).

The relative distributions of affected workers in 1973 are very similar whether we use our own or Gramlich's tabulations. Both are above the 45 degree line, but below the 1990 relative distribution. Thus, relative to workers who were affected by the 1974 increase in the minimum wage, workers affected by the 1990 and 1991 increases were more likely to come from *further down* the family-income distribution.[12] There are a number of explanations for the relative decline in the family incomes of affected workers. First, the increase in the fraction of individuals who live alone (see Blank and Card [1993]) has strengthened the connection between low individual earnings and low family income. Second, changes in fertility patterns, transfer programs, and other factors have led to a decline in the incomes of families with children relative to the incomes of other families.[13] This trend could have contributed to a decline in the relative family incomes of teenagers, who comprised about 30 percent of all affected workers in both 1973 and 1990. Furthermore, within the working teenage population, the correlation between low family income and low wages has changed. In 1973, Gramlich (1976) found that teenagers who were earning between the old and the new minimum-wage rates had *higher* family incomes than did other teenagers. In 1990, however, teenagers earning between $3.35 and 4.24 per hour had *lower* family incomes than did those earning other wage rates.[14] A final factor in the changing relative distribution of affected workers is the steady decline in real wages for less-educated workers during the past two decades. We suspect that this trend has led to a relative decline in the family incomes of nonteenage workers who are at or near the minimum wage.

Although our finding that minimum-wage workers are drawn disproportionately from lower-income families is consistent with the findings of Gramlich (1976) and Kohen and Gilroy (1982), it is inconsistent with a more recent study by Horrigan and Mincy (1993). Horrigan and Mincy used March 1988 data to compare the family incomes of all workers and of those earning between $3.35 and 4.71 per hour (the minimum wage that would have prevailed in 1987 if the minimum had been indexed to the Consumer Price Index after 1981). Unlike us, they concluded that affected workers essentially are uniformly distributed across the family-income distribution (Horrigan and Mincy [1993, Table 8.6]).

A number of important differences between their procedures and ours account for the dramatic difference in conclusions about the relative family-income distribution of workers who are affected by an increase in the minimum wage. First, their sample includes only hourly-rated, private-sector workers who report the same industry and occupation in March as for the previous year, whereas our samples include all paid, non-self-employed workers. Second, we compare the family-income distribution of affected workers with the distribution of *all* workers, whereas Horrigan and Mincy compared the family incomes of hourly-rated workers who earned between $3.35 and 4.71 per hour with the family incomes of all hourly-rated workers. By excluding salaried workers from their tabulations of the income distribution for all workers, Horrigan and Mincy have underrepresented the upper half of the family income distribution.[15] We believe that this procedure, in combination with their narrower sample of workers, accounts for their conclusion that minimum-wage workers are evenly distributed across the family-income distribution.

To summarize, we find that 17 percent of workers whose wages were affected by the most recent increases in the federal minimum wage live in families with incomes in the bottom decile of (overall) family incomes, and that another 13 percent live in families in the second decile of family incomes. We also find that the relative family-income distribution of workers who are affected by a rise in the minimum wage has deteriorated during the past two decades. It should be noted that the decline in the *relative* income position of affected workers might actually understate the fall in the real standard of living for many affected workers. Between 1973 and 1990, real incomes of families in the bottom 20 percent of the income distribution shrank.[16] Thus, the 30 percent of affected workers in the two lowest family-income deciles in 1990 were somewhat poorer in real terms than were their counterparts in the early 1970s.

The Effect of the Minimum Wage on the Distribution of Wages

As we have already seen in chapters 2–4, an increase in the minimum wage has a substantial effect on the earnings of less-skilled workers (including fast-food workers, retail-trade employees, and teenagers). More generally, the minimum wage serves as a "backstop" for the wages of a significant fraction of *all* wage and salary workers. Figure 9.3.A, for example, shows the relative frequency distribution of wages in the U.S. economy during the first three months of 1990—immediately before the April 1 rise in the mini-

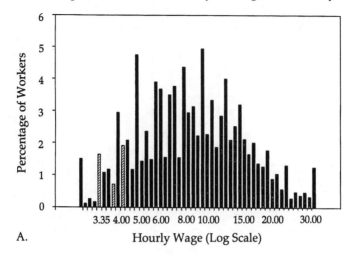

A.

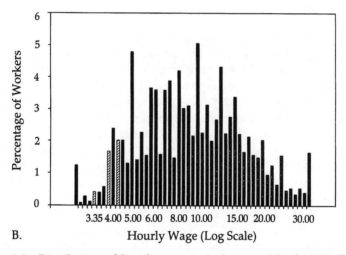

B.

Figure 9.3 Distribution of hourly wages. A. January–March 1990. B. January–March 1991. Highlighted bars represent $3.35 per hour, $3.80 per hour, and $4.25 per hour.

mum wage from $3.35 to 3.80 per hour went into effect.[17] Even though the federal minimum had remained frozen for almost a decade, and almost one-half of the states had legislated state wage floors above $3.35 per hour, 1.2 percent of all workers earned exactly $3.35 per hour during the first quarter of 1990. Figure 9.3.B shows the wage distribution for the first three months of 1991, nine months

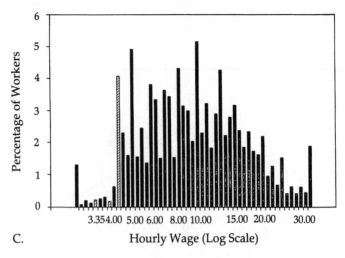

C.

Figure 9.3 *Continued* C. January–March 1992.

after the effective date of the new minimum. The lower tail of the wage distribution has been "swept" to the right, and the previous spike in the wage distribution at $3.35 per hour has been largely replaced by a spike at $3.80 per hour. The fraction of workers earning less than $3.35, however, remains relatively constant. Finally, Figure 9.3.C shows the wage distribution for the first three months of 1992, almost one year after the second (April 1991) increase in the federal minimum wage, to $4.25 per hour. Now, the fraction of workers earning the minimum wage has risen to 3.0 percent, and the spikes at $3.35 and $4.00 per hour virtually have disappeared.

If the distribution of wages remained stable over time in the absence of an increase in the minimum wage, then a simple comparison of Figures 9.3.A and 9.3.C could be used to estimate the effect of the minimum wage on the overall wage distribution. Over a two-year period, however, wage inflation and other macroeconomic forces normally would be expected to lead to some shift in the wage distribution, even if the minimum wage was fixed. As in the study of the employment effects of the minimum wage, what is needed is a credible counterfactual. Following the logic developed in chapter 4, a natural approach is to use regional or interstate variation in the level of wages to compare the effects of the federal minimum wage across labor markets.

Figure 9.4 tracks the 5th and 10th percentiles of wages between the first quarter of 1989 and the last quarter of 1991 in three groups

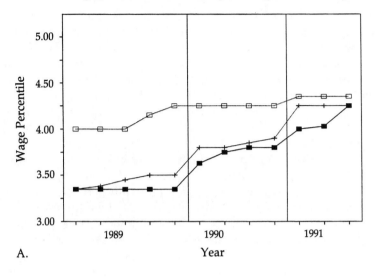

A.

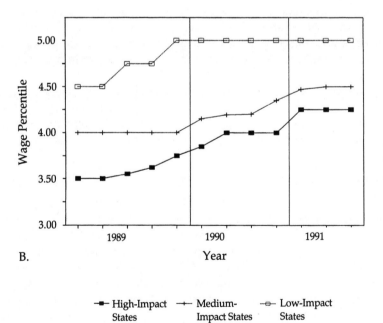

B.

━■━ High-Impact ━+━ Medium- ━▱━ Low-Impact
States Impact States States

Figure 9.4 Changes in 5th and 10th wage percentiles in three groups of states, 1989–1991. A. 5th percentile. B. 10th percentile.

of states: (1) a set of 13 low-wage states (where the minimum wage had a high impact); (2) a set of 22 medium-wage states; and (3) a set of 16 high-wage states (where it had a low impact). The classification of states is the same as the one used in chapter 4 to study the effect of the minimum wage on teenage employment and is based on the fraction of teenagers earning between $3.35 and 3.79 per hour during 1989. For reference, the April 1990 and April 1991 minimum-wage increases are shown in the figure by vertical lines between the first and second quarters of 1990 and 1991, respectively.

Both the 5th and 10th percentiles of wages in the low-impact states drifted upward during the three-year sample period. However, most of the increases in the 5th and 10th percentiles in these states occurred *before* the first increase in the federal minimum wage took effect.[18] This feature of the timing of the increases suggests that the structure of wages in the low-impact states largely was unaffected by the federal minimum-wage hikes. Thus, the changes in wage percentiles in the low-impact states can serve as a counterfactual for the growth of the wage percentiles in the other states. On this basis, the data in Figure 9.4 suggest that the 1990 and 1991 increases in the federal minimum wage raised the 5th percentile of wages in the lowest-wage (i.e., high-impact) states by 60 cents (18 percent); and raised the 10th percentile of wages in these states by 25 cents (7 percent).[19] The estimated effect of the minimum wage on the 5th percentile of wages in the middle group of states is similar, but the estimated effect on the 10th percentile of wages in these states is zero (because the rise in the 10th percentile of wages during the sample period is the same in the middle group of states and the low-impact states).

Comparisons Across States

Although the grouped analysis in Figure 9.4 is straightforward and highlights the precise timing of changes in the wage percentiles, aggregation into only three groups makes statistical inference rather difficult. An alternative approach is to aggregate several months of data at the beginning and end of the 1989–1991 sample period for each state, and to use information on the changes in wages across all 50 states (and the District of Columbia). This approach is followed in the graphical analysis in Figure 9.5, and in the regression models reported in Table 9.3 (see p. 296). For each state, we used data for April–December 1989 and corresponding data for 1991 to compute the 5th, 10th, 25th, 50th, and 90th percentiles of wages before and after the most recent round of minimum-wage increases. We also

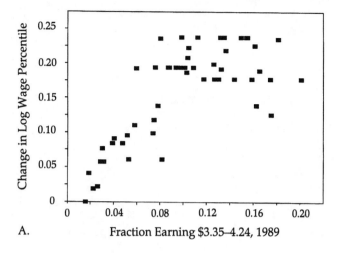

A.

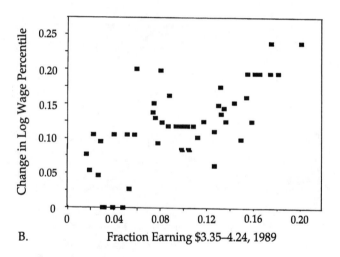

B.

Figure 9.5 Changes in wage percentiles, 1989–1991. A. Change in 5th percentile. B. Change in 10th percentile.

used the April–December 1989 data to compute the fraction of affected workers in the state—those who were earning between the old $3.35 minimum wage and the new $4.25 rate. Each panel of Figure 9.5 plots the changes in the indicated wage percentiles for the 50 states (and the District of Columbia) against the fraction of affected workers in the state.[20] Corresponding regression models, with and without an additional control variable representing the change in the

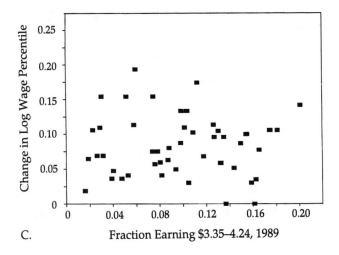

C.

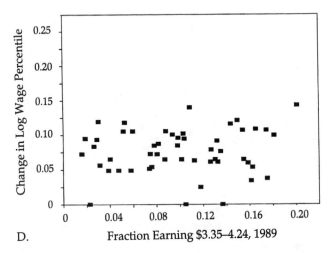

D.

Figure 9.5 *Continued* C. Change in 25th percentile. D. Change in 50th percentile.

overall employment–population rate in the state, are reported in Table 9.3.

The graphs and the estimated regression models tell a similar story. The changes in the 5th and 10th percentiles of wages across states are strongly positively correlated with the fraction of workers who initially were earning between $3.35 and 4.24 per hour in the state. At the higher wage percentiles, by comparison, there is little evidence of a correlation between wage growth and the fraction-

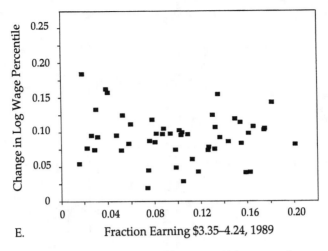

Figure 9.5 *Continued* E. Change in 90th percentile.

affected variable. A possible exception is the 50th percentile shown in Figure 9.5.D. Although the graph shows no obvious relation between the growth rate of median wages and the fraction of affected workers in 1989, the regression models reveal a marginally significant effect. The explanation for this apparent discrepancy is the influence of the data for California. In the regression models, which are estimated by weighted least squares, using relative population sizes as weights, California (which had a low fraction affected and no change in the median wage) is a "leverage point," and its influence drives up the magnitude and statistical significance of the estimated regression coefficient. If we eliminate California from the data set, the estimated coefficient is small and statistically insignificant. Given this result, and the results for the 25th and 90th percentiles of wages, we suspect that the increase in the minimum wage probably had little effect on the distribution of wages at or above the 25th percentile.

The addition of the employment–population rate as a control variable for differing labor-market trends across states has little influence on the estimated models in Table 9.3. We have also estimated specifications that include the change in the state's unemployment rate, and models that include the levels of the state employment–population rate for 1989, 1990, and 1991. All of these specifications lead to similar coefficient estimates for the critical fraction-affected variable.

Panel B of Table 9.3 reports estimates of regression models in

TABLE 9.3
Estimated Models for Changes in the Percentiles of Log Wages Across States, 1989–1991

Panel A: Models for Changes in the 5th, 10th, 25th, 50th, and 90th Percentiles

	5th Percentile		10th Percentile		25th Percentile		50th Percentile		90th Percentile	
	(1)	(2)	(3)	(4)	(5)	(6)	(7)	(8)	(9)	(10)
1. Fraction Affected	1.23	1.18	0.78	0.69	-0.03	0.00	0.22	0.21	0.01	0.06
	(0.13)	(0.16)	(0.11)	(0.14)	(0.11)	(0.14)	(0.10)	(0.12)	(0.08)	(0.10)
2. Change in Employment Rate	—	0.27	—	0.46	—	-0.15	—	0.03	—	-0.27
		(0.50)		(0.42)		(0.41)		(0.36)		(0.31)
3. R-Squared	0.63	0.63	0.49	0.50	0.00	0.00	0.09	0.09	0.00	0.02

Note: Standard errors are shown in parentheses. Models are estimated on 51 state observations, using data from the 1989 and 1991 Current Population Surveys. The dependent variable is the change in the logarithm of the indicated wage percentile from April–December 1989 to April–December 1991. Fraction Affected represents the fraction of wage and salary earners in the state who earned between $3.35 and 4.24 per hour in April–December 1989. Change in Employment Rate is the change in the employment–population rate for all workers in the state between 1989 and 1991. All models include an unrestricted constant.

Panel B: Models for the Relative Change in the Percentiles of Log Wages

	90th − 10th Percentile		50th − 10th Percentile		90th − 50th Percentile	
	(1)	(2)	(3)	(4)	(5)	(6)
1. Fraction Affected	-0.76	-0.63	-0.56	-0.48	-0.20	-0.14
	(0.15)	(0.18)	(0.15)	(0.19)	(0.10)	(0.12)
2. Change in Employment Rate	—	-0.74	—	-0.44	—	-0.30
		(0.54)		(0.57)		(0.38)
3. R-Squared	0.35	0.38	0.21	0.22	0.07	0.09

Note: See note to Panel A. The dependent variable is the change in the differential between the logarithms of the indicated wage percentiles from April–December 1989 to April–December 1991.

which the dependent variable is the state-specific log wage *gap* between the 90th and 10th percentiles of wages (columns 1 and 2); the 50th and 10th percentiles of wages (columns 3 and 4); or the 90th and 50th percentiles of wages (columns 5 and 6). These models indicate that the increase in the federal minimum wage was responsible for a significant compression of the wage distribution in states with a high fraction of workers who were affected by the minimum-wage increases. For example, the estimates imply that the $90-10$ log wage gap closed by 0.09–0.11 in New Mexico (fraction affected = 0.17) relative to California (fraction affected = 0.02) as a consequence of the federal minimum wage. This represents a reduction of approximately 7 percent in the log wage gap.

We can also use the estimates in Table 9.3 to get a rough sense of the size of the effect of the 1990 and 1991 minimum-wage hikes on economy-wide wage dispersion. During 1989, the fraction of affected workers in the United States as a whole was 0.087. Multiplying this fraction by the estimated coefficients in columns 1 and 2 of panel B in Table 9.3, we obtain an estimated effect of -0.055 to -0.066 on the economy-wide $90-10$ log wage gap.[21] During the period from 1979 to 1989, the $90-10$ log wage gap for male wage and salary workers in the United States rose by 0.185 (see Figure 9.1.B). Ignoring the difficulty of aggregating wage percentiles across states, we estimate that the 1990 and 1991 minimum-wage hikes rolled back some 30 percent of the previous decade's accumulated increase in wage dispersion. It is interesting to note that this estimate is very similar to DiNardo, Fortin, and Lemieux's estimate of the share of the increase in male wage dispersion over the 1980s attributable to the decline in the real minimum wage between 1979 and 1989.

EFFECTS ON THE DISTRIBUTION OF FAMILY EARNINGS FOR WORKING FAMILIES

As we noted in the introduction to this chapter, one of the main issues concerning the effect of the minimum wage is whether the earnings gains generated by an increase in the minimum tend to be distributed toward families with higher or with lower incomes. Because the minimum wage can affect the incomes *only* of families that have at least one worker, and because most families obtain a large fraction of their income from labor earnings, it is important to understand how the minimum wage affects the distribution of earnings across families. Fortunately, the monthly CPS data files that we used to construct state-specific estimates of the distribution of hourly wages in the late 1980s and early 1990s can be used to construct estimates of the distribution of total weekly family earnings before and after the increase in the federal minimum wage. This data source has the important feature that both the individual wage information and the family-earnings information pertain to the survey week. By comparison, the March CPS data (used in Table 9.2, and by previous researchers who have attempted to study the distributional effect of the minimum wage) combines individual wage information for the survey week in March with total family earnings or income measured over the previous year.

In constructing our estimates of the family-earnings distribution, we have made allowances for two features of the CPS family earnings data: (1) the overrepresentation of families that have multiple earners; and (2) the undercount of earnings for families that have self-employed workers. Details of the procedures that we used to handle these features are presented in the Appendix. In brief, we adjust for multiple earners per family by weighting each individual's data by the number of earners in his or her family. We adjust for the nonreporting of self-employment earnings by deleting information for any wage-earner whose family includes a self-employed worker, and reweighting the remaining observations.[22]

The potential effect of the minimum wage on the distribution of family earnings depends on how affected workers are allocated across families. This distribution is illustrated in Table 9.4, which is based on data for all wage and salary earners in January–March 1990 (just prior to the 1990 minimum-wage increase). The first column of the table shows the percent of all workers in a given decile group with wages in the affected range ($3.35–4.24 per hour). The second column shows the family-earnings distribution of affected workers. A key fact that emerges from the two columns is the high concentration of affected workers in low-earnings families: 34 percent of all workers in the first decile are affected by the minimum wage, and 36 percent of all affected workers live in families in the lowest earnings decile.

The family-earnings gains generated by an increase in the minimum wage are proportional to the fraction of total family *hours* in the affected range. As shown in the third and fourth columns of Table 9.4, affected and unaffected workers in the various earnings deciles tend to work slightly different numbers of hours. On average across all deciles, affected workers work fewer hours per week. In the lowest earnings decile, however, affected workers actually work more than do other wage earners. These patterns imply that the overall fraction of "affected hours" (i.e., the fraction of hours

TABLE 9.4

Distribution of Workers and Hours Affected by the 1990 and 1991
Increases in the Minimum Wage, by Family-Earnings Decile

	Percentage of Workers in Decile Who Are Affected (1)	Distribution of Affected Workers (percent) (2)	Hours per Week		Percentage of All Hours Worked in the Decile that are Affected (5)	Distribution of Affected Hours (percent) (6)
			Affected Workers (3)	Unaffected Workers (4)		
Family-Earnings Decile						
All	7.4	100.0	28.5	39.1	5.5	100.0
1	34.4	35.6	28.3	26.7	35.7	35.4
2	7.5	7.6	32.5	37.7	6.5	8.7
3	6.6	7.5	31.7	39.2	5.5	8.4
4	7.1	8.4	33.5	39.8	6.1	9.9
5	6.8	8.4	30.6	39.8	5.3	9.1
6	5.4	7.0	28.8	39.8	4.0	7.1
7	5.0	7.4	26.3	40.0	3.3	6.8
8	3.9	6.1	25.1	40.3	2.5	5.4
9	3.6	6.3	23.2	40.2	2.1	5.1
10	3.0	5.6	21.4	41.3	1.6	4.2

Note: Derived from tabulations of January–March 1990 Current Population Surveys. Affected workers are those whose hourly wage is between $3.35 and 4.24 per hour. Affected hours are hours worked by those whose wage rate is between $3.35 and 4.24 per hour.

worked by those with wages between $3.35 and 4.24 per hour) is less than the overall fraction of affected workers (5.5 percent of hours versus 7.4 percent of workers), but that, for families in the first decile, the fraction of affected hours is slightly higher than the fraction of affected workers (35.7 percent versus 34.4 percent). On the basis of the distribution of affected hours in the last column (column 6), we conclude that about one-third of the earnings gains attributable to the 1990 and 1991 increases in the federal minimum wage accrued to families in the lowest decile of the family-earnings distribution.

To quantify the effect of the minimum-wage hikes on the distribution of family earnings, we computed state-specific estimates of the 10th, 50th, and 90th percentiles of total weekly family earnings for April–December 1989 and April–December 1991. We then correlated state-specific growth rates in the various earnings deciles with the fraction of workers in the state who were affected by the minimum-wage increase—the same measure of the impact of the minimum wage used in the previous section. Figure 9.6 presents plots of the

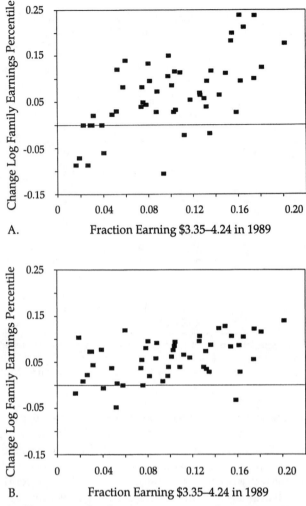

Figure 9.6 Changes in family earnings percentiles, 1989–1991. A. Change in 10th percentile. B. Change in 50th percentile.

changes in the various earnings percentiles against the fraction-affected measure. Table 9.5 reports estimated regression models (analogous to the models in Table 9.3) that relate the change in a specific percentile of total family earnings to the fraction-affected variable and a control variable representing the change in the state employment–population rate between 1989 and 1991.

Again, the plots and the regression models tell a similar story. They show a strong, positive correlation between the change in the

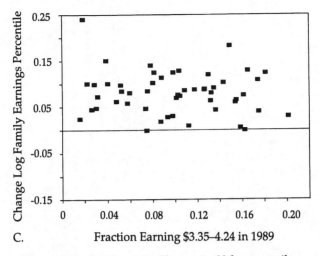

Figure 9.6 *Continued* C. Change in 90th percentile.

10th percentile of family earnings and the fraction of workers affected by the minimum wage in the state. The relationship is somewhat attenuated, but still highly significant, when state-specific employment trends are taken into account, suggesting (as in chapter 4) that the fraction-affected variable is positively correlated with state-specific economic growth patterns between 1989 and 1991. The estimated coefficients imply that the federal minimum-wage hike led to an increase in the 10th percentile of weekly family earnings that was 10 to 14 percent larger in a highly affected state (like New Mexico) than in a less-highly affected state (like California). This range is fairly similar to our estimate of the relative effect of the minimum wage on the 10th percentile of wages in the two states (10 to 11 percent, using the estimates in columns 3 and 4 of Table 9.3). On the basis of the evidence in Table 9.4, one might have expected a smaller effect of the minimum wage on the 10th percentile of *family earnings* than on the 10th percentile of *wages*, as not all the wage earners in families at the 10th percentile of family earnings are affected directly by the minimum wage. However, this intuition is misleading, because the effect of the minimum wage on a given percentile of family earnings depends on what fraction of total earnings are contributed by affected workers in families at that point in the earnings distribution. For example, suppose that the minimum wage affects the wages of only the lowest 5 percent of workers in a given state and therefore has no effect on the 10th percentile of wages. If some of the affected workers live in families whose total earnings equal

TABLE 9.5
Estimated Models for Changes in the Percentiles of Log Weekly Family Earnings Across States, 1989–1991

	10th Percentile		50th Percentile		90th Percentile		90th − 10th Percentile		50th − 10th Percentile	
	(1)	(2)	(3)	(4)	(5)	(6)	(7)	(8)	(9)	(10)
1. Fraction Affected	1.01	0.72	0.42	0.35	−0.06	−0.14	−1.07	−0.86	−0.58	−0.37
	(0.18)	(0.21)	(0.11)	(0.13)	(0.13)	(0.16)	(0.20)	(0.24)	(0.19)	(0.23)
2. Change in Employment Rate	—	1.55	—	0.45	—	0.43	—	1.12	—	−1.10
		(0.64)		(0.40)		(0.48)		(0.73)		(0.69)
3. R-Squared	0.38	0.45	0.24	0.26	0.00	0.02	0.36	0.39	0.16	0.20

Note: Standard errors are shown in parentheses. Models are estimated on 51 state observations, using data from the 1989 and 1991 Current Population Surveys. The dependent variable is the change in the logarithm of the indicated percentile of total weekly family earnings from April–December 1989 to April–December 1991. See text for derivation of this variable. Fraction Affected represents the fraction of wage and salary earners in the state who earned between $3.35 and 4.24 per hour in April–December 1989. Change in Employment Rate is the change in the employment–population rate for all workers in the state between 1989 and 1991. All models include an unrestricted constant.

the 10th percentile, then the increase in the minimum wage will raise the 10th percentile of family earnings, but not the 10th percentile of wages.

The estimated coefficients of the fraction-affected variable in models for the change in median family earnings (columns 3 and 4 of Table 9.5) suggest that the increase in the minimum wage also had a significant effect on median family earnings in states with a high fraction of affected workers. For example, the coefficients imply that, between 1989 and 1991, median weekly family earnings rose 5 to 6 percent more rapidly in New Mexico than in California. On the other hand, our estimates for the 90th percentile of family earnings (columns 5 and 6) suggest that the minimum-wage increase had no effect on the upper tail of the family-earnings distribution.[23] The estimated models for the $90 - 10$ and $50 - 10$ percentile gaps (columns 7–10) indicate that the federal minimum wage had a substantial effect on the dispersion in weekly family earnings.

Although these results are interesting, it is difficult to get a sense of the overall impact of the minimum wage by examining only the percentiles of the family-earnings distribution. To further quantify the distributional effect of the minimum wage, we calculated the share of total family earnings earned by the lowest 10 percent of families, using data for April–December 1989 and 1991. We divided states into the same three state groups used in the analysis in Figure 9.4, according to whether the 1990 and 1991 minimum-wage increases had a high-, medium-, or low-impact on wages in the state. The results are summarized in Table 9.6. During 1989, families in the lowest decile earned between 1.9 and 2.0 percent of total family earnings in the three different state groups. Between 1989 and 1991, the earnings share of the lowest 10 percent of families rose by 0.08 percentage points (or 4.3 percent) in the high-impact states, but fell by 0.03 and 0.06 percentage points in the medium- and low-impact states, respectively. A difference-of-differences of the 1989–1991 changes suggests that the minimum wage increased the earnings share of the lowest decile by 0.14 percentage points (6 percent) in the high-impact states relative to the low-impact states. The overall effect on the lowest 10 percent of families in the United States as a whole is perhaps only one-third to one-half as large, because the minimum wage had smaller effects in the low- and medium-impact states.

How reasonable is this calculation? Recall from Table 9.1 that, prior to the increase in the federal minimum wage, 7.4 percent of all workers were earning between $3.35 and 4.24 per hour, and that the average wage of these affected workers was $3.77 per hour. If the

TABLE 9.6
Shares of Total Earnings Earned by Families in the Lowest Decile
of Family Earnings, Before and After the 1990 and 1991 Increases
in the Federal Minimum Wage

| | Earnings Share of Families in First Decile | | |
State Group	1989 (1)	1991 (2)	Change (3)
1. High-Impact	1.87	1.95	0.08
2. Medium-Impact	1.88	1.85	−0.03
3. Low-Impact	1.98	1.92	−0.06

Note: Table entries represent the share of total weekly family earnings earned by families in the first decile of the family-earnings distribution. The three state groups are defined by the impact of the minimum wage on wages in the state.

minimum-wage increase raised wages for workers in the affected wage to $4.25 per hour (with no effect on subminimum-wage workers, no "ripple effect" on higher-wage workers, and no employment effects), then affected workers would receive an average 48 cent per hour pay raise. Multiplying this hourly raise by the average number of hours worked per week (28.1), and assuming a total work force of 105 million wage and salary workers in early 1990, the recent increase in the federal minimum wage raised wages by $105 million per week, or $5.5 billion per year. During 1990, there were approximately 81 million families with earnings (counting individuals living alone as families), with average family earnings of approximately $650 per week. Thus, ignoring any employment effects or wage effects on higher- or lower-wage workers, the minimum-wage increase was equivalent to a transfer of approximately 0.20 percent of total family earnings. According to Table 9.4, 35 percent of the earnings gains from the minimum-wage hike, or approximately 0.07 percentage points of total earnings, should have accrued to families in the lowest decile of earnings. Assuming that the federal minimum wage had no effect on family earnings in the low-impact states, this is roughly consistent with the simple shares analysis in Table 9.6, which indicates a redistribution of about 0.14 percent of total earnings in the high-impact states and 0.03 percent of total earnings in the medium-impact states. Nevertheless, some caution is required in interpreting Table 9.6, since the 1990–1991 recession was less severe in the high- and medium-impact states, possibly leading us to overstate the effect of the minimum wage increase.

EFFECTS OF THE INCREASE IN THE MINIMUM WAGE
ON POVERTY RATES

We turn to a final aspect of the potential effect of the minimum wage: its affect on the fraction of individuals living in poverty. The poverty rate is defined as the fraction of individuals whose family income falls short of a family-composition-specific poverty threshold.[24] As noted in the introduction to this chapter, the connection between the poverty rate and the minimum-wage rate is necessarily limited, because two-thirds of adults who live in poverty do not work. Nevertheless, the minimum wage sometimes is defined as an "antipoverty program," and much of the political rhetoric from supporters of the minimum wage focuses on its supposed antipoverty effects.

We used CPS files for March 1990 (one month before the 1990 increase in the minimum wage) and March 1992 (11 months after the 1991 increase) to compute individual poverty rates, by state, for all individuals aged 16 and older, and for workers (i.e., people who had worked at any time during the previous year). Because the March CPS uses family income in the previous calendar year to define poverty status, our poverty rates are properly interpreted as rates for 1989 and 1991. As in our analysis of the distributions of wages and family earnings, we then regressed the change in the state-specific poverty rate on a measure of the fraction of workers in the state affected by the 1990 and 1991 minimum wage hikes, and on variables meant to control for state-specific economic trends—either the change in the state employment–population rate between 1989 and 1991, or the change in the state unemployment rate over the same interval.

The results are presented in Table 9.7. In the models without any other control variables, the effects of the minimum-wage variable on either the overall poverty rate or the poverty rate of workers are negative and marginally significant, suggesting that poverty rates fell faster in states in which the minimum wage had a bigger impact. In the models with controls for changes in economic conditions, the estimated effects are uniformly negative, but not different from zero at conventional significance levels. To further analyze the determinants of poverty, we also estimated models that included both the change in the state employment rate and a set of indicator variables for the major Census regions (northeast, south, northcentral, and west). The latter pick up any unobserved regional trends in economic conditions, government support programs, or family composition that might affect poverty rates. In these models (reported in

TABLE 9.7
Estimated Models for Changes in the Poverty Rate Across States, 1989–1991

	Overall Poverty Rate				Poverty Rate for Workers			
	(1)	(2)	(3)	(4)	(5)	(6)	(7)	(8)
1. Fraction Affected	−0.15 (0.08)	−0.06 (0.10)	−0.14 (0.12)	−0.03 (0.11)	−0.13 (0.07)	−0.12 (0.08)	−0.18 (0.10)	−0.12 (0.10)
2. Change in Employment Rate	—	−0.48 (0.31)	—	−0.57 (0.31)	—	−0.06 (0.26)	—	−0.08 (0.27)
3. Change in Unemployment Rate	—	—	0.09 (0.42)	—	—	—	−0.26 (0.36)	—
4. Region Controls	No	No	No	Yes	No	No	No	Yes
5. R-Squared	0.07	0.12	0.07	0.22	0.07	0.07	0.08	0.11

Note: Standard errors are shown in parentheses. Models are estimated on 51 state observations, using data from the March 1990 and March 1992 Current Population Surveys. The dependent variable in columns 1–4 is the change in the fraction of individuals aged 16 and older whose total family income is below the appropriate poverty line (taking into account family size). The dependent variable in columns 5–8 is the change in the fraction of individuals aged 16 and older who worked last year and whose total family income is below the appropriate poverty line. Fraction Affected represents the fraction of wage and salary earners in the state who earned between $3.35 and 4.24 per hour in April–December 1989. Change in Employment Rate is the change in the employment–population rate for all workers in the state between 1989 and 1991. Change in Unemployment Rate is similar. Region controls represent indicator variables for three Census regions. All models include an unrestricted constant.

columns 4 and 8), the estimated coefficients of the fraction-affected variable are negative and small for the overall poverty rate, and negative and somewhat larger for the poverty rate among workers. The coefficient in column 8 implies that the increase in the federal minimum wage led to a 1.6 percentage point decline in the fraction of "working poor" in a state where a high fraction of workers were affected by the minimum wage (such as New Mexico) relative to a state where a low fraction of workers were affected (such as California). Because the poverty rate for workers in New Mexico in 1991 was 11 percent, this effect is relatively large.

To better understand the magnitude of the coefficients in the poverty models in Table 9.7, we used March 1990 CPS data to estimate the *maximum* fraction of working-poor individuals who could be moved out of poverty by an increase in the minimum wage to $4.25 per hour. Specifically, for each individual, we calculated the ratio of the family poverty gap (i.e., the amount of money necessary to raise the individual's family out of poverty) to individual earnings in the previous year. We then compared this ratio with the percentage increase in wages that an individual who previously had earned less than $4.25 per hour would receive if his or her wages were "topped up" to $4.25 per hour. Using this method, we estimate that a maximum of 12 percent of working-poor individuals could be moved out of poverty by the minimum wage.[25] Across states, the fraction of "potentially moveable" working poor is positively correlated with the fraction of workers who earned between $3.35 and 4.24 per hour: an increase in the fraction of workers in the affected wage range from 2 to 17 percent (e.g., comparing California and New Mexico) is associated with a 7 percentage point increase in the fraction of "potentially moveable" working poor (the *t*-statistic for this estimate is 1.5). Our estimates of the coefficient of the fraction-affected variable in models for the change in the fraction of working poor suggest that all of these potentially moveable individuals were in fact moved out of poverty by the increase in the federal minimum wage.

In summary, we find some evidence that poverty rates, particularly for working adults, fell more quickly between 1989 and 1991 in states in which the increase in the minimum wage had the largest impact on wages. The imprecision of our estimates makes it difficult to assert confidently that this change was attributable to the minimum wage. Nevertheless, there is certainly no evidence that the increase in the minimum wage led to an *increase* in poverty. Rather, our analysis points to a modest poverty-reducing effect of the minimum wage.

CONCLUSIONS

Contrary to the opinion proffered by many analysts, our empirical results suggest that the most recent round of increases in the federal minimum wage had a narrowing effect on the distributions of wages and family earnings, and that it may have led to a modest reduction in the rate of poverty among workers.

The effect of the minimum wage on the distribution of wages is direct and easily measured. Consistent with recent research by Di-Nardo, Fortin, and Lemieux (1994), we find that the minimum wage serves as a backstop for the wages of a significant fraction of *all* wage and salary workers, not just teenagers. Our estimates indicate that the 1990 and 1991 increases in the minimum wage led to a significant compression of wages in the lower tail of the overall wage distribution—effectively rolling back a significant share of the increased wage inequality that developed during the 1980s.

The effect of the minimum wage on the distribution of family earnings is somewhat less direct, as not all workers who are affected by an increase in the minimum wage live in families with low earnings. Perhaps surprisingly, however, inspection of the distribution of affected workers across families suggests that more than 35 percent of the earnings gains generated by the 1990 and 1991 minimum wage hikes were concentrated among families in the bottom 10 percent of the family-earnings distribution. Direct estimates of the effect of the minimum wage on the lower decile of family earnings, based on the natural experiment provided by interstate variation in the fraction of workers affected by the federal minimum-wage hike, are large and relatively precise. We also compare changes in the share of total earnings paid to families in the lowest decile of the family-earnings distribution across groups of states that were more affected and less affected by the increase in the federal minimum wage. We find that the earnings share of the poorest families rose more rapidly in states in which the minimum wage had the biggest effect on wages, although the actual increase in earnings was relatively modest.

The connection between minimum wages and poverty is even less direct, because most people who live in poverty are nonworkers, and the minimum wage can affect only families with workers. Again, we use the interstate variation in the impact of the 1990 and 1991 minimum-wage increases to estimate the effect of the minimum wage on poverty. Our estimates point to small poverty reductions for the working poor. However, the estimates are relatively imprecise.

On balance, our conclusions echo those of Gramlich, whose 1976 study first opened up the issue of the distributional impact of the minimum wage to systematic empirical analysis. As Gramlich noted, it seems that a modest rise in the minimum wage ". . . may in fact have slightly beneficial effects both on low-wage workers and on the overall distribution of income."

APPENDIX

The analysis in this chapter is based on wage, income, and family-earnings data drawn from two sets of Current Population (CPS) data files. Wage and family-earnings data are taken from the merged monthly outgoing rotation group files for various months of 1989, 1990, and 1991. In our extracts of these files, we include individuals aged 16 and older who were employed as paid workers at the time of the CPS survey. Individuals in the extracts who reported being paid by the hour on their main job are assigned their reported hourly pay as a "wage." Individuals who reported being paid by the week, month, etc. are assigned the ratio of their reported weekly earnings to their reported usual weekly hours as a "wage." Individuals with allocated hourly or weekly earnings are assigned a missing wage, as are those whose reported or constructed hourly wage is less than $1.00 per hour or greater than $75 per hour.

The outgoing rotation group files include a measure of total family wage and salary earnings for each individual, as well as information on the number of wage and salary earners in the individual's family, and an indicator for whether any other family members are self-employed. In calculating the distributions of family earnings, we performed three adjustments to the family earnings data and the CPS sample weights to account for the fact that self-employment earnings are not included in CPS data. First, we set family earnings equal to missing for any individual living in a family with one or more self-employed workers. This change affects approximately 6 to 8 percent of all individuals who are working as paid workers. Second, we adjusted upward the sampling weights of individuals living in families with no self-employed family members to account for the missing data for individuals with self-employed family members. Third, we divided each individual's sample weight by the number of earners in his or her family. This adjustment reweights the individual data to take into account the fact that a family with N earners will be included in the sample N times.

Data on poverty and total family income are taken from the March 1990, 1991, and 1992 CPS files. In our extracts from these files, we include individuals aged 16 and older. Family income is based on reported income from all sources for the previous calendar year. The

March CPS files include a measure of the appropriate poverty threshold for each family, based on the number of family members and the age composition of the family. Poverty status is defined by comparing actual family income with the poverty threshold.

Notes

1. This calculation is described later in this chapter.

2. For example, Peter Passell wrote in the February 18, 1993, *New York Times* that "much of the gain from a higher minimum wage would go to surfboards and stereos—not into rent and baby formula."

3. These figures are taken from Card and Lemieux (1994) and are based on wage rates reported for each individual's main job.

4. Our evidence suggests that the fraction of the earnings gains from a higher minimum wage that goes to families with lower incomes is larger than the fraction reported in a recent study by Horrigan and Mincy (1993). We discuss the reasons for the discrepancy later in this chapter.

5. Note that some of the workers who were earning between $3.35 and 4.24 per hour during March 1990 may have been out of the labor market in 1991, and that others may have gained enough experience to raise their wages beyond $4.25 per hour. However, the set of workers in the labor market is constantly being replenished by others with about the same age, education, and skill characteristics. Thus, when we refer to affected workers, we actually are referring to a class of workers—say, 16- to 24-year-olds with fewer than 12 years of schooling—rather than to a specific set of individuals.

6. Self-employed workers are exempt from the minimum wage and are excluded from the tabulations. By "wage and salary workers," we mean those people who report themselves as working for pay for a private or government employer.

7. We use the term "family" to include both multiperson families and individuals who live alone.

8. Subminimum-wage workers are more likely than those earning between $3.35 and 4.24 per hour to report being paid by the week or month. For salaried workers, we must compute an hourly wage by dividing average weekly earnings by average weekly hours. Because weekly hours often are misreported, this procedure induces some extra measurement error in the wages of salaried workers.

9. Note that this definition of family income deciles is somewhat unorthodox, as 10 percent of individuals, rather than 10 percent of families, are in each decile.

10. Formally, this is similar to a Kolmorogov test for equality of two distribution functions. See Cox and Hinkley (1974, pp. 198–202).

11. Note that the income deciles in Table 9.2 are for all individuals, rather than all workers. Thus, about 4.5 percent of all workers are in the first decile group.

12. A similar trend is revealed in a recent study by Burkhauser and Glenn (1994). Data in their Table 1 show that, in 1979, 34 percent of all low-wage workers (those whose average hourly earnings during the previous year were less than one-half of the overall average wage) lived in families that were poor or near-poor. In 1989, this fraction had risen to 39 percent.

13. For example, real median family income of all families with children fell by 20 percent between 1974 and 1990, while the real median income of families without children remained constant. See U.S. Department of Commerce (1993, Table B-12).

14. For example, the average family income of teenagers who earned between $3.35 and 4.24 per hour in March 1990 was 10 percent less than the average family income of higher-wage teenagers. Gramlich (1976, Table 12) reported that, during 1973, family income of teenagers earning between $1.60 and 2.00 per hour was 10 percent higher than that of teenagers earning more than $2.00 per hour.

15. During March 1990, the average family incomes of hourly-rated workers and salaried workers were $37,300 and $51,360, respectively.

16. The real average family income of families in the bottom fifth of the income distribution fell from $11,069 in 1973 to $10,555 in 1990 (in 1992 dollars). Over the same time period, the average income–poverty ratio for families in the bottom fifth of the income distribution fell from 1.12 to 0.99. See U.S. Department of Commerce (1993, Tables B-7 and B-8).

17. The data sources for this figure are the monthly Current Population Surveys conducted in 1989, 1990, and 1991, as described in the Appendix to this chapter.

18. Some of the 1989 increases in the fifth and tenth percentiles in the high-wage states might be a result of state-specific minimum-wage laws that took effect in many of these states during that year.

19. These estimates are based on a comparison of the relative changes in the wage percentiles in the low-wage and high-wage states, from the first quarter of 1989 to the fourth quarter of 1992.

20. We use the changes in the logarithms of the wage percentiles.

21. Because the wage percentiles for the United States as a whole cannot be written as weighted averages of the wage percentiles in each of the states, this procedure is not strictly correct. Nevertheless, it gives a sense of the potential effect of the minimum-wage hikes.

22. This procedure implicitly assumes that the incidence of self-employment is randomly distributed across the working population.

23. We also have analyzed the 5th and 25th percentiles of family earnings. The estimated coefficients of the fraction-affected variable for the 5th percentile of family earnings are positive and highly significant, but slightly lower than the coefficients for the 10th percentile (e.g., the estimate is 0.78, with a standard error of 0.30, for a model with no control variables). The estimated coefficients in the models for the 25th percentile are likewise slightly smaller than the estimated coefficients for the 50th percentile (e.g., 0.38, with a standard error of 0.13, for a model with no controls).

CHAPTER 10

How Much Do Employers and Shareholders Lose?

> While we believe large increases (10 percent or so) in either food or labor costs are very manageable for most industry participants, the combination of large increases in both food and labor costs at the same time could have a negative effect on industry profitability.
>
> —Montgomery Securities Report

MOST RESEARCH THAT has been conducted on the distributional impact of the minimum wage has focused on the consequences for workers. Less is known about the impact on employers. We lack answers to such basic questions as: How much do minimum-wage increases reduce employers' profits? Which employers are most likely to suffer reduced profits as a result of a minimum-wage increase? Are any employers forced into bankruptcy because of the minimum wage? Employers and their representatives often strongly oppose minimum-wage increases. Nevertheless, we have little data to assess the quantitative impact of minimum-wage increases on employer profits.

Economists generally agree that a minimum-wage increase will raise the costs of business for employers of low-wage workers. Indeed, if the minimum wage increases by 10 percent, and other things are held constant, then employers' costs will increase by the share of minimum-wage labor in their total costs, times 10 percent. These higher costs can be accommodated in several ways: First, the profits of firms that hire minimum-wage workers could decline. Second, firms may raise prices, and pass on the cost of the minimum-wage hike to consumers. Third, an increase in the minimum wage may induce firms to eliminate inefficiencies, or may interact with pre-existing economic distortions, to generate greater revenues. Of course, all of these effects may occur simultaneously.[1]

We begin this chapter with a statistical profile of the kinds of employers who hire minimum-wage workers, and are most directly affected by an increase in the minimum-wage. Not surprisingly, our results indicate that employers who pay wages at or near the minimum tend to be relatively small, and concentrated in the retail-trade sector, especially the restaurant industry. We then present a summary of alternative theoretical models of the effect of the minimum wage on profits.

The bulk of this chapter presents a series of stock market event studies, exploring the reaction of the stock market to news about impending minimum-wage legislation. We identify a series of events, beginning in early 1987, that may have altered investors' expectations about the future course of the minimum wage. For example, when then-Vice President George Bush announced that he could support a minimum-wage increase, informed analysts may have raised their forecast of the likelihood of a higher minimum wage. If the stock market accurately reflects the value of publicly traded firms, then the market's reaction to news about the minimum wage provides a direct measure of how the minimum wage affects low-wage employers' profits. We focus on a large sample of publicly traded firms, including McDonald's, Kmart, and Sears, that pay many of their workers close to the minimum wage. After adjusting for overall market returns, our results provide mixed evidence that the value of these firms changes in response to legislative maneuvering on the minimum wage. News associated with the November 1989 federal minimum wage legislation had little systematic effect on the market valuation of low-wage employers. News concerning more recent proposals to increase the minimum wage may have had a small negative effect on the value of such firms—on the order of 1 or 2 percent. One difficulty in interpreting these results is the fact that investors might have anticipated the news before it was released. Another is that the event-study approach relies heavily on the assumption that the market responds rationally to new information. Nevertheless, our findings suggest that stock prices of low-wage employers are *not* affected severely on the day, or on the surrounding days, that new information on the minimum wage is released.

PROFILE OF MINIMUM-WAGE EMPLOYERS

Table 10.1 presents a summary of the characteristics of employers that paid the minimum wage, and other wage rates, in April 1993.[2] The first four columns present the fraction of workers in selected wage ranges who were employed by firms in various size classes and industries. The first row of column 2, for example, shows that 59.7 percent of *all* workers who were paid an hourly wage rate equal to the minimum wage in 1993 ($4.25 per hour) were employed in establishments that had fewer than 25 workers. The corresponding fraction for subminimum-wage employees (column 1) is 59.2 percent. Individuals who earned more than the minimum wage are divided into two categories: near-minimum-wage workers (those earning between $4.26 and 4.75 per hour), in column 3, and higher-wage workers (those earning more than $4.75 per hour) in column 4.

A number of striking patterns emerge from Table 10.1. Relative to those who earned a higher wage, minimum-wage workers and near-minimum-wage workers were more likely to work at small establishments. Interestingly, however, about 64 percent of minimum wage workers were employed at multi-establishment firms (i.e., firms like McDonald's that operate many smaller establishments). This percentage is not far below the 71 percent of higher-wage employees at multi-establishment firms, and substantially above the 38.2 percent rate for subminimum-wage workers. Thirty-five percent of minimum-wage workers were employed in firms with fewer than 25 employees at all locations, compared to 20 percent of workers who were paid more than $4.75 per hour. Thus, the relative concentration of minimum-wage and near-minimum-wage workers at small firms is only partially offset when one measures employer size by the total number of employees at all locations.

The industrial distribution of minimum-wage workers is also notably different from that of higher-wage workers. Companies in the retail trade and service industries together employ 83 percent of minimum-wage workers, with over half of all minimum-wage workers employed in the retail trade sector alone. By contrast, retail trade and services employed just under one-half of all workers who are paid more than $4.75 per hour. Using a finer industrial breakdown, we find that minimum-wage workers are unusually prevalent in the restaurant, hotel, grocery store, variety merchandise store, and department store industries. Fully 28.5 percent of all minimum-wage employees in 1993 worked for a restaurant.

The entries in the last four columns of Table 10.1 give the distribution of employees across the various wage categories for each row category. For example, row 1 of column 6 indicates that 3.9 percent of all workers who were employed in firms with fewer than 25 employees were paid the minimum wage. Although this percentage may seem low, note that only 2.5 percent of workers nationwide were paid exactly the minimum wage in 1993. Small businesses were much more likely to pay the minimum wage than were large businesses, but the percentage of workers who were paid the minimum is low in either case.[3]

The wage distributions for each industry reveal a similar result:

TABLE 10.1
Description of Firms that Employ Minimum-Wage and Near-Minimum-Wage Workers, April 1993

Employer Characteristics	Percent of Workers in Each Wage Range Employed at Employer Type				Wage Distribution of Workers Employed at Each Employer Type			
	<4.25 (1)	4.25 (2)	4.26–4.75 (3)	>4.75 (4)	<4.25 (5)	4.25 (6)	4.26–4.75 (7)	>4.75 (8)
Establishment Size								
1. 1–24	59.2	59.7	51.4	32.0	5.0	3.9	6.2	85.0
2. 25–99	27.3	24.2	27.4	24.7	3.2	2.2	4.6	90.1
3. 100–249	6.7	7.9	12.0	15.1	1.3	1.2	3.4	94.1
4. 250+	6.8	8.3	9.2	28.1	0.7	0.7	1.5	97.1
Multiple Establishments								
5. Yes	38.2	63.9	59.4	71.3	1.6	2.0	3.5	92.9
6. No	61.8	36.1	40.6	28.8	5.8	2.7	5.5	86.0
Firm Size								
7. 1–24	50.5	35.3	35.0	20.2	6.6	3.4	6.2	83.9

8. 25–99	16.9	14.9	11.9	13.0	3.7	2.4	3.6	90.4
9. 100–249	4.3	3.7	8.2	8.8	1.4	0.9	3.7	93.9
10. 250+	28.2	46.1	44.9	58.0	1.4	1.7	3.1	93.8

Industry

11. Agriculture	6.1	2.7	3.0	1.3	11.5	4.5	8.1	76.0
12. Mining	0.1	0.0	0.0	0.7	0.7	0.1	0.2	99.1
13. Construction	1.6	1.1	1.1	5.2	1.0	0.6	0.9	97.5
14. Manufacturing	5.7	8.9	9.3	19.1	0.9	1.2	2.1	95.7
15. Transportation/Communication/ Public Utilities	2.6	1.0	1.7	8.2	1.0	0.3	0.9	97.8
16. Wholesale Trade	1.3	1.2	1.3	4.0	1.0	0.8	1.5	96.8
17. Retail Trade	39.1	51.3	50.6	13.9	6.6	7.5	12.3	73.5
18. Finance, Insurance, Real Estate	3.2	1.0	1.7	7.2	1.4	0.4	1.1	97.2
19. Services	38.9	31.7	30.4	34.4	3.3	2.3	3.7	90.7
20. Public Administration	1.4	1.3	0.9	6.0	0.7	0.6	0.7	98.0
21. All	100.0	100.0	100.0	100.0	2.9	2.5	4.2	90.4

Note: Estimates by establishment and firm size are based on the April 1993 Current Population Survey (CPS) Employee Benefit Supplement. Estimates by industry are based on the 1993 CPS outgoing rotation group files.

the percentage of workers who were paid the minimum wage does not exceed 8 percent in any industry. In the retail-trade sector, for example, only 7.5 percent of workers were paid exactly the minimum, although another 12.3 percent were paid between the minimum and $4.75 per hour. In the restaurant industry, 13.4 percent of workers were paid the minimum wage, and another 18 percent were paid between the minimum and $4.75 per hour. Assuming full compliance, an increase in the minimum wage to $4.75 per hour in 1993 would have directly affected the pay of 31.5 percent of restaurant employees.

One could argue that the minimum wage has a larger impact than these figures indicate, because many workers start at the minimum, and then receive raises. As discussed in chapter 5, the entire wage structure at some firms could ratchet up as a result of a minimum wage hike. An examination of wage data on a given date, as in Table 10.1, ignores the fact that the minimum wage may provide an anchor for the firm's wage structure. To address this issue, we have recalculated the figures in Table 10.1, including only workers who were hired within the preceding year. We find that 7.4 percent of recently-hired workers were paid exactly the minimum wage—a rate that is more than three times the rate for all workers. Another 12 percent of recently-hired workers were paid between the minimum and 50 cents more than the minimum. Ten percent of recent hires in establishments with fewer than 25 employees were paid the minimum wage, compared with 2.9 percent of recent hires at establishments with 250 or more employees. Thus, the minimum wage influences a substantially higher fraction of employees when one considers only entry-level workers.

THE EFFECT OF THE MINIMUM WAGE ON PROFITS

How would an increase in the minimum wage affect the profitability of firms? We first consider the impact of imposing a minimum wage, or of increasing the minimum wage, on a single employer that operates in a competitive industry. We then consider the effect of a minimum wage on the profits of an entire industry. Next, we illustrate the theoretical insights from this analysis with a hypothetical example based on a "typical" fast food restaurant. Finally, we discuss the effect of the minimum wage on employer profits under alternative economic models.

Competitive, Wage-Taking Firm

The neoclassical model assumes that each firm chooses its level of employment so as to maximize profits. We denote the firm's output by $F(L)$, where $F(\cdot)$ is an increasing, concave function of the amount of labor, L, that the firm employs.[4] The product price, p, and the wage, w, are assumed to be *fixed*. The optimized profit function, $\pi(w)$, is

$$\pi(w) = \max_L p\, F(L) - wL. \tag{10.1}$$

Let w^0 represent the initial wage in the absence of a minimum wage (or before an increase in the minimum), let $\pi^0 = \pi(w^0)$, and let $w^M > w^0$ represent the minimum wage. The discrete second-order approximation to the change in the firm's profit ($\Delta\pi$) is given by

$$\frac{\Delta\pi}{\pi^0} \approx -\frac{w^0 L^0}{\pi^0}\left(\frac{w^M - w^0}{w^0}\right) + \frac{1}{2}\frac{w^0 L^0}{\pi^0}\,\eta\left(\frac{w^M - w^0}{w^0}\right)^2, \tag{10.2}$$

where L^0 is the optimal level of employment at wage w^0, and η is the absolute value of the elasticity of demand for labor. The first term in equation (10.2) indicates that the first-order effect of an increase in the minimum wage is to reduce the profit of the firm in proportion to the ratio of payroll costs to profits. The second term in (10.2) is positive, indicating that the effect of the minimum-wage increase on shareholder wealth will be less than the first-order term if the employer reduces employment (i.e., if $\eta > 0$). The intuitive explanation for this result is that, other things being equal, if a profit-maximizing firm chooses to reduce employment when the minimum wage rises, then it must be able to increase its profit relative to a situation in which it is constrained to maintain the same level of employment. The greater the scope for substituting capital or skilled labor for minimum-wage labor (i.e., the greater the elasticity of demand), the less the minimum-wage increase will eat into profit. Indeed, in the extreme case, in which a firm can costlessly substitute capital or skilled workers without increasing costs or cutting output, profit will be unaffected by the minimum-wage hike.

Industry Level

The preceding analysis is based on the assumption that a minimum wage is applied to a single firm. More realistically, many firms in an affected industry are covered by the minimum wage. In this case, increasing the minimum wage will increase the labor costs of the entire industry, leading to an increase in the market price of output. Specifically, if the industry experiences a substantial decline in employment as a result of a rise in the minimum wage, then output will decline, and, consequently, the product price will rise. Any increase in the product price will partially offset the decline in employers' profit. Indeed, in the standard case where the industry is made up of perfectly competitive firms with constant returns to scale, the product price will eventually rise by just enough to fully cover the increase in payroll costs. In the neoclassical model, however, industry prices will rise *only* if industry output and employment fall.

A search of company annual reports revealed many instances where managers reported raising prices to offset the effect of the minimum wage. For example, Sandwich Chef Incorporated stated in their annual report:

> Many of the Company's employees are paid hourly rates related to the federal minimum wage. Accordingly, inflation related annual increases in the minimum wage have historically increased the Company's labor costs. . . . In most cases, the Company has been able to increase prices sufficiently to match increases in its operating costs, but there is no assurance that it will be able to do so in the future.

Hypothetical Example

The following example serves to illustrate the impact of a minimum-wage increase on a hypothetical firm's profits in the neoclassical model. Consider a restaurant that employs only minimum-wage workers, and that has $2.0 million in revenues per year.[5] Column 1 of Table 10.2 presents a hypothetical balance sheet for this firm prior to an increase in the minimum wage. We assume that labor costs equal 30 percent of revenues ($600,000), and that other costs, including rent, food, and materials, equal $1.2 million. The firm's annual profit is 10 percent of revenues, or $200,000. The value of the firm equals the present discounted value of its profit. If we assume that the firm's balance sheet will continue as described indefinitely and use a real interest rate of 3 percent to discount future profit, then the present discounted value of the firm's profits would be $6.67 million.

Now suppose that Congress increases the minimum wage by 15 percent. If the restaurant does not change its level of employment, then its labor costs will increase by 15 percent, to $690,000. Furthermore, if the firm continues to charge the same price and does not cut its other inputs, its annual profit will fall by 45 percent, to $110,000 per year. A new balance sheet for this firm is presented in the second column of Table 10.2. How will this decline in profit affect the present value of the firm's profits? The answer to this ques-

TABLE 10.2

Effect of Minimum-Wage Increase on Value of a Hypothetical Firm

Balance Sheet Item	Before Minimum-Wage Increase (1)	After Minimum-Wage Increase (2)
1. Sales	$2,000,000	$2,000,000
2. Labor Cost	600,000	690,000
3. Other Costs (food, materials, rent, etc.)	1,200,000	1,200,000
4. Profit	200,000	110,000
5. Present Value of Profits (3 percent interest rate)	6,666,667	6,332,128[a]
6. Decline in Value	—	5.0%

[a]This calculation assumes that the minimum-wage increase causes labor costs to increase by 15 percent for four years and has no effect on labor costs thereafter.

tion depends on how long the minimum-wage increase is in effect. Suppose, for example, that the 15 percent increase in the minimum wage is abruptly eroded by a burst of inflation after four years. In this scenario, the firm's profit would be $110,000 for the next four years, and $200,000 thereafter. If we continue to discount future profit with a 3 percent real interest rate, then the present value of the firm's profit would now be $6.3 million, 5 percent lower than its value in the absence of the minimum-wage increase.[6]

Of course, the firm may not be passive in responding to the minimum wage. The neoclassical model predicts two responses. First, the firm might cut employment. Cutting employment obviously would offset the increase in labor costs, but it would also result in lower revenue at a fixed price. For example, if employment is cut by 10 percent (i.e., the elasticity of labor demand is 0.67), then labor costs would increase by only $21,000, rather than by $90,000. However, if the restaurant hires fewer workers it will be able to serve fewer customers, and revenue would decline. For example, if a 10 percent reduction in employment causes sales to decline by 3.6 percent, then all the savings from cutting employment will be erased by foregone revenue. Because of the decline in revenue, any buffer provided by cutting employment will have a second-order effect on profits. Moreover, the material in chapters 2–4 strongly suggests that most firms do not reduce employment very much in response to an increase in the minimum wage. Thus, there is little evidence that the first-order loss in profit is moderated.

Second, the restaurant might be able to raise prices of its meals, if other restaurants cut back on employment and raise their prices, as well.[7] A rise in the meal price might increase the firm's revenue relative to a situation in which the price did not rise, and thus could increase profits. Indeed, if customers would tolerate a 4.5 percent price hike without buying fewer restaurant meals, then restaurants could increase revenues by an amount sufficient to offset the entire minimum-wage increase. If, more realistically, some customers would choose to eat at home rather than pay more to dine out, then the demand for the entire restaurant industry will shrink as prices rise. In this case, prices will not rise by enough in the short run to fully offset the higher costs created by the increase in the minimum wage. In the longer run, the reduction in profits will lead some restaurants to close down, allowing prices to eventually rise by enough to restore industry profits to a "normal" level.

Alternative Models

A variety of models that have received much attention from economic theorists in recent years have different implications for the effect of the minimum wage on profitability. First, we consider situations in which firms have the power to set wage rates because of efficiency wage considerations, monopsony, search, or other reasons. Second, we consider models in which firms do not necessarily maximize profits.

The standard neoclassical model of a competitive firm implies that firms do not have "wage policies"; instead every firm is assumed to be able to hire all the workers it wants at the going "market wage rate." In other words, in the standard model, firms have no discretion over the wages that they pay. As we have seen, in the standard model, the profit that the employer loses as a result of a minimum-wage hike is, to a first approximation, equal to the amount of labor multiplied by the increase in the wage. By contrast, any model in which firms determine the level of their wages to maximize profits will imply that, to a first-order approximation, an increase in the minimum wage has no effect on profits.

For example, suppose that, as part of a strategy to keep vacancies low, reduce turnover, improve morale, or for other reasons, the firm sets its initial wage at w^*, rather than at w^0. We capture the notion that the wage rate affects the firm's revenue by assuming that output depends positively on L and w. The firm now selects its employment *and wage* to maximize profits:

$$\pi = \max_{w,L} p\, F(w,L) - wL. \tag{10.3}$$

This yields two first-order conditions:

$$pF_L = w^* \tag{10.4a}$$

$$pF_w = L^0. \tag{10.4b}$$

The first equation is the familiar first-order condition for profit maximization in which the value of the marginal revenue product of labor is equal to the wage rate. The second equation requires that the wage is set so that, on the margin, the revenue generated by paying a slightly higher wage is equal to the amount of labor that must be paid that higher wage.

Assuming that these equations characterize the optimal wage and employment levels, then to a first-order approximation, the loss in profits if the firm is required to pay more (or less) than the wage that it chooses is zero. We can see this by considering the derivative of equation (10.3) with respect to w at the optimal level of w^* and L^0:

$$d\pi/dw = p\, F_w(w^*,L^0) - L^0 = 0. \tag{10.5}$$

By the first-order condition (10.4b), this is equal to zero. The intuitive explanation for this result is that if a minimum-wage increase forces the firm to pay slightly more than its optimally-selected wage, then the firm will offset virtually all of this extra cost by savings from being able to fill vacancies more rapidly, having lower turnover, improved morale, etc. Any decline in profitability is of a second-order magnitude, although in this case the second-order effect is negative.

There is some anecdotal support for this kind of a model. Companies often report that paying higher wages results in improved employee productivity. For example, Dollar General Corporation noted in its 1992 annual report that the impact of the 1992 minimum-wage hike was minimized due to "greater employee productivity."

ELIMINATION OF SLACK

The neoclassical model assumes that firms operate in such a way as to minimize costs on every margin. The second class of models relaxes the assumption that firms are strict profit-maximizers. In this case, a minimum-wage increase could force firms to implement cost-saving measures or to generate additional revenue with fixed resources. Firms might operate with some slack for a variety of reasons. First, a literature in corporate finance suggests that agency relationships may drive a wedge between shareholders' interests and managers' interests, so that managers pursue objectives other than that of pure profit maximization. Second, operating with some productivity slack might be an optimal strategic choice for a firm if it can use this slack as a strategic threat against potential competitors. Third, managers simply might lack sufficient information to maximize profits.

The hypothetical restaurant described in Table 10.2 could attempt to offset the cost of a minimum-wage increase by reducing its nonlabor costs. According to the balance sheet, the firm pays $1.2 million for such nonlabor costs as supplies and rent. The neoclassical model assumes that no savings can be generated by reducing these expenditures. If there is some slack, however, the firm might be able to negotiate lower prices from suppliers or use nonlabor inputs more efficiently to lower costs. If the firm could reduce these expenditures by 7.5 percent, it would recoup the entire $90,000 cost increase resulting from the minimum-wage hike.

Although the neoclassical model assumes that firms have negotiated the lowest possible prices from suppliers, and have used inputs at peak efficiency levels before an increase in the minimum wage, annual company reports provide many examples of ways in which managers claim to take advantage of quantity discounts or improved efficiency to offset the effect of a minimum-wage increase. For example, GB Foods Corp. noted in its 1992 annual report that, "The Company has been able to offset the effects of inflation to date, including increases in the statutory minimum wage, through small price increases and economies resulting from the purchase of food products in increased numbers due to the increased number of Green Burrito stores, and efficiencies in the preparation of food in the Company's Commissary." The *Nation's Restaurant News* (July 18, 1988, p. 66) reported that the International House of Pancakes "would attempt to recoup increased labor costs [from the California minimum wage increase] through intensified efforts to eliminate waste and save energy." Gary Gerdemann, a KFC spokesman, recently stated that his company has the ability to "engineer out" a one-half percent cost increase by switching suppliers, reducing packaging, shipping materials in bigger lots, and changing recipes.[8] This slack seems to exist even though a minimum-wage hike recently was imposed.

Stock Market Valuation

According to modern finance theory, the stock market value of a firm represents investors' forecasts of the present discounted value of the firm's future profits. Investors are forward looking, and base their prediction of the firm's profits on all relevant information that is available at the time that they make their forecasts. In an "efficient market," the shareholders' wealth is determined by the present value of the firm's future profits.

How would the stock market valuation of firms that hire minimum-wage workers change in response to news about a minimum-wage increase? The answer depends on two issues. The first issue relates to the impact that investors expect a minimum-wage increase to have on company profits. On the one hand, as we have seen in the hypothetical example in Table 10.2, if the labor market behaved according to the standard model, the present value of profits of firms that hire minimum-wage workers would be expected to decline considerably. On the other hand, if investors expect that the increased labor costs will be offset by improved recruitment, lower turnover, or the elimination of slack, then the minimum-wage increase would be expected to have a much smaller effect on profits. One difficulty with relying on investor sentiment as a measure of profitability is that investors' valuations of a particular company might stray from its true value, either because of idiosyncratic errors in valuations, or because investors use the wrong model to forecast the impact of certain events. By using data on a large sample of firms that are affected by the minimum wage, however, we average out idiosyncratic factors that might influence an individual firm's stock market valuation.

The second major issue is whether investors anticipate increases in the minimum wage, and incorporate these expectations into their forecasts of the firm's profitability, in advance of key events. One would not expect the value of affected firms to change on the day of a minimum-wage increase, because investors would have anticipated the increase since the time the legislation was passed, and probably earlier. The market should respond only to news, which, by definition, involves previously unknown information. The difficulty is in identifying events that contain news about the minimum wage. For example, consider the news that Congress has voted to increase the minimum wage by 15 percent. In the days and weeks before the vote, investors have already had a chance to assign probabilities to the possible vote outcomes. Suppose that, on the day before the vote, market participants believe that the bill has an 80 percent chance of success. Therefore, on the day of the actual vote, if the bill is passed the "news" leads to a 20 percent upward revision of the likelihood of a higher minimum wage. If a 15 percent rise in the minimum lowers the value of a company by 5 percent, then the "news" on the day of the vote accounts for a reduction in the value of the firm of only 1 percent (= 20 percent × 5 percent). The problem is that it is difficult for a researcher to know what investors expected in advance of the vote, and how the outcome of the vote changed investors' forecasts of the likelihood of a minimum-wage increase.

Another example of expectational effects concerns the timing of future minimum-wage increases. Suppose that, at time t, the market fully anticipates that the minimum wage will eventually increase by 15 percent, but that it does not expect the increase to occur for another four years. Suppose further that, contrary to expectations, Congress votes to increase the minimum wage immediately. In this case, the fact that the minimum wage will be 15 percent higher during the next four years is news. One could, for example, interpret the results presented in Table 10.2 as implying that the minimum wage is permanently increased by 15 percent in year t, but that the market previously had expected the increase to occur in year $t + 4$. Profits are lower than expected for four years, but return to the expected level thereafter. Under this scenario, the news of a sooner-than-expected increase would lower the stock market value of the hypothetical restaurant by 5 percent.

EVIDENCE ON THE EFFECT OF THE MINIMUM WAGE ON PROFITS

Stock Market Event Study Methodology

Increasingly, economists are using stock-market data to evaluate the impact of labor-market interventions on shareholder wealth. Recent studies have examined the effects of the passage of the Wagner Act, unionization drives, and strikes on the stock-market values of affected firms.[9] Abowd (1989) found that unexpected increases in union wages result in a dollar-for-dollar tradeoff with shareholder wealth. As far as we are aware, however, no study has estimated the impact of the minimum wage on shareholder wealth.

We have collected daily stock data on two samples of publicly-traded firms that are especially likely to have been affected by recent minimum-wage increases. Membership in Sample A is based on a company's primary industry affiliation. This sample consists of 110 firms in the restaurant, department store, grocery store, merchandise store, variety store, hotel and motel, linen supply, and motion picture theater industries. Companies in these industries tend to employ a disproportionate number of minimum-wage workers. A complete list of Sample A firms is included in Appendix Table A.10.1.

Firms in Sample B were identified by conducting a computerized search of text fields in 1992 company annual reports to find all firms that cited the 1990 or 1991 minimum-wage increase as a reason for increased labor costs. Sample B consists of 28 companies, most of which are restaurants. They are listed in Appendix Table A.10.2. Many of Sample B companies also belong to Sample A. Because Sample B firms volunteered that the minimum-wage hike raised their payroll costs, there is little doubt that they were directly affected by legislation to increase the minimum wage.

We have identified a total of 23 news events that might have led investors to revise their expectations about the likelihood or magnitude of a minimum-wage increase. Twenty of these news events, from early 1987 to mid-1989, pertain to the progress of a bill to raise the federal minimum wage from $3.35 per hour. This bill was ultimately passed in November 1989, leading to the 1990 and 1991 increases in the minimum wage that are studied in chapter 4. Three additional news events pertain to the more recent (1993) debate about raising the minimum wage above $4.25 per hour.

Daily stock return information for companies in the two samples was obtained from the Center for Research in Security Prices (CRSP). In examining stock price movements in response to news about the minimum wage, we remove the effect of overall market factors by estimating a standard market model.[10] Formally, for each of the companies in Sample A and Sample B, we estimate a daily return model of the form:

$$R_{it} = \alpha_i + \beta_i R_{mt} + \epsilon_{it} \tag{10.6}$$

where R_{it} is the return on the common stock of firm i on day t, adjusted for stock splits and dividends; R_{mt} is the return on the equally weighted NYSE/AMEX index on day t; α_i and β_i are regression coefficients; and ϵ_{it} is an error term for firm i on day t. For our initial analysis of events between 1987 and 1989, the market model is estimated using data on returns for 1987. For our subsequent analysis of events in 1993, we estimate the market model using data for 1992. Estimated excess returns (ER), also known as prediction errors, are calculated for each firm for each day in the analysis period by

$$ER_{it} = R_{it} - (\hat{\alpha}_i + \hat{\beta}_i R_{mt}) \tag{10.7}$$

where $\hat{\alpha}_i$ and $\hat{\beta}_i$ are estimates of α_i and β_i.

The excess returns are estimates of the abnormal returns to the stockholders of the sample of firms on each trading day. Average excess returns across all firms are calculated for each day in the analysis period.[11] These averages are then cumulated to provide a series of cumulative average excess returns around each event. We focus on the average excess return and cumulative average excess return surrounding days in which news about the minimum wage was released.[12]

A Brief History of Events Leading to the 1989 Minimum-Wage Legislation

To examine the stock market's reaction to news about the minimum wage, it is important to identify events that change investor's expectations about the future course of the minimum wage. We used past issues of the *Wall Street Journal* and other sources in order to identify key events connected to recent legislation on the minimum wage. Because the *Journal* is the nation's largest business newspaper, this source should provide a record of the news on the minimum wage that was available to most investors. Here, we briefly summarize the evolution of recent minimum-wage legislation.

Periodically since 1938, Congress has amended the Fair Labor Standards Act (FLSA) to increase the level of the minimum wage. In the years between increases, the real value of the minimum wage has been eroded by inflation, causing a sawtooth pattern in the real value of the minimum over time. In 1977, Congress amended the FLSA to raise the minimum wage to $2.65 per hour in 1978, to $2.90 per hour in 1979, to $3.10 per hour in 1980, and to $3.35 per hour in 1981. Under President Reagan, the historical pattern of periodic increases in the minimum wage was halted. In all likelihood, investors came to regard the prospects of a minimum-wage increase in the Reagan era as remote and lowered their forecasts of the long-run level of the minimum wage.

In March 1987, Senator Edward Kennedy and Representative Augustus Hawkins introduced legislation to increase the minimum wage to $4.65 per hour by 1990.[13] In June 1987, President Reagan signalled that he might soften his opposition to a minimum-wage increase if the legislation were weakened to include a subminimum wage for youths.[14] Hearings lasting several months were held on the proposed increase. On September 19, 1988, then-Vice President Bush announced during the presidential campaign that he could support an increase in the minimum wage.[15] Later that month, however, a Republican-led filibuster in the Senate thwarted the Kennedy and Hawkins effort to increase the minimum wage. The vote fell five votes short of reaching cloture.[16]

In early March of 1989, Congress and President Bush again considered the issue. The Bush administration signalled that it would propose increasing the hourly minimum to $4.25 by 1992, provided that employers were allowed to pay a short-term "training wage" of

$3.35 to youths.[17] Shortly thereafter, the Senate Labor Panel voted 11 to 6 in favor of raising the minimum to $4.65 per hour.[18] The administration signalled its resolve to veto any legislation that would "go beyond its proposal of raising the minimum to $4.25 per hour, with a training wage of $3.35."[19] On March 23, 1989, the House voted by a 248 to 171 margin on H.R. 2 to raise the minimum wage to $4.55 per hour by 1991. The White House reiterated its resolve to veto this legislation.[20] Nonetheless, the Senate followed the lead of the House and, on April 12, 1989, voted 62 to 37 in favor of the Senate minimum-wage increase bill, S-4. In mid-May 1989, after a conference, both houses of Congress approved a bill to raise the minimum wage to $4.55 per hour.[21] The number of votes in favor of this legislation in both the Senate and the House, however, fell short of the margin required to override a presidential veto. President Bush vetoed the legislation on June 13, 1989.[22] Although a veto had been threatened, the actual veto was significant because it was the first of Bush's Presidency. The following day, the House again voted on H.R. 2, and, as expected, the vote fell short of the required number to override a veto.

The Congress took up the minimum wage again in the fall of 1989. The House Labor Panel voted to increase the minimum to $4.25 per hour over two years, and to set a 60-day subminimum wage. Labor Secretary Elizabeth Dole reiterated the President's intention to veto any bill that increased the minimum wage to more than $4.25 per hour in less than three years.[23] On November 1, 1989, the *Wall Street Journal* reported that President Bush and Congressional Democrats had reached a compromise agreement on the minimum wage, clearing the way for eventual passage of the legislation. On November 1, 1989, the House passed H.R. 2710 by a margin of 382 to 37. This bill increased the minimum wage to $3.80 per hour on April 1, 1990, and to $4.25 per hour on April 1, 1991, and created a 60–day youth subminimum wage. One week later, the Senate passed identical legislation by a vote of 89 to 8.

Unfortunately, it is difficult to identify the exact events that conveyed new information on the future course of the minimum wage. Although it is likely that many investors considered it a certainty, or near certainty, that President Bush would deliver on his threatened veto of H.R. 2, the actual act of signing the veto probably induced some investors to revise their expectations about the President's resolve to block minimum-wage legislation that did not conform to his conditions. We suspect that the successful Republican filibuster of the Kennedy-Hawkins bill also provided new information about the prospects of a minimum-wage increase, in this case lowering expectations that a higher minimum would be imposed. Furthermore, the compromise agreement reached by the President and Congressional Democrats and reported on November 1 probably took many investors by surprise. In the next section, we examine how the stock market reacted to these events, as well as to other events relating to the 1989 legislation.

Results for the 1989 Legislation: Sample A

The left-hand column of Table 10.3 briefly describes 20 newsworthy events leading up to the 1989 amendments to the FLSA. The descriptions are generally based on the title of the *Wall Street Journal's* article on the event. The date corresponds to the publication date of the article; the event usually occurred on the preceding day. In column 1, next to each event we present our *ex ante* prediction as to whether investors would have interpreted the event as positive or negative with respect to minimum-wage employers' future profits. These predictions are based on the assumption that a minimum-wage increase will be perceived as having a negative effect on profits, and try to take into account investors' expectations of the future course of the minimum prior to the event. For example, we expect that President Bush's veto of H.R. 2 would have slightly lowered the probability that some investors attached to a minimum-wage increase, even though the veto had been threatened.

In the remaining columns of Table 10.3, we present estimates of the average excess return for stocks in Sample A (the sample of 110 firms in low-wage industries). The excess returns in column 2 correspond to a particular day (denoted $t = 0$), usually the day that the event was reported in the *Wall Street Journal*. Because information about the event could have leaked out prior to the publication date, or could have been slow to affect market prices, we have also calculated excess returns over longer windows around the event dates. We present cumulative excess returns between the day of the event and five trading days after the event (in column 3), between five days prior to the event and five days after the event (in column 4), and between ten days prior to the event and ten days after the event (in column 5).

A striking feature of Table 10.3 is that almost all the average excess returns are small and statistically insignificant. On the day that the event was described in the *Wall Street Journal*, for example, only 2 of the 20 average excess returns are statistically significantly different from zero at the 10 percent level. In a sample of 20 events, one would expect 2 events to achieve statistical significance at the 10 percent level merely as a result of chance. Nevertheless, on the two days in which the average excess return achieves statistical significance, the value of the low-wage firms declined, as we hypothesized. The decline in the average value of the firms on these days was 0.6 and 0.7 percent.

When we expand the interval to within 10 trading days of the day of the event, the average excess return is statistically significant for four events. The average excess return on each of these four days is positive, even though the news conveyed by three of the four events probably would have been interpreted as unfavorable for profits. The cumulative return moves in the direction that we predicted in fewer than one-half of the 16 events for which we give an unambiguous prediction. The predictions also perform poorly if the window is limited to the five-day period surrounding the event.

Figures 10.1–10.7 provide graphs of the cumulative excess returns over the period starting ten trading days before the event and ending ten days after the event for seven particularly newsworthy events. Figure 10.1 indicates that stock prices of Sample A firms began to *rise* about three days before the *Wall Street Journal* reported that Ronald Reagan might ease his stance on the minimum wage. The modest rally for firms in the low-wage industries continued after the story appeared. Another perverse pattern is evident in Figure 10.3, which indicates that the growth in the average excess return for the Sample A firms continued unabated after the *Wall Street Journal* ran a story claiming that the prospects for a minimum-wage hike had increased as a result of President Bush's support.

Figure 10.4 probably contains the strongest evidence that investors view a minimum-wage hike as having negative consequences for corporate profits. This figure shows the cumulative excess stock market returns around the time of the final cloture vote on the Republican-led filibuster of the Kennedy-Hawkins minimum-wage bill. The cumulative excess return in the ten-day interval around the successful filibuster was nearly 4 percent. Moreover, negative excess returns are apparent a few trading days before the final cloture vote, which coincides with the date of an earlier vote on cloture. Nevertheless, the inconsistent results with respect to the other events lead one to wonder whether this pattern of excess returns truly reflects the market reaction to news about the minimum wage, or to some other factors.

Figure 10.8 provides a longer-term perspective on the value of Sample A firms. The figure shows the cumulative excess return from 1986 through 1993, with the initial value normalized to 100 on the last trading day of 1985.[24] Days marked 1–20 on the graph corre-

TABLE 10.3
Cumulative Excess Returns of Sample A Firms, 1987–1989

Event	Predicted Effect (1)	Cumulative Excess Returns			
		t = 0 (2)	t = 0 to 5 (3)	t = −5 to 5 (4)	t = −10 to 10 (5)
1. March 26, 1987 Democrats seek higher min. wage, White House quickly opposes it.	?	0.000	−0.002	0.008	0.018
2. June 12, 1987 Reagan may ease min. wage stand.	−	−0.003	0.011	0.021*	0.027*
3. September 22, 1987 Move in Congress to boost min. wage revives perennial debate on possible loss of jobs.	?	−0.006*	−0.005	−0.013	−0.020
4. March 4, 1988 Panel votes bill to sharply boost min. wage.	−	−0.007*	−0.017**	−0.015	−0.013
5. March 11, 1988 Panel delays wage vote; raises minimum to $5.05.	−	−0.005	−0.012	−0.024**	−0.019
6. June 3, 1988 Labor's push to boost min. wage draws unexpected opposition from some Democrats.	+	−0.005	−0.003	0.000	0.001
7. September 19, 1988 Prospects wax for minimum-wage rise, helped by Bush's support for increase.	−	0.000	0.010	0.021*	0.045***
8. September 27, 1988 Democrats' bid to boost min. wage this year is thwarted by GOP filibuster.	+	−0.003	0.018**	0.028**	0.039**
9. March 3, 1989 Bush to propose raising min. wage to $4.25 an hour, a lower training pay.	−	0.004	0.007	0.010	0.017

10. March 9, 1989 Congress moves to increase min. wage.	−	0.002	0.007	0.016	0.017
11. March 24, 1989 House votes major increase in hourly wage.	−	0.001	0.007	0.012	0.021
12. April 12, 1989 Senate votes to raise min. wage, but measure faces a threatened veto.	?	0.000	0.007	0.008	0.018
13. May 3, 1989 Conferees agree on min. wage of $4.55, hope for accord with Bush.	−	0.003	0.007	0.026**	0.039**
14. May 12, 1989 Minimum-wage rise is approved by House.	−	0.003	0.004	0.010	0.022
15. May 18, 1989 Senate clears a wage bill Bush opposes.	−	0.000	−0.001	0.005	0.021
16. June 14, 1989 Bill on raising min. wage vetoed by Bush.	+	0.002	−0.002	0.000	0.015
17. June 15, 1989 Bush's veto on wage bill survives House.	+	0.004	−0.004	0.001	0.010
18. September 20, 1989 House Labor Panel passes bill to raise min. wage.	−	−0.004	−0.003	−0.007	−0.009
19. November 1, 1989 Compromise on min. wage reached.	−	−0.004	−0.005	−0.004	0.002
20. November 10, 1989 Bush criticized for minimum-wage compromise.	?	0.001	0.003	0.002	−0.007

Note: The sample size ranges between 102 and 108. The coefficients for the market model are estimated with data on 1987 returns.
*Significant at the .10 level.
**Significant at the .05 level.
***Significant at the .01 level.

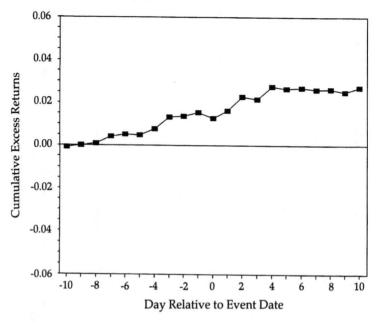

Figure 10.1   June 12, 1987: Reagan may ease minimum wage stand.

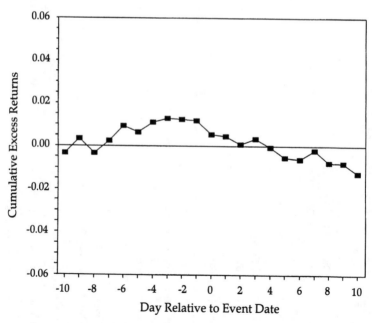

Figure 10.2   March 4, 1988: Panel votes to sharply boost minimum wage.

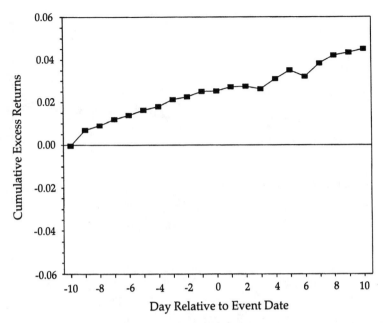

Figure 10.3   September 19, 1988: Bush supports minimum-wage increase.

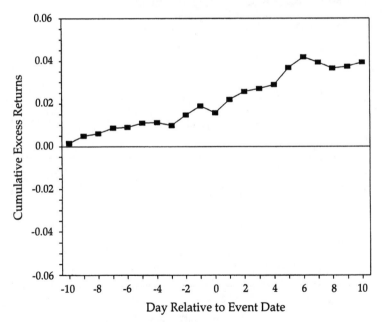

Figure 10.4   September 27, 1988: Democrats' bid to boost minimum wage thwarted by GOP filibuster.

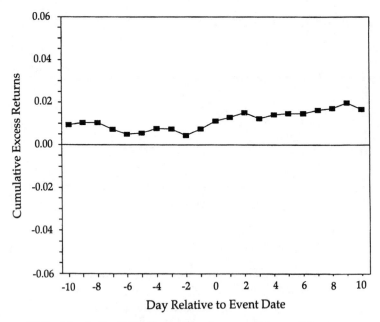

Figure 10.5   March 3, 1989: Bush to propose raising minimum wage to $4.25, a lower training wage.

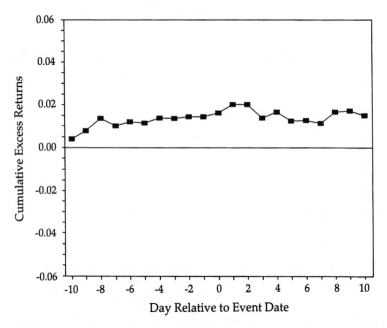

Figure 10.6   June 14, 1989: Bill on raising minimum wage vetoed by Bush.

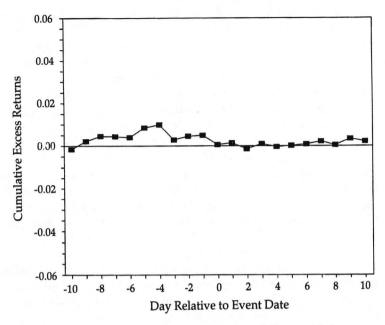

Figure 10.7 November 1, 1989: Compromise bill on minimum wage reached.

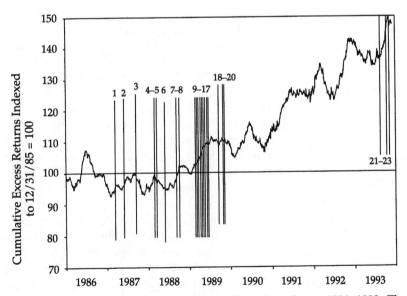

Figure 10.8 Cumulative excess return for Sample A firms, 1986–1993. The numbers refer to events in Tables 10.3 and 10.5.

spond to the events listed in Table 10.3. (Days marked 21–23 correspond to events listed in Table 10.5, described later.) Four important conclusions can be drawn from the figure. First, the Sample A portfolio of stocks is highly variable. Second, these low-wage employers have outperformed the market since 1988. Third, during the 1987–1989 period, when the prospects of a minimum-wage increase rose, the Sample A firms tended to outperform the market. Fourth, in the four years since the minimum-wage increase actually took effect, Sample A firms outperformed the market by some 40 percent.

It is worth noting that, in 1988, many analysts were predicting that stock prices of restaurants and other low-wage employers would fall as a result of a possible rise in the minimum wage. For example, on July 18, 1988, securities analyst Steven Rockwell predicted in the *Nation's Restaurant News* (p. 64) that there was "little hope" for the restaurant industry "from an investor's point of view." He elaborated that, "Investors are focusing on several issues to justify their negative stance toward the group. Most prominent among them are concerns over an increase in the minimum wage and the possibility of rising food costs." The positive excess returns shown in Figure 10.8 do not seem to bear out this concern.

Results for Sample B

A possible criticism of the results in Table 10.3 is that Sample A might include some firms that are not affected significantly by a minimum-wage increase, because their employees' wages are well above the minimum. Although the sample was constructed by choosing firms in industries that tend to employ low-wage workers, one can not be certain whether minimum-wage labor contributes a large share of costs in these firms. We attempt to overcome this criticism by examining Sample B. Because the 28 firms in Sample B specifically mentioned the minimum-wage increase in connection with their labor costs, we are more confident that each of these firms was affected by the 1989 minimum-wage legislation.

Table 10.4 presents results from the market analysis that we applied to Sample B companies. On the day of the event, the excess returns are all small and statistically insignificant. Because the size of this sample is smaller than that of Sample A, the average excess returns are less precisely estimated. Nevertheless, the typical daily standard error for the estimates is about 0.007, so an excess return of 1.4 percent or more would be detectable. Moreover, expanding the interval around the day of the event does not provide stronger evidence that news about a minimum-wage hike lowers shareholder wealth for this sample. On 11 of the 16 days in which we make an unambiguous prediction as to the sign of the event, the cumulative excess stock market return during the ten-day period surrounding the event has the opposite sign.

Figure 10.9 shows the cumulative excess return for Sample B firms from 1986 through 1993, with the initial value normalized to 100 on the last trading day of 1985. Although the general impression given by Figure 10.9 is similar to that of the comparable figure for Sample A firms (see Figure 10.8), there are some notable differences. First, the value of Sample B firms was relatively stable during the 1987–1989 period, when the minimum-wage legislation was inching forward. Second, during the 1990–1993 period, Sample B firms far outperformed both the market and the Sample A firms. On the other hand, as was the case for Sample A firms, it is difficult to conclude that Sample B stocks performed poorly in 1989, a year in which investors' expectations about a minimum-wage increase most likely were revised upward.

Evidence from Recent Minimum-Wage Proposals

As we have noted, in a stock market event study it is difficult to know whether a particular event conveyed new information to the market. One interpretation of the results in Tables 10.3 and 10.4 is that market values of low-wage employers do not respond to news about minimum-wage hikes. Another is that the events conveyed no new information. The information contained in the events could have been leaked prior to their publication dates in the *Wall Street Journal*, or the events could have been anticipated prior to publication. We address this issue by performing an event study to examine the effect of a memorandum on the minimum wage written by Labor Secretary Robert Reich and later leaked to the media.

The memorandum to the President from Secretary Reich was dated July 20, 1993, and was reported in the *Wall Street Journal* on August 12, 1993.[25] The substance of the memo was that the Labor Department would step up efforts to review the minimum wage, with an interest in raising the minimum to at least $4.50 per hour, and then indexing the minimum to inflation. Although the memo stated that the Labor Department would report back in 90 days with initial recommendations, it also stated that, "To achieve the goal of making work pay, the minimum should be raised and then indexed." We suspect that many investors were surprised by Secretary Reich's interest in raising the minimum wage at this time, because the administration concurrently was attempting to pass a bill on

TABLE 10.4
Cumulative Excess Returns of Sample B Firms, 1987–1989

Event	Predicted Effect (1)	Cumulative Excess Returns				
		$t = 0$ (2)	$t = 0\ to\ 5$ (3)	$t = -5\ to\ 5$ (4)	$t = -10\ to\ 10$ (5)	
1. March 26, 1987 Democrats seek higher min. wage, White House quickly opposes it.	?	−0.009	0.020	0.044*	0.046	
2. June 12, 1987 Reagan may ease min. wage stand.	−	−0.010	0.012	0.022	0.018	
3. September 22, 1987 Move in Congress to boost min. wage revives perennial debate on possible loss of jobs.	?	−0.006	−0.009	−0.035	−0.031	
4. March 4, 1988 Panel votes bill to sharply boost min. wage.	−	−0.002	0.003	−0.004	0.007	
5. March 11, 1988 Panel delays wage vote; raises minimum to $5.05.	−	0.004	0.002	0.001	0.002	
6. June 3, 1988 Labor's push to boost min. wage draws unexpected opposition from some Democrats.	+	−0.003	−0.014	−0.018	−0.026	
7. September 19, 1988 Prospects wax for minimum-wage rise, helped by Bush's support for increase.	−	0.002	0.016	0.032	0.040	
8. September 27, 1988 Democrats' bid to boost min. wage this year is thwarted by GOP filibuster.	+	0.003	0.004	0.019	0.028	
9. March 3, 1989 Bush to propose raising min. wage to $4.25 an hour, a lower training pay.	−	0.001	0.008	0.017	0.035	

10. March 9, 1989 Congress moves to increase min. wage.	—	0.001	−0.001	0.015	0.030
11. March 24, 1989 House votes major increase in hourly wage.	—	0.001	−0.001	0.017	0.027
12. April 12, 1989 Senate votes to raise min. wage, but measure faces a threatened veto.	?	0.005	0.002	0.022	0.059*
13. May 3, 1989 Conferees agree on min. wage of $4.55, hope for accord with Bush.	—	0.002	0.001	0.032	0.066*
14. May 12, 1989 Minimum-wage rise is approved by House.	—	0.001	−0.005	0.015	0.025
15. May 18, 1989 Senate clears a wage bill Bush opposes.	—	−0.001	−0.006	0.005	0.006
16. June 14, 1989 Bill on raising min. wage vetoed by Bush.	+	0.010	0.004	0.004	0.024
17. June 15, 1989 Bush's veto on wage bill survives House.	+	0.001	−0.003	0.009	0.021
18. September 20, 1989 House Labor Panel passes bill to raise min. wage.	—	−0.006	0.001	−0.006	−0.016
19. November 1, 1989 Compromise on min. wage reached.	—	0.002	0.002	0.009	−0.010
20. November 10, 1989 Bush criticized for minimum-wage compromise.	?	0.001	−0.005	0.000	−0.004

Note: The sample size is 28. The coefficients for the market model are estimated with data on 1987 returns.

*Significant at the .10 level.

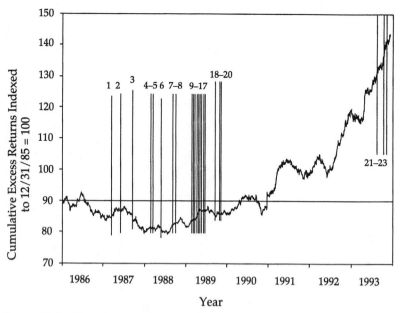

Figure 10.9 Cumulative excess return for Sample B firms, 1986–1993. The numbers refer to events in Tables 10.3 and 10.5.

universal health insurance—largely funded by an employer mandate.

Two subsequent events related to this episode can also be analyzed. On October 13, 1993, the *Wall Street Journal* reported that, "Labor Secretary Robert Reich is ready to propose raising the minimum wage to $4.75 an hour, an even bigger boost than he was expected to recommend." On November 1, however, the *Journal* (p. A11A) reported that Secretary Reich had issued a statement on October 29 "recommending that the administration wait until next year to seek an increase in the minimum wage."[26]

An unusual feature of this episode is that we know the exact date on which the memorandum was written, the date on which it was leaked, and the dates of subsequent statements on the minimum wage. We use these events to conduct our event study. Excess returns on the days surrounding the three main events are reported in Table 10.5 for Sample A firms, and in Table 10.6 for Sample B firms.[27] On the day that Secretary Reich's memorandum was first reported in the *Wall Street Journal*, the average excess return was −0.6 percent for Sample A firms, and 0.1 percent for Sample B firms; neither change was statistically significant, however. Figure 10.10 shows the cumulative excess returns during the ten days before and after this event. The figure does not indicate that firms in either sample ex-

TABLE 10.5
Cumulative Excess Returns of Sample A Firms, 1993

Event	Predicted Effect (1)	Cumulative Excess Returns				
		t = 0 (2)	t = 0 to 5 (3)	t = −5 to 5 (4)	t = −10 to 10 (5)	
21. August 12, 1993 Reich plans a push to raise min. wage.	−	−0.006	−0.007	0.013	0.006	
22. October 13, 1993 Reich to seek rise in min. wage to $4.75 an hour, an increase of 12 percent.	−	−0.004	0.001	0.004	0.013	
23. October 29, 1993 Reich advises President to delay min. wage recommendation until next year.	+	0.008*	0.019*	0.030**	0.046*	

Note: The sample size is 110. The coefficients for the market model are estimated with data on 1992 returns.
  *Significant at the .10 level.
  **Significant at the .05 level.

TABLE 10.6
Cumulative Excess Returns of Sample B Firms, 1993

Event	Predicted Effect (1)	Cumulative Excess Returns				
		$t = 0$ (2)	$t = 0\ to\ 5$ (3)	$t = -5\ to\ 5$ (4)	$t = -10\ to\ 10$ (5)
21. August 12, 1993 Reich plans a push to raise min. wage.	−	0.001	−0.021	−0.010	−0.013
22. October 13, 1993 Reich to seek rise in min. wage to $4.75 an hour, an increase of 12 percent.	−	−0.021*	−0.030	−0.018	0.004
23. October 29, 1993 Reich advises President to delay min. wage recommendation until next year.	+	0.021*	0.016	0.028	0.042

Note: The sample size is 27. The coefficients for the market model are estimated with data on 1992 returns.
*Significant at the .05 level.

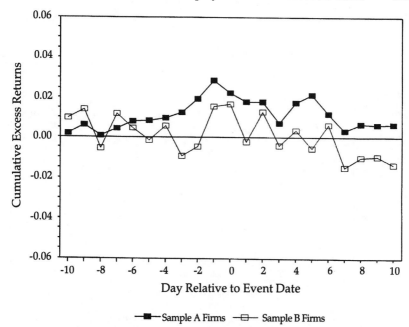

Figure 10.10   August 12, 1993: Reich plans a push to raise minimum wage.

perienced any abnormal movement in returns around the time that the memorandum was leaked to the press. If we cumulate excess returns over the period between the date that the memorandum was written and the date that it was leaked (July 19–August 12), we find that the stock values of Sample A firms increased by 2.4 percent, and those of Sample B firms increased by 0.9 percent. These findings suggest that the memorandum had surprisingly little impact on the stock market values of affected firms.

The two subsequent event dates connected to this episode provide more support for the view that news about minimum-wage hikes lowers the value of affected firms. Cumulative returns for these events are shown in Figures 10.11 and 10.12. In both samples, the average excess return was negative on the day that the *Wall Street Journal* reported that Secretary Reich would seek an increase in the minimum wage to $4.75 per hour. Furthermore, the average excess return was positive in both samples on the day that Secretary Reich stated that he would recommend that the administration postpone seeking an increase in the minimum wage. In the first event, the value of Sample B firms declined by 2.1 percent; in the second, it increased by 2.1 percent. It is also worth noting that the abnormal returns were greater in Sample B firms than in Sample A firms,

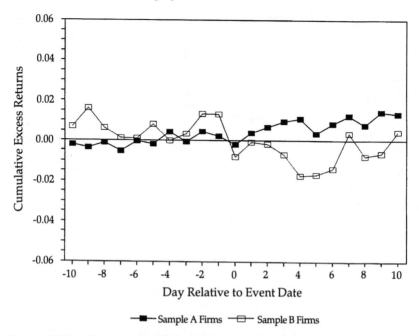

Figure 10.11 October 13, 1993: Reich to seek rise in minimum wage to $4.75 an hour, an increase of 12 percent.

which makes sense, because Sample B companies are more likely to be affected by a minimum-wage increase. These results suggest that news about a possible minimum-wage hike does influence investors' valuations of companies.

To probe this result further, we examined whether the daily excess returns on October 13 and 29 were correlated across companies. Within our sample, the profitability of some companies is likely to be more sensitive to changes in the minimum wage than is that of others. If stock movements on October 13 and 29 were partially a response to changes in profit forecasts linked to new information about the minimum wage, then we would expect a negative correlation in excess returns across companies for the two events, as the information in the first event increased the probability of a minimum-wage hike, and the information in the second event decreased the probability. The correlation across Sample B firms between the excess returns on these two days is in fact large and negative ($r = -0.70$).[28] Curiously, however, the cumulative excess returns over 5-day windows around the two events are virtually uncorrelated across companies. Nevertheless, our finding that those stocks that

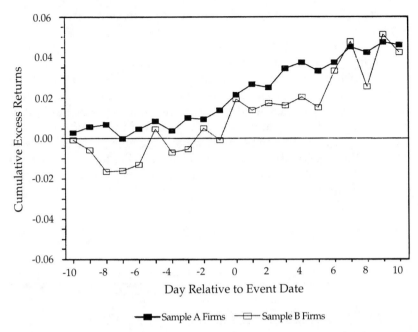

Figure 10.12   October 29, 1993: Reich advises President to delay minimum wage recommendation until next year.

declined on October 13th tended to rebound on October 29th suggests that the valuations were responding to news about the minimum wage.

Summary

Our event studies provide an initial attempt to quantify the impact of minimum-wage legislation on the value of firms. Because it is difficult to identify an event that unambiguously raises or lowers investors' expectations about the future level of the minimum wage, the conclusions that we draw from this analysis must be viewed as tentative. That said, the results provide mixed evidence that news about a minimum-wage hike induces investors to adjust their valuation of firms downward. We have obtained our strongest evidence from an examination of excess returns in response to recent news about revisions of the minimum wage. By comparison, excess returns associated with news about the 1989 minimum-wage legislation are generally unsystematic. In the sample of events that we have examined, news about a minimum-wage hike rarely seems to coincide with movements of more than 1 or 2 percent in shareholder wealth.

It would be fruitful if future research could supplement this analysis with a study of how minimum wages influence accounting measures of firm profitability. In addition, it would be worthwhile to study how minimum-wage changes influence the transaction prices of firms such as franchise restaurants that tend to hire minimum-wage workers. Finally, more research is needed on the effects of the minimum wage on business openings and closings. Our analysis of data for the McDonald's restaurant chain in chapter 2 showed no effect of the minimum wage on new openings, but broader evidence is clearly required.

APPENDIX

TABLE A.10.1
Sample A: 110 Companies Used in Event Study

Company Name	Primary Industry	Market Value ($1,000s)
Albertson's Inc.	Grocery Stores	6,776,443
AMC Entertainment Inc.	Motion Picture Theaters, Except Drive-ins	221,508
American Stores Co.	Grocery Stores	3,062,890
Ampal American Israel Corp.	Hotels and Motels	178,284
Angelica Corp.	Linen Supply	256,594
Arden Group Inc.	Grocery Stores	82,263
Ark Restaurants Corp.	Eating Places	34,305
Bayport Restaurant Group Inc.	Eating Places	40,220[a]
Benihana National Corp.	Eating Places	17,874
Brendle's Inc.	Variety Stores	10,067
Brinker International Inc.	Eating Places	2,107,858
Bruno's Inc.	Grocery Stores	692,436
Buffets Inc.	Eating Places	788,465
Carl Karcher Enterprises Inc.	Eating Places	194,717
Carmike Cinemas Inc.	Motion Picture Theaters, Except Drive-ins	143,460
Carter Hawley Hale Stores Inc.	Department Stores	427,272[a]
Casey's General Stores Inc.	Grocery Stores	272,195
Cineplex Odeon Corp.	Motion Picture Theaters, Except Drive-ins	278,795
Cintas Corp.	Linen Supply	1,586,882

TABLE A.10.1
(continued)

Company Name	Primary Industry	Market Value ($1,000s)
Chart House Enterprises Inc.	Eating Places	97,476[b]
Club Med Inc.	Hotels and Motels	328,161
Consolidated Products Inc.	Eating Places	62,120
Consolidated Stores Corp.	Variety Stores	923,458
Cracker Barrel Old Country Store Inc.	Eating Places	1,638,780
Craig Corp.	Grocery Stores	75,208
Crowley Milner & Co.	Department Stores	11,640
Dairy Mart Convenience Stores Inc.	Grocery Stores	34,512
Dayton Hudson Corp.	Variety Stores	4,761,264
Delchamps Inc.	Grocery Stores	97,873
Dial Corp. DE	Eating Places	1,895,411
Dillard Department Stores Inc.	Department Stores	4,284,690
Dollar General Corp.	Variety Stores	1,254,030
El Chico Restaurants Inc.	Eating Places	66,591
Family Dollar Stores Inc.	Variety Stores	957,984
Family Steak Houses of Florida Inc.	Eating Places	6,569
Federated Department Stores Inc.	Department Stores	NA[a]
Food Lion Inc.	Grocery Stores	3,202,107
Foodarama Supermarkets Inc.	Grocery Stores	16,065
Frisch's Restaurants Inc.	Eating Places	91,551
G & K Services Inc.	Linen Supply	212,252
Gander Mountain Inc.	Miscellaneous Merchandise Stores	38,849
Giant Food Inc.	Grocery Stores	1,537,352
Gottschalks Inc.	Department Stores	83,288
Ground Round Restaurants Inc.	Eating Places	87,317
Hannaford Bros Co.	Grocery Stores	885,155
Healthcare Services Group Inc.	Linen Supply	92,249
Hilton Hotels Corp.	Hotels and Motels	2,904,943
Ingles Markets Inc.	Grocery Stores	198,022
Jamesway Corp.	Department Stores	11,261
JB's Restaurants Inc.	Eating Places	28,320
Kahler Corp.	Hotels and Motels	23,037

TABLE A.10.1
(*continued*)

Company Name	Primary Industry	Market Value ($1,000s)
Kmart Corp.	Department Stores	8,776,708
Kroger Co.	Grocery Stores	2,157,688
L. Luria & Son Inc.	Miscellaneous Merchandise Stores	80,820
La Quinta Inns Inc.	Hotels and Motels	712,719
Luby's Cafeterias Inc.	Eating Places	612,607
Mac Frugal's Bargain Close Outs Inc.	Variety Stores	581,674
Marcus Corp.	Hotels and Motels	360,167
Max & Erma's Restaurants Inc.	Eating Places	32,556
May Department Stores Co.	Department Stores	9,780,846
McDonald's Corp.	Eating Places	20,121,684
Mercantile Stores Co. Inc.	Department Stores	1,335,595
Morgan's Foods Inc.	Eating Places	52,151
Morrison Restaurants Inc.	Eating Places	948,150
Motts Holdings Inc.	Grocery Stores	16,503
National Convenience Stores Inc.	Grocery Stores	NA[a]
National Pizza Co.	Eating Places	162,669
Neiman Marcus Group Inc.	Department Stores	711,487
Orient Express Hotels Inc.	Hotels and Motels	14,634
Pancho's Mexican Buffet Inc.	Eating Places	53,373
PEC Israel Economic Corp.	Grocery Stores	586,218
Penn Traffic Co.	Grocery Stores	392,551[b]
Pepsico Inc.	Eating Places	32,586,264
Piccadilly Cafeterias Inc.	Eating Places	123,724
Proffitt's Inc.	Department Stores	205,556
Quality Food Centers Inc.	Grocery Stores	478,739
Rio Hotel & Casino Inc.	Hotels and Motels	333,504
Riser Foods Inc.	Grocery Stores	56,567[b]
Rose's Stores Inc.	Variety Stores	12,755
Ruddick Corp.	Grocery Stores	530,633
Ryan's Family Steak Houses Inc.	Eating Places	480,636
S K I Ltd.	Hotels and Motels	68,772
Sbarro Inc.	Eating Places	596,899
Schultz Sav O Stores Inc.	Grocery Stores	41,053[b]
Sears Roebuck & Co.	Department Stores	18,540,504
Seaway Food Town Inc.	Grocery Stores	26,910

TABLE A.10.1
(*continued*)

Company Name	Primary Industry	Market Value ($1,000s)
Service Merchandise Co Inc.	Miscellaneous Merchandise Stores	993,420
Shoney's Inc.	Eating Places	938,810
Sizzler International Inc.	Eating Places	265,665
Smith's Food & Drug Centers Inc.	Grocery Stores	623,303
Spaghetti Warehouse Inc.	Eating Places	55,597
Stop & Shop Cos. Inc.	Grocery Stores	NA[a]
Strawbridge & Clothier	Department Stores	232,852
Stuarts Department Stores Inc.	Variety Stores	11,976
Thousand Trails Inc.	Hotels and Motels	31,814
TPI Enterprises Inc.	Eating Places	199,166
Tuesday Morning Corp.	Variety Stores	43,703
Unifirst Corp.	Linen Supply	317,781
United Inns Inc.	Hotels and Motels	20,784
Unitog Co.	Linen Supply	148,344[b]
Uno Restaurant Corp.	Eating Places	86,349
Vicorp Restaurants Inc.	Eating Places	182,083
Vie de France Corp.	Eating Places	66,100
Volunteer Capital Corp.	Eating Places	56,254
Vons Cos. Inc.	Grocery Stores	693,424
Wal Mart Stores Inc.	Department Stores	57,463,050
Wall Street Deli Inc.	Eating Places	48,125
Walt Disney Co.	Amusement Parks	22,805,280
Warehouse Club Inc.	Miscellaneous Merchandise Stores	3,401
Weis Markets Inc.	Grocery Stores	1,182,708
Wendy's International Inc.	Eating Places	1,733,612
Winn Dixie Stores Inc.	Grocery Stores	4,018,121
Woolworth Corp.	Variety Stores	3,346,226
WSMP Inc.	Eating Places	11,786

Note: Market values are as of December 31, 1993. The sample was selected on the basis of primary industry affiliation.

[a]Not included in the 1993 period.
[b]Not included in the 1987–1989 period.

TABLE A.10.2
Sample B: 28 Companies that Mention Minimum Wage
in Company Report

Company Name	Primary Industry	Market Value ($1,000s)
Brinker International Inc.	Eating Places	2,107,858
Buffets Inc.	Eating Places	788,465
Chefs International Inc.	Eating Places	63,846
Ciatti's Inc.	Eating Places	NA
Consolidated Products Inc.	Eating Places	62,120
Cuco's Inc.	Eating Places	4,481
Dairy Mart Convenience Stores Inc.	Grocery Stores	34,512
Dollar General Corp.	Variety Stores	1,254,030
El Chico Restaurants Inc.	Eating Places	66,591
Family Steak Houses of Florida Inc.	Eating Places	6,569
Hancock Fabrics Inc.	Sewing, Needlework and Piece Goods	203,366
JB's Restaurants Inc.	Eating Places	28,320
Kenwin Shops Inc.	Women's Clothing Stores	2,389
Morgan's Foods Inc.	Eating Places	52,151
Morrison Restaurants Inc.	Eating Places	948,150
National Pizza Co.	Eating Places	162,669
One Price Clothing Stores Inc.	Women's Clothing Stores	159,823
Pancho's Mexican Buffet Inc.	Eating Places	53,373
Piccadilly Cafeterias Inc.	Eating Places	123,724
Ryan's Family Steak Houses Inc.	Eating Places	480,636
Sizzler International Inc.	Eating Places	265,665
Sunbelt Nursery Group Inc.	Retail Nurseries and Garden Stores	NA[a]
Sunshine Jr. Stores Inc.	Gasoline Service Stations	10,416
Valhi Inc.	Beet Sugar	559,037
Vicorp Restaurants Inc.	Eating Places	182,083
Volunteer Capital Corp	Eating Places	56,254
Wall Street Deli Inc.	Eating Places	48,125
Wendy's International Inc.	Eating Places	1,733,612

Note: Market value is as of December 31, 1993. The sample was selected by a search for the term "minimum wage" in the text fields of the annual reports. The sample includes companies that volunteered that the 1990 or 1991 minimum-wage increase led to higher labor costs.

[a]Not included in the 1993 period.

Notes

1. Actually, a fourth possibility is that prices of other inputs, such as land, could decline. Because minimum-wage employers are a small part of the market for most of these other inputs, however, this effect is unlikely to be too important.

2. The table was calculated from 1993 Current Population Survey data. Information on employer size was taken from the April 1993 Employee Benefits Supplement. Industry data were taken from the 1993 outgoing rotation group file. The April sample consists of 13,986 workers aged 16 and older, and the outgoing rotation group sample consists of 168,423 workers aged 16 and older. Hourly earnings data were truncated below at $1.00 per hour, and above at $150.00.

3. Several studies have found that, on average, smaller employers pay lower wages than do larger employers, after adjusting for the characteristics of their workers. See, for example, Brown and Medoff (1989).

4. The discussion in this subsection closely follows Abowd (1989). For simplicity, we ignore nonlabor inputs. The main conclusions are unchanged if output also depends on nonlabor inputs.

5. Although this example is meant to be hypothetical, these figures are in the ballpark for a large fast-food restaurant.

6. If we assume a real interest rate of 10 percent, rather than 3 percent, then the present value of the firm would have declined by 13 percent, not 5 percent.

7. Any one firm might find it difficult to raise its meal prices, because it would lose business to competitors. However, if competitors also raised prices, then the relevant product-demand curve would be at the industry level, not at the firm level.

8. See New York Times, "Hardest Task of the 1990's: Raising Prices," March 1, 1994, p. D1.

9. For examples, see Becker and Olson (1989) on the Wagner Act, Neumann (1980) and Becker and Olson (1986) on strikes, Liberty and Zimmerman (1986) on contract renegotiations, and Ruback and Zimmerman (1984) on unionization.

10. The event study methodology is common in the finance literature. See Brown and Warner (1985) for a description of this methodology. We calculate standard errors for the estimates using the formula provided by Brown and Warner.

11. In some cases, data on returns are not available for every trading day of 1987. In these cases, we used data for the sample of available days in 1987 to estimate the coefficients of the market model. Moreover, some stocks were not available for every trading day subsequent to 1987. We used the sample of stocks that was available each day. As a result, the sample changes slightly on some days.

12. We also have performed the analysis under the assumption that the excess return is the difference between the stock's return and the market return. These results were quite similar to estimates based on the market

models. In addition, we found similar results when we used the value-weighted market return, rather than the equally-weighted market return.

13. See *Wall Street Journal*, March 26, 1987, p. 5.

14. See *Wall Street Journal*, June 12, 1987, p.3.

15. See *Wall Street Journal*, September 19, 1988, p. 16.

16. See *Wall Street Journal*, September 26, 1988, p. 20.

17. See *Wall Street Journal*, March 3, 1989, p. A3.

18. See *Wall Street Journal*, March 9, 1989, p. A6.

19. See *Wall Street Journal*, March 9, 1989, p. A2.

20. See *Wall Street Journal*, March 24, 1989, p. A3.

21. See *Wall Street Journal*, May 18, 1989, p. A10.

22. See *Wall Street Journal*, June 14, 1989, p. A3.

23. See *Wall Street Journal*, September 20, 1989, p. A14.

24. Each day in this period, excess returns were calculated as the stock's return minus the market return. We then cumulated the average excess returns, using the formula $\Pi_t \, 100(1 + AER_t)$, where AER_t is the average excess return on day t. We obtained similar results when we used a market model to estimate excess returns.

25. See *Daily Labor Report*, August 19, 1993, D1–D2, for the text of the memorandum.

26. Because of the lag in the *Journal's* reporting on this issue, in our analysis, we dated the event as occurring on October 29, 1993.

27. For this analysis, we estimated the coefficients for the market model using data for 1992, the preceding calendar year.

28. One company in the sample (Family Steak Houses of Florida, Inc.) had an excess return of 0.19 on October 13, and of -0.24 on October 29. If we eliminate this company, the correlation becomes -0.51.

CHAPTER 11

Is There an Explanation? Alternative Models of the Labor Market and the Minimum Wage

> In economics it takes a theory to kill a theory; facts can only dent a theorist's hide.
>
> —Paul A. Samuelson

THROUGHOUT THIS BOOK, we have emphasized the gap between the predictions from the "standard," or "textbook," model of the minimum wage, and the actual experiences of firms and labor markets under minimum-wage legislation. In our view, the empirical evidence suggests that the standard model is incomplete. The most important discrepancy between the theory and the evidence concerns the employment effect of a higher minimum wage. Several different experiments, described in detail in chapters 2–4, fail to show that employment losses occur after the minimum wage is increased. Moreover, as we have seen in chapters 6–8, the evidence in the literature of employment losses is surprisingly fragile. We also have documented a variety of other features of the low-wage labor market that are inconsistent with the simple model described in introductory textbooks.

Many economists are reluctant to abandon the elementary model of the labor market that lies behind the conventional analysis of minimum wages. The standard model is simple and powerful. Indeed, it is this combination of attributes that makes the model so pervasive in introductory textbooks, and so amenable to empirical testing. Furthermore, we suspect that the standard model *does* provide a good description of some labor markets, and *does* correctly predict the effect of the minimum wage on some firms. We also suspect that, at sufficiently high levels of the minimum wage, the predicted employment losses of the standard model will be borne out. Nevertheless, we believe that the evidence presented in this book is compelling enough to justify rethinking the nature of low-wage labor markets, and the applicability of the standard model for describing the effects of modest levels of the minimum wage.

Many alternative models depart only slightly from the standard model, and yet yield very different predictions about the effect of the minimum wage. During the past 20 years, a virtual revolution has occurred in economic theory, focusing on the effects of incomplete information, search costs, and other "imperfections" that are ruled out in the standard model. Expanded models that incorporate these features can lead to the prediction that a moderate increase in the minimum wage has an ambiguous effect on firm- and market-level employment. These models also can explain other aspects of the labor market that are difficult to reconcile with the standard model, including systematic wage differences for similar workers across firms.

In this chapter, we review some of these alternative models and assess their applicability to the kinds of labor markets affected by the minimum wage. Before turning to the alternatives, however, we present a detailed description of "the" standard model (including several variants), highlighting its main predictions about the effects of the minimum wage.

THE STANDARD COMPETITIVE MODEL

A Single Firm with One Type of Labor

The basic building block of the standard model is a representative firm that uses labor inputs, L, and nonlabor inputs, K, to produce output, y, using a neoclassical production function:

$$y = F(L, K). \tag{11.1}$$

This equation specifies that output depends only on the *quantities* of inputs, with no possibility of varying the effort or efficiency of labor by varying wages. The firm is assumed to take the wage rate of labor, w, and the price of nonlabor inputs, r, as parametric; that is, the firm is a price taker in the input markets. The firm's optimal labor input choice, *conditional* on a given output choice, is

$$L = h(y, w, r). \tag{11.2}$$

Assuming that the production function exhibits constant returns to scale, it is well-known (see, for example, Allen [1938, pp. 369–374]) that the elasticity of the conditional labor-demand function with respect to the wage, η, is related to the elasticity of substitution exhibited by the production function, σ, and labor's share of total cost, α, by

$$\eta = -(1 - \alpha)\sigma. \tag{11.3}$$

If the wage paid by the firm increases as a result of an increase in the minimum wage, then, *holding output constant*, the impact on firm-level employment is characterized by η. Estimates in the literature on static employment demand surveyed by Hamermesh (1993, chapter 3) suggest that η is between -1 and 0 for most types of employers, with -0.3 representing a "best guess."

For purposes of analyzing the effect of the minimum wage in most situations, however, equation (11.3) is too simple. First, it ignores the output response of firms that are affected by the minimum wage. Normally, one would expect firms to respond to a rise in the marginal cost of production by lowering their desired level of output, leading to an additional "scale effect" on the demand for labor. Second, equation (11.3) ignores heterogeneity in the labor force. Most employers hire workers at a variety of different skill levels and wage rates. Furthermore, even within a relatively homogeneous group, such as teenagers, some workers earn more than others. Thus, in predicting the effects of a rise in the minimum wage on a firm's total employment, or on the total number of teenagers employed, we must consider a heterogeneous labor force. Third, an analysis based on equation (11.3) ignores the fact that some employers are exempt from minimum-wage laws, or choose not to comply with them. We consider each of these extensions in turn.

Output Effects for a Competitive Industry

The simplest way to derive the output effect of a change in the cost of labor is to consider a competitive industry composed of identical firms, each facing the same input and output prices, and each with the same constant-returns-to-scale production technology. In such an industry, the distribution of output and employment across firms is arbitrary. However, the output of the *industry* as a whole is well determined, and it is therefore possible to characterize the demand for labor by the entire industry.

Suppose that the industry's output is sold in a competitive market, with inverse demand function $p = P(Y)$ (where p denotes the industry selling price, and Y denotes total industry output), and let ϵ represent the elasticity of demand for industry output ($\epsilon < 0$). Then an increase in the wage will lead to an increase in the industry selling price, which is proportional to labor's share of cost:

$$d \log p = \alpha \, d \log w. \tag{11.4}$$

This price increase will be accompanied by a reduction in total industry output:

$$d \log Y = \epsilon \, d \log p = \epsilon \, \alpha \, d \log w, \tag{11.5}$$

and a proportional output, or scale, effect on the demand for labor in the industry. The *unconditional* elasticity of industry-level employment with respect to the wage is therefore

$$\eta' = \eta + \epsilon \alpha = -[(1 - \alpha) \sigma - \alpha \epsilon], \qquad (11.6)$$

where we use the prime to distinguish the unconditional elasticity, η' (defined for the industry as a whole), from the conditional or output-constant elasticity, η (defined at both the firm-level and the industry-level).[1] Note that the unconditional elasticity is necessarily larger (in absolute value) than is the conditional elasticity. For example, if wages comprise 30 percent of costs, and the product demand elasticity is -1.0, then a conditional elasticity of -0.3 is associated with an unconditional elasticity of -0.6.

What is an appropriate elasticity of product demand for forecasting the effects of a minimum-wage hike? As noted in Tables 9.1 and 10.1, approximately one-half of workers whose wages are affected or potentially affected by the minimum wage are employed in retail trade, and another 30 percent are employed in services. Thus, the relevant demand elasticities are mainly in the retail-trade and service industries. Houthakker and Taylor (1970) present a variety of demand elasticities for various trade and service products. For example, they estimate that the elasticity of demand for restaurant meals is -1.4, that the elasticity of demand for apparel is -1.0, and that the elasticity of demand for car repair services is -0.4. These estimates suggest that the output effect associated with an increase in the minimum wage is potentially large. On the other hand, labor's share of cost in these industries may be smaller than in other sectors of the economy. We noted in chapter 2 that labor's share of cost in the fast-food industry is approximately 30 percent. It may be higher in other types of restaurants and in the service industry, and may be much smaller in department stores and similar retail outlets.

Assuming that the critical parameters—σ, α, and ϵ—are known, we can easily summarize the predicted effect of a minimum wage on an industry that employs a single type of labor. Suppose that a 1 percent increase in the minimum wage generates a k percent increase in the industry wage (where k can range between 0 and 1 percent, depending on the initial level of wages in the industry relative to the new minimum wage). Then, the predicted percentage effect on the industry's selling price is αk, the predicted percentage effect on the industry's total output is $\alpha k \epsilon$, and the predicted percentage effect on industry employment is $k \eta'$. Note that, for similar values of σ, α, and ϵ, the output, price, and employment effects of the minimum wage are all larger for more heavily impacted industries, where "impact" is measured by the rate, k, at which industry wages rise in response to the minimum wage. A similar prediction applies across regional labor markets: the greater the increase in wages for low-wage workers in a particular region induced by a rise in the minimum wage, the greater the predicted effects on the employment rate of the group of workers, and on the output and prices of the products that they produce.

Output Effects for a Firm with Market Power

In a competitive industry with a linearly homogeneous production function, only the industry-level employment-demand function is well defined. A different industry model is one in which each employer has some degree of market power in the output market. For example, if consumers and firms differ in their physical locations, then each firm in the industry has a natural market area consisting of nearby consumers, and firm-specific output and employment-demand functions are well defined.[2] Suppose that a firm faces a firm-specific product-demand function with constant elasticity, ϵ. Then, with the substitution of the appropriate demand elasticity, equation (11.6) continues to describe the *firm's* unconditional employment demand elasticity with respect to a firm-specific wage increase.[3]

For purposes of modeling the effect of an industry-wide wage increase, however, the relevant product-demand elasticity is one that takes into consideration simultaneous price adjustments at all firms. This elasticity will tend to be smaller (in absolute value) than the elasticity of demand for a firm's output with respect to its own price.[4] In the case of the restaurant industry, for example, any individual restaurant presumably faces a relatively elastic demand for its product, holding constant prices at nearby restaurants. When the minimum wage increases, however, prices will tend to rise at all restaurants, resulting in a smaller net reduction in demand at any particular firm. Indeed the appropriate product-demand elasticity is precisely the kind of industry-wide elasticity typically estimated in the consumer-demand literature. For our purposes, then, the distinction between a model with perfectly competitive firms and one with market power based on geographically differentiated products is probably small.

Heterogeneous Labor

A potentially more important consideration than the structure of the output market is the extent of heterogeneity in the labor force. We consider two, alternative models of heterogeneous labor: (1) one with discrete "types" of labor; and (2) one with a continuum of perfectly substitutable types.

TWO TYPES OF LABOR

One way to extend the simple model described by equations (11.1) through (11.6) is to introduce two types of labor, skilled (L_1) and unskilled (L_2), which are imperfect substitutes for each other and for nonlabor inputs. It is natural to assume that the wage for unskilled labor (w_1) is affected by the minimum wage, whereas the wage for skilled labor (w_2) is not. In this case, the derivatives of the *unconditional* demands for skilled and unskilled workers at the industry level satisfy

$$\text{d} \log L_1 = (\alpha_1 \sigma_{11} + \alpha_1 \epsilon) \, \text{d} \log w_1, \tag{11.7a}$$

$$\text{d} \log L_2 = (\alpha_1 \sigma_{21} + \alpha_1 \epsilon) \, \text{d} \log w_1, \tag{11.7b}$$

where α_1 represents the share of unskilled labor in total cost, and σ_{11} and σ_{21} are the Allen partial elasticities of substitution associated with the production function $F(L_1, L_2, K)$.[5] The term $\alpha_1\epsilon \, \text{d} \log w_1$ represents the scale effect generated by the increase in w_1 and is proportional to the product of the unskilled-labor-cost share and the output-demand elasticity. The term $\alpha_1\sigma_{11}$ represents the "own-substitution" effect of an increase in w_1 and is necessarily negative, because $\sigma_{11} \leq 0$.[6] Finally, the term $\alpha_1\sigma_{21}$ represents the "cross-substitution" effect between unskilled and skilled labor and may be negative or positive, depending on the degree of complementarity between the two types of labor.

Equations (11.7a) and (11.7b) have two implications with respect to the observed employment effects of a minimum wage. As in the simpler case with only one kind of labor, employment of workers whose wages are affected by the minimum wage will necessarily fall. No such unambiguous statement is possible for total employment ($L_1 + L_2$), because, in principle, the increase in employment of skilled workers could offset the decrease in employment of unskilled workers. Total employment *will* decline with a rise in the unskilled wage, however, if $\sigma_{31} > 0$—that is, if nonlabor inputs are a substitute for unskilled labor.[7]

CONTINUOUS TYPES OF LABOR

The division of the labor force into discrete types of workers is analytically convenient, but not very appealing empirically. The main difficulty is posed by the fact that observed wage distributions tend to be relatively smooth. Among teenage workers in a particular state, for example, there is no obvious division into "high-wage" and "low-wage" workers. Rather, the teenage wage distribution is more or less continuous (albeit with spikes at certain wage values). Even among the nonsupervisory workers at a single fast-food restaurant, one typically observes a wide range of entry-level wages (see chapter 5).

A useful conceptual approach to this observed wage diversity is suggested by the human capital model (see, for example, Welch [1969]). Suppose that different workers possess different amounts of human capital (an amalgam of such factors as schooling, experience, motivation, and ability). Suppose further that the total productivity of a given collection of workers is simply the sum of their individual human-capital stocks. In this situation, the labor market is characterized by a single wage rate for an "efficiency unit" of human capital, and each individual receives a wage that equals the product of his or her human-capital stock and the price of an efficiency unit

$$w_i = h_i w, \tag{11.8}$$

where w_i is the wage rate observed for individual i, h_i represents his or her human capital stock, and w is the standardized wage rate. If h_i is log-normally distributed, for example, then this model readily can account for the observed cross-sectional dispersion of observed wages. Equation (11.8) might be described as a "one-factor human-capital model," because the only relevant determinant of wages is the amount of human capital possessed by a given worker, and all workers are perfect substitutes in production.

To derive the implications of this model, consider a modified version of the production function (11.1) that depends on total human capital, H, and nonlabor inputs, K, where $H = \Sigma_i h_i$ is the sum of the human capital of the firm's labor force. If each worker is paid according to equation (11.8), then firms will be indifferent as to the composition of their labor force, although each firm will have an optimal stock of total human capital.[8] Indeed, the model of equations (11.1)–(11.6) can be reinterpreted as a model of the derived demand for human capital, and equation (11.6) can be reinterpreted as the elasticity of the demand for human capital with respect to the standardized wage.

The predictions of this kind of model for the effect of a minimum wage are illustrated most easily with the aid of a figure. Figure 11.1.A shows a hypothetical wage distribution corresponding to equation (11.8) in a market with no minimum wage. Adopting the normalization that $E(h_i) = 1$, the standardized wage (i.e., the wage

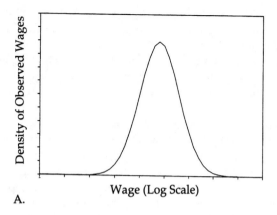

A.

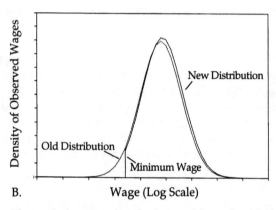

B.

Figure 11.1 Theoretical wage distribution, with and without minimum wage. A. Without minimum wage. B. With minimum wage.

for an individual with one unit of human capital) is simply the mean of observed wages. Figure 11.1.B shows the effect of imposing a minimum wage of m. The minimum wage leads to two changes in the wage distribution. First, the entire distribution of wages shifts right, reflecting an increase in the market price of human capital from w to w'. Second, the distribution of wages is truncated on the left at the minimum wage. Any individual with $h_i < m/w'$ is excluded from the market. This prediction is one that Stigler (1946, p. 358) emphasized, arguing that "workers whose services are worth less than the minimum wage are discharged . . ." after an increase in the minimum wage is imposed.

The change in the market price of human capital after the imposition of a minimum wage can be determined by noting that the change in the total supply of human capital is

$$dH = - \int_{-\infty}^{m/w'} h \, f(h) \, dh,$$

where $f(h)$ is the density function of the human capital distribution. This quantity is proportional to the total earnings of individuals who are excluded from the market by the increase in the minimum wage. Using equation (11.6),

$$(w' - w)/w = 1/\eta' \, (dH/H).$$

With the substitution of the previous expression for dH, this equation can be solved for w'. It is easy to see that the increase in the market price of human capital will be larger, the smaller in absolute value is the elasticity of demand for human capital. Indeed, in the limiting case of a perfectly inelastic demand, the standardized wage will rise by the ratio of the minimum wage to the lowest wage that was previously observed in the labor market, and the total number of employed workers will remain constant. With less than perfectly inelastic demand, the rise in the minimum wage will reduce the employment of low-wage workers and will lead to an increase in wages for all other workers.

An interesting aspect of this model is the predicted pattern of employment losses after a minimum-wage increase. Individuals whose wages are the farthest below the minimum are the most likely to lose their jobs, whereas individuals whose wages are just short of the new minimum are likely to receive a raise sufficient to ensure their continued employment.

A comparison of Figure 11.1 with the observed distribution of wages (e.g., Figure 9.3) suggests an important weakness of the one-factor model of the labor market. Specifically, the assumption of perfect substitutability of different types of labor is inconsistent with a spike in the distribution of wages at the minimum wage. The spike *can* be rationalized by the presence of nonwage offsets that smooth out the distribution of total compensation relative to the distribution of hourly wages. As we noted in chapter 5, however, it is difficult to find concrete evidence of such offsets. A second weakness of the one-factor model is the prediction that wages will rise by the same amount for *all* workers who originally were earning more than the minimum wage. In chapters 4 and 5, we presented some evidence of spillover effects for workers who had been earning more than the new minimum wage. However, these spillovers are limited to workers whose wages fall within a narrow range above the minimum. Both weaknesses suggest that a strict one-factor human-capital model is inconsistent with the nature of observed wage changes occurring after a rise in the minimum wage.

The one-factor human-capital model has been generalized by Heckman and Sedlacek (1981) to allow for several different types of skills, each of which is used in one sector (or industry). The predictions of their generalized model are similar to those of a one-factor model. An increase in the minimum wage is predicted to raise the standardized price of skills in affected industries, leading to wage increases throughout the wage distribution, and causing some low-wage workers in these industries to lose their jobs.

Allowing for an Uncovered Sector

Currently, more than 90 percent of all workers in the U.S. economy are covered by the federal minimum wage. The coverage rate for teenagers is only slightly lower (see chapter 6). Even with these high rates of coverage, however, a substantial amount of subminimum-wage employment exists. During 1992, for example, 3.3 percent of all workers and 10.2 percent of all teenagers reported earning less than $4.25 per hour.[9] This phenomenon suggests that theoretical models of the minimum wage should make allowance for employment opportunities in the uncovered sector. Such models were proposed and analyzed by Welch (1974 and 1976), Mincer (1976), and Gramlich (1976), among others. The two-sector models in the literature typically ignore heterogeneity across workers and assume instead that all workers in both sectors are identical. We adopt this simplification.

We begin by positing labor-demand functions for the covered and uncovered sectors:

$$\log L_c = \eta_c \log w_c + \text{constant}, \tag{11.9a}$$

$$\log L_u = \eta_u \log w_u + \text{constant}, \tag{11.9b}$$

where L_c and L_c represent covered and uncovered employment, w_c and w_u represent covered and uncovered wage rates, and η_c and η_u represent the (unconditional) elasticities of employment demand in the two sectors.[10] These equations ignore the possible effects of uncovered wages on covered-sector employment demand, and vice versa. Nevertheless, cross-substitution effects could be potentially significant if the two sectors supply the same products—for example, in the case of covered and uncovered restaurants.

Suppose that an increase in the minimum wage leads to an increase in the covered-sector wage. From equation (11.9a), it is clear that *covered sector employment necessarily will decline.* The effect on uncovered-sector employment depends on the assumed model of labor supply to the two sectors. A useful benchmark model is one in which the total supply to both sectors depends on the average wage in the two sectors (with a weight reflecting the relative size of the sectors), and the supply to the uncovered sector is simply the residual between total supply and demand in the covered sector. In this benchmark case, if wages in the two sectors start off approximately equal, then

$$d \log w_u = -\frac{c}{1-c} \times \frac{\zeta - \eta_c}{\zeta - \eta_u} \times d \log w_c, \qquad (11.10)$$

where c is the initial fraction of workers in the covered sector, and ζ is the elasticity of supply to the combined market.[11] Because both η_c and η_u are negative, equation (11.10) predicts that wages will fall in the uncovered sector after a change in the minimum wage is imposed that raises covered-sector wages. Indeed, if the covered sector is larger than the uncovered sector, then this equation predicts significant wage declines in the uncovered sector, unless demand in the uncovered sector is extraordinarily elastic. The reasoning behind this conclusion is simple: if the covered sector is larger, a given percentage employment *loss* in the covered sector creates a larger percentage increase in labor supply to the uncovered sector, which can be absorbed only with a substantial wage cut.

Relatively little research has been conducted on how wages in the uncovered sector respond to a change in the minimum wage. One of the few studies, by Tauchen (1981), estimated the effect of the federal minimum wage on hourly wages in agriculture, using quarterly data, by region, from the late 1940s to the mid-1960s. His results showed varying effects by region, with a significantly negative effect in one of nine regions, and a significantly positive effect in two regions.[12] As pointed out by Mincer (1976), however, the prediction that uncovered-sector wages will fall in response to a rise in the wage in the covered sector is *not* robust to alternative stories about sectoral choice and unemployment. Following the example of Todaro's (1969) model of rural-urban migration, Mincer proposed that individuals who lose their jobs in the covered sector could either move to uncovered jobs or queue up for covered-sector jobs. In equilibrium, the expected utilities of these two alternatives must be equal, implying (under risk neutrality) that

$$w_u = \frac{L_c}{L_c + U} w_c + \left(1 - \frac{L_c}{L_c + U}\right) b, \qquad (11.11)$$

where U is the number of workers in the queue for covered-sector jobs, and b is the dollar value of nonparticipation.[13] Given the sector-specific employment-demand functions, the model is closed by an expression for U. A simple assumption is that $L_c + L_u + U = S(w_u)$, where S is a supply function to both sectors (see, for example, Brown, Gilroy, and Kohen [1982, p. 492]). Combining these equations leads to the following expression for the derivative of the wage in the uncovered sector with respect to an increase in w_c:

$$\frac{dw_u}{dw_c} = \frac{c(1 + \eta_c R_c)}{1 + \zeta R_u - (1 - c - u) \times (1 + \eta_u R_u)}, \tag{11.12}$$

where $c = L_c/S$ is the fraction of the labor force in the covered sector, $u = U/S$ is the fraction of the labor force in unemployment, $R_c = (w_c - b)/w_c$ is the gap between covered-sector wages and b, $R_u = (w_u - b)/w_u$ is the gap between uncovered-sector wages and b, and ζ is the elasticity of supply. The sign of this expression depends on whether $|\eta_c| > 1/R_c$.[14] If employment demand in the covered sector is relatively inelastic, then a rise in w_c leads to a rise in w_u, a fall in employment in both sectors, and an increase in unemployment. Using (11.12), it is possible to derive expressions for the elasticity of total employment (in both sectors) to the covered-sector wage change induced by a minimum wage.

Before concluding, it is worth underscoring a comment made by Brown, Gilroy, and Kohen (1982) on the nature of the equilibrium condition (11.11). As in Todaro's model, this equation embodies the assumption that individuals can queue for covered-sector jobs *only* if they are unemployed. Although this assumption may be appropriate if covered-sector jobs and uncovered-sector jobs are in different geographic locations, we believe that it is less appropriate in the context of the U.S. minimum wage.[15] If workers can queue for covered-sector jobs *and* simultaneously hold an uncovered-sector job, however, then the model boils down to the simpler model characterized by equation (11.10), with the unambiguous prediction that a rise in the covered-sector wage will lead to a decline in the wage in the uncovered sector. We emphasize that, regardless of the impact on the uncovered sector, a rise in the minimum wage is predicted to lead to a decline in employment in the covered sector.

Long-Run Versus Short-Run Effects

In the discussion so far, we have made no distinction between short-run and long-run responses to the minimum wage. All the theoretical models are essentially long-run models that assume employers can costlessly adjust to a change in the price of labor. Over the short run, however, some nonlabor inputs may be costly to adjust or may be "sunk" (an example is the physical structure of a fast-food restaurant). With costly adjustment or sunk inputs, employment will not necessarily respond immediately to an increase in the minimum wage. Rather, adjustments will take place over the long run, as some firms exit the industry, others gradually downsize, and potential entrants are deterred from starting new firms.

A simple and extreme version of short-run adjustment cost arises in a so-called "putty-clay" model, in which capital, once installed, has a rigid capital–labor requirement.[16] Prior to the installation of capital, a firm is free to choose any capital–labor ratio. Afterward, the firm is constrained to use labor and capital in fixed proportions up to the capacity constraint dictated by the size of the capital stock. One can show in such a model that the optimal employment response to an unexpected increase in wages is zero, at least for wage increases that are less than a maximum threshold determined by the ratio of capital costs per worker to the wage. Installed capital in a putty-clay model acts like a sunk training investment in Oi's (1962) model of labor as a quasi-fixed factor and creates a discontinuity in the short-run employment-demand function. Another aspect of this model is that all the short-run costs of a higher minimum wage are borne by the owners of firms. In the short run, industry selling prices do not respond to an increase in wages.

We believe that the distinction between short-run and long-run responses to the minimum wage is potentially important. Unfortunately, there is no easy way to judge what fraction of employment adjustments in service and retail-trade industries are accomplished within a "short" time frame (say, 6 months), and what fraction are realized over several years. One way to form a rough estimate is to examine the length of time between renovations at a typical retail or service establishment. For example, if firms normally install new capital or renovate their stores on a three-year cycle, then at least one-third of firms will have fully adjusted to a minimum-wage change within 12 months. Another way to judge the length of the "long run" is to examine the pattern of employment responses to a minimum-wage hike over increasingly long time intervals. Some evidence of this type is provided by our study of teenage employment rates between 1989 and 1992. Our reading of the evidence is that the estimated employment effects are very similar (and very close to zero) over one-, two-, and three-year time horizons. Clearly, more-detailed studies of the effects of minimum wages on longer-run employment decisions and the entry and exit of firms are desirable. Our study of restaurant openings in the McDonald's chain is a step in this direction. In the meantime, one must recognize that the "standard model" does not necessarily preclude a zero employment effect of the minimum wage in the short run. In cases in which the employment effect of the minimum wage is zero, however, the price effects also should be zero.

Summary and Scorecard for the Conventional Model

We are now in a position to evaluate the predictions of the standard model for the effects of an increase in the minimum wage. The first four columns of Table 11.1 present a tabular summary of the main implications of the various versions of the standard model. We present the predictions of the different models for the wages and employment outcomes of both "directly affected" workers—workers in covered-sector jobs who previously were earning less than the new minimum wage—and "indirectly affected" workers—higher-wage workers or those in the uncovered sector. In the bottom rows of the table, we also present the predictions of the various models regarding industry prices and the characteristics of the wage distribution, including the spike at the minimum wage, wage spillovers for workers who were earning more than the new minimum wage, and the use of subminimum-wage provisions. A dash in the table indicates that the model in question makes no prediction about the particular phenomenon. For comparison purposes, column 7 presents our best guess as to the actual patterns in the labor market, based on the analyses in the previous chapters of this book.

The most obvious difficulty associated with any long-run version of the standard model is that of explaining the existence of zero, or even positive, employment changes for affected workers following a minimum-wage increase. Each alternative version of the standard model posits the existence of a decreasing employment-demand function for directly affected workers. As shown in the table, our reading of the evidence is that the employment effects are either zero or, if anything, slightly positive. The models, particularly the model with a continuum of perfectly substitutable skill types, do a better job of matching the evidence with respect to wages, although even here, none of the models is consistent with the presence of a spike in the wage distribution, limited wage spillovers to higher-wage workers, and negligible use of the subminimum wage. Standard models predict that a rise in the minimum wage will lead to an increase in prices that is large enough to cover the cost of the higher wage. The available evidence is generally consistent with this prediction, although the pattern of price changes that we found at fast-food restaurants within New Jersey and Texas is not.

MODELS IN WHICH FIRMS SET WAGES

A common feature of the standard models that we have discussed is the assumption that the firm is a price-taker in the labor market—in other words, that there is no firm-specific component of wages. In the standard model, a worker with a given set of characteristics receives exactly the same wage at any potential employer (holding constant the nature of the job). Casual observation and a variety of other kinds of evidence suggest that this assumption is an oversimplification (see chapter 5 for an overview of this evidence). In this section, we pursue the implications of firm-specific wage-setting for the effects of a minimum wage. The analysis revolves around a relatively simple question: Do employers have to pay a higher wage in order to maintain and motivate a larger work force? If the answer is "yes," then a modest increase in wages induced by a minimum-wage hike can lead to an increase in employment.

A Static Model—Traditional Monopsony

Textbook discussions of the minimum wage often present a supplementary analysis of the case in which an employer faces an upward-sloping supply schedule of labor (see, for example, Baumol and Blinder [1991, pp. 788–791]). The exercise usually is motivated by the example of a one-company town. With only one buyer of labor (a so-called monopsonist), the supply schedule to the firm is the labor supply-function for the market as a whole and is presumed to be upward sloping. We summarize this traditional monopsony model here.

Assume that workers are homogeneous, and suppose that the wage rate that the firm must pay to attract and retain L workers is $w = g(L)$. The function $g(L)$ is simply the inverse supply function of labor, and its logarithmic derivative (d log w/d log L) is the inverse of the elasticity of supply. The standard textbook model corresponds to the extreme assumption that the elasticity of supply is infinite, implying that $g'(L) = 0$.

As was first established by Joan Robinson (1933), a monopsonist sets a wage such that the marginal revenue product of labor $MRP(L)$ is equated to the marginal cost of labor:[17]

TABLE 11.1
Alternative Models of the Effect of the Minimum Wage: Summary and Scorecard

	Alternative Versions of the Standard Model				Models with Firm Wage-Setting		
	Homogeneous Labor (1)	Two or More Discrete Types of Labor (2)	Continuum of Perfect Substitutes (3)	Two-Sector Model with Homogeneous Labor (4)	Single-Firm Model (5)	Equilibrium Wage-Dispersion Model (6)	Evidence (7)
Predicted Effect of Minimum Wage on Wages							
1. Covered Affected Workers[a]	Positive	Positive	Positive	Positive	Positive	Positive	Positive
2. Uncovered or Higher-Wage Workers[b]	—	Zero	Positive	Negative or ?	—	Positive	Positive
Predicted Effect of Minimum Wage on Employment							
3. Covered Affected Workers[a]	Negative	Negative	Negative	Negative	Positive or negative	Positive or negative	Zero or positive
4. Uncovered or Higher-Wage Workers[b]	—	?	Zero	Positive or ?	—	Positive or ?	Negative or ?

Predicted Effect of Minimum Wage on Wage Distribution

5. Existence of Spike at Minimum	—	No (excluding offsets)	—	—	No	Yes
6. Wage Spillovers to Higher-Wage Workers	—	Yes	—	—	Yes	Yes, but limited to narrow range

Subminimum Wage

7. Used, if Possible?	Yes	Yes	Yes	No (monitoring version)	No (wage-policy version)	Hardly ever

Predicted Effect of Minimum Wage on Product Prices

8. Products Produced by Affected Workers	Positive	Positive	Positive	Negative or positive	Negative or positive	Positive (across states)

Predicted Effect of Minimum Wage on Firm Profits

9. Profits of Employers of Affected Workers	Negative	Negative	Negative	Negative (first-order effect = 0)	Negative (first-order effect = 0)	Weak negative

Note: A question mark means that the model's prediction is ambiguous. A dash means that the model makes no prediction.
[a] Workers who previously earned less than the new minimum wage and worked in the covered sector.
[b] Higher-wage workers (in models with more than one skill type) or workers in the uncovered sector.

$$MRP(L) = d [L g(L)]/dL$$
$$= w (1 + 1/\zeta),$$

(11.13)

where ζ is the elasticity of supply. If ζ is infinite, then this expression reduces to the standard case of setting $MRP(L) = w$. Otherwise, the inverse elasticity of supply generates a wedge between the marginal product and the wage. For example, a supply elasticity of ten implies a ten percent gap between $MRP(L)$ and the observed wage.

In a monopsonistic equilibrium, the employer is "supply constrained." Such an equilibrium is illustrated in Figure 11.2. The curve labeled $MC(L)$ represents the marginal cost of hiring an additional worker. As shown by equation (11.13), $MC(L) > w$. Starting from a situation in which the wage is monopsonistically determined at a level w^o, a k percent increase in the wage caused by an increase in the minimum wage will lead to a $k\zeta$ percent *increase* in employment along the supply curve of labor, and to a commensurate increase in the firm's output.[18] As the figure makes clear, however, this calculation is valid only for a "small" increase in the minimum wage. Indeed, the employment response to higher wages is inverse-U shaped, with a maximum increase in employment for a wage increase of $-\eta/[\zeta(\zeta - \eta)]$, and a reduction in employment (relative to the initial equilibrium) for any increase greater than $1/\zeta$, where η is the labor-demand elasticity that would be exhibited if the firm were a price taker in the labor market (i.e., the inverse of the logarithmic derivative of the marginal-revenue-product function).

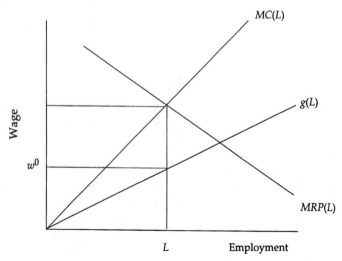

Figure 11.2   Illustration of monopsony equilibrium.

Textbook discussions of monopsony usually dismiss it as an intellectual curiosity. The reasoning behind this harsh judgment is the intuitive belief that the elasticity of labor supply to a particular firm is close to infinity unless the firm actually employs a significant fraction of the total pool of potential workers. This intuition is borrowed from the field of industrial organization, where the degree of market power enjoyed by a particular seller is thought to be correlated with the seller's market share.[19] In the market for such relatively unskilled workers as teenagers or high school dropouts, the buyers of labor typically are small firms—restaurants, service stations, and retail outlets. Because each firm employs only a tiny fraction of the unskilled workers in its local market, their degree of monopsony power is often thought to be negligible.

A Simple Dynamic Model: A Reinterpretation of Monopsony

The belief that individual firms can take wages as given is grounded in a static "perfect information" view of the labor market. In a market with complete information, where each worker makes a once-and-for-all decision about which job to choose, an employer who offered a 10 percent higher wage than other employers obviously would attract a large queue of qualified applicants. Finding this queue, the employer could reduce the offered wage until it was only trivially above the market rate and still attract enough workers to fill the required positions. In practice, however, information about job opportunities is imperfect, and workers move between jobs and in and out of the labor force at a rapid pace. The turnover rate among low-wage workers is especially high. At a typical fast-food restaurant, for example, fewer than one-half of the nonsupervisory workers have been on the job more than six months.[20] These high turnover rates mean that low-wage employers are fighting a constant "war of attrition." Unlike the idealized situation of the standard model, in which an employer can announce a job opening at the going market wage and instantly fill the position, low-wage employers spend a great deal of time and energy recruiting and training new workers.

A variety of evidence suggests that vacancies are a pervasive phenomenon in the low-wage labor market. In mid-1988, just prior to the minimum-wage increases that we study in chapters 2–4 of this book, a Gallup Poll commissioned by the National Restaurant Association recorded 200,000 vacancies nationwide in the eating and drinking industry, implying a vacancy rate of about 3 percent.[21] A survey of fast-food restaurants conducted by the Bureau of National Affairs (1985) found that more than 80 percent of fast-food stores had vacancies at any point in time. Low-wage employers use several different incentive mechanisms to reduce turnover and increase recruiting rates, including hiring bonuses and transportation assistance (Bureau of National Affairs, 1985, Table 8). In our survey of fast-food restaurants in New Jersey and Pennsylvania, we found that about one-third of the restaurants paid bonuses to employees who brought in a friend to work in the restaurant. It is difficult (although not impossible) to justify the existence of these programs and the corresponding attention paid to vacancies and recruiting in a model in which as many workers as needed can always be found at the going wage.

Apart from bonuses and other recruiting incentives, firms can offer higher wages to attract more workers. A higher wage has both costs and benefits. On the cost side, the firm obviously has to pay more to new workers and to its existing labor force. On the benefit side, a higher wage attracts a greater number of applicants and helps to reduce the turnover rate of existing workers. To formalize the trade-offs involved, suppose that a firm that offers a wage, w, can expect to be able to hire $H(w)$ new (suitably qualified) workers per month, where $H'(w) > 0$. Suppose, in addition, that the monthly quit rate is $q(w)$, where $q'(w) \leq 0$. If the firm wants to maintain a work force of L employees, it must set a wage such that the number of new hires per month just balances the number of quits. This condition is

$$H(w) = q(w) \, L. \qquad (11.14)$$

Equation (11.14) implies a relation between the offered wage and the steady-state size of the work force, with elasticity

$$\frac{d \log w}{d \log L} = \frac{1}{\theta_H - \theta_q}, \qquad (11.15)$$

where $\theta_H \geq 0$ is the wage elasticity of the hiring function and $\theta_q \leq 0$ is the wage elasticity of the quit function. The standard model corresponds to the assumption that θ_H is infinite, in which case the firm is a price taker in the labor market. More realistically, if a higher wage generates only a finite addition to the applicant flow, and if the quit rate is not infinitely elastic with respect to the wage, then the required wage is strictly an increasing function of the size of the desired work force.

The implicit constraint posed by having to equate monthly hiring and quit rates plays a role that is just like the supply function in the traditional, static monopsony model. In particular, the analytical results developed for the traditional monopsony model carry over to this simple dynamic model by setting the labor-supply elasticity $\zeta =$ $(\theta_H - \theta_q)$. In a dynamic model, the question of whether the firm has any monopsony power is equivalent to the question of whether either the elasticity of the hiring function or the elasticity of the quit function is infinite.

The literature presents considerable evidence on the magnitude of the quit-rate elasticity. Campbell (1993) used data from the Employment Opportunity Pilot Project (EOPP) survey of recently filled job positions to estimate the elasticity of the quit rate with respect to the wage. This data set is especially relevant for our purposes, because the survey was targeted at low-wage, entry-level jobs. Campbell's base specification yields an elasticity of the monthly quit rate with respect to the wage rate of -0.96 (with a standard error of 0.22). This is a sizable, but certainly finite, number. Campbell's other specifications yield slightly smaller estimates. Other estimates of the elasticity of the quit rate based on data from the EOPP have been reported by Meitzen (1986) and tend to be smaller in magnitude than Campbell's.

Quit-rate functions have been estimated using individual-level longitudinal data in a large number of studies, including studies by Blau and Kahn (1981), Viscusi (1979 and 1980), Shaw (1985), and Light and Ureta (1992) (see Devine and Kiefer [1991, chapter 8] for a partial survey). Our reading of these studies is that the elasticity of the quit rate with respect to the wage is usually negative and statistically significant, but rarely as large as -1.0. Finally, Parker and Burton (1967), Pencavel (1970), and Parsons (1973) reported estimates of the effect of industry-level wages on industry-average monthly quit rates for firms in manufacturing. These studies all suggest that quit rates are negatively related to wages, with an elasticity in the range of -1.0. For example, Pencavel's pooled estimates (Table I) imply an elasticity of the quit rate with respect to wages of between -0.90 and -1.10. We conclude that the elasticity of the quit rate with respect to wages is significant, but not much larger than -1.0.

Much less research has been conducted on the elasticity of the hiring rate with respect to the offered wage. Holzer, Katz, and Krueger (1991) used data from the EEOP survey on the number of applications that employers reported for their last filled job vacancy. They regressed the log of the number of applicants on a variety of information about the employer's local labor market, the nature of the job, the type of worker who ultimately filled the job, and the offered wage rate. Recognizing the potential endogeneity of the offered wage, Holzer, Krueger, and Katz presented estimation results using alternative sets of instrumental variables for the wage. Their estimates of the elasticity of applications with respect to wages are uniformly positive and generally statistically significant. The point estimates range from about 0.5 (standard error = 0.3), using two-digit-industry dummies as instruments, to 4.1 (standard error = 0.9), using establishment-size dummies as instruments. The latter set of instruments is theoretically appropriate if one believes that firms with a larger steady-state employment target offer higher wages in order to raise hiring rates.

A related study of the application rate for jobs in the federal civil service was conducted by one of us—Krueger (1988). The annual number of applications for federal job openings posted through the Office of Personnel Management's Open Competitive Appointment System is available from 1950 onward, as is the number of jobs filled through this system. The log of the number of applicants per new job was regressed on the ratio of the average federal government wage to the average private-sector wage, measures of cyclical conditions in the labor market, and various trend terms. The estimated elasticities of the overall application rate with respect to the relative federal wage range from 1.8 to 2.7, with standard errors of 0.4 to 0.5, depending on the choice of control variables. The estimated elasticity is higher (4.0, with a standard error of 0.5) when the application rate is redefined to include only "qualified" applicants in the numerator. For our purposes, this specification is probably the preferred one, because the theoretical hiring rate in the monopsony model refers to the hiring rate of suitably qualified workers.[22]

On the basis of these studies, a rough estimate of the elasticity of the application rate with respect to offered wages would be between 0.5 and 4.0, with the upper range of these estimates arising from specifications that more closely correspond to the theoretical structure of a dynamic monopsony model. Combining a quit rate elasticity of -1.0 with an application elasticity of 4.0, we obtain an estimate of the combined elasticity $(\theta_H - \theta_q) = 5.0$. Given the sampling errors on the estimates, we probably can rule out a combined elasticity of greater than 10. If $(\theta_H - \theta_q)$ is between 5 and 10, the gap between marginal productivity and wages is between 10 and 20 percent—a range that is potentially plausible.

Assuming that the hiring and quit rates are *not* infinitely elastic with respect to the offered wage, what are the implications of a simple dynamic model for the characteristics of the low-wage labor market, and the effect of the minimum wage? First, the model suggests that larger firms must pay a higher wage, on average—at least in markets in which the minimum wage is not binding. Of course, this prediction must be interpreted carefully, as the relation between work-force size and wages holds only when other factors are held constant. If we write the hiring and quit functions as $H(w/w^a)$ and $q(w/w^a)$, where w^a is a relevant alternative wage, then the predicted relation is

$$\log w = \log w^a + (\theta_H - \theta_q)^{-1} \log N. \qquad (11.16)$$

Unobserved heterogeneity in the alternative wage obviously can lead to difficulties in the estimation of an equation like (11.16). Furthermore, the assumption that the hiring and quit-rate elasticities are constant across firms may be misleading. For example, differences in the nature of the local labor market may lead to differences not only in w^a, but in the sensitivity of applicant flows and quit rates to the wage rate offered by individual employers. Variation across employers in the relevant elasticities will lead to wage variation across firms that is not directly correlated with employment. Finally, and perhaps most importantly, observed firm size in equation (11.16) is endogenous. In principle, it is necessary to have a suitable set of exogenous determinants of firm size, such as the size of the product market, in order to obtain reliable estimates of this "structural" equation.

Despite these difficulties, we estimated models such as the one in (11.16), using the samples of fast-food restaurants from our New Jersey–Pennsylvania study, and from the earlier Texas study. In each case, we used data collected *before* the rise in the minimum wage (i.e., from February–March 1992 for the New Jersey–Pennsylvania sample, and from the period preceding April 1990 for the Texas sample). The results are summarized in Table 11.2. For each sample, we report ordinary least squares (OLS) estimates of a specification like (11.16), and estimates from an alternative Tobit specification that recognizes the "truncation" of observed wages at the minimum wage.[23] The estimation results show that wages are significantly related to establishment size.[24] The estimated coefficients, however, are relatively small, ranging from 0.02 to 0.05.[25] Taken literally, these estimates imply that $(\theta_H - \theta_q)$ ranges from 20 to 50. This range is inconsistent with the range implied by the direct estimates of θ_H and θ_q that we have discussed and may reflect difficulties in the OLS estimation of equation (11.16). Ideally, we would like to instrument establishment size with some exogenous determinants of size, such as highway location. This analysis is beyond the limitations of our data.

A second implication of the monopsony model is that the imposition of a binding minimum wage will lead to employment gains for

Table 11.2
Effect of Establishment Size on Wages

Variable	NJ − PA		Texas	
	OLS (1)	Tobit (2)	OLS (3)	Tobit (4)
1. Intercept	1.493	1.461	1.183	1.099
	(0.033)	(0.048)	(0.039)	(0.058)
2. Log Number of FTE Employees	0.020	0.025	0.030	0.053
	(0.010)	(0.014)	(0.014)	(0.021)
3. Store in New Jersey	−0.001	0.002	—	—
	(0.009)	(0.013)		
Indicators for Store Characteristics				
4. Company Owned	0.016	0.021	0.034	0.055
	(0.009)	(0.012)	(0.012)	(0.018)
5. Burger King	−0.046	−0.066	−0.023	−0.044
	(0.011)	(0.016)	(0.014)	(0.021)
6. KFC	−0.025	−0.031	0.028	0.028
	(0.014)	(0.020)	(0.016)	(0.023)
7. Roy Rogers	−0.021	−0.022	—	—
	(0.013)	(0.018)		
8. R-Squared	0.075	—	0.184	—
9. Sample size	379	379	157	157

Note: Standard errors are shown in parentheses. The dependent variable in all models is the log of the starting wage rate. The starting wage pertains to February–March 1993 for the New Jersey–Pennsylvania sample, and to pre-April 1990 for the Texas sample. FTE employment is full-time equivalent employment. Roy Rogers restaurants were not sampled in Texas.

moderate increases in the minimum, but eventual employment losses if the minimum wage is pushed up "too far." The intuitive explanation for this positive employment effect is based on the observation that, in a monopsonistic equilibrium, the firm maintains a positive stock of vacancies. The firm would gladly hire additional workers at the offered wage but, because it would have to pay a higher wage to its existing workers, is not willing to increase the wage in order to attract more workers. When the minimum wage rises slightly, the recruiting rate also rises, and the firm is able to fill some of its vacancies. If the minimum wage increases too much, however, the firm will have to cut employment in order to raise the marginal revenue product of labor up to the level of the minimum.

In our analysis of the effect of the New Jersey minimum wage on fast-food restaurants in the state, we found that employment increased among restaurants that initially were paying the lowest wages, but was stable (relative to trends in Pennsylvania) for restaurants that already were paying more than the new minimum wage. We found no evidence of a "backward-bending" effect of the minimum wage after dividing restaurants that were affected by the minimum wage into a high-impact group (those that previously were paying the old minimum wage) and a medium-impact group (those that were paying more than the old minimum, but less than the new minimum). In the context of a monopsony model, these findings suggest that at least some firms have a significant degree of monopsony power.[26]

A third implication of the monopsony model concerns the relation between firms' profitability and increases in the minimum wage. As we noted in chapter 10, if firms have discretion over the wages that they set, then the first-order effect of an increase in the wage on the firms' profitability is zero. Our evidence on the stock market's reaction to news of minimum-wage legislation suggests that the value of low-wage employers is not very sensitive to announcements of minimum-wage changes. This finding may be more consistent with a monopsony-like model than with the standard competitive model.

Equilibrium Wage-Setting Models

An important limitation of the simple dynamic model described in the last section is the ad hoc nature of the hiring and quit-rate functions. An increase in the minimum wage presumably affects the wages offered by other firms in the market and therefore shifts the hiring and recruiting functions of any particular firm. Depending on the nature of these shifts, the final equilibrium may be different from the one implied by the analysis of a single firm, taking the hiring and recruiting functions as given. Recently, a number of authors have developed *equilibrium* wage-dispersion models, in which each firm chooses a wage, conditional on the distribution of wages in the market, thereby endogenously determining their hiring and turnover rates. Papers in this vein include those by Burdett and Mortensen (1989), Mortensen and Vishwanath (1991), Chalkley (1991), Lang and Dickens (1993), Burdett and Wright (1994), and Manning (1993).[27] Burdett and Mortensen (1989) and Mortensen and Vishwanath (1991) assumed that workers and firms are homogenous (apart from differences in reservation wages and job-contact rates), whereas Manning (1993) allowed for differences in productivity across workers, and Burdett and Wright (1994) allowed for match-specific heterogeneity across workers and firms.

Burdett and Mortensen's (1989) model is the simplest example of these models. In their basic specification, workers receive a continuous flow of new information about the labor market in the form of "draws" from the distribution of offered wages.[28] Unemployed workers follow a conventional search strategy, adopting an optimal reservation wage and accepting any wage that is higher than their reservation wage. Employed workers also accept any wage offer that is higher than the wage they currently receive. Each worker has the same level of productivity at any firm, and each firm must decide what wage to post. Although firms can choose to pay a lower wage, the result is a lower "recruiting rate" (i.e., a lower rate of acceptance of their wage offer by presently employed workers) and a higher quit rate (i.e., a higher rate of acceptance of outside job offers by their current employees). Because firms are identical, all wage choices yield the same level of profits, and Burdett and Mortensen showed that the equilibrium is characterized by a nondegenerate distribution of wages across firms, with the property that higher-wage firms are larger than lower-wage firms. In a version of the model in which equally productive workers have different reservation wages, Burdett and Mortensen also showed that the imposition of a minimum wage will lead to an decrease in equilibrium unemployment, and to an increase in equilibrium employment, with the employment gains concentrated at the initially smaller/lower-wage firms.

Many of these properties carry over to Manning's (1993) model, although he allowed workers to differ in their relative productivities and in their relative valuations of leisure. Manning assumed that firms post a single wage offer, and then accept any applicant whose productivity level is higher than the offered wage. This "company wage policy" assumption corresponds to the stylized nature of low-wage labor markets and differs from the ex-post bargaining that is assumed in the Diamond (1982a and 1982b) matching model. Manning argued that the posting of a single "take-it-or-leave-it" wage allows the firm to avoid bargaining with individual employees, and also satisfies within-firm fairness constraints. One implication of this policy is that the productivity level of any workers who are actually hired by a firm exceeds their wage, as in a standard monopsony model. This follows directly from the observation that workers are hired *only* if their productivity level is equal to or greater than the offered wage. Manning showed that, as the arrival rate of job information tends to infinity, however, wages converge to individual-specific productivity levels.[29]

In Manning's model, the imposition of a binding minimum wage results in a shift to the right in the entire distribution of wage offers (as in the standard model with a continuum of perfectly substitutable skill types). The effect on unemployment and on the employment rate is ambiguous and can be positive for modest minimum-wage levels (as in Burdett and Mortensen), or negative (as in the standard model with a continuum of skills).

Equilibrium wage-dispersion models provide three important insights about the role of "informational frictions" in the labor market. First, even if workers and firms are identical ex ante, the monopsony power that firms hold over their current employees in a labor market that has search costs leads to an equilibrium in which wages differ systematically across firms. Second, different wage policies can coexist in equilibrium, with some firms choosing a "low-wage/high-turnover" policy, and others choosing a "high-wage/low-turnover" policy. Interestingly, this principle is one that is widely accepted in the personnel field. Personnel textbooks regularly introduce the concept of a wage policy and analyze the costs and benefits of high-wage and low-wage policies (see, for example, Milkovitch and Newman [1987]). Third, even allowing for the endogenous determination of the wage distribution, a minimum wage sometimes can increase employment by forcing the low-wage/high-turnover firms to reduce turnover, and to expand their steady-state labor force. Even if a minimum-wage hike increases employment, however, the welfare implications are ambiguous. In the simplest case of identical workers and identical jobs, the search that arises in the labor market is "inefficient," and a suitably determined minimum wage can improve efficiency. In more complicated models (such as Manning's), a minimum wage could easily increase *or* reduce economic efficiency.

Monopsonistic Effects Arising from Monitoring

The static and dynamic monopsony models considered so far are driven by the assumption that firms can attract and retain more workers if they pay a higher wage. A different source of monopsony-like behavior arises in a model in which workers have some discretion over the level of effort exerted on the job, and firms use a combination of direct monitoring and efficiency wage premiums to induce a higher level of effort. Such a model was presented by Rebitzer and Taylor (1991).[30] Following Shapiro and Stigliz (1984), Rebitzer and Taylor assumed that a worker who loses a higher-paying job suffers a greater loss of utility than does a worker who loses a lower-paying job. Firms can therefore induce a greater level of effort by paying a wage premium and threatening to fire workers who are caught shirking. The firm's optimal policy is to pay a "no-shirking" wage sufficiently high so that the cost of losing the job, multiplied by the probability of detection, just equals the monetized disutility of exerting effort on the job.

Rebitzer and Taylor then assumed that the probability of detection is a strictly decreasing function of the number of nonsupervisory workers hired by the firm. A simple explanation for this assumption is that each firm has one manager, and that, as employment expands, the manager's ability to monitor the effort level of any individual employee decreases. Therefore, it follows directly that the no-shirking wage increases with the number of employees hired by the firm. In choosing an optimal level of employment, the firm sets the marginal revenue product equal to the marginal cost of hiring an additional worker. If the no-shirking wage is an increasing function of employment, then marginal cost is higher than the offered wage, and just as in a standard monopsony model, a gap emerges between marginal productivity and the wage. Also, as in the standard monopsony model, a firm that is forced to increase its offered wage as a result of a minimum-wage hike will *increase* employment, at least for small-enough wage increases.

An interesting aspect of this model is that it potentially can explain why firms do not pay subminimum wages, even if they are legally permitted to do so, and there is a queue of workers who are willing to work for a subminimum. Just as in Shapiro and Stiglitz's original model, employers who fear that low-wage workers will shirk on the job will not necessarily pay wages that are as low as possible.

Summary and Scorecard for Monopsonistic Models

The main implications of the monopsonistic models that we have discussed are summarized in the fifth and sixth columns of Table 11.1. We present the implications of the simple "isolated firm" model in column 5, and the implications of the equilibrium wage dispersion models (Burdett and Mortensen [1989] and Manning [1993]) in column 6. In contrast to the various versions of the standard model in columns 1–4, monopsonistic models have ambiguous predictions with respect to the employment effects of the minimum wage. The monitoring version of the simple monopsony model and Manning's "company wage policy" model also predict nonutilization of subminimum-wage provisions. Like the standard model with a continuum of skills, equilibrium wage dispersion models predict spillover effects of a minimum-wage hike throughout the entire wage distribution. The equilibrium wage dispersion models also rule out a spike at the minimum wage. Otherwise, equilibrium search models can potentially match the observed characteristics of the labor market fairly well.

On the price side, monopsony models generally imply that prices move inversely with employment. Thus, if a minimum wage has no employment effect (or a positive effect), it must have no effect on prices (or a negative effect). This prediction is inconsistent with the patterns of price increases in the restaurant industry that we observed across states and cities (discussed in chapter 4), and in New Jersey relative to Pennsylvania (discussed in chapter 2). It is more consistent with the patterns of price increases that we observed at fast-food restaurants within New Jersey and within Texas.

CONCLUSIONS

We began this chapter by arguing that the standard labor-market model that is routinely presented in the textbooks is incomplete. As we have seen, "the standard model" is actually a rich collection of models, all sharing the fundamental assumption that firms take wages as given. This assumption leads to the unambiguous prediction that an increase in the minimum wage will reduce the employment of workers whose wages are affected by the law. Different versions of the standard model make different predictions about other effects of the minimum wage—its effects on the wages and employment rates of higher-wage workers, for example, or its effects on firms in the uncovered sector. Simple variants of the standard model are also consistent with the absence of a *short-run* effect of the minimum wage on employment.

On the basis of our research in chapters 2–4, we believe that, on average, the employment effects of a minimum-wage increase are close to zero. Sometimes, as in the case of the fast-food industry in New Jersey, an increase in the minimum wage seems to be associated with modest employment gains. Other times, it may well be associated with small employment losses. This range of employment responses, centering on zero, is inconsistent with the proposition that the standard model is *always* correct. Models that depart from the standard model by allowing firms some discretion in the setting of wages have very different implications about the employment effects of a minimum wage. In particular, these models are consistent with a range of employment responses to a modest increase in the minimum wage, including employment gains at some firms, and losses at others. It is possible that the standard model is correct, and that the employment effects that we observed are not true long-run effects. However, this interpretation requires us to treat any positive employment effect as a statistical aberration.

A variety of other evidence on the nature of low-wage labor markets is also more consistent with the view that firms have some control over wage setting than with the extreme view embodied in the standard model that they take the "market wage" as given. Much of this evidence centers on the importance of turnover and recruiting, and the resources that low-wage employers devote to these activities. We suspect that dynamic models, in which firms set wages to balance their hiring and quit rates, capture the essence of the low-wage market better than do static models, which assume that employers can recruit all the workers they want at the going wage. Dynamic models may also prove useful in explaining the wide variation in wages that is observed for seemingly identical low-wage workers. Nevertheless, a rigorous evaluation of the alternative models must await additional research.

NOTES

1. We are assuming that, as the industry adjusts its input demands, the prices of other inputs do not change.

2. Models with local market power are described in Tirole (1988, chapter 7).

3. This follows from the fact that, with a constant demand elasticity, the firm's price is a constant markup over its marginal cost. The assumption of a constant firm-specific demand elasticity is crucial.

4. A simple model to illustrate this point can be constructed as follows. Suppose the demand function facing a particular firm is log-linear: $\log y = A + \epsilon \log p + \delta \log p'$, where p' is the geometric average of prices charged by other firms in the industry, and $\delta > 0$. Assuming that marginal cost, c, is constant, and that each firm chooses its own price, taking the others' prices as given, the first-order condition yields $p = \epsilon/(1+\epsilon)c$ (note that $|\epsilon| > 1$). If a 1 percent increase in wages causes marginal cost to rise by α (labor's share of cost), then each firm's price rises by α percent, and each firm's output declines by $(\epsilon + \delta)\alpha$ percent. Thus, the "effective" demand elasticity for an industry-wide wage increase is $(\epsilon + \delta)$.

5. See Dixit (1976, pp. 78 and 79) for a simple derivation of these equations. Unlike the elasticity of substitution in the two-input case, with more than two inputs, the Allen partial elasticities do not have a simple interpretation in terms of the curvature of the isoquants of the production function (see Blackorby and Russell [1989]).

6. In the case of one labor input and one nonlabor input, the Allen partial elasticity is $\sigma_{11} = -\sigma(1 - \alpha)/\alpha$, where σ is the more-familiar Hicksian

elasticity of substitution between labor and other inputs, and α is labor's cost share.

7. This statement can be proved by showing that a weighted average of skilled and unskilled employment, using as weights the relative wages of the two groups prior to the minimum-wage change, will necessarily fall with a rise in the minimum if $\sigma_{31} > 0$. See Brown, Gilroy, and Kohen (1982, page 493) for another bound on the elasticity of total employment with respect to w_1.

8. The firm's first-order conditions require that the marginal product of human capital equals the standard wage, w.

9. Of course, some fraction of subminimum-wage workers are misclassified because of errors in their reported earnings or hours data.

10. For simplicity, we drop the prime notation distinguishing the conditional and unconditional demand elasticities.

11. This equation follows from the equilibrium condition for the uncovered sector:

$$S(cw_c + (1 - c)w_u) - D^c(w_c) = D^u(w_u),$$

where $D^j(w_j)$ represents demand in sector j and $S(\cdot)$ represents supply.

12. Curiously, Tauchen's results suggest that, in regions in which a higher minimum wage reduces agricultural wages, it also reduces agricultural employment—a correlation that is inconsistent with a simple two-sector model.

13. This formulation differs in some aspects from those of Mincer (1976) and Gramlich (1976) while retaining the basic flavor of their models.

14. Technically, the denominator of (11.12) could be negative. This is unlikely if the uncovered sector is relatively small.

15. The assumption is similar to the assumption in the early search literature that individuals can only search for a better job if they are unemployed (see Devine and Kiefer [1991, chapter 8]).

16. We are grateful to George Johnson for bringing this model to our attention.

17. In the notation of the first section, $MRP(L) = pF_L (L, K^*(L))$ for a firm in a perfectly competitive output market, where $K^*(L)$ is the optimal level of nonlabor inputs (obtained by setting $pF_K(L, K^*(L)) = r$, where r is the price of nonlabor inputs). We suppress the dependence of the marginal revenue product on output and input prices.

18. Because the marginal product of labor is $w^o(1 + 1/\zeta)/p$ (where p is the product price), a k percent increase in wages leads to a $k(1 + \zeta)w^o/p$ increase in output.

19. Modern industrial organization theory is filled with counterexamples, however (see Tirole [1988]).

20. This figure is from our New Jersey–Pennsylvania study.

21. *Nation's Restaurant News* August 8, 1988, p. F46.

22. Meurs (1992) presented an analysis of the application rate for jobs in

the French civil service that is very similar to Krueger's (1988). Her estimates show an elasticity of the application rate with respect to the relative salary of government workers that is comparable to the ones for the United States.

23. The Tobit specification treats wage observations at the minimum wage as if the "true" wage would be lower in the absence of the minimum.

24. Models similar to the one in column 3 of Table 11.2 are reported in Katz and Krueger (1992). The specifications differ in the inclusion of local labor-market variables (which were unavailable for our New Jersey—Pennsylvania sample).

25. Interestingly, this range is very similar to the range of estimates for the establishment-size elasticity reported by Brown and Medoff (1989), using much broader samples of workers and firms.

26. Recall that the maximum employment effect in a monopsony model arises when the wage is raised by a factor of $|\eta|/(\zeta + |\eta|)$. The New Jersey minimum wage rose by 20 percent. If the full 20 percent increase generated the largest possible employment response, and if $|\eta| = 1$, then $\zeta = 3$, implying about a 30 percent gap between wages and marginal productivity among the lowest-wage firms in the state prior to the minimum-wage hike.

27. An earlier paper, by Albrecht and Axell (1984), is similar in some respects. The papers by Diamond (1982a and 1982b) also study a similar issue.

28. In Mortensen and Vishwanath (1990), workers receive draws from the offer distribution *and* from the distribution of "filled" jobs. The latter are interpreted as job leads supplied by friends or social contacts.

29. Technically, the arrival rate must increase relative to the (exogenous) job-dissolution rate.

30. Oi (1990) uses a similar model to explain why wages are higher in larger firms.

CHAPTER 12

Conclusions and Implications

IN THIS CHAPTER, we review our major findings on the effect of the minimum wage and ask "What does it all mean?" Specifically, we highlight some of the implications of our research for public policy discussions about the minimum wage, and for the direction of future research on the minimum wage and the nature of the labor market.

SUMMARY OF BASIC FINDINGS

Our strongest and most important findings concern the effect of the minimum wage on employment. In chapters 2–4, we explored a variety of different "policy experiments" in which an increase in the minimum wage led to an increase in wages for a specific group of workers. The results are summarized in Table 12.1. For each study, we describe the source of the underlying minimum-wage change, the nature of the comparison that is used to infer the effects of the minimum wage, the average wage increase associated with the increase in the minimum wage, and the average effect of the minimum wage on employment. To facilitate comparisons across studies, we have converted all wage and employment effects to proportional changes relative to the preincrease period.

The first two studies, described in chapter 2, use firm-level data from individual fast-food restaurants collected before and after an increase in the minimum wage. As shown by the average wage impacts in rows 1 and 2 of Table 12.1, starting wages in the fast-food industry are directly affected by changes in the minimum wage. We estimate that the April 1992 minimum-wage increase in New Jersey raised starting wages for fast-food restaurants in the state by 11 percent, whereas the April 1991 increase in the federal minimum wage raised starting wages in Texas restaurants by 8 percent. In both cases, contrary to the predictions of the simple textbook model of the minimum wage, our results indicate that the increase in wages was accompanied by an *increase* in employment.

Because of a concern that the long-run impact of the minimum wage might be different from the short-run impact, and a recognition that higher minimum wages might deter the entry of new res-

TABLE 12.1
Summary of Estimated Employment Effects

Analysis	Source of Wage Change (1)	Nature of Comparison (2)	Proportional Effects on	
			Wages (3)	Employment (4)
1. New Jersey–Pennsylvania Fast-Food Restaurants	New Jersey minimum wage rises to $5.05 April 1992	Across states and within NJ between high- and low-wage restaurants	0.11*	0.04
2. Texas Fast-Food Restaurants	Federal minimum wage rises to $4.25 April 1991	Between high- and low-wage restaurants	0.08*	0.20*
3. California Teenagers	California minimum wage rises to $4.25 July 1988	Between teenagers in California and comparison areas	0.10*	0.12
4. Cross-States, Teenagers, 1989–1992	Federal minimum wage rises from $3.35 to 4.25	Across states with higher and lower fractions earning $3.35–4.24 in 1989	0.08*	0.00
5. Cross-States, Workers with Low Predicted Wages, 1989–1992	Federal minimum wage rises from $3.35 to 4.25	Across states with higher and lower fractions earning $3.35–4.24 in 1989	0.07*	0.02
6. Cross-States, Employees in Retail Trade, 1989–1992	Federal minimum wage rises from $3.35 to 4.25	Across states with higher and lower fractions earning $3.35–4.24 in 1989	0.05*	0.01
7. Cross-States, Employees in Restaurant Industry, 1989–1992	Federal minimum wage rises from $3.35 to 4.25	Across states with higher and lower fractions earning $3.35–4.24 in 1989	0.07*	0.03*

Note: Estimated wage and employment effects are proportional changes relative to pre-minimum-wage period. In rows 1 and 2, the wage effects are for starting wages only. In other rows, the wage effects are for mean log wages of the specified group.

*Indicates that the estimate is based on an underlying model in which the effect of the minimum-wage impact variable is statistically significant at the 5 percent level.

taurants, we also examined the rate of restaurant openings and closings in the McDonald's restaurant chain between 1986 and 1991. By comparing restaurant-opening rates across states that followed different minimum-wage policies during the late 1980s, we are able to test whether a higher minimum wage (either state specific or federal) deterred the growth of firms. The results show no evidence that higher minimum wages led to a decrease in the net number of McDonald's restaurants in a state, or to a slower rate of restaurant openings between 1986 and 1991.

The third analysis, presented in chapter 3, uses statewide microdata for workers in California and a group of comparison areas from before and after the July 1988 increase in California's minimum wage. The rise in the minimum wage in California led to a 10 percent increase in wages for teenagers in the state relative to those in the comparison areas. As in the New Jersey–Pennsylvania and Texas studies, we find that the increase in average wages was associated with a relative increase in the employment–population rate of California teenagers. We have also compared teenage employment trends in California with those in other states and continue to find a relative increase in teenage employment after the rise in the minimum wage.

All four analyses presented in chapter 4 make use of statewide data for the 50 states from before and after the 1990 and 1991 increases in the federal minimum wage. In these studies, the effect of the minimum wage is deduced by comparing changes in labor-market outcomes between high-wage states, where the increase in the federal minimum wage had little or no effect on wages, and low-wage states, where the increase pushed further into the existing wage distribution. Again, we find that the rise in the minimum wage led to increases in wages for affected workers. The wages of teenagers, other workers with low predicted wages, and employees in the retail trade and restaurant industries increased as a result of the increase in the federal minimum wage. In every case, however, the estimated effect of the minimum wage on the corresponding employment outcome was either zero or positive.

The absence of negative employment effects in all the studies in Table 12.1 provides reasonably strong evidence against the prediction that a rise in the minimum wage invariably leads to a fall in employment. Although most of the estimated employment effects are insignificantly different from zero, the results are uniformly positive, and relatively precisely estimated. We find zero or positive employment effects for different groups of low-wage workers in different time periods, and in a variety of regions of the country. The weight of this evidence suggests that it is very unlikely that the minimum wage has a large, negative employment effect.

Our second set of findings pertains to the effect of higher minimum wages on prices in the restaurant industry. A comparison of price changes at fast-food restaurants in New Jersey and Pennsylvania after the increase in the New Jersey minimum wage suggests that average prices rose in New Jersey by about enough to cover the costs of the higher minimum wage. Within New Jersey, however, we find that prices rose just as quickly at restaurants that were affected by the law as at higher-wage restaurants that already were paying as much as or more than the new minimum wage. A similar finding emerges in the Texas study. Prices rose at about the same rate at fast-food restaurants that had to make larger or smaller wage adjustments after the rise in the federal minimum wage. Finally, we used two different sources of price data to compare the rates of increase of average restaurant prices across cities and states where the 1990 and 1991 changes in the federal minimum wage had bigger and smaller effects on the wages of restaurant workers. The findings are imprecise, but point toward price increases of about the magnitude required to cover the higher cost of labor associated with the rise in the minimum wage.

Our third set of findings concerns other features of the labor market that are difficult to reconcile with the simplest textbook model. We identify four important anomalies in the low-wage labor market: (1) the presence of a large "spike" in the wage distribution at the minimum wage; (2) the tendency for a minimum-wage hike to generate pay increases for workers who previously were earning more than the new minimum (a so-called ripple effect); (3) the absence of systematic evidence that employers reduce nonwage benefits in order to offset an increase in the minimum wage; and (4) the extremely low utilization rate of youth and training subminimum provisions. Considered individually, each feature can be explained by a suitably modified version of the textbook model. It is more difficult to develop a unified explanation for their coexistence. Perhaps as importantly, the textbook model assumes that equally skilled workers are paid the same wage at all employers. It is difficult (although not impossible) to reconcile this assumption with the range of wages that exist in the labor market for seemingly identical workers. As Heckman and MaCurdy (1988, p. 232) observed with respect to labor-supply theories, "A soft protective belt of plausible omitted (unobserved) variables can always be erected to rationalize any empirical outcome." At some point, however, the underlying theoretical model presumably loses its usefulness as an analytical tool.

Our last set of new empirical results concerns the distributional effect of the minimum wage. Using a methodology similar to the cross-state employment comparisons presented in chapter 4, we measure the effect of the minimum wage on the distribution of hourly wages, the distribution of family earnings, and the poverty rate. We find that the most recent increases in the federal minimum wage led to significant increases in wages for workers at the bottom of the wage distribution, and to a reduction in overall wage dispersion. We estimate that the 1990 and 1991 increases in the minimum wage rolled back a significant fraction of the cumulated increase in wage inequality from the previous decade.

Workers who earn the minimum wage or slightly more than the minimum wage are disproportionately drawn from families in the lower portion of the earnings distribution. Indeed, about one-third of workers whose wages were affected by the 1990 and 1991 increases in the federal minimum wage lived in families in the bottom 10 percent of the earnings distribution. Consistent with this high degree of concentration, we find that the increase in the minimum wage led to increases in the lower percentiles of family earnings, and to an increase in the share of earnings going to families at the bottom of the distribution. Nevertheless, given the relatively small magnitude of the earnings transfers generated by the 1990–1991 increases in the federal minimum wage—about 0.2 percent of total earnings, or $5.5 billion per year—the actual effects of the minimum wage on the standard of living of families with low earnings are modest.

We also study the effects of the minimum wage on the value of firms, using a standard event study methodology to correlate changes in the market value of firms that are likely to employ minimum-wage workers with news about legislative changes in the minimum wage. Our results are mixed. Most of the news about the impending minimum-wage increases during the late 1980s led to little or no change in the market value of low-wage employers. In contrast, more recent news of possible revisions in the minimum wage may have led to small declines in the market value of these firms.

A final aspect of our work is the reanalysis of the previous literature, both for the U.S. and abroad, that has concentrated on measuring the employment effects of the minimum wage. Our reevaluation suggests that the evidence in the previous literature is less compelling, and less decisive, than many economists recognize. Some of the studies are flawed by a failure to consider the source of the wage variation that drives their empirical findings. Other studies suffer from the absence of a credible control group, whose employment experiences can be used as a "counterfactual" for the experiences of workers affected by the minimum wage. Perhaps the strongest, and certainly the most widely cited, evidence of a negative employment effect of the minimum wage comes from time-series studies of the aggregate teenage employment rate. Unlike the analyses summarized in Table 12.1, time-series studies rely on the assumption that observations from other time periods (during which the minimum wage was lower or higher) can be used as a counterfactual for the present. We view this as a less compelling methodology than the use of other labor markets in the *same* time period as a counterfactual. In any case, our update of the time-series evidence shows that the estimated employment effect of an increase in the minimum wage is smaller, and no longer statistically distinguishable from zero, after data from the 1980s have been added. Wellington (1991) and Klerman (1992) reached similar conclusions. In addition, a meta-analysis of the previous time-series literature suggests that the statistical significance of the earlier findings might have been overstated by specification searching and/or publication bias.

These findings have implications both for minimum-wage policy and for the direction of future research on the labor market and the minimum wage. We consider these two sets of implications in turn.

Policy Implications

Despite the generally negative opinion of the minimum wage held by most professional economists, minimum wages remain politically popular. Depending on how the question is phrased, and when it is asked, opinion polls consistently show that 65 to 90 percent of the general public favor an increase in the minimum wage. Support for a minimum-wage increase is surprisingly broad and tends to be even higher among younger people, nonwhites, and those with lower family incomes. A 1987 Gallup poll found that 66 percent of Republicans and 84 percent of Democrats favored an increase in the minimum wage, to $4.65 per hour (*The Gallup Poll* [1987]). More recently, an October 1993 NBC–Wall Street Journal poll found 64 percent of adults in favor of another increase in the minimum wage. It is probably safe to assume that the minimum wage will continue to attract the attention of policymakers in the foreseeable future.

Another feature that contributes to the popularity of the minimum wage is the fact that a change in the minimum wage does not affect government spending directly. The minimum wage is a classic example of an employer mandate. In an era during which the government budget constraint is very tight, and increases in direct taxation are politically infeasible, the minimum wage and other mandate programs are more attractive policy options.

What are the implications of our findings for policy discussions of the minimum wage? At the outset, it should be noted that many economists view the minimum wage as a highly inefficient transfer program and, therefore, usually recommend its repeal. Our findings suggest that the efficiency aspects of a modest rise in the minimum wage are overstated. In the diverse set of policy experiments summarized in Table 12.1, we find no evidence for a large, negative employment effect of higher minimum wages. Even in the earlier literature, however, the magnitude of the predicted employment losses associated with a typical increase in the minimum wage are relatively small. This is not to say that the employment losses from a much higher minimum wage would be small: the evidence at hand is relevant only for a moderate range of minimum wages, such as those that prevailed in the U.S. labor market during the past few decades. Within this range, however, there is little reason to believe that increases in the minimum wage will generate large employment losses.

For moderate levels of the minimum wage, we believe that our findings suggest a reorientation of policy discussions away from the efficiency aspects of the minimum wage and toward distributional issues, such as the characteristics of workers and families who receive pay increases from an increase in the minimum wage, and the effect of the minimum wage on profits and prices. Chapters 9 and 10 of this book attempt to fill in some of the gaps in our knowledge about the distributional impact of the minimum wage. Our findings suggest that the distributional effects of a typical increase in the minimum wage are relatively small, although they tend to reduce inequality. For example, ignoring any employment effects or ripple effects, we estimate that the 1990 and 1991 increases in the federal minimum wage transferred about $5.5 billion per year to low-wage workers. This is a very small fraction of the total wage bill in the economy (0.2 percent). Even if all these transfers were received by low-income families (which they were not), such a modest sum can make only a small difference in the overall distribution of incomes in the economy. By the same token, the potential effects of such an increase in wages on economy-wide prices is also small. For example, if *all* the costs of a higher minimum wage were passed through to consumer prices, the net effect would be a once-and-for-all increase in retail prices of only about 0.3 percent.

Another aspect of the minimum wage that warrants additional policy discussion is its effect on the supply side of the labor market.

Working from the standard textbook model of the labor market, economists have tended to concentrate on the demand-side effects of a higher minimum wage. Our finding that the employment effects of a higher minimum wage are negligible, or even sometimes positive, calls for more attention to the supply side of the labor market. An increase in the minimum wage clearly affects the value of work for a sizable fraction of less-skilled workers in the economy. Relative to some other transfer programs, the minimum wage has the feature of "making work pay," rather than discouraging labor-market participation. In our view, the supply-side effects of the minimum wage deserve more attention in the policy arena.

A third issue that is brought into focus by our analysis of "anomalies" in the labor market is the fact that the minimum wage is a floor on total *wage payments*, rather than on total compensation. At present, federal law permits tipped employees to count tips for as much as 50 percent of the minimum wage, and also allows a subminimum for a small fraction of workers.[1] An interesting question is whether medical insurance premiums or other nonwage benefits should also be credited toward meeting the minimum wage. If the relative costs of health insurance and other nonwage benefits continue to rise, this question may take on added importance.

A final issue that is often raised in policy discussions about the minimum wage is the question of indexation.[2] Many economists have opposed indexation on the same grounds that they oppose the minimum wage itself, arguing that, even if the minimum wage cannot be repealed by legislation, it should be gradually repealed by inflation. Again, the evidence in this book suggests the need for a reconsideration of the costs and benefits of indexation. On the one hand, our findings suggest that the efficiency costs of the minimum wage are probably small. On the other hand, they also show that the minimum wage is an important determinant of the level of wage dispersion in the economy. Recent work by DiNardo, Fortin, and Lemieux (1994) has shown that the decline in the real value of the minimum wage throughout the 1980s accounted for 20 to 30 percent of the increase in wage inequality during the decade. Our own findings indicate that the 1990 and 1991 increases in the federal minimum wage eliminated a roughly equivalent share of overall wage dispersion. As in the more general policy discussion on the minimum wage, we believe that discussions about indexation should place greater emphasis on distributional issues.

A practical question concerning indexation must be addressed as well: If the minimum wage is indexed, what should it be indexed to? One possible answer is the Consumer Price Index (CPI). However, this choice poses a difficulty. During the past two decades, average wages for less-skilled workers—even those who typically would earn more than the minimum wage—have not kept pace with inflation. A minimum wage indexed to the CPI runs the risk of eventually rising much farther into the wage distribution than its current level.[3] Such an increase may push the minimum wage outside the moderate range of the past and could well have adverse consequences for employment.

An alternative that is sometimes suggested is to index the minimum wage to the average wage in the economy. Because an increase in the minimum wage has some effect on the average level of wages, indexation of the minimum wage to the average wage might result in an unintended spiral effect. Furthermore, if recent trends toward widening wage inequality continue, indexation of the minimum wage to the average wage may push the minimum wage further up the wage distribution. A third alternative is to index the minimum wage to a lower percentile of the wage distribution, such as the 25th or the 30th percentile. Obviously, this choice would prevent the minimum wage from rising too quickly relative to the lower tail of the wage distribution.

Regardless of the precise formula, however, indexation of the minimum wage raises two political issues. On the one hand, a debate over the minimum wage gives politicians a clear opportunity to take a stand on a simple and well-understood issue, and to signal their position to various constituency groups.[4] Indexation of the minimum wage would eliminate these potentially valuable opportunities. On the other hand, once written into law, an indexation formula becomes extremely difficult to change, even if circumstances change, or if obvious problems with application of the formula become apparent.[5] Thus, there may be some political risk in codifying a specific indexation formula.

It is worth stressing that the intensity of the political debate surrounding the minimum wage—on both sides of the issue—is out of proportion to its real importance in the economy. Our findings suggest that the minimum wage is a modest transfer program with relatively small efficiency losses. Opponents tend to exaggerate its adverse employment effects, while proponents tend to exaggerate its effects on poverty. Similar observations have led Charles Brown (1988) to question whether the minimum wage is overrated as a subject of public policy concern.

IMPLICATIONS FOR ECONOMIC RESEARCH

The minimum wage is a favorite topic of economic research. As shown in Table 12.2, a computerized search of the economics litera-

TABLE 12.2
Number of Economics Articles Published on Selected Programs, 1969–1994, and Annual Spending on the Programs

Program	Number of Journal Articles (1)	Annual Program Spending (Billions, 1993) (2)
1. Minimum Wage	327	—
2. Aid to Families with Dependent Children (AFDC)	89	22.3
3. Food Stamps	47	26.3
4. Medicaid	132	132.0
5. Head Start	8	2.8
6. Occupational Safety and Health Act (OSHA)	51	—
7. Unemployment Insurance	707	35.3
8. Workers' Compensation Insurance	38	62.0
9. Federal Job-Training Programs (e.g., Job Training Partnership Act, Job Corps)	34	3.6

Source: Column 1: authors' tabulations based on a search of *EconLit*, March 1994, Silver Platter 3.0. Column 2: 1993 *Green Book*, except row 8, which is taken from *John Burton's Workers' Compensation Monitor*, volume 6 (March/April 1993). All cost estimates are for the 1993 fiscal year, except the estimate in row 8, which is for 1992.

ture reveals that more than 300 journal articles have been published on the minimum wage during the past 25 years. By comparison, the number of articles on most other labor-market programs is far smaller: fewer than 100 articles have been published on AFDC, and even fewer have been published on Food Stamps, the Occupational Safety and Health Act, Workers' Compensation, Head Start, or federal job-training programs. Among the programs surveyed in the table, only Unemployment Insurance has attracted more professional attention from economists. The number of articles written on the minimum wage is even more remarkable when the relative size of the transfer created by the minimum wage is taken into account. Although there is no easy way to estimate the total cost of the minimum wage, recall that the 1990 and 1991 *increases* in the federal minimum, which raised the minimum by 27 percent, transferred about $5.5 billion. A minimum wage increase probably generates a smaller transfer than many other government programs.

What accounts for economists' fascination with the minimum wage? Perhaps the main reason is that the minimum wage provides a simple and direct test of the kind of theoretical reasoning that economists routinely apply to other, more complicated phenomena, and to many policy questions. Irrespective of the exact parameters determining supply and demand behavior, the standard model makes the unambiguous prediction that an increase in the minimum wage will lead to a reduction in employment. By comparison, the predictions of the standard model for the effects of a cyclical demand shock, or a change in the tax code, depend crucially on specific modeling assumptions and unknown behavioral parameters.

The findings summarized in Table 12.1 suggest that the direct test posed by the minimum wage fails to confirm the predictions of the conventional model. In addition, several other anomalies in the low-wage labor market are difficult to reconcile with the simplest versions of the standard model. The conventional model is somewhat more successful in describing the effects of the minimum wage on restaurant prices. Even here, however, our findings with respect to price changes in New Jersey and Texas after increases in the minimum wage are inconsistent with the standard model. All this evidence suggests to us that the conventional model is *incomplete*. A similar view of the evidence is expressed by Richard Freeman (1994):

> If your prior was that moderate increases in the U.S. minimum risk large job losses, the new evidence should move you to a major rethink. . . . If your prior was that U.S. minimums have only marginal negative effects on employment, the new evidence should move you to wonder about monopsony, disequilibrium situations in the market and the like . . .

We believe there is a need to reformulate the set of theoretical models that are applied to the low-wage labor market, taking into account the fact that increases in the minimum wage do not necessarily lead to decreases in employment, and perhaps other characteristics of the labor market, such as the spike in the wage distribution at the minimum wage, the frequent failure of employers to use the subminimum, and the variability of wages across firms. As we noted in chapter 11, models in which firms have some discretionary power over wages are potentially capable of explaining a broader range of reactions to an increase in the minimum wage. This modification and/or other extensions to the standard model may prove useful in improving the predictive abilities of economic theory in the labor market.

Our findings also have a number of implications for the direction of future empirical work on the labor market and the minimum wage. One leading implication is the importance of a credible research design. In our studies, we have emphasized the so-called natural-experiments approach, which makes use of a well-defined comparison group (or groups) to estimate the labor-market outcomes that would have been observed in the absence of a change in the minimum wage. The minimum wage is a policy that is particularly amenable to this approach, because minimum wages often vary across states, and even a uniform federal minimum-wage increase has varying effects across states, depending on the overall level of wages in a state. Perhaps as important as the concept of a comparison group is the notion of an *a priori* research design. In seeking to test a simple theoretical prediction such as the employment effect of a higher minimum wage, it is important to be able to spell out the comparisons that will constitute the "test" well in advance of the data analysis. This is especially true if the test concerns a generally accepted theory. By prespecifying the research design, analysts can hope to obtain broad agreement on the methodology, even if the interpretation of the findings is controversial. Prespecified research designs are widely used in the natural sciences and may eventually see wider acceptance in economics.

A second broad implication of our research findings is the value of firm-level microdata for testing hypotheses about employment demand. During the past three decades, the field of labor economics has been revolutionized by the widespread availability of individual microdata. These data have led to a vast improvement in our understanding of the determinants of wages and have altered significantly the analysis of such topics as discrimination, unionism, and education. Comparable data on the demand side are as yet unavailable. It is clear to us, however, that additional progress in modeling the labor market will depend in part on the availability of firm-level data.

A number of specific issues strike us as high-priority areas for future empirical work. First, the need for additional long-term analysis of the effects of the minimum wage is clear-cut. Although we have presented some longer-term comparisons, the bulk of the evidence in this book is based on changes that have occurred over a period of one to three years. It is possible that the full impact of a higher minimum wage will become apparent only after a relatively long time. A major difficulty confronting this type of analysis, however, is that most of the impact of a typical increase in the minimum wage is eroded by inflation after three or four years. Furthermore, over the course of several years, many other factors might impinge on the labor market, making it difficult to sort out the effect of a modest change in the minimum wage.

A second and related topic is the effect of minimum wages on the profitability and output of firms. Economists have access to relatively good employment data for specific groups of low-wage workers, and for specific low-wage industries. We have much weaker data on the outputs of firms and industries that are affected by the minimum wage, and on the determinants of profitability. More and better firm-specific data would greatly improve our knowledge about the effects of the minimum wage on productivity and profits.

A third area in which our evidence is ambiguous, and in which additional research would be valuable, is in the realm of prices. Our analysis of pricing in the fast-food industry is based on a limited set of prices. It is an open question whether firms tend to raise all their product prices together in response to an increase in the minimum wage, or whether a higher fraction of cost increases is shifted to certain types of customers (for example, lunch-time customers versus breakfast or dinner customers).

Finally, we believe that future empirical work on the low-wage labor market and the minimum wage should focus explicitly on modeling the sources of wage variation across firms, and on measuring the degree of discretion that individual employers have in setting wages. To conduct this analysis, it will be necessary to combine data on turnover, vacancies, and recruiting flows with data on the hiring standards and skill characteristics of workers at different firms.

Although many economists may disagree with our interpretation of the findings in this book, we hope that they will at least agree on the value of testing the implications of standard economic theory, and on the validity of our empirical approach. We think that the methods we have laid out—committing to an *ex ante* research design, attempting to mimic experimental conditions, identifying and testing alternative comparison groups, and using a number of different data sets and policy experiments—can lead to a clearer understanding of the validity of economic hypotheses and, ultimately, to a more complete description of the labor market.

NOTES

1. The youth subminimum provision that figured so prominently in the 1989 amendments to the Fair Labor Standard Act was phased out of existence in 1993.

2. Indexation of the federal minimum wage has been proposed (and defeated) on several occasions. The original version of the Fair Labor Standard Amendments Bill of 1977 (S. 1871) contained an indexing provision that was defeated. See Krehbiel and Rivers (1988).

3. A similar concern has arisen with respect to the indexation of Social

Security benefits. Because Social Security benefits are indexed to the CPI, the level of benefits relative to the hourly earnings of the median worker in the economy has risen during the past 20 years. Relative to hourly earnings of workers at the 25th percentile of the earnings distribution, the increase has been even greater.

4. A similar point is sometimes raised in reference to the use of cost-of-living escalation clauses in union contracts (see, for example, Garbarino [1962]). An indexed contract reduces union leaders' opportunity to show their value to union members, because most wage increases become "automatic."

5. For example, the original indexation formula for Social Security benefits resulted in "double indexation" for a cohort of recipients. See McKay and Schnobel (1981).

References

Abowd, John M. 1989. "The Effect of Wage Bargains on the Stock Market Value of the Firm." *American Economic Review*, 79:774–90.

Abowd, John M., and Mark R. Killingsworth. 1981. "Structural Models of the Effects of Minimum Wages on Employment by Age Groups." In *Report of the Minimum Wage Study Commission*, vol. 5. Washington, D.C.: U.S. Government Printing Office.

Adams, F. Gerard. 1989. "The Macroeconomic Impacts of Increasing the Minimum Wage." *Journal of Policy Modeling*, 11:179–90.

Albrecht, James W., and Bo Axell. 1984. "An Equilibrium Model of Search Unemployment." *Journal of Political Economy*, 92:824–40.

Allen, Roy George Douglas. 1938. *Mathematical Analysis for Economists*. London: Macmillan.

Alpert, William T. 1986. *The Minimum Wage in the Restaurant Industry*. New York: Praeger.

American Chamber of Commerce Research Association. 1990. *Cost of Living Index: Comparative Data for 291 Urban Areas* (First Quarter 1990). Louisville, KY: ACCRA.

Angrist, Joshua D. 1991. "The Draft Lottery and Voluntary Enlistment in the Vietnam Era." *Journal of the American Statistical Association*, 86:584–95.

Angrist, Joshua D., and Alan B. Krueger. 1991. "Does Compulsory School Attendance Affect Schooling and Earnings?" *Quarterly Journal of Economics*, 106:979–1014.

————. 1994. "Split Sample Instrumental Variables." Technical Working Paper, no. 150. Cambridge, MA: National Bureau of Economic Research, Inc.

Ashenfelter, Orley, and David Card. 1981. "Using Longitudinal Data to Estimate the Employment Effects of the Minimum Wage." Discussion Paper, no. 98. London: London School of Economics.

Ashenfelter, Orley, and Timothy Hannan. 1986. "Sex Discrimination and Product Market Competition: The Case of the Banking Industry." *Quarterly Journal of Economics*, 101:149–73.

Ashenfelter, Orley, and Robert Smith. 1979. "Compliance with the Minimum Wage Law." *Journal of Political Economy*. 87:333–50.

Baumol, William, and Alan Blinder. 1979. *Economics: Principles and Policy*. New York: Harcourt Brace Jovanovich, Inc.

————. 1991. *Economics: Principles and Policy*. New York: Harcourt Brace Jovanovich, Inc.

Baumol, William, and Edward Wolff. 1993. "Puerto Rican Catch Up in the Postwar Period." Unpublished paper. New York: New York University Department of Economics.

Becker, Brian E., and Craig A. Olson. 1986. "The Consequences of Strikes for Shareholder Equity." *Industrial and Labor Relations Review*, 39:425–38.

———. 1989. "Unionization and Shareholder Interests." *Industrial and Labor Relations Review*, 42:246–61.

Becker, Gary, and George Stigler. 1974. "Law Enforcement, Malfeasance and the Compensation of Enforcers." *Journal of Legal Studies*, 3:1–18.

Begg, Colin B., and Jesse A. Berlin. 1988. "Publication Bias: A Problem in Interpreting Medical Data." *Journal of the Royal Statistical Society*, 151:419–63.

Berlin, Jesse A., Colin B. Begg, and Thomas A. Louis. 1989. "An Assessment of Publication Bias Using a Sample of Published Clinical Trials." *Journal of the American Statistical Association*, 84:381–92.

Betsey, Charles L., and Bruce H. Dunson. 1981. "Federal Minimum Wage Laws and the Employment of Minority Youth." *Papers and Proceedings of the American Economic Association*, 71:379–84.

Blackburn, McKinley L., David E. Bloom, and Richard B. Freeman. 1990. "The Declining Economic Position of Less-Skilled American Males." In *A Future of Lousy Jobs?* edited by Gary Burtless. Washington, D.C.: The Brookings Institution.

Blackorby, Charles, and R. Robert Russell. 1989. "Will the Real Elasticity of Substitution Please Stand Up? (A Comparsion of the Allen/Uzawa and Morishima Elasticities)." *American Economic Review*, 79:882–88.

Blank, Rebecca, and David Card. 1993. "Poverty, Income Distribution, and Growth: Are They Still Connected?" In *Brookings Papers on Economic Activity*, edited by William C. Brainard and George L. Perry, vol. 2. Washington, D.C.: The Brookings Institution.

Blau, Francine, and Lawrence M. Kahn. 1981. "Race and Sex Differences in Quits by Young Workers." *Industrial and Labor Relations Review*, 34:563–77.

Bloch, Farrell E. 1980. "Political Support for Minimum Wage Legislation." *Journal of Labor Research*, 1:245–53.

———. 1989. "Political Support for Minimum Wage Legislation: 1989." *Journal of Labor Research*, 13:187–90.

Boschen, John F., and Herschel I. Grossman. 1981. "The Federal Minimum Wage, Employment, and Inflation." In *Report of the Minimum Wage Study Commission*, vol. 6. Washington, D.C.: U.S. Government Printing Office.

Brown, Charles. 1988. "Minimum Wage Laws: Are They Overrated?" *Journal of Economic Perspectives*, 2:133–47.

Brown, Charles, Curtis Gilroy, and Andrew Kohen. 1982. "The Effect of the Minimum Wage on Employment and Unemployment." *Journal of Economic Literature*, 20:487–528.

———. 1983. "Time Series Evidence on the Effect of the Minimum Wage on Youth Employment and Unemployment." *Journal of Human Resources*, 18:3–31.

Brown, Charles, and James Medoff. 1989. "The Employer Size-Wage Effect." *Journal of Political Economy*, 97:1027–59.

Brown, Jared J., and Jerold B. Warner. 1985. "Using Daily Stock Returns: The Case of Event Studies." *Journal of Financial Economics*, 14:3–31.

Burdett, Kenneth, and Dale T. Mortensen. 1989. "Equilibrium Wage Differentials and Employer Size." Discussion Paper, no. 860. Evanston, IL: Northwestern University Center for Mathematical Studies in Economics and Management Science.

Burdett, Kenneth, and Randall Wright. 1994. "Two-Sided Search." Staff Report, no. 169. Minneapolis, MN: Federal Reserve Bank of Minneapolis, Research Department.

Bureau of National Affairs. 1985. *Retail/Services Labor Report* (Special Supplement on Employee Relations in the Fast Food Industry), 72, June 10. Washington, D.C.: Bureau of National Affairs, Inc.

———. 1987a. *Daily Labor Report*, August 17. Washington, D.C.: Bureau of National Affairs, Inc.

———. 1987b. *Daily Labor Report*, December 24. Washington, D.C.: Bureau of National Affairs, Inc.

———. 1988a. *Daily Labor Report*, July 1. Washington, D.C.: Bureau of National Affairs, Inc.

———. 1988b. *Daily Labor Report*, July 14. Washington, D.C.: Bureau of National Affairs, Inc.

———. 1988c. *Daily Labor Report*, November 7. Washington, D.C.: Bureau of National Affairs, Inc.

———. 1989. *Daily Labor Report*, June 14. Washington, D.C.: Bureau of National Affairs, Inc.

———. 1993. *Daily Labor Report*, March 18. Washington, D.C.: Bureau of National Affairs, Inc.

———. 1994. *Daily Labor Report*, April. 14. Washington, D.C.: Bureau of National Affairs, Inc.

———. Undated. *Labor Relations Reporter Wages and Hours Manual.* Washington, D.C.: Bureau of National Affairs, Inc.

Burkhauser, Richard V., and Andrew J. Glenn. 1994. "Public Policies for the Working Poor: The Earned Income Tax Credit Versus Minimum Wage Legislation." Income Security Policy Series Paper, no. 8. Syracuse, NY: Maxwell School of Citizenship and Public Affairs.

Burtless, Gary. 1993. "The Case for Randomized Field Trials in Economic and Policy Research." Unpublished paper. Washington, D.C.: The Brookings Institution.

Buse, A. 1992. "The Bias of Instrumental Variables Estimators." *Econometrica*, 60:173–80.

Campbell, III, Carl M. 1993. "Do Firms Pay Efficiency Wages? Evidence with Data at the Firm Level." *Journal of Labor Economics*, 11:442–70.

Campbell, Donald T. 1957. "Factors Relevant to the Validity of Experiments in Social Settings." *Psychological Bulletin*, 54:297–312.

———. 1969. "Reforms as Experiments." *American Psychologist*, 24:409–29.

Card, David. 1989. "Deregulation and Labor Earnings in the Airline Industry." Working Paper, no. 247. Princeton, NJ: Princeton University Industrial Relations Section.

———. 1990. "The Impact of the Mariel Boatlift on the Miami Labor Market." *Industrial and Labor Relations Review*, 44:245–57.

Card, David. 1992a. "Using Regional Variation in Wages to Measure the Effects of the Federal Minimum Wage." *Industrial and Labor Relations Review*, 46:22–37.

———. 1992b. "Do Minimum Wages Reduce Employment? A Case Study of California, 1987– 1989." *Industrial and Labor Relations Review*, 46:38–54.

Card, David, Lawrence F. Katz, and Alan B. Krueger. 1994. "Comment on David Neumark and William Wascher, 'Employment Effects of Minimum and Subminimum Wages: Panel Data on State Minimum Wage Laws.'" *Industrial and Labor Relations Review*, 48:487–96.

Card, David, and Alan B. Krueger. 1994. "Minimum Wages and Employment: A Case Study of the Fast-Food Industry In New Jersey and Pennsylvania." *American Economic Review*, 84:772–93.

Card, David, and Thomas Lemieux. 1994. "Changing Wage Structure and Black–White Wage Differentials." *Papers and Proceedings of the American Economic Association*, 84:29–33.

Castillo-Freeman, Alida, and Richard Freeman. 1990. "Minimum Wages in Puerto Rico: Textbook Case of a Wage Floor?" *Industrial Relations Research Association Proceedings*, 43:243–53.

———. 1992. "When the Minimum Wage Really Bites: The Effect of the U.S.-Level Minimum on Puerto Rico." In *Immigration and the Work Force*, edited by George Borjas and Richard Freeman. Chicago: University of Chicago Press.

Chalkley, Martin. 1991. "Monopsony Wage Determination and Multiple Unemployment Equilibria in a Non-Linear Search Model." *Review of Economic Studies*, 58:181–93.

Charner, Ivan, and Bryna Shore Fraser. 1984. *Fast Food Jobs*. Washington, D.C.: National Institute for Work and Learning.

Cochran, William G. 1957. "Analysis of Covariance: Its Nature and Uses." *Biometrics*, 13:261–81.

Colander, David, and Arjo Klamer. 1987. "The Making of an Economist." *Journal of Economic Perspectives*, 1:95–111.

Cox, D. R., and D. V. Hinkley. 1974. *Theoretical Statistics*. London: Chapman and Hall, Ltd.

Cullen, Donald E. 1961. "Minimum Wage Laws." Bulletin 43. Ithaca, NY: New York State School of Industrial and Labor Relations.

Currie, Janet, and Bruce C. Fallick. 1994. "The Minimum Wage and the Employment of Youth: Evidence from the NLSY." Unpublished paper. Los Angeles: University of California at Los Angeles Department of Economics.

Davis, Eleanor. 1936. "Minimum Wage Legislation in the United States: Summary of Fact and Opinion." Princeton, NJ: Princeton University Industrial Relations Section.

De Long, J. Bradford, and Kevin Lang. 1992. "Are All Economic Hypotheses False?" *Journal of Political Economy*, 100:1257–72.

Devine, Theresa J., and Nicholas M. Kiefer. 1991. *Empirical Labor Economics: The Search Approach*. Oxford: Oxford University Press.

Diamond, Peter A. 1982a. "Wage Determination and Efficiency in Search Equilibrium." *Review of Economic Studies*, 49:217–27.

_____. 1982b. "Aggregate Demand Management in Search Equilibrium." *Journal of Political Economy*, 90:881–94.

Dickens, Richard, Stephen Machin, and Alan Manning. 1994. "The Effects of Minimum Wages on Employment: Theory and Evidence from the UK." Working Paper, no. 4742. Cambridge, MA: National Bureau of Economic Research, Inc.

DiNardo, John, Nicole M. Fortin, and Thomas Lemieux. 1994. "Labor Market Institutions and the Distribution of Wages, 1973–92: A Semiparametric Approach." Unpublished paper. Montreal: University of Montreal Department of Economics.

Dixit, A. K. 1976. *Optimization in Economic Theory*. Oxford: Oxford University Press.

Dollar General Corporation. 1992. *10-K Report Filed with the U.S. Security and Exchange Commission*. Taken from *Disclosure SEC Database* (1994 edition). Bethesda, MD: Disclosure Incorporated.

Ehrenberg, Ronald G., and Alan J. Marcus. 1980. "Minimum Wage Legislation and the Educational Outcomes of Youths." In *Research in Labor Economics*, edited by Ronald Ehrenberg, vol. 3. Greenwich, CT: JAI Press.

_____. 1982. "Minimum Wages and Teenagers' Enrollment–Employment Outcomes: A Multinomial Logit Model." *Journal of Human Resources*, 17:39–52.

Ehrenberg, Ronald, and Robert Smith. 1994. *Modern Labor Economics: Theory and Public Policy*. New York: HarperCollins Publishers, Inc.

Fisher, Alan A. 1973. "The Minimum Wage and Teenage Unemployment: A Comment on the Literature." *Western Economic Journal*, 11:514–24.

Fitoussi, Jean-Paul. 1994. "Wage Distribution and Unemployment: The French Experience." *Papers and Proceedings of the American Economic Association*, 84: 59–64.

Flaim, Paul. Undated. "Employment and Unemployment in Puerto Rico." Mimeograph. Washington, D.C.: U.S. Department of Commerce, Bureau of the Census.

Fleisher, Belton. 1970. *Labor Economics: Theory and Evidence*. Englewood Cliffs, NJ: Prentice-Hall, Inc.

Freedman, David, Robert Pisani, and Roger Purves. 1978. *Statistics*. New York: W.W. Norton and Company.

Freeman, Richard B. 1981. "Black Economic Progress After 1964: Who Has Gained and Why?" In *Studies in Labor Markets*, edited by Sherwin Rosen. Chicago: University of Chicago Press.

_____. 1982. "Economic Determinants of Geographic and Individual Variation in the Labor Market Position of Young Persons." In *The Youth Labor Market: Its Nature, Causes and Consequences*, edited by Richard B. Freeman and David A. Wise. Chicago: University of Chicago Press.

_____. 1994. "Minimum Wages—Again!" *International Journal of Manpower*, 15:8–25.

Freeman, Richard B., Wayne Gray, and B. Casey Ichniowski. 1981. "Low Cost Student Labor: The Use and Effects of the Subminimum Wage Provisions for Full-Time Students." In *Report of the Minimum Wage Study Commission*, vol. 5. Washington, D.C.: U.S. Government Printing Office.

Freeman, Richard B., and James L. Medoff. 1984. *What Do Unions Do?* New York: Basic Books.

Fritsch, Conrad. 1981. "Exemptions from the Fair Labor Standards Act, Retail Trade and Services." In *Report of the Minimum Wage Study Commission,* vol. 5. Washington, D.C.: U.S. Government Printing Office.

Gallup, Jr., George. 1987. *The Gallup Poll: Public Opinion 1987.* Wilmington, DE: Scholarly Resources Inc.

Garbarino, Joseph W. 1962. *Wage Policy and Long Term Contracts.* Washington, D.C.: The Brookings Institution.

GB Foods Corporation. 1992. *10-K Report Filed with the U.S. Security and Exchange Commission.* Taken from *Disclosure SEC Database* (1994 edition). Bethesda, MD: Disclosure Incorporated.

Gibbons, Robert, and Lawrence F. Katz. 1992. "Does Unmeasured Ability Explain Inter-Industry Wage Differentials?" *Review of Economic Studies,* 59:515–35.

Gramlich, Edward M. 1976. "Impact of Minimum Wages on Other Wages, Employment and Family Incomes." In *Brookings Papers on Economic Activity,* edited by Arthur M. Okun and George L. Perry, vol. 2. Washington, D.C.: The Brookings Institution.

Grenier, Gilles, and Marc Séguin. 1991. "L'incidence du Salaire Minimum sur le Marché du Travail des Adolescents au Canada: Une Reconsidération des Résultats Empiriques." *L'Actualité Economique,* 67:123–43.

Grossberg, Adam, and Paul Sicilian. 1994. "Minimum Wages, On-the-Job Training and Wage Growth." Unpublished paper. Hartford, CT: Trinity College Department of Economics.

Grossman, Jean B. 1983. "The Impact of the Minimum Wage on Other Wages." *Journal of Human Resources,* 18:359–78.

Hamermesh, Daniel S. 1980. "Factor Market Dynamics and the Incidence of Taxes and Subsidies." *Quarterly Journal of Economics,* 95:751–64.

———. 1981. "Minimum Wages and Demand for Labor." Working paper, no. 656. Cambridge, MA: National Bureau of Economic Research, Inc.

———. 1993. *Labor Demand.* Princeton, NJ: Princeton University Press.

Hamermesh, Daniel S., and Jeff E. Biddle. 1994. "Beauty and the Labour Market." *American Economic Review.*

Hamermesh, Daniel S., and Albert Rees. 1993. *The Economics of Work and Pay.* New York: HarperCollins Publishers, Inc.

Hashimoto, Masnori. 1982. "Minimum Wage Effects on Training on the Job." *American Economic Review,* 72:1070–87.

Hashimoto, Masanori, and Jacob Mincer. 1970. "Employment and Unemployment Effects of Minimum Wages." Working paper. Cambridge, MA: National Bureau of Economic Research, Inc.

Heckman, James J., and Guilherme Sedlacek. 1981. "The Impact of the Minimum Wage on the Employment and Earnings of Workers in South Carolina." In *Report of the Minimum Wage Study Commission,* vol. 5. Washington, D.C.: U.S. Government Printing Office.

Heckman, James J., and Thomas E. MaCurdy. 1988. "Empirical Tests of Labor-Market Equilibrium: An Evaluation." *Carnegie Rochester Conference Series on Public Policy,* 28:231–58.

Heckman, James J., and Joseph V. Hotz. 1989. "Choosing Among Alternative Nonexperimental Methods for Estimating the Impact of Social Programs: The Case of Manpower Training." *Journal of the American Statistical Association*, 84:862–74.

Heckman, James J., and Brooks Paynor. 1989. "Determining the Impact of Federal Anti-discrimination Policy on the Economic Status of Blacks." *American Economic Review*, 79:138–77.

Heilbroner, Robert, and Lester Thurow. 1987. *Economics Explained*. New York: Simon and Schuster.

Holzer, Harry J., Lawrence F. Katz, and Alan B. Krueger. 1991. "Job Queues and Wages." *The Quarterly Journal of Economics*, 106:739–68.

Horrigan, Michael W., and Ronald B. Mincy. 1993. "The Minimum Wage and Earnings and Income Inequality." In *Uneven Tides*, edited by Sheldon Danziger and Peter Gottshalk. New York: Russell Sage Foundation.

Houthakker, H. S., and Lester D. Taylor. 1970. *Consumer Demand in the United States: Analyses and Projections*. Cambridge, MA: Harvard University Press.

Iden, George. 1980. "The Labor Force Experience of Black Youth: A Review." *Monthly Labor Review*, 103:10–16.

International Labor Organization. 1983 and 1993. *Yearbook of Labor Statistics*. Geneva, Switzerland: International Labor Organization.

Kaitz, Hyman. 1970. "Experience of the Past: The National Minimum." In *Youth Unemployment and Minimum Wages*, U.S. Department of Labor, Bureau of Labor Statistics, Bulletin 1657:30–54. Washington, D.C.: U.S. Government Printing Office.

Katz, Lawrence, and Alan B. Krueger. 1990. "The Effect of the New Minimum Wage Law in a Low-Wage Labor Market." *Industrial Relations Research Association Proceedings*, 43:254–65.

———. 1992. "The Effect of the Minimum Wage on the Fast Food Industry." *Industrial and Labor Relations Review*, 46:6–21.

Kearl, J. R., Clayne L. Pope, Gordon C. Whiting, and Larry T. Wimmer. 1979. "What Economists Think: A Confusion of Economists?" *American Economic Review*, 69:28–37.

Kelly, Terrence. 1975. "Youth Employment Opportunities and the Minimum Wage: An Econometric Model of Occupational Choice." Working Paper, no. 3608-01. Washington, D.C.: The Urban Institute.

———. 1976. "Two Policy Questions Regarding the Minimum Wage." Working Paper, no. 3608-05. Washington, D.C.: The Urban Institute.

Kerr, Clark. 1994. "Introduction: Labor in the Course of the Development of Economic Thought." In *Labor Economics and Industrial Relations: Markets and Institutions*, edited by Clark Kerr and Paul D. Staudohar. Cambridge, MA: Harvard University Press.

Kim, Taeil, and Lowell J. Taylor. 1994. "The Employment Effect in Retail Trade of California's 1988 Minimum Wage Increase." Unpublished paper. Pittsburgh: Carnegie Mellon University Department of Economics.

Klerman, Jacob. 1992. "Study 12: Employment Effect of Mandated Health Benefits." In *Health Benefits and the Workforce*, U.S. Department of Labor,

Pension and Welfare Benefits Administration. Washington, D.C.: U.S. Government Printing Office.

Kohen, Andrew I., and Curtis L. Gilroy. 1982. "The Minimum Wage, Income Distribution, and Poverty." In *Report of the Minimum Wage Study Commission*, vol. 7. Washington, D.C.: U.S. Government Printing Office.

Kosters, Marvin, and Finis Welch. 1972. "The Effects of the Minimum Wage by Race, Sex, and Age." In *Racial Discrimination in Economic Life*, edited by Anthony Pascal. Lexington, MA: D.C. Heath.

Krehbiel, Keith, and Douglas Rivers. 1988. "The Analysis of Committee Power: An Application to Senate Voting on the Minimum Wage." *American Journal of Political Science*, 32:1151–74.

Krueger, Alan B. 1988. "The Determinants of Queues for Federal Jobs." *Industrial and Labor Relations Review*, 42:567–81.

———. 1991. "Ownership, Agency, and Wages: An Examination of Franchising in the Fast Food Industry." *Quarterly Journal of Economics*, 106:75–102.

———. 1995. "The Effect of the Minimum Wage When It Really Bites: A Reexamination of the Evidence from Puerto Rico." In *Research in Labor Economics*, edited by Solomon Polachek. Greenwich, CT: JAI Press.

Krueger, Alan B., and Lawrence H. Summers. 1987. "Reflections on the Inter-Industry Wage Structure." In *Unemployment and the Structure of Labor Markets*, edited by Kevin Lang and Jonathan Leonard. Oxford: Blackwell.

Lalonde, R. J. 1986. "Evaluating the Econometric Evaluations of Training Programs with Experimental Data." *American Economic Review*, 76:604–20.

Lang, Kevin. 1994. "The Effect of Minimum Wage Laws on the Distribution of Employment: Theory and Evidence." Unpublished paper. Boston: Boston University Department of Economics.

Lang, Kevin, and William T. Dickens. 1993. "Bilateral Search as an Explanation for Labor Market Segmentation and Other Anomalies." Working Paper, no. 4461. Cambridge, MA: National Bureau of Economic Research, Inc.

Lazear, Edward P. 1981. "Agency Earnings Profiles, Productivity and Hours Restrictions." *American Economic Review*, 71:606–20.

Lazear, Edward P., and Frederick H. Miller. 1981. "Minimum Wage Versus Minimum Compensation." In *Report of the Minimum Wage Study Commission*, vol. 5. Washington, D.C.: U.S. Government Printing Office.

Leamer, Edward E. 1978. *Specification Searches: Ad Hoc Inference with Nonexperimental Data*. New York: John Wiley and Sons, Inc.

Leighton, Linda, and Jacob Mincer. 1981. "The Effects of the Minimum Wage on Human Capital Formation." In *The Economics of Legal Minimum Wages*, edited by Simon Rottenberg. Washington, D.C.: American Enterprise Institute for Public Policy Research.

Lester, Richard A. 1946. "Shortcomings of Marginal Analysis for Wage-Employment Problems." *American Economic Review*, 36:62–82.

———. 1964. *The Economics of Labor*. New York: Macmillan.

———. 1994. "Wage Differentials and Minimum-Wage Effects." In *Labor Economics and Industrial Relations: Markets and Institutions*, edited by Clark Kerr and Paul D. Staudohar. Cambridge, MA: Harvard University Press.

Lewis, H. Gregg. 1963. *Unionism and Relative Wages in the United States.* Chicago: University of Chicago Press.

———. 1986. *Union Relative Wage Effects: A Survey.* Chicago: University of Chicago Press.

Liberty, Susan E., and Jerold L. Zimmerman. 1986. "Labor Union Contract Negotiations and Accounting Choices." *Accounting Review,* 61:692–712.

Light, Audrey, and Manuelita Ureta. 1992. "Panel Estimates of Male and Female Job Turnover Behavior: Can Female Nonquitters Be Identified?" *Journal of Labor Economics,* 10:156–81.

Linneman, Peter. 1982. "The Economic Impacts of Minimum Wage Laws: A New Look at an Old Question." *Journal of Political Economy,* 90:443–69.

Love, John F. 1986. *McDonald's Behind the Arches.* New York: Bantam Books.

Machin, Stephen, and Alan Manning. 1994. "The Effects of Minimum Wages on Wage Dispersion and Employment: Evidence from the U.K. Wage Councils." *Industrial and Labor Relations Review,* 47:319–29.

Maddala, G. S. 1977. *Econometrics.* New York: McGraw-Hill, Inc.

Manning, Alan. 1993. "Labour Markets with Company Wage Policies." Unpublished paper. London: London School of Economics.

Martin, Richard. 1987. "NRA Blasts McDonald's on Wage Issue." *Nation's Restaurant News,* 21:1.

Mattila, J. Peter. 1978. "Youth Labor Markets, Enrollments, and Minimum Wages." *Industrial Relations Research Association Proceedings,* 31:134–40.

———. 1981. "The Impact of Minimum Wages on Teenage Schooling and on the Part-Time/Full-Time Employment of Youths." In *The Economics of Legal Minimum Wages,* edited by Simon Rottenberg. Washington, D.C.: American Enterprise Institute for Public Policy Research.

McDonald's Corporation. 1986 and 1991. *McDonald's Restaurant Guide.* Chicago: McDonald's Corporation.

———. 1991. *1991 Annual Report.* Chicago: McDonald's Corporation.

McKay, Steven F., and Bruce D. Schnobel. 1981. "Effects of the Various Social Security Benefit Computation Procedures." Actuarial Study, no. 86. Washington, D.C.: Social Security Administration.

Meitzen, Mark E. 1986. "Differences in Male and Female Job-Quitting Behavior." *Journal of Labor Economics,* 4:151–67.

Meurs, Dominique. 1992. "Étude des Déterminants de L'Offre de Travail dans la Fonction Publique en France." Communication aux XIIèmes Journées d'Economie Sociale.

Meyer, Bruce. 1994. "Natural and Quasi- Experiments in Economics." Unpublished paper. Evanston, IL: Northwestern University Department of Economics.

Meyer, Robert H., and David A. Wise. 1983a. "Discontinuous Distributions and Missing Persons: The Minimum Wage and Unemployed Youth." *Econometrica,* 51:1677–98.

———. 1983b. "The Effects of Minimum Wage on Employment and Earnings of Youth." *Journal of Labor Economics,* 1:66–100.

Milkovitch, George, and Jerry Newman. 1987. *Compensation.* McAllen, Texas: Success Business Publications.

Mincer, Jacob. 1976. "Unemployment Effects of Minimum Wages." *Journal of Political Economy*, 84:87–105.

Mortensen, Dale T., and Tara Vishwanath. 1991. "Information Sources and Equilibrium Wage Outcomes." Discussion Paper, no. 948. Evanston, IL: Northwestern University Center for Mathematical Studies in Economics and Management Science.

Murphy, Kevin M., and Robert H. Topel. 1987. "Unemployment, Risk, and Earnings." In *Unemployment and the Structure of Labor Markets*, edited by Kevin Lang and Jonathan Leonard. London: Basil Blackwell.

National Restaurant Association. 1990. *Restaurants USA*. Washington, D.C.: National Restaurant Association.

Nagar, A. L. 1959. "The Bias and Moment Matrix of the General k-class Estimators of the Parameters in Simultaneous Equations." *Econometrica*, 27:575–95.

Neumann, George R. 1980. "The Predictability of Strikes: Evidence from the Stock Market." *Industrial and Labor Relations Review*, 33:325–35.

Neumark, David, and William Wascher. 1992. "Employment Effects of Minimum Wages and Subminimum Wages: Panel Data on State Minimum Wage Laws." *Industrial and Labor Relations Review*, 46:55–81.

———. 1994. "Employment Effects of Minimum and Subminimum Wages: Reply to Card, Katz, and Krueger." *Industrial and Labor Relations Review*, 48:497–512.

Oi, Walter Y. 1962. "Labor as a Quasi-Fixed Factor of Production." *Journal of Political Economy*, 70:538–55.

———. 1990. "Employment Relations in Dual Labor Markets (It's Nice Work if You Can Get It)." *Journal of Labor Economics*, 8:124–49.

Parker, John E., and John F. Burton, Jr. 1967. "Voluntary Labor Mobility in the U.S. Manufacturing Sector." *Industrial Relations Research Association Proceedings*, 20:61–70.

Parsons, Donald O. 1973. "Quit Rates Over Time: A Search and Information Approach." *American Economic Review*, 63:390–401.

Pencavel, John H. 1970. *An Analysis of the Quit Rate in American Manufacturing Industry*. Princeton, NJ: Princeton University Industrial Relations Section.

Puerto Rico Office of the Governor, Planning Board. Various years. *Informe Económico al Gobernador*. San Juan, Puerto Rico: Estado Libre Asociado de Puerto Rico.

Ragan, James F. 1977. "Minimum Wages and the Youth Labor Market." *Review of Economics and Statistics*, 59:129–36.

———. 1981. "The Effect of a Legal Minimum Wage on the Pay and Employment of Teenage Students and Nonstudents." In *The Economics of Legal Minimum Wages*, edited by Simon Rottenberg. Washington, D.C.: American Enterprise Institute for Public Policy Research.

Rebitzer, James B., and Lowell J. Taylor. 1991. "The Consequences of Minimum Wage Laws: Some New Theoretical Ideas." Working Paper, no. 3877. Cambridge, MA: National Bureau of Economics Research, Inc.

Reynolds, Lloyd, and Peter Gregory. 1965. *Wages, Productivity, and Industrialization in Puerto Rico*. Homewood, IL: Richard D. Irwin, Inc.

Robinson, Joan. 1933. *The Economics of Imperfect Competition*. London: St. Martin's Press.

Roper Center. 1994. *Public Opinion Online*. Storrs, CT: Roper Center at the University of Connecticut.

Ruback, Richard S., and Martin B. Zimmerman. 1984. "Unionization and Profitability: Evidence from the Capital Market." *Journal of Political Economy*, 92:1134–57.

Sandwich Chef Incorporated. 1992. *10-K Report Filed with the U.S. Security and Exchange Commission*. Taken from *Disclosure SEC Database* (1994 edition). Bethesda, MD: Disclosure Incorporated.

Samuelson, Paul. 1951. "Economic Theory and Wages." In *The Impact of the Union*, edited by D.M. Wright. New York: Harcourt, Brace and Company.

Santiago, Carlos. 1989. "The Dynamics of Minimum Wage Policy in Economic Development: A Multiple Time-Series Approach." *Economic Development and Cultural Change*, 38:1–30.

Sargent, James D., and David G. Blanchflower. 1994. "Obesity and Stature in Adolescence and Earnings in Young Adulthood." *Archives of Pediatrics and Adolescent Medicine*, 148:681–87.

Schaafsma, Joseph, and William D. Walsh. 1983. "Employment and Labour Supply Effects of the Minimum Wage: Some Pooled Time-Series Estimates from Canadian Provincial Data." *Canadian Journal of Economics*, 16:86–97.

Schultz, Theodore. 1964. *Transforming Traditional Agriculture*. New Haven: Yale University Press.

Shapiro, Carl, and Joseph E. Stiglitz. 1984. "Equilibrium Unemployment as a Worker Discipline Device." *American Economic Review*, 74:433–44.

Shaw, Kathryn L. 1985. "The Quit Decision of Married Men." *Journal of Labor Economics*, 5:533–60.

SG&A Company. 1992. *10-K Report Filed with the U.S. Security and Exchange Commission*. Taken from *Disclosure SEC Database* (1994 edition). Bethesda, MD: Disclosure Incorporated.

Sicilian, Paul, and Adam J. Grossberg. 1993. "Do Legal Minimum Wages Create Rents? A Re-examination of the Evidence." *Southern Economic Journal*, 60:201–9.

Siskind, Frederic. 1977. "Minimum Wage Legislation in the United States: Comment." *Economic Inquiry*, January:135–38.

Slichter, Sumner. 1950. "Notes on the Structure of Wages." *Review of Economics and Statistics*, 32:80–91.

Solon, Gary. 1985. "The Minimum Wage and Teenage Employment: A Reanalysis with Attention to Serial Correlation and Seasonality." *Journal of Human Resources*, 20:292–97.

Spriggs, William E., David Swinton, and Michael Simmons. 1992. "The Effect of Changes in the Federal Minimum Wage: Restaurant Workers in Mississippi and North Carolina." Unpublished paper. Washington, D.C.: Employment Policy Institute.

Stafford, Frank. 1986. "Forestalling the Demise of Empirical Economics: The Role of Microdata in Labor Economics Research." In *Handbook of Labor Economics*, vol. 1, edited by Orley C. Ashenfelter and Richard Layard. Netherlands: Elsevier Science Publishers B.V.

Stigler, George J. 1946. "The Economics of Minimum Wage Legislation." *American Economic Review*, 36:358–65.

———. 1947. "Marginalism and Labor Markets: A Rejoinder." *American Economic Review*, 37:154–56.

Swidinsky, Robert. 1980. "Minimum Wage and Teenage Unemployment." *Canadian Journal of Economics*, 13:158–71.

Tauchen, George E. 1981. "Some Evidence on Cross-Sector Effects of the Minimium Wage." *Journal of Political Economy*, 89:529–47.

Tirole, Jean. 1988. *The Theory of Industrial Organization.* Cambridge, MA: MIT Press.

Todaro, Michael P. 1969. "A Model of Labor Migration and Urban Unemployment in Less Developed Countries." *American Economic Review*, 59: 138–48.

Tversky, Amos, and T. Gilovich. 1989. "The Cold Facts About the 'Hot Hand' in Basketball." *Chance*, 2:16–21.

U.S. Department of Commerce. Bureau of the Census. 1984. *Census of Population: Detailed Population Characteristics, Puerto Rico*, PC80-1-D53. Washington, D.C.: Government Printing Office.

———. 1990a. *1987 Census of Retail Trade*, Subject Series, Miscellaneous Subjects, RC87-S-4. Washington, D.C.: U.S. Government Printing Office.

———. 1990b. *1987 Economic Censuses of Outlying Areas: Puerto Rico*, OA87-E-4. Washington, D.C.: U.S. Government Printing Office.

———. 1993. *Money Income of Households, Families, and Persons in the United States: 1992.* Current Population Reports Series P60-184. Washington, D.C.: U.S. Government Printing Office.

———. Various years. *County Business Patterns.* Washington, D.C.: Government Printing Office.

U.S. Department of Education. Office of Educational Research and Improvement. 1991. *Digest of Education Statistics 1991.* Washington, D.C.: U.S. Government Printing Office.

U.S. Department of Labor. Bureau of International Labor Affairs. 1992, 1993. *Foreign Labor Trends.* Washington, D.C.: Government Printing Office.

U.S. Department of Labor. Bureau of Labor Statistics. 1993. *Employment and Earnings.* February. Washington, D.C.: Government Printing Office.

U.S. Department of Labor. Bureau of Labor Statistics. Various years. *Employment and Wages—Annual Averages.* Washington, D.C.: U.S. Government Printing Office.

———. Various years. *Geographic Profiles of Unemployment and Employment.* Washington, D.C.: U.S. Government Printing Office.

U.S. Department of Labor. Women's Bureau. 1928. *The Development of Minimum Wage Laws in the United States, 1912 to 1927.* Washington, D.C.: U.S. Government Printing Office.

U.S. House of Representatives. Committee on Ways and Means. 1994. *1994 Green Book.* Washington, D.C.: U.S. Government Printing Office.

U.S. Office of the President. 1981. *Report of the Minimum Wage Study Commission* (Seven Volumes). Washington, D.C.: Government Printing Office.

———. 1993. *Economic Report of the President.* Washington, D.C.: Government Printing Office.

Viscusi, W. K. 1979. "Job Hazards and Worker Quit Rates: An Analysis of Adaptive Worker Behavior." *International Economic Review*, 20:29–58.

———. 1980. "Sex Differences in Worker Quitting." *Review of Economics and Statistics*, 62:388–97.

Wachter, Michael L., and Choongsoo Kim. 1979. "Time-Series Changes in Youth Joblessness." Working Paper, no. 384. Cambridge, MA: National Bureau of Economic Research, Inc.

Weidenbaum, Murray. 1993. "How Government Reduces Employment." Unpublished paper. St. Louis: Washington University Center for the Study of American Business.

Welch, Finis. 1969. "Linear Synthesis of Skill Distribution." *Journal of Human Resources*, 4:311–24.

———. 1974. "Minimum Wage Legislation in the United States." *Economic Inquiry*, 12:285–318.

———. 1976. "Minimum Wage Legislation in the United States." In *Evaluating the Labor Market Effects of Social Programs*, edited by Orley Ashenfelter and James Blum. Princeton, NJ: Princeton University Press.

———. 1977. "Minimum Wage Legislation in the United States: Reply." *Economic Inquiry*, 15:139–42.

———. 1993. "The Minimum Wage." *Jobs and Capital*, vol. 2. Santa Monica, CA: The Milken Institute.

Wellington, Allison. 1991. "Effects of the Minimum Wage on the Employment Status of Youths: An Update." *Journal of Human Resources*, 26:27–46.

Wessels, Walter J. 1980. *Minimum Wages, Fringe Benefits, and Working Conditions*. Washington, D.C.: American Enterprise Institute for Public Policy Research.

West, E.G., and Michael McKee. 1980. *Minimum Wages: The New Issues in Theory, Evidence, Policy and Politics*. Ottawa, Canada: Economic Council of Canada and the Institute for Research on Public Policy.

Williams, Nicolas. 1993. "Regional Effects of the Minimum Wage on Teenage Employment." *Applied Economics*, 25:1517–28.

Zaidi, Albert. 1970. *A Study of the Effects of the $1.25 Minimum Wage Under the Canada Labour (Standards) Code*. Task Force of Labour Relations, study no. 16. Ottawa: Privy Council Office.

Index